Augsburg College
George Sverdrup Library
Minneapolis, Minnesota 55454

MODERN AMERICAN HISTORY ★ A Garland Series

Edited by
FRANK FREIDEL
Harvard University

WISCONSIN VOTING PATTERNS IN THE TWENTIETH CENTURY, 1900 TO 1950

David L. Brye

Garland Publishing, Inc.
New York & London ★ 1979

© 1979 David L. Brye

All rights reserved

Library of Congress Cataloging in Publication Data
Brye, David L   1938–
  Wisconsin voting patterns in the twentieth century, 1900 to 1950.

  (Modern American history)
  Bibliography: p.
  1. Elections—Wisconsin—History. 2. Voting —Wisconsin—History. 3. Wisconsin—Politics and government—1848–1950. I. Title. II. Series.
  JK6095.B78   329′.023′77504   78-62376
  ISBN 0-8240-3627-1

All volumes in this series are printed on acid-free, 250-year-life paper.
Printed in the United States of America

TABLE OF CONTENTS

	Preface	iv
I.	Method	1
II.	Research Design	34
III.	Settlement of Wisconsin	81
IV.	The Wisconsin Political Scene in 1900	163
V.	Wisconsin and Progressivism, 1900 to 1925	225
VI.	Wisconsin Votes, 1925 to 1950	295
	Conclusion	347
	Appendices:	
	A Sources of Data	354
	B Wisconsin Social and Economic Data	360
	C Wisconsin Elections, 1888 to 1952	371
	D Wisconsin Ethnic Voting, 1898 to 1952	377
	E Ethnic Voting Units	400
	Bibliography	426

To my parents

Emil and Alice Brye

who kept faith

PREFACE

This study began as an effort to discuss the electoral sources of support for the Wisconsin progressive movement by applying the methods of voting behavior analysis from political science and political sociology. It has both broadened and narrowed in scope since its origin so many years ago. Broadened in the sense that it is now an effort to discuss in general Wisconsin voting patterns in the first half of the Twentieth Century; narrowed in that it concentrates on specific parts of the electorate and on specific electoral trends. Rather than calling it Wisconsin Voting Patterns in the Twentieth Century, I should label it Essays on Wisconsin Voting in the Twentieth Century.

A few explanatory notes will aid the reader in pursuing Wisconsin voters through the pages of this volume. First of all, progressivism is not defined as equalling reform or efforts at business control or social control, but rather as the movement in Wisconsin which centered around Robert M. La Follette and his political ventures. The work of Sam Hays, Richard Hofstadter, Gabriel Kolko, Robert Wiebe, and others makes clear the need for a better definition and understanding of progressive reform.

Equally necessary is a new understanding of the

internationalist-isolationist dichotomy. If Robert
La Follette and his two sons are to be defined as isolationists then the author finds it a more congenial
attitude toward foreign policies than that of their
opponents. The entire discussion by historians of
the "hyphenate" vote is replete with value judgments
against those groups whose vote is affected by their
ethnic background.

Partly because of the need to remove this assimilationist bias, partly because it represents contempory
usage, and partly because it is less clumsy, ethnic
references in this study omit "-American." Thus,
"German vote" and "German attitudes" refer, of course,
to the vote and attitudes of those of German background resident in the United States.

When one spends ten years of research and writing--
with time out for teaching, running for political
office, and occasional rest and relaxation--one accumulates a long list of people who deserve recognition
for their assistance at various points along the way.

My dissertation adviser, Frank Freidel, in addition
to an obvious sense of patience, has given me much
encouragement and moral support over the years. Ernest
May read and critiqued the dissertation on which
this manuscript is based. Lee Benson and Sam Hays
provided both scholarly inspiration and personal en-

couragement at early stages of research and writing. Harlan Hahn first introduced me to the mysteries of voting behavior research when we were beginning our graduate work. Al Bogue, Merle Curti, Paul Faler, Erling Jorstad, Paul Kleppner, and Roger Wyman aided me at crucial moments in the course of the development of my ideas and the expression of those ideas in written form.

A number of students at Luther College assisted me in my research--Tom Berkland, Paul Hesterman, Dennis Linderbaum, Dave Woodward, and Jorge Zurita. Ralph Kloske most ably served as my research assistant and computer programmer in the final revision of the manuscript. Carol Jenson read and critiqued the first two chapters, Jeanyne Bezoir Slettom edited several of the later chapters; whatever gracefulness may have crept into the writing owes much to their vigilance. Dag Ingvoldstad deserves special credit for translating my handwriting into legible typescript in early drafts of the work. Bert Arneson gave her personal touch to the arduous task of reproducing the additional copies of the final draft. Greg Vanney prepared the index.

Danforth and Woodrow Wilson Foundations helped finance the education and the research which led ultimately to the completed product. The American

Lutheran Church and Luther College also provided financial assistance at various stages in the writing. John Linnell, former Dean of Academic Affairs at Luther College, John Christianson, Chairman of the Luther College History Department, Earl and Virginia Leland, Jim and Elaine Hippen, Ron and Kathy Christenson, Leonard and Sharon Smith, and a host of friends and colleagues provided intellectual stimulation and personal friendship along the way.

The two people most intimately involved in the production of this, the finished product, are my sisters Sue Frydenlund and Elizabeth Hellwig. Both aided in the arduous task of collecting, calculating, and transposing data onto data sheets. Sue proved especially adept as my primary research assistant; while Elizabeth, in addition to her earlier research tasks, is responsible for typing the final copy you see before you. Adrian Pollock prepared the maps in Chapter III. My parents deserve a special vote of gratitude for their encouragement of my scholarly pursuits over the years and for their faith in the eventual appearance of the final product. But they, along with all the others mentioned above, have graciously left responsibility for any errors to me.

David L. Brye
Decorah, Iowa

WISCONSIN

VOTING

1900 TO 1950

CHAPTER I   METHOD

Application of the methods and insights of the social sciences to the study of past human behavior looms ever larger on the horizon of the historical profession. This development is to the benefit of all disciplines involved. Theories of human behavior can be verified, or modified, by studying past societies. Certainly deviations or variations from general laws of behavior must include the historical dimension as a major factor in explanation.

At the same time, historians can gain valuable concepts around which to organize their research--and even more importantly--gain new methods to help explain the past. Especially valuable, at least for modern historians, are the methods of quantification combined with the use of computers. As William Aydelotte suggests in an article on "Quantification in History":

> When all reservations have been made, quantification has still shown itself, in the light of the considerable experience we now have, to be a powerful tool in historical analysis. It helps to make the work both easier and more reliable, and, in some cases, it provides a means of dealing with questions that could not be attacked in any other way. Those wrestling with problems for which this approach is appropriate can ill afford to dispense with it.[1]

Aydelotte is exceedingly cautious in the case he makes for the use of quantitative methods. Not so Lee Benson! Benson has long been calling for the systematic analysis of American history, even taking the audacious step of suggesting Henry Buckle as the patron saint and 1984 as the end of the millenium to be marked by Buckle's return to rule in the hearts and minds of historians.[2] Samuel Hays has also been a consistent supporter of the use of quantitative data, calling it the "most promising current methodological innovation in the social analysis of political history."[3]

All three of these men, and most other people involved in quantitative historical research, caution against mere reliance on numbers to give us the answers to historical problems. Before the quantification must come the research design, or in Benson's words, the establishment of "potentially verifiable hypotheses."[4] From quantification we can answer the "who" questions of history; we can only find suggestions for getting at the "why" questions. These queries must then be explored by using the standard historical methods and the theories developed by the social sciences. This is not to diminish the relevance of quantification because it deals with the lesser question. There are a large number of "who" questions which have been inadequately or wrongly answered by historians. And most "what" questions should be rephrased into "who" questions. For example, "What caused the Civil War?" as usually dealt with by historians should be rephrased, "Who caused the Civil War?" or "What groups supported and opposed the move toward war?" Only when we have answered these questions adequately can we proceed to formulate and test hypotheses for dealing with the "why" questions.[5]

Once one accepts the method of quantification, the need to use computers is obvious. The magnitude of data is frequently such that it can only be conveniently stored in a computer. Also any effort to systematically organize the data beyond the simplest statistical table, an operation which should be labelled counting rather than statistics, requires so many mathematical operations as to make a computer essential.[6]

At present, political history is the area of historical analysis which is undergoing the greatest change under the impact of both the theories and the statistical methods developed by social scientists. Thus far this investigation has taken three main directions: the study of legislative behavior using roll-call analysis, the study of political elites by means of collective biographies, and the study of electoral or voting behavior.

Very few American historians have published studies using roll-call analysis. However, a number of recent books and articles on Congress have employed the method beyond the level of using a few selected votes: Joel Silbey and Thomas Alexander on the Pre-Civil War Congresses, David Donald on Reconstruction Congresses from 1863-1867, and Allan Bogue on the Civil War Congresses.[7] Howard Allen in writing on the Senate from 1911 to 1916 is one of the few American historians to break away from the apparent obsession with the Civil War period.[8] William Aydelotte has made extensive use of roll-call analysis in his studies of the English Parliament in the mid-Nineteenth Century.[9] Most of the theoretical work involving roll-calls has been done by political scientists.[10]

The most extensive work on political elites has taken place in the examination of progressive leadership of the early Twentieth Century. Pioneering--and misleading--research in this area was done by George Mowry in his work on the California progressives and by Alfred Chandler in his essay on "The Origins of Progressive Leadership," published as an Appendix to The Letters of Theodore Roosevelt.[11] The Mowry-Chandler thesis was canonized by Richard Hofstadter in The Age of Reform, and by Mowry himself in The Era of Theodore Roosevelt, 1900-1912, despite a major methodological error--the failure to do a comparative study of conservative leadership. Recent research by Richard Sherman, William Kerr, Samuel Hays, Daniel Potts, Bonnie Fox, and James Crooks has quite effectively demolished the earlier conclusions by using this comparative method.[12] David Thelen, in a detailed study of the Wisconsin legislature from 1897 to 1903 combining both roll-call analysis, to determine the degree of progressivism, and collective biography, to pinpoint characteristics of progressives, moderates and conservatives, concluded, "The social origins of Wisconsin legislators between 1897 and 1903 clearly suggest that no particular manner of man became a progressive."[13] The Thelen essay includes a critique on the applying of concepts in one field, social stratification, to another field, the historical origins of progressivism. Michael Rogin goes beyond elite studies to voting behavior analysis to challenge the Mowry-Chandler-Hofstadter thesis on Mowry's own ground, California.[14]

An example of the problems involved in elite studies can also be seen in Otis Graham's <u>An Encore for Reform: The Old Progressives and the New Deal</u>. From a variety of sources, Graham draws up a list of 400 progressives, 168 of whom survived through the first four years of the New Deal. Graham concludes that there was a basic discontinuity between progressive reform and New Deal reform because sixty of his sample opposed the New Deal while only forty-five supported or were to the left of it. The numbers are impressive but the study suffers from a lack of definition of progressivism, a very rigorous test for New Dealism, and from an insistence that men's ideas do not change.[15]

Since this study fits under the category of electoral or voting behavior studies, it is well to find its location in this genre of historical interpretation. Most research done by historians in this area grows directly out of the insights and methods of political science and to a lesser degree of political sociology. Voting behavior research falls into two branches differentiated by the kind of data used. The most popular approach among political scientists has been the use of survey data. The studies made at the Survey Research Center of the University of Michigan, especially *The American Voter* (1960) and the series of articles collected in *Elections and the Political Order* (1966), are among the most recent contributions of this collaborative effort to explain American electoral behavior.[16]

In terms of methodology or data these studies contribute little to the study of political history prior to 1940. However, they have contributed a number of concepts which have aided historians both in interpretation and in establishing hypotheses to verify. A primary example would be their stress on the importance of tradition in determining a man's vote. As Angus Campbell and his colleagues say in *The American Voter*:

> The most important factor differentiating responses is not economic status, social milieu, or variations in deep-seated temperament, but quite simply the political party, which more often than not has been espoused years before the candidate takes up a position as an object in the psychological field. Thus prior party attachments form the great watershed for public reaction to current events.[17]

Along with this emphasis has come a downplaying of the effect of political campaigns. The pioneering Erie County study of the 1940 election was instrumental in showing this lack of effect.[18] Both of these insights have led to the beginning of a major reorientation of American political history away from the traditional presidential campaign and election approach. Campaign slogans and election victories or losses are being downgraded; emphasis is being placed on the changing responses over time of the electorate and the groups of which it is composed. As Hays suggests,

> The important long-range historical fact about elections is not necessarily the outcome of any one contest, but the degree to which they reveal shifts or continuities in political attitude.[19]

This approach leads to a greater use of off-year election returns in order to peg more precisely electoral changes. For example, 1894 becomes more important than the Bryan campaign of 1896 in describing and explaining the arrival of the Republican majority which lasted basically until the 1930's.[20]

Of great importance to historians has been the realization that the electorate must be divided into groups, each of which responds differently to the ongoing political process. Thus Benson in his call for studying elections over time and space states that "no interpretations of an election outcome can begin to be verified until the description of what happened is translated into who caused it to happen."[21]

While much of the impetus for this kind of investigation has come from survey research, the historian must look to the other branch of voting behavior for a relevant methodology. He has few surveys before the 1930's and only rare direct evidence of the responses of individual voters.

Consequently, he must rely on aggregate data, data which "consists of distributions of whole populations [at the state, congressional district, county, minor civil division, or precinct level] among the categories of various systems of classification without providing information about which category any <u>particular</u> unit of population falls into."[22]

In the past, historians who dealt with group responses to politics based their interpretations either on observers: a ward boss saying, "The Irish deserted us!" or a newspaper noting, "The Catholics flocked to the Democratic banner like pigs to a trough."; or on the behavior of elite members of groups. For example, an historical truism has been that Germans voted Republican in the 1860 election. This conclusion was arrived at from the support given the Republican party by Carl Schurz and a number of German journalists. Thus, two prominent historians concluded in their popular textbook as recently as 1962:

> The German-Americans for the most part had joined the Democratic party as soon as they became naturalized; but they had suffered too much from tyranny in the fatherland to support it in any new shape. The personality of Lincoln and the free homestead issue swept them into a new party allegiance, and in conjunction with the New England element they carried the Northwestern states.[23]

Two generally ignored studies of the early 1940's based on analyses of election returns from homogeneous German areas contained enough information to discredit this interpretation.[24] Recent studies, using more sophisticated statistical techniques should finally lay it in the grave.[25]

The earliest of these quantitative works on German voting in 1860 was by Joseph Schafer, the Superintendent of the Wisconsin State Historical Society from 1920 to 1941.[26] Schafer had received his training under Frederick Jackson Turner at Wisconsin. This was appropriate as Turner was one of the first historians to be alerted to differing voting behavior patterns. In a letter to Schafer when the latter was planning his Domesday Book Series on Wisconsin, Turner said:

> I should make in selected areas detailed studies of the correlations between party votes, by precincts, wards, etc., soils, nationalities and state-origins of the voter, assessment rolls, denominational groups, illiteracy, etc. What kind of people tend to be Whigs, what Democrats, Abolitionists, etc. This can be ascertained by such studies and it would be the first time such correlations have been worked out on any considerable scale.[27]

A number of Turner's students turned to this approach including Orrin Libby[28] and Edgar Robinson[29] in addition to Schafer. But historians at this time failed to go much beyond mapmaking and raw data gathering and did not assimilate the new field of statistics into their methodology.

Thus, the main development of electoral analysis using aggregate data has come from the fields of political science and sociology. Franklin Giddings, the pioneering sociologist at Columbia, trained William Ogburn and Stuart Rice. Ogburn did an intensive study of initiative and referenda voting in Oregon and wrote a series of articles on presidential elections.[30] Rice produced the first classic in American voting behavior, Quantitative Methods in Politics, in 1928.[31]

Other political scientists who made important contributions to the study of electoral behavior using aggregate data were Charles Merriam, Harold Gosnell, and V. O. Key.[32] Gosnell made extensive use of statistical methods, including the ever-popular correlation analysis, in Machine Politics: Chicago Model published in 1937 and in Grass Roots Politics in 1942.[33]

V. O. Key's works, including the monumental Southern Politics published in 1949, have provided some of the most useful insights into how the American electorate functions. Unlike most political scientists and sociologists, Key firmly grounded his work in the historical dimension. In Southern Politics he made extensive use of interviews to determine the unique historical development of the politics of each state in the South. However, Key shied away from using correlation analysis. In his Primer on Statistics for the Political Scientist he even suggested in his chapter on simple correlation that:

> To most audiences to which one directs his findings, the coefficient of determination or correlation is a symbol devoid of content. Often the entire conclusion can be translated into English and the statistical analysis discarded. . . . By the exercise of a modicum of ingenuity, the most hardened audience of

> skeptics about statistics may be seduced into
> following the findings of a correlation
> analysis. In the process it is often just
> as well to avoid employing the term correla-
> tion.³⁴

Key preferred the more easily visualized map and scattergram.

Key was not the only worker who remained in the vineyards of aggregate data as the survey people took over the rest of the field. Rudolf Heberle who emigrated from Nazi Germany in 1938 brought a thorough grounding in the methods originated by Andre Siegfried in his study of French electoral patterns published in 1913.³⁵ Heberle's methodological essays present the clearest case for the use of aggregate data, for taking the whole social context into account, for looking at elections over time, and for using small, homogeneous units of population.³⁶ Strikingly, almost none of the recent works on voting behavior either in history or political science and sociology cite these essays even though Heberle's work based on this method, From Democracy to Nazism: A Regional Case Study on Political Parties in Germany, is referred to frequently.³⁷

Regional and state studies provide the best arena for those who would probe into the who and why of voting. The state of Wisconsin has often served as guinea pig in this laboratory. Because of this past research and the nature of the current project, studies of Wisconsin voting patterns will be used to illustrate the development and controversies in voting behavior analysis.

The pioneering effort in Wisconsin political ecology is, of course, Joseph Schafer's work on the 1860 election which culminated in his article on "Who Elected Linclon?" published posthumously in the American Historical Review of October, 1941.[38] While effectively demolishing the myth of German support for Lincoln by looking at several townships which were solidly German, Schafer did not systematically examine the question of ethnic voting in 1860. He failed even to take the elementary step of percentaging the vote. With Schafer's death, the Turner historical tradition of empirical voting analysis died, not only in Wisconsin but elsewhere as well until revived by Lee Benson in his study of Jacksonian democracy.

The next tie-in of Wisconsin with voting behavior research came from political science, as one of the case studies in the Gosnell work already cited. Gosnell made extensive use of correlation analysis in his study of Wisconsin voting patterns in the 1930's.[39] Using county level data, Gosnell located areas of Democratic, Republican, and Progressive strength in Wisconsin. He used correlations to check the strength of party discipline and party tradition as well as the nature of party support. It is in his effort at the latter that Gosnell fell into the pit of the "ecological fallacy."

Statistical correlation is based on the relationship

between two variables over a series of units such as the seventy-one counties in Wisconsin. If the dependent variable, for example, the Democratic vote, can be seen to vary as the independent variable, the percent Catholic, German, rural, etc., does, a correlation is said to exist between the two variables. The coefficient of correlation can be computed to measure mathematically the degree of association between the two variables. This coefficient can vary from +1.0 to -1.0, that is to say, from a perfect association to a perfect non-association. Thus Gosnell found the coefficient of correlation between the vote for Franklin D. Roosevelt in 1936 and the rural-farm percentage from the 1930 census to be -.53. Assuming a causal relationship, he concluded that the more rural a county the less likely it was to vote for Roosevelt in 1936. The problem, as W. S. Robinson pointed out in his famous article on "Ecological Correlations and the Behavior of Individuals," is that the variation may be explained by other variables which may not have been measured or in Robinson's words, "an ecological correlation is almost certainly not equal to its corresponding individual correlation."[40] A good example of this problem can be seen in correlations between the Democratic vote and the percent Catholic. This correlation frequently turns out to be very high but may be so because in fact the Democratic vote is highly correlated with social class which in turn is highly correlated with percent Catholic.

This can be accounted for by holding the one variable constant and by doing a partial correlation. Ultimately, however, it is impossible to hold all variables but one constant without getting into statistical manipulation which is far beyond the limits of the data.[41]

One way of avoiding the ecological fallacy or false relationship between variables is to turn to survey research as most political scientists and sociologists have done. Another way of avoiding it is to go to smaller geographical units which will be more nearly homogeneous therefore giving one the ability to hold more variables constant. This study has done the latter by going to the minor civil division--township, village, city, and ward--rather than the usual county level data. Very few studies of voting behavior have taken this approach because of the lack of data on the minor civil division level.

Almost all studies of Wisconsin voting behavior since Gosnell have been done by use of county level data, or more recently, by use of survey data. Examples of the former are the studies by Louis Bean of the Joe McCarthy elections of 1946 and 1952; by Andrew Baggaley of "Voting Changes in Wisconsin Counties" in the 1950's; and by John Fenton in his Midwest Politics.[42] The Fenton book which has much of value on recent Wisconsin politics illustrates the problem of ecological correlations using large units such as counties. At one point Fenton defines Scandinavian counties as those with 6% or more Scandinavian-born in the 1930 census. One historian of Wisconsin progressivism has also used county level data to "investigate to what extent different social and economic groups in society supported this movement."[43]

The most recent study of Wisconsin politics appears in The Intellectuals and McCarthy: The Radical Specter by Michael Paul Rogin. In one of the most insightful books written on the nature of McCarthy's support, Rogin includes a chapter on "Wisconsin: McCarthy and the Progressive Tradition" which by use of county statistics demolishes the idea of continuity between Robert La Follette and Joe McCarthy.[44]

To avoid the problems involved in the use of county level data, Leon Epstein and others have turned to survey data gathered under the auspices of the Wisconsin Survey Research Laboratory. This has led to a number of electoral studies: "Religion and Wisconsin Voting in 1960," Votes and Taxes on the 1962 gubernatorial election, "Who Voted for Goldwater: The Wisconsin Case," and "The Two Electorates: Voters and Non-Voters in a Wisconsin Primary."[45]

Austin Ranney, co-author with Epstein of the last two articles, argues elsewhere that there is a place for scholars using aggregate data although for Ranney this place is very minor compared with the users of survey data:

> They are most likely to make valuable contributions if they bypass questions about particular individuals and types of individuals

and adopt as their sole object of inquiry the
behavior of electorates.[46]

Ranney glosses over the question of the reliability of survey data even though in one of the studies he co-authored, 39% of those interviewed said they had voted in the 1964 gubernatorial primary compared wih an actual estimated turnout of 28.5%--an over-report of 10.5%.[47] In fact, surveys yield any number of problems: the conceptual framework and phrasing of the questions may greatly affect the responses and their interpretation; the sample cannot be broken down into small enough cells to isolate all but a few variables; and, most importantly for the historian, surveys are of limited use in dealing with historical questions as they are oriented toward general laws of human behavior and often ignore the historical context.

This has led a number of political scientists to return to the methods of Frederick Jackson Turner and Joseph Schafer in their use of minor civil division level data. Even Epstein did this in his "Size of Place and the Division of the Two-Party Vote in Wisconsin," and Politics in Wisconsin.[48] Rather than use ecological correlations to determine the rural-urban party split, Epstein divided the electorate according to size-of-place varying from Milwaukee County and "Urbanized areas and cities over 50,000" to "townships with more than 50% farm population."[49] One of his students did a follow-up on the size-of-place analysis after it was challenged by a Michigan study.[50] Although he ignores ethnicity in his major work on Wisconsin politics, Epstein had dealt with it in an earlier work, The Wisconsin Farm Vote for Governor, 1948-1954.[51] In this brief study Epstein divided the state's 1077 townships according to ethnic groups and computed the partisan split for each group for elections from 1948 to 1954.

Two other recent studies also use minor civil divisions in order to isolate homogeneous units. Andrew Baggaley in "Religious Influence on Wisconsin Voting, 1928-1960" isolated townships and villages which voted strongly for or against state aid for busing parochial school students in a 1946 referendum and then examined the votes of these units for Al Smith in 1928, for Adlai Stevenson in 1956, and for John F. Kennedy in the 1960 Wisconsin presidential primary and presidential election. Michael Rogin, in "Wallace and the Middle Class: the White Backlash in Wisconsin," examined the vote for Wallace in the 1964 Wisconsin primary in Milwaukee's 18 suburbs. By looking at the vote on the minor civil division level Rogin was able to prove that Wallace scored more heavily in Republican middle class suburbs than he did in Democratic working class suburbs.[52]

Historians are also beginning to use minor civil divisions as Roger Wyman's article on "Wisconsin Ethnic Groups and the Election of 1890" indicates. In addition to correlation analysis at the county level, Wyman investigated voting in specific townships in an election which had high salience for foreign-born voters.[53] Paul Kleppner and Richard Jensen have studied ethnic and religious groups in Wisconsin and several other Midwest states by use of detailed demographic data on the minor civil division level.[54]

One would be remiss in discussing studies of Wisconsin voting patterns if he ignored the work of Samuel Lubell. In two general studies of voting behavior in the United States, <u>The Future of American Politics</u> and <u>Revolt of the Moderates</u>, Lubell used the Wisconsin political scene as an example of the role of progressive third parties during the interwar period and of McCarthyism or "The Politics of Revenge" in the 1950's.[55] Lubell writes as an informed political analyst but not a scholar. However, many of his insights into the nature of American voting were borne out in this research, as will become clear in subsequent chapters.

NOTES

[1]Aydelotte, American Historical Review, LXXI (April, 1966), 825. Aydelotte also discusses quantification and its relationship to generalization in history in "Notes on the Problem of Historical Generalization," in Louis Gottschalk, ed., Generalization in the Writing of History (Chicago, 1963), 145-177. Both of these articles appear in Aydelotte, Quantification in History (Reading, Massachusetts, 1971). See also Aydelotte's "Introduction" to this collection of his essays.

[2]See Benson, "Quantification, Scientific History, and Scholarly Innovation," AHA Newsletter, IV (June, 1966), 11-16; "Research Problems in American Political Historiography," in Mirra Komarovsky, ed., Common Frontiers of the Social Sciences (Glencoe, Ill., 1957), 113-181; The Concept of Jacksonian Democracy: New York as a Test Case (Princeton, 1961); "An Approach to the Scientific Study of Past Public Opinion," Public Opinion Quarterly, XXXI (Winter, 1967-68), 522-567. These articles, along with several others, are collected in Benson, Toward the Scientific Study of History: Selected Essays of Lee Benson (Philadelphia, 1972).

[3]Hays, "New Possibilities for American Political History: The Social Analysis of Political Life," paper presented at the American Historical Association, December 29, 1964, mimeo Inter-University Consortium for Political Research, Ann

Arbor, Michigan, 36. Published in Seymour Martin Lipset and Richard Hofstadter, eds., <u>Sociology and History: Methods</u> (New York, 1968), 181-227. See also "The Use of Historical Statistical Inquiry," <u>Prologue: The Journal of the National Archives,</u> I (Fall, 1969), 7-16; "Computers and Historical Research," in Edmund A. Bowles, ed., <u>Computers in Humanistic Research</u> (Englewood Cliffs, New Jersey, 1967), 62-72; and "A Systematic Social History," in George Athan Billias and Gerald N. Grob, ed., <u>American History: Retrospect and Prospect</u> (New York, 1971), 315-360.

[4]Benson, "Research Problems," 113-122.

[5]In addition to the above essays on quantification and history, see Stephan Thernstrom, "Quantitative Methods in History: Some Notes," in Lipset and Hofstadter, eds., <u>Sociology and History: Methods</u>, 59-78; Allan G. Bogue, "United States: The 'New' Political History," <u>Journal of Contemporary History</u>, III (January, 1968), 5-27; Joel H. Silbey, "Clio and Computers: Moving into Phase II, 1970-1972," <u>Computers and the Humanities</u>, VII (November, 1972), 67-79; Robert D. Swierenga, "Clio and Computers; A Survey of Computerized Research in History," <u>Ibid</u>., V (Sept., 1970), 1-21, and "Computers and American History: The Impact of the 'New' Generation," <u>Journal of American History</u>, LX (March, 1974), 1045-1070; Morton Rothstein, <u>et al</u>., "Quantification and American History: An Assessment," in Herbert J. Bass, ed., <u>The State of American History</u> (Chicago, 1972), 298-329; and Robert F.

Berkhofer, Jr., A Behavioral Approach to Historical Analysis (New York, 1969). In addition to articles on computer use in history, Computers and the Humanities also publishes an annual bibliography of books and articles in history using quantification. (See I: 145-149; II: 169-170; III: 219-221; IV: 320-322; V: 229-232; VI: 246-249; VII: 246-249.) Note also the continuing treatment of quantitative methods in the rather ingeniously named Historical Methods Newsletter (originally subtitled Quantitative Analysis of Social, Economic and Political Development) which has been published quarterly at the University of Pittsburgh since December, 1967. Charles Dollar and Richard J. Jensen, The Historian's Guide to Statistics (New York, 1971), the best of recent statistics textbooks for historians, contains a lengthy bibliography, 236-297.

[6]For this study most of the work was done without the use of a computer. The amount of statistical manipulation of the data was insufficient to justify punching it all on IBM cards. Relevant county electoral and demographic data have been key punched and coefficients of correlation determined by use of computer. Eli S. Marks cautions against the overuse of computers in "You Can Do It on a Computer, But Should You?" Public Opinion Quarterly, XXVII (Fall, 1963), 481-485.

[7]Silbey, The Shrine of Party: Congressional Voting Behavior, 1841-1852 (Pittsburgh, 1967); Alexander, Sectional

Stress and Party Strength: A Study of Roll-Call Voting Patterns in the United States House of Representatives, 1836-1860 (Nashville, 1967); Donald, The Politics of Reconstruction, 1863-1867 (Baton Rouge, 1965); Bogue, "Bloc and Party in the United States Senate, 1861-1803," Civil War History, XIII (September, 1967), 221-241; "Senators, Sectionalism, and the 'Western' Measures of the Republican Party," in David M. Ellis, ed., The Frontier in American Development: Essays in Honor of Paul Wallace Gates (Ithaca, New York, 1969), 20-46; and "Some Dimensions of Power in the Thirty-Seventh Senate," in William O. Aydellotte, Allen G. Bogue, and Robert William Fogel, eds., The Dimensions of Quantitative Research in History (Princeton, 1972), 285-318.

[8]Allen, "Geography and Politics: Voting on Reform Issues in the United States Senate, 1911-1916," Journal of Southern History, XXVII (May, 1961), 216-228; and, with Jerome M. Clubb, "Party Loyalty in the Progressive Years: The Senate, 1909-1915," Journal of Politics, XXIX (August, 1967), 567-584.

[9]Aydelotte, "A Statistical Analysis of the Parliament of 1841: Some Problems of Method," Bulletin of the Institute of Historical Research, XXVII (November, 1954), 141-155; "Voting Patterns in the British House of Commons in the 1840's," Comparative Studies in Society and History, V (January, 1963), 134-163; and "Parties and Issues in Early

Victorian England," *Journal of British Studies*, V (May, 1966), 95-114. See Aydelotte, *Quantification in History*, 181, for a more complete list of his articles.

[10] See Lee F. Anderson, Meredith W. Watts, Jr., and Allen R. Wilcox, *Legislative Roll-Call Analysis* (Evanston, Illinois, 1966); Duncan MacRae, Jr., *Issues and Parties in Legislative Voting: Methods of Statistical Analysis* (New York, 1970); and the studies in John C. Wahlke and Heinz Eulau, eds., *Legislative Behavior: A Reader in Theory and Research* (Glencoe, Illinois, 1959).

[11] Mowry, *The California Progressives* (Berkeley, 1951), ch. V, and "The California Progressive and His Rationale: A Study in Middle Class Politics," *Mississippi Valley Historical Review*, XXXVI (September, 1949), 239-250. Chandler, "The Origins of Progressive Leadership," in Elting E. Morrison, ed., *The Letters of Theodore Roosevelt* (Cambridge, 1954), VIII, Appendix III, 1462-1465.

[12] Sherman, "The Status Revolution and Massachusetts Progressive Leadership," *Political Science Quarterly*, LXXVIII (March, 1963), 59-65; Kerr, "The Progressives of Washington, 1910-12," *Pacific Northwest Quarterly*, LV (October, 1964), 157-169; Potts, "The Progressive Profile in Iowa," *Mid-America*, XLVII (October, 1965), 257-268; Fox, "The Philadelphia Progressives: A Test of the Hofstadter-Hays Thesis," *Pennsylvania History*, XXXIV (October, 1967), 372-394; and Crooks, *Politics and Progress: The Rise of Urban Progressivism in*

Baltimore, 1895-1911 (Baton Rouge, 1968). Burton W. Folsom discusses the studies of progressives and other elites in "The Collective Biography as a Research Tool," Mid-America, LIV (April, 1972), 108-122.

[13] Thelen, "Social Tensions and the Origins of Progressivism," Journal of American History, LVI (September, 1969), 323-341. The quote is from page 332. Collective biography has also been used by Gerald Prescott in "Wisconsin Farm Leaders in the Gilded Age," Agricultural History, XLIV (April, 1970), 183-199, and "Gentlemen Farmers in the Gilded Age," Wisconsin Magazine of History, LV (Spring, 1972), 197-212.

[14] Rogin, "Progressivism and the California Electorate," Journal of American History, LV (September, 1968), 297-314. This article has been reprinted with minor changes in Rogin and John L. Shover, Political Change in California: Critical Elections and Social Movements, 1890-1966 (Westport, Connecticut, 1970), 35-61. See also Rogin's The Intellectuals and McCarthy: The Radical Specter (Cambridge, 1967).

[15] Graham, An Encore For Reform (New York, 1967). All of these problems come to the fore in examining the Wisconsin progressives used (and not used) in the Graham study.

[16] Angus Campbell, Philip E. Converse, Warren E. Miller, and Donald E. Stokes, The American Voter (New York, 1960) and Elections and the Political Order (New York, 1966). Earlier studies of this nature were done at the Survey Research Center and at the Bureau of Applied Social Research

of Columbia University. Surveys of the literature in this field are contained in The American Voter, 12-17; Samuel J. Eldersveld, "Theory and Method in Voting Behavior Research," Journal of Politics, XIII (February, 1951), 70-87; Peter H. Rossi, "Four Landmarks in Voting Research," in Eugene Burdick and Arthur J. Brodbeck, eds., American Voting Behavior (Glencoe, Ill., 1969), 5-54; Seymour M. Lipset, Paul F. Lazarsfeld, Allan H. Barton, and Juan Linz, "The Psychology of Voting: An Analysis of Political Behavior," in Gardner Lindsey, ed., Handbook of Social Psychology (Cambridge, 1954), II, 1124-75; and Walter Berns, "Voting Studies," in Herbert J. Storing, ed., Essays on the Scientific Study of Politics (New York, 1962), 3-62.

[17]Campbell, et al., The American Voter, 292.

[18]Paul F. Lazarsfeld, Bernard Berelson, and Hazel Gaudet, The People's Choice: How the Voter Makes up His Mind in a Presidential Campaign (New York; 1944).

[19]Hays, "New Possibilities for American Political History," 5. An earlier discussion of this approach appeared in Robert T. Bower, "Opinion Research and Historical Interpretation of Elections," Public Opinion Quarterly, XII (Fall, 1948), 455-464.

[20]See J. Rogers Hollingsworth, "The Historian, Presidential Elections, and 1896," Mid-America, XLV (July, 1963), 185-192. Samuel P. Hays has also stressed this, though mainly in lectures, such as those delivered at the Research

Conference on Political Data: Historical Analysis of Quantitative Data, sponsored by the Inter-University Consortiuim for Political Research, at Ann Arbor, Michigan, July 26 to August 13, 1965. See Hays, "Political Parties and the Community-Society Continuum," in William Nisbet Chambers and Walter Dean Burnham, eds., The American Party Systems: Stages of Political Development (New York, 1967), 152-181.

[21] Benson, "Research Problems," 120. In italics in original.

[22] Austin Ranney, "The Utility and Limitations of Aggregate Data in the Study of Electoral Behavior," in Austin Ranney, ed., Essays on the Behavioral Study of Politics (Urbana, Illinois, 1962), 91. The emphasis is Ranney's.

[23] Samuel Eliot Morison and Henry Steele Commager, The Growth of the American Republic, 5th ed. (New York, 1962), I, 665. It is interesting to note that this is virtually unchanged from the third edition (1942; 1947 printing, I, 637) cited by Lee Benson in his challenge of this interpretation in "Research Problems," 173. In the most recent revision of Morison and Commager, done mainly by William E. Leuchtenburg, this error has finally been corrected:

> Many German-Americans remained in the Democratic party; Catholics distrusted the radicalism of Republican leaders like Carl Schurz, older Lutherans supported slavery, and in general Germans were suspicious of the nativist and temperance strains in the Republican party. But in 1860 the personality of Lincoln and the free homestead issue swept large numbers of Germans into the Republican fold; they were probably decisive in swinging Illinois to Lincoln.

Morison, Commager, and Leuchtenburg, The Growth of the American Republic, 6th ed. (New York, 1969), I, 606.

[24]Joseph Schafer, "Who Elected Lincoln?" American Historical Review, XLVIII(October, 1941), 51-63; Andreas Dorpalen, "The German Element and the Issues of the Civil War," Mississippi Valley Historical Review, XXIX (July, 1942), 55-76.

[25]George H. Daniels, "Immigrant Vote in the 1860 Election: The Case of Iowa," Mid-America, XLIV (July, 1962), 146-162; Paul J. Kleppner, "Lincoln and the Immigrant Vote: A Case of Religious Polarization," Ibid., XLVIII (July, 1966), 176-195. These articles and others have been gathered together with a most useful introduction in Frederick C. Luebke, ed., Ethnic Voters and the Election of Lincoln (Lincoln, Nebraska, 1971).

[26]Schafer's main work on the German vote was the article published in the American Historical Review of October, 1941, eight months after his death. However, he had written extensively on the relationship between ethnicity and voting in two volumes of the Wisconsin Domesday Book Series: Four Wisconsin Counties: Prairie and Forest (Madison, 1927), 140-170; and The Wisconsin Lead Region (Madison, 1932), 213-217. See Chapter III for more on Schafer's Domesday Book Series, an ambitious effort to describe completely the settlement and development of Wisconsin, township by township. It is interesting in light of his later analysis of the subject

that Schafer's first work on ethnicity, a series of articles entitled, "The Yankee and Teuton in Wisconsin," had concluded with the standard interpretation of the German vote going to Lincoln. See "The Yankee and Teuton in Wisconsin: Social Harmonies and Discords," Wisconsin Magazine of History, VII (December, 1923), 170-171.

[27] Quoted in Joseph Schafer, "The Wisconsin Domesday Book," Wisconsin Magazine of History, IV (September, 1920), 63-4. Turner's interest in voting patterns went back to his college days when he wrote in his Commonplace Book; "Need of Study of Foreign groups. . .Votes by districts. Why are Nor[wegians] rep[ublican], Irish dem[ocrats]." Quoted in Ray A. Billington, "Young Fred Turner," Wisconsin Magazine of History, XLVI (Autumn, 1962, 47.

[28] Turner wrote the introduction to Libby's The Geographical Distribution of the Vote of the Thirteen States on the Federal Constitution, 1787-1788 (Madison, 1894), which, although little read itself, became famous as the basis for a part of Charles Beard's Economic Interpretation of the Constitution.

[29] Robinson collected election data on the county level which he published in The Presidential Vote, 1896-1932 (Stanford, California, 1934), and They Voted for Roosevelt (Stanford, 1947). I am indebted to Richard Jensen, "The Development of Historical Psephology in America," unpublished manuscript, Ann Arbor, Michigan, August 5, 1965, for these

insights into the history of voting behavior studies. Much of what appeared in his essay has since been published by Jensen, as "History and the Political Scientist," and "American Election Analysis: A Case Study of Methodological Innovation and Diffusion," in Seymour Martin Lipset, ed., Politics and the Social Sciences (New York, 1969), 1-28, 226-243.

[30]See Ogburn and Delvin Peterson, "Political Thought of Social Classes," Political Science Quarterly, XXXI (June, 1916), 300-317, for the Oregon study. For a complete bibliography of Ogburn's writings see Otis Dudley Duncan, ed., William F. Ogburn on Culture and Social Change (Chicago, 1964), 349-360.

[31]See Rossi, "Four Landmarks in Voting Research," 307-313. Rice had earlier studied American farmer-labor politics in Farmers and Workers in American Politics (New York, 1924).

[32]Merriam was head of the Political Science Department at the University of Chicago and trained Gosnell who in turn trained Key.

[33]Gosnell, Machine Politics: Chicago Model (Chicago, 1937) and Grass Roots Politics: National Voting Behavior of Typical States (Washington, 1942), which includes detailed studies of voting patterns in California, Illinois, Iowa, Louisiana, Pennsylvania, and Wisconsin in the 1930's.

[34]Key, A Primer on Statistics for the Political Scientist (New York, 1954), 125-126. The emphasis is added. In ad-

dition to his Southern Politics in State and Nation (New York, 1949), Key's path-breaking work includes "A Theory of Critical Elections," Journal of Politics, XVII (February, 1955), 3-18; "Secular Realignment and the Party System," Journal of Politics, XXVI (May, 1959), 198-210; and The Responsible Electorate: Rationality in Presidential Voting, 1936-1960 (Cambridge, 1966).

[35]Siegfried, Tableau Politique de la France de l'Ouest sous la Troisieme République (Paris, 1913).

[36]Heberle, "Principles of Political Ecology," in Karl G. Specht, ed., Sociologishe forschur in Unserer Zeit (Koln, 1951), 187-196; "On Political Ecology," Social Forces, XXXI (October, 1952), 31-39; and Social Movements: An Introduction to Political Sociology (New York, 1951), Part IV, 193-265.

[37]Heberle, From Democracy to Nazism (Baton Rouge, 1945). See Seymour Martin Lipset, Political Man (Garden City, New York, 1960), 140-149, for a discussion based on the book. The Heberle influence is also clear in Heberle and A. L. Bertrand, "Factors Motivating Voting Behavior in a One-Party State," Social Forces, XXVII (May, 1949), 343-350; Perry H. Howard, Political Tenderness in Louisiana 1812-1952 (Baton Rouge, 1956); Heberle, Howard, and William G. Havard, The Louisiana Election of 1960 (Baton Rouge, 1963).

[38]See footnotes 24 and 26.

[39]Gosnell and Morris H. Cohen, "Progressive Politics:

Wisconsin an Example," *American Political Science Review*, XXXIV (October, 1940), 920-935; also published as a chapter of *Grass Roots Politics*.

[40] Robinson, *American Sociological Review*, XV (June, 1950), 351-357, citation from 357.

[41] See Arnold M. Rose, "A Weakness of Partial Correlation in Sociological Studies," *American Sociological Review*, XIV (August, 1949), 536-539.

[42] Bean, *Influences in the 1954 Mid Term Elections*. Washington, D. C., 1954); Baggaley, "Patterns of Voting Change in Wisconsin Counties, 1952-1957," *Western Political Quarterly*, XII (March, 1959), 141-144; Fenton, *Midwest Politics* (New York, 1966), 44-74.

[43] Jorgen Weibull, "The Wisconsin Progressives, 1900-1914," *Mid-America*, XLVII (July, 1965), 191-221. The quote is from 191. This study by a Swedish scholar was done at the University of Wisconsin in 1962.

[44] Rogin, *The Intellectuals and McCarthy*, 59-103. The work of Louis Bean cited above also dealt with the nature of McCarthy's support.

[45] Epstein and Harry M. Scoble, "Religion and Wisconsin Voting in 1960," *Journal of Politics*, XXVI (May, 1964), 381-96; Epstein, *Votes and Taxes* (Madison, 1964); Epstein and Austin Ranney, "Who Voted for Goldwater: The Wisconsin Case," *Political Science Quarterly*, LXXXI (March, 1966), 82-99; Epstein and Ranney, "The Two Electorates: Voters and

Non-Voters in a Wisconsin Primary," Journal of Politics, XXVIII (August, 1966), 598-616.

⁴⁶Ranney, "The Utility and Limitations of Aggregate Data," 99. The emphasis is Ranney's.

⁴⁷Epstein and Ranney, "Two Electorates," 600-601.

⁴⁸Epstein, "Size of Place," Western Political Quarterly, IX (March, 1956), 138-150; Politics in Wisconsin (Madison, 1958), Ch. IV. This chapter, "Size of Place and the Two-Party Vote," is largely a rewrite of the article.

⁴⁹See the tables on 60 and 62 of Epstein's Politics in Wisconsin for the results for the gubernatorial elections from 1948 to 1954.

⁵⁰David Adamany, "Size of Place Analysis Reconsidered," Western Political Quarterly, XVII (September, 1964), 477-487; N. A. Masters and D. S. Wright, "Trends and Variations in the Two-Party Vote: The Case of Michigan," American Political Science Review, LII (December, 1958), 1078-1090.

⁵¹Epstein, Wisconsin Farm Vote, a University of Wisconsin Extension Division Publication, Mimeographed. (Madison, 1954). See Chapter III and Appendix A for the source of ethnic data on the minor civil division level.

⁵²Baggaley, "Religious Influence in Wisconsin Voting," American Political Science Review, LVI (March, 1962), 66-70; Rogin, "Wallace and the Middle Class: The White Backlash in Wisconsin," Public Opinion Quarterly, XXX (Spring, 1966), 98-108, and "Politics, Emotion, and the Wallace Vote,"

British Journal of Sociology, XX (March, 1969), 27-49.

[53]Wyman, "Wisconsin Ethnic Groups," Wisconsin Magazine of History, LI (Summer, 1968), 269-293. Wyman used a similar method in his doctoral dissertation on Wisconsin Progressivism from 1900 to 1914, "Voting Behavior in the Progressive Era: Wisconsin as a Case Study," (University of Wisconsin, Ph. D. Dissertation, 1970), three vols.

[54]Kleppner, The Cross of Culture: A Social Analysis of Midwestern Politics, 1850-1900 (New York, 1970). Jensen, The Winning of the Midwest: Social and Political Conflict, 1888-1896 (Chicago, 1971).

[55]Lubell, Future of American Politics, 3rd. ed. (New York, 1965), 142-145; Revolt of the Moderates (New York, 1952), 64-74.

CHAPTER II   RESEARCH DESIGN

At the heart of this study is a detailed analysis of Twentieth Century voting patterns in Wisconsin based on minor civil divisions--cities, villages, townships, and wards--for selected elections from 1898 to 1950. The main concentration is on electoral behavior of ethnic groups combined with analysis by size-of place. Townships, city wards, and villages and cities grouped according to size have been categorized by ethnic and religious composition. Voting percentages have been computed for these units in nineteen elections and four referenda during the period in question. With these data as the basic source, but using other primary sources as well as secondary accounts of ethnic groups and electoral behavior during this period, a series of questions forms the framework for the study: What was the nature of the political universe in Wisconsin prior to the advent of the progressive movement? What groups provided the basis of support for and opposition to Robert La Follette and the progressive movement prior to World War I? How did these groups respond to the War and to the decade of the 1920's? How did they respond to the Depression of the 1930's, the New Deal, and the left-of-New Deal Wisconsin Progressive Party led by La Follette's two sons? How did the political response of these groups to World War II compare with their response to World War I?

And, finally, how did the groups align themselves in the political spectrum as the half-century came to an end?

The method of getting at the composition of the electorate supporting a party or individual involves computing the median vote (or the mean vote for the 1908 to 1920 Presidential contests) for each grouping of voting units, based on ethnic, religious and size-of-place differences. While the largest groupings--German Catholics, German Lutherans, Yankee Protestants, and Norwegians--yield sizable samples, sufficient concentrations of Swedes, Danes, Finns, Bohemians, Belgians, Poles, and Irish exist to allow conclusions to be reached on these segments of the population also. In addition, small samples of English, Welsh, Swiss, Reformed and Catholic Hollanders, French Canadians, Italians, and Austrians yield partial information on those groups which appear in lesser numbers on the roll-call of Wisconsin's foreign-born population.

Any quantitative study proceeds from certain methodological assumptions. A basic assumption underlying this study of voting patterns is that there is a need to study politics at the state and local level both as case studies to determine general patterns and because American politics is organized at that level. While there are basic national trends which determine national and even state and local elections, there are also sectional, state, and local variations in these patterns. V. O. Key in his writing does much to point this out:

> Viewed over the entire nation, the party organization constitutes no disciplined army. It consists rather of many state and local points of power, each with its own local following and each comparatively independent of external control. Each of the dispersed clusters of party professionals has its own concerns with state and local nominations and elections. Each has a base for existence independent of national politics. Each in fact enjoys such independence that more than a tinge of truth colors the observation that there are no national parties, only state and local parties.[1]

The first dozen chapters of Key's <u>Southern Politics</u> consist of a state-by-state analysis of the so-called solid South which yielded "if not eleven types of factionalism [the Southern version of two-party politics in the days before the Republican resurgence] at least great variation."[2]

Survey research underplays these variations since it is based on a national population sample and very seldom pays attention to geographical differences beyond the division of the country into four sections. At the same time, a danger to avoid in state and local studies is generalization to other areas or to the entire political universe. As Lee Benson suggested in his study of New York politics in the Jacksonian period, systematic studies of other states would be necessary before his assault on the Turner-Beard-Schlesinger economic determinist interpretation could be generalized beyond New York. At best a state or local study provides a working hypothesis to be further tested.[3]

A second assumption is that small homogeneous units--

city wards or precincts, villages, and townships--must be used in order to isolate homogeneous social groups. This method is most successful in isolating ethnic groups. Pinpointing economic variables is more difficult as Benson's study on Jacksonian democracy indicates. While his argument that ethno-cultural groupings are primary determinants of voting behavior is convincing, his study is hampered by the difficulty of measuring economic status. Occupational groupings--except for rural-farm--are very difficult to pinpoint with certainty even using the smallest electoral units.

A third assumption is that the units must be studied over time to pinpoint variation from election to election after first separating out the overall secular or long-range trend. For example, a 10% shift on the part of German-dominated areas may be explained by the general trend for that election, or it may be a shift peculiar to German voters. The problem, especially in a study covering fifty years, is to find homogeneous units which have not changed either by shifts in boundaries or by shifts in population. Boundary changes include the creation of new townships, uncommon in Wisconsin after 1895 except in the northern counties of the cutover area where town creating lasted into the 1910's; the creation of villages especially from 1890 to 1920; the annexation of neighboring areas by cities, primarily in the 1950's and 1960's; and the continual changes in city ward lines.

Population turnover is more difficult to deal with and deserves special attention in a study of this nature covering a period of more than fifty years. A number of studies using manuscript census data discuss this problem for the Nineteenth Century. The most detailed study of turnover, or geographical mobility or persistence as it is also called, is Merle Curti's study of Trempealeau County in Wisconsin. Basing his study on the 1850 to 1880 manuscript census,[4] Curti found a high rate of turnover among all population groups during this, the frontier period in Trempealeau County. Curti noted that this mobility was as great for foreign-born and their descendants as it was for native-born thus countering the standard picture of the foreign-born as a more stable population element.[5]

Allan Bogue looking at the turnover in four Iowa townships found that "a high proportion of each new group of farmers dropped out early, leaving a core of much more persistent men."[6] In a detailed study of an Iowa township and the village at its center, Rodney Davis also discovered much mobility in the formative period of settlement. Davis' findings support the "general agreement among all students of population behavior of new communities that more people moved on during the formative years of a locality than stayed. Only as places grew older did their population tend to stabilize."[7] Davis noted that farmers tended to stabilize by 1880, but that farm laborers and townsmen had not yet arrived at stability in that year.

Stephan Thernstrom in his study of social mobility in Newburyport, Massachusetts from 1850 to 1880 was surprised to find extensive geographical mobility yielding a "floating population" of workers but also affecting the kind of families to be found in city directories: "of the 2025 families recorded in 1849, only 360 were to be found in Newburyport in 1879. <u>Within the span of a generation</u> the community had experienced something very close to a complete turnover of its population."[8]

One problem of population studies is the lack of manuscript U. S. censuses after 1880. This has been overcome in some cases by the use of manuscript state censuses. The pioneering study in persistence by James C. Malin on Kansas used the manuscript Kansas state census for the years 1865 to 1935. Malin found 1915 to be the transitional year between relative mobility and a significantly higher degree of stabilization for Kansas.[9] Peter Coleman used the Wisconsin state censuses for 1885 and 1895 to look at village turnover in Grant County. He found a very high rate of turnover of households varying from 35% to 59% between 1880 and 1885 despite a relatively small population change. Coleman, like Davis, tied the high rate of village turnover to economic conditions, to "the unsettling influence of the profound social and economic transformation sweeping America in the late Nineteenth Century."[10]

Unfortunately, with the exception of Malin's work on Kansas, an area with a later settlement pattern than that of Wisconsin, all of these studies stopped prior to 1900, the beginning date of this study. In fact, they are all primarily concerned with mobility during the frontier and early industrial period. More work needs to be done on the transitional period from frontier area to stable community and the degree of persistence in the Twentieth Century.

One further weakness remains in these studies--the stress on individual persistence as opposed to group persistence. Even a simple correction for normal generational turnover would add 33% to the persistence figures for each ten-year period, assuming each generation to be about thirty years. Beyond this, stabilization can reach a very high level for groups even if individual persistence is not that great. A number of illustrations support this conclusion.

The Norwegian experience in the Midwest was probably similar to that of most ethnic groups. Certain early-settled communities served as staging areas for further movement west. A typical individual or family would stop first in Muskego or Koshkonong, Wisconsin before moving to the western part of the state or on to Iowa to settle. At a later period, he would stop at the Coon Valley-Coon

Prairie settlement on his way to the Dakotas.[11] A very high rate of turnover would appear in what almost immediately became a solidly Norwegian community. In his study of Dane and Vernon Counties, the Koshkonong and Coon Prairie settlements, to determine the degree of "segregation and assimilation of Norwegian settlements," sociologist Peter Munch found the Norwegian settlement of Coon Prairie actually consolidating from 1878 to 1930, "the tendency having been to get rid of alien elements within the area of settlement itself."[12] In a detailed look at four Norwegian neighborhoods in Dane County, Munch found the same persistence, and even intensification of ethnic solidarity both in a geographical and associational sense. Indeed, 96% of all associations of people interviewed in the early 1950's were with fellow Norwegians.[13]

Joseph Schafer also found this to be true in his Wisconsin Domesday Book research. In a detailed study of Newton township in Manitowoc County, Schafer found a remarkable rate of family persistence from 1860 to 1903.

> On the map of the year 1903 we identify 82 names of persons who owned land in the township in 1860. In most cases the land held was in the same sections and constituted in part or in whole the original farms. Recalling that the number of farm owners in 1860, according to the census, was 228, we see that the proportion of persisting families must have been very large. The biographies in the county history include the names of 18 persons who resided in the town of Newton in 1910. In all cases they were then living on the farms on which they were born.[14]

A further indication of group persistence applied specifically to Wisconsin comes from studies in rural sociology published by the Agricultural Experiment Station of the University of Wisconsin. Rural sociologists have been greatly interested in the changing patterns of rural neighborhoods. Neighborhoods in Dane County, 121 in all, were first mapped in 1921. At that time, ninety-five of those were classified as active, that is "carrying on group activities or having recognizable factors holding the group together and giving it some sense of unity or group consciousness."[15] Sixty-three of these remained active in 1931, along with twenty-four new neighborhoods; seventy-two of the 1931 neighborhoods carried over into 1941. Forty-seven of the ninety-five neighborhoods active in 1921 were still active in 1951.[16] Writing in 1944, John Kolb and Douglas Marshall concluded:

> When the 24 neighborhoods, open-country and hamlet, classed as active for the first time in 1931 were excluded, it is surprising how stable in form and regular in activity the other active neighborhoods were throughout the whole 20-year period. Considering seven major institutions, for example, we find no significant changes; in fact 68% of these neighborhoods had the same institutional activities in each of the three periods--1921, 1931, 1941. . . .The boundaries of the neighborhoods had not changed significantly.[17]

The most useful evidence on turnover comes from the very work on nationality groups which forms the basis for isolating the ethnic areas in this study. In the late

1930's, the Agricultural Experiment Station of the University of Wisconsin in cooperation with the Works Progress Administration mapped on a township level Wisconsin's ethnic areas as of 1940. The basis of the study was a re-tabulation by nativity of the heads-of-household listed in the 1905 manuscript state census. Use of extensive, if impressionistic, field work brought this up-to-date as of 1940. George W. Hill, one of the co-directors of the project concluded:

> Outside of the northern cutover counties, a great deal of persistence does appear to exist. There is also a high degree of relationship between social isolation and culture fixation. Some groups, notably the Polish and Bohemian, have spread over much more territory in the passing generation.[18]

An ethnic mapping in 1969 of the seven county tobacco growing area of Southwestern Wisconsin based on field surveys and on platbooks found that "The 1969 ethnic map, when compared with those based on 1905 data, reveals only small changes in ethnic distribution despite the passage of nearly two-thirds of the century."[19] A study of Lafayette County in 1960 also concluded that while "many small changes have occurred . . . the situation regarding the major ethnic groups still remains the same as in 1905."[20]

With the general pattern of persistence established it is possible to look at specific problems of boundary changes and population shifts in this study, since a major part of the task has been the location of homogeneous voting units which remained relatively stable over the fifty years covered.

The beginning point for selection of voting units to be included in the study was 1900. By this time all but one of Wisconsin's seventy-one counties had been created and most had assumed final boundaries.[21] These counties contained 1045 townships, 145 villages, and 115 cities. Most townships which were divided to form new townships, which had villages created from their midst, or which lost significant area to cities by annexation after 1900 were eliminated from the sample used in this study.[22] Almost all townships in the fifty-three southern counties had been created by the beginning of the Twentieth Century. The northernmost counties were still undergoing settlement, however. These counties had been the scene of Wisconsin's logging operation from prior to the Civil War until 1900.[23] In the decade prior to World War I, this cutover region began to attract agricultural settlers, reaching population stability by the 1920 census.[24] Still, some fifty voting units from the eighteen counties of the cutover area maintained sufficient stability to be used in this study.

Villages and cities incorporated after 1905 were included if the townships from which they were created were sufficiently of a single ethnic group to indicate that the village would fall within the same category. While most of the villages and cities were in existence by 1905, this method allowed the addition of forty-seven units including twenty-eight German, seven Norwegian, three Swedish, two Danish, two Polish, two Bohemian, and single Dutch, French-Canadian, and Italian villages. Those villages and cities which grew so rapidly as to change their basic character were eliminated from the study.

The urban vote proved to be the most difficult with which to deal. Larger cities lacked homogeneity and grew so rapidly that analysis of the cities themselves was usually impossible. Although wards often found solid ethnic communities nestled in their midst, changes in boundaries, demographic characteristics, and size made analysis even at this level no easy task. Fortunately, the period under study occurred after most cities arrived at maturity and before the great pressure for reapportionment arrived. Thus, Ashland and La Crosse, for example, made almost no changes in ward line-up for the entire fifty-year period, and even Milwaukee reapportioned only twice--in 1912 and in 1931. In each case most of the city's wards retained their basic outlines.[25] As for demographic characteristics, these too changed very little once large-scale immigration ceased in 1914. Bayrd Still, writing on Milwaukee, noted:

> Apart from some movement prompted by this colored invasion [sic] of the Sixth and Tenth wards, the foreign-born continued by 1940 to inhabit generally the colonies in which they had resided twenty years earlier.[26]

A total of sixty-seven wards, forty-one of them German, can

be used with due caution for at least part of the study.

With the pool of voting units which did not change boundary over most of the period from 1898 to 1950 determined, the next task was to select homogeneous units. The first division was by size-of-place. Five categories were used: rural-farm townships; villages and cities with a population under 2,500; cities from 2,500 to 10,000; cities over 10,000, and urban wards. The definition of rural-farm township was 70% or more rural-farm throughout the fifty-year period.[27] Cities and villages were placed in the population category in which they fit during most of the time period under consideration.

Size-of-place analysis has not received extensive attention from political scientists. The most important study in this area is Leon Epstein's Politics in Wisconsin. Dealing primarily with the gubernatorial elections from 1948 to 1954, Epstein set up ten categories into which all voting units in the state were placed:[28]

    Milwaukee County
    Other urbanized area and cities over 50,000
    Cities of 25,000 to 50,000
    Cities of 10,000 to 25,000
    Cities of 5,000 to 10,000
    Cities of 2,500 to 5,000
    Cities and villages of 1,000 to 2,500
    Cities and villages under 1,000
    Townships with less than 50% farm population
    Townships with more than 50% farm population

Epstein in later research involving survey rather than the aggregate data used in his Politics in Wisconsin compressed his categories as follows:[29]

> Milwaukee and Madison
> Cities of 50,000 to 100,000
> Cities of 10,000 to 50,000
> Cities of 2,500 to 10,000
> Villages and cities to 2,500
> Unincorporated

Most discussions of elections lump together people from communities of under 2,500 with those from unincorporated areas as rural. Farmers are separated out in occupational analysis which in turn ignores size-of-place analysis.[30]

Samuel Lubell in his <u>Future of American Politics</u> makes clear the need to separate rural-farm from village voters. In describing the gradual movement of farmers toward the Democratic party as a "long-brewing political revolution," Lubell noted that this was:

> A quiet sort of revolution, its force has been obscured by the parties lumping all rural residents, townspeople as well as farmers, as part of the same farm vote. Separating these two voting elements, one discovers that the mainstay of Republican strength in the countryside has not been the farmer at all. The citadel of the Republican farm vote has been the courthouse ring rather than the "grass roots" farmer, the man on Main Street rather than the man with the hoe.[31]

Using data on Iowa gathered by <u>Wallace's Farmer</u>, Lubell illustrates the gap between farmer and small town from 1916 to 1948:[32]

Table I   Democratic Percentage of Total Vote in Iowa

Year	State	Farmers	Towns	Cities
1916	44%	44%	41%	49%
1920	25%	24%	25%	29%
1924	23%	26%	21%	22%
1928	38%	43%	31%	37%
1932	59%	70%	51%	53%
1936	56%	61%	48%	56%
1940	48%	49%	42%	51%
1944	48%	47%	43%	52%
1948	52%	54%	45%	53%

When economic issues are most salient the gap widens, when foreign policy issues move to the fore, the gap narrows. A long-term change has been from dependence on the town for political leadership to farm protest directed at the town to a growing realization on the part of Main Street businessmen that the continuance of their livelihood depends on the stability of rural America.

> Conflicts between town and country still persist, of course. Among the townspeople many still feel linked with business emotionally, economically, and ideologically. But a greater proportion than ever before now identify their own welfare with higher farm income and government price supports.[33]

Despite Lubell's stress on the farm vs. small town dimension most historians have ignored this factor in their analysis of farm protest. Robert Dykstra has called attention to this oversight in an article entitled "Town-Country Conflict: A Hidden Dimension in American Social History." After a search of the historical literature, Dykstra concluded that "with a few isolated exceptions, the his categories as follows:[29]

> Milwaukee and Madison
> Cities of 50,000 to 100,000
> Cities of 10,000 to 50,000
> Cities of 2,500 to 10,000
> Villages and cities to 2,500
> Unincorporated

Most discussions of elections lump together people from communities of under 2,500 with those from unincorporated areas as rural. Farmers are separated out in occupational analysis which in turn ignores size-of-place analysis.[30]

Samuel Lubell in his Future of American Politics makes clear the need to separate rural-farm from village voters. In describing the gradual movement of farmers toward the Democratic party as a "long-brewing political revolution," Lubell noted that this was:

> A quiet sort of revolution, its force has been obscured by the parties lumping all rural residents, townspeople as well as farmers, as part of the same farm vote. Separating these two voting elements, one discovers that the mainstay of Republican strength in the countryside has not been the farmer at all. The citadel of the Republican farm vote has been the courthouse ring rather than the "grass roots" farmer, the man on Main Street rather than the man with the hoe.[31]

Using data on Iowa gathered by Wallace's Farmer, Lubell illustrates the gap between farmer and small town from 1916 to 1948:[32]

Table I Democratic Percentage of Total Vote in Iowa

Year	State	Farmers	Towns	Cities
1916	44%	44%	41%	49%
1920	25%	24%	25%	29%
1924	23%	26%	21%	22%
1928	38%	43%	31%	37%
1932	59%	70%	51%	53%
1936	56%	61%	48%	56%
1940	48%	49%	42%	51%
1944	48%	47%	43%	52%
1948	52%	54%	45%	53%

When economic issues are most salient the gap widens, when foreign policy issues move to the fore, the gap narrows. A long-term change has been from dependence on the town for political leadership to farm protest directed at the town to a growing realization on the part of Main Street businessmen that the continuance of their livelihood depends on the stability of rural America.

> Conflicts between town and country still persist, of course. Among the townspeople many still feel linked with business emotionally, economically, and ideologically. But a greater proportion than ever before now identify their own welfare with higher farm income and government price supports.[33]

Despite Lubell's stress on the farm vs. small town dimension most historians have ignored this factor in their analysis of farm protest. Robert Dykstra has called attention to this oversight in an article entitled "Town-Country Conflict: A Hidden Dimension in American Social History." After a search of the historical literature, Dykstra concluded that "with a few isolated exceptions, the cleavage between small town and hinterland has been overlooked."[34]

Arthur Vidich and Joseph Bensman in <u>Small Town and Mass Society</u> also point out the clashes between farmers and the community which services them, although they are very aware of the means by which village political leaders dominate the politics of the rural area around them.[35] Again, few sociologists have followed their example in separating out and examining villages and the rural areas around them.

In addition to separating out the rural-farm vote from the "rural-small town" vote, this study originally divided the small town vote into communities under 1,000 and communities from 1,000 to 2,500. This closely corresponds to the state's legal distinction between villages and cities as most villages in Wisconsin fall under the 1,000 category; few cities do.[36] However, the smallness of the samples and the lack of meaningful differences between these two categories led to their combination. The use of the 2,500 division is most useful because it coincides with the census distinction between urban and rural.

Epstein's size-of-place analysis for cities over 2,500 has drawn more criticism than the rural-farm, rural-nonfarm division on the grounds that there is too broad a distribution of the vote within each size category suggesting that other variables than size-of-place might explain the distribution. A study of Michigan cities led to the conclusion that "the size of place in which the Michigan voter resides is not a reliable guide to his voting behavior . . . instead a large part of the variation in the two-party vote in a city can be explained in terms of the occupational structure."[37]

The size-of-place analysis was retained in an effort to verify its validity over a whole range of elections. The Michigan study covered only one election, Epstein's Wisconsin study and the Adamany followup covered eight elections.

For this study, urban areas over 2,500 have been divided into two categories, 2,500 to 10,000 and 10,000 and over. Most of the larger cities are treated on a ward level because of their lack of homogeneity. Five cities over 10,000 find their way into the study as they minimally meet the requirement of being sufficiently German. None of the five are over 50,000 in population by the end limit of the study.[38]

One additional factor must be mentioned. Political units which met the basic criteria of no boundary change and minimal demographic change for most but not all of the fifty years of this study were still used for the years during which they maintained stability. Thus, the number of units in each category from 1898 to 1950 was as follows:

Table II   Voting Units by Size-of-Place, 1898-1950[39]

	1898	1905	1924	1940	1950	Total Units
Rural-farm townships	228	264	312	312	260	312
Villages and cities to 2,500	64	102	146	149	146	149
Cities 2,500 to 10,000	27	28	28	28	28	28
Cities over 10,000	5	5	5	5	5	5
City wards	50	50	59	53	50	67
Total Units	374	449	550	547	489	561

More basic in determining voting behavior than size-of-place is ethno-cultural background. Voting behavior analysts and political historians have turned increasingly to this factor to explain voting not only during the period of immigration in the Nineteenth Century but into the Twentieth Century as well. A number of the studies cited in Chapter I pay attention to ethnicity or nationality background. One of the first to really point people in this direction was Samuel Lubell who stressed the importance of the appeal of Franklin Roosevelt and the New Deal to the second- and third-generation urban immigrant. Historians have more readily followed up these insights than have political scientists. The two major publications of the Survey Research Center at the University of Michigan, The American Voter and Elections and the Political Order, ignore almost completely the effect of ethnicity.[40]

V. O. Key originally pointed to the importance of the

ethnic voter in his landmark "A Theory of Critical Elections."
Describing the voter realignment in the critical election
of 1928, Key examined the percent foreign-born as one of his
main variables, concluding:

> Examination of the characteristics of the two
> groups of cities and towns. . . those with the
> most marked Democratic gains, 1920-1928, and
> those with the widest movement in the opposite
> direction--reveals the expected sorts of dif-
> ferences. Urban, industrial, foreign-born,
> Catholic areas make up the bulk of the first
> group of towns, although an occasional rural
> Catholic community increased its Democratic
> vote markedly. The towns with a contrary
> movement tended to be rural Protestant,
> native-born.[41]

However, in his <u>Politics, Parties and Pressure Groups</u>,
Key stresses the acculturation and assimilation aspect of
the immigration experience:

> The American political system has absorbed
> wave after wave of immigration. As each new
> influx of migrants arrived peoples of like
> national origin, language, and culture formed
> political blocs attached to this or that
> party as circumstances, immediate self-interest,
> or a stratey of self-protection dictated. . .
> Although from time to time specific events
> of issues activate memories linked to the
> homeland even across several generations, over
> the long run the cohesiveness of national-
> origin groups declines. . . the gradual
> weakening of the cohesion of ethnic groups
> is paralleled by changes in voting behavior.
> A secular decline in the partisan solid-
> arity of the group occurs as members of each
> generation become more susceptible to the
> political appeals to which people generally
> respond rather than to group-directed appeals.[42]

Key admits that there is little data in this area, though
his posthumously published study of voting from 1936 to

1960 almost entirely ignores the increased attention being paid to ethnic groups.[43]

In fact, a number of studies by political scientists and sociologists have pointed to the continued importance of ethnicity well into the middle of the Twentieth Century. Nathan Glazer and Daniel Moynihan in Beyond the Melting Pot stress its impact on New York City politics. In general Glazer and Moynihan down-play the acculturation-assimilation interpretation and stress the continuity of ethnic consciousness.[44] Moses Rischin used the Survey Research Center's data from its earlier studies to give ethnicity much more credence than the Center itself had, concluding:

> In the next generation two major unresolved domestic issues--segregation and the relations between church and state--will test the American capacity for growth. Experience warrants the prophecy that ethnic attitudes toward these issues, as towards foreign policy, will be affected by the legacy of the past as it is shaped by the present and that the voting returns will continue to reflect ethnic influences. As the different ethnic groups ascend the social and economic ladder, these cultural influences assume a different guise, but they persist as shapers of the voting habits of the American people. The proposition that the ethnic factor is second only to the economic factor in influencing an American's vote is unlikely to be overthrown in the near future.[45]

Lucy Dawidowicz and Leon Goldstein in a series of studies on the 1960 election tested not only the obvious effect of religion but also the ethnic variable. They found significant differences among Catholic ethnic groups and among Protestant groups in responding to the campaign of John F.

Kennedy. For example, Baptists and Methodists in Tennessee broke more strongly with the Democratic Party than did Lutherans in Minnesota. The Dawidowicz-Goldstein study concluded that "broad statements about the Protestant vote are surely pointless. No one will be surprised to find the varieties of American Protestantism with their manifold ethnic and cultural association reflected in variegated voting behavior."[46]

In a study of the Italians of New Haven since the 1930's, Raymond Wolfinger found great persistence in the political orientation of this ethnic group, in this case in the Republican direction. Four points made by Wolfinger are also borne out by this study:

1. Members of ethnic groups tend to vote for one party or another in numbers which cannot be explained by other demographic characteristics.

2. The salience of ethnicity varies from election to election with the issues of each election. Foreign policy and cultural issues such as prohibition and nativism are often salient to the ethnic groups affected by them. Economic issues such as depressions and general foreign policy questions not related to one's ethnic group tend to diminish ethnic voting.

3. Ethnic partisanship remains even after the issues which first induced it have subsided: "One of the most remarkable tendencies in political behavior is the persis-

tence of partisan affiliations for generations after the
reasons for their formation have become irrelevant to contemporary society."

4. Ethnic group members tend to vote for a fellow-member of their group on whatever political ticket he appears. More importantly they will support the party which gives them political recognition. Since the latter usually comes only as the ethnic group moves into the middle class, it is a more important issue to second- and third-generation ethnics than to the first-generation.[47]

More research has been done on the effect of religion on voting than on the effect of ethnicity. Most of this assumes the similarity of groupings within one religion, a view canonized by Will Herburg in Protestant, Catholic, Jew.[48] Seymour Martin Lipset, the political sociologist, also stresses religious conflict in a number of insightful essays which omit discussion of ethno-cultural variations.[49]

Historians also have been slow in breaking with the assimilationist school of immigration studies and in moving to study the persistence of nationality traits—including the acquisition of basic political orientation. Lee Benson pioneered in this effort in his work on Jacksonian democracy. Benson concluded that:

> at least since the 1820's when manhood suffrage became widespread, ethnic and religious differences have tended to be relatively the most important sources of political differences . . . the sharpest political

cleavages occurred, not between immigrants
and Yankees, but between different groups of
immigrants.[50]

Sam Hays in his work on the late Nineteenth Century also
stresses ethno-cultural issues as they affect ethnic groups:

> Party divisions after the Civil War grew out
> of the impact of evangelical Protestantism
> on the political world of the late 1840's and
> the early 1850's. In the form of Prohibition,
> nativism, and antislavery, that movement pro-
> duced both a sharp realignment of voting
> behavior and a cultural unity for the Repub-
> lican party. The Democratic party, in turn,
> combined Catholics and German Lutherans and
> nonevangelical Protestant native-born Ameri-
> cans in a common hostility to evangelical im-
> perialism and the alignment persisted with
> little change until the depression of 1893. . .
> The years from 1893 to 1896 witnessed the first
> major voting realignment in American politics
> since the 1850's. This realignment seems to
> have been a product of the depression of 1893
> and of the shifting attractiveness of parties
> and candidates to ethno-cultural groups.[51]

Excellent surveys of literature in this field have
been published by Robert Swierenga and Samuel McSeveney.[52]
The pre-Civil War period has seen a number of quantitative
studies reflecting the move toward an ethno-cultural explanation of American voting patterns[53] as has the period
in which politics became truly nationalized, 1880-1900.[54]
Three studies in the latter period deal with Wisconsin, along
with other Midwestern states, all laying great stress on
ethno-cultural issues.[55]

The Twentieth Century has been less studied by historians in terms of ethnic voting partly because of the earlier
assumption that ethnicity lost salience with the passage

of time and partly because demographic data is more difficult to acquire on the minor civil division level after 1890. Most studies have been of individual cities.[56] Exceptions have been Joseph Huthmacher's study of Massachusetts, Michael Rogin and John Shover's work on California, and Rogin's _tour de force_ on Wisconsin and the Dakotas.[57] Jorgen Weibull also studied Wisconsin during the early progressive period, placing some stress on ethnic factors.[58]

However, none of the statewide Twentieth Century studies have looked at ethnic voting on the minor civil division level in a systematic way. This study aims at doing just that. The final stage after identifying voting units which remained constant over the fifty years and categorizing them by size-of-place was to identify homogeneous ethno-cultural areas which remained so over the same period. Wisconsin lends itself to this typology for a number of reasons. First, it was largely settled by 1900. It had passed beyond the frontier stage of high geographical mobility into a stage of relative stability. Second, most of the people settling the state were immigrants from Europe, thus giving a suitable laboratory for investigating ethno-cultural groups. In fact, people from an Eastern, Yankee background form just one of several ethnic groups despite their dominance of the Wisconsin political scene prior to 1900. Finally, Wisconsin has good data with which to measure ethnicity on the minor civil division level.

This data is contained in the retabulation of the 1905 state census carried out under the auspices of the Works Progress Administration in the late 1930's. The study retabulated all heads-of-household in that census according to a number of characteristics--one of which was country or state of birth <u>and</u> country or state of parent's birth. By combining these two categories, a fair index of ethnicity could be obtained for each voting unit in the state existent in 1905.[59] Since most of Wisconsin's settlement came after 1840 only a few third-generation heads-of-household would have appeared in the 1905 retabulation listed as native-born of native-born parents. Two examples should suffice to illustrate the point:

Newton township in Manitowoc County was settled in the 1840's by Germans who soon totally displaced the few Yankee settlers already there.[60] According to the published 1905 state census, 242 of Newton's 1,741 residents were born in Germany with 1,451 listed as native-born.[61] This gives a breakdown of 14% German compared with 83% native-born. However, the retabulation of the census shows that 85% of the 327 family heads were born in Germany, or had parents from Germany, while only 2% were native-born of native-born parents.

The township of Coon in Vernon County was settled in the 1850's by Norwegians. It finds its way into our sample both as a township and as the village of Coon Valley which was incorporated in 1907, two years after the census was taken. The 1905 published census records the township, including the future village, as having 416 Norwegian-born and 1,009 native-born out of a total of 1,438 residents, 29% and 70% respectively. The retabulated census gives a somewhat different picture, with 95% of the town of Coon, and village of Coon Valley's 214 heads-of-household listed as Norwegian, native-born of native-born parents not even showing up in this listing.

Table III on the next page indicates the number of units for each ethnic group falling under each size-of-place category. The minimum percent refers to the percent of heads-of-household in the given ethnic stock necessary before the political unit was used in this study. Generally, for larger groups this was 60%; for smaller groupings the percentage dropped as low as 28%--and in two cases, to 17%. Obviously the lower the minimum--and the smaller the number of units in each category--the more cautious one must be in making generalizations. In almost every case, of course, these figures under-represent the actual purity of the given voting units.

Persistence of ethnicity throughout the fifty years was checked in a number of ways. The WPA study in the 1930's led to the publishing of a map of Wisconsin ethnic areas as of 1940. This was based on the retabulation of

Table III Voting Units by Ethnic Group and Size-of-Place

	Rural Townships		Villages and Cities						Wards	
			Under 2,500		2,500–10,000		Over 10,000			
	N=*	Min.%**	N=	Min.%	N=	Min.%	N=	Min.%	N=	Min.%
German	165	60%	86	50%	22	40%	5	50%	41	60%
Native-born	22	60%	20	60%	2	60%	0	--	5	50%
Norwegian	35	60%	19	50%	1	50%	0	--	4	35%
Swedish	14	50%	5	43%	1	37%	0	--	1	30%
Danish	8	38%	3	50%	1	30%	0	--	4	35%
Finnish	12	43%	0	--	0	--	0	--	0	--
Polish	12	60%	2	35%	0	--	0	--	8	(29%)
Bohemian	11	46%	2	40%	0	--	0	--	0	--
Irish	9	37%	0	--	0	--	0	--	1	35%
Belgian	7	47%	0	--	0	--	0	--	1	35%
Swiss	3	47%	2	48%	1	28%	0	--	0	--
Hollanders	4	48%	3	50%	0	--	0	--	0	--
English	3	45%	2	50%	0	--	0	--	0	--
Welsh	2	29%	2	35%	0	--	0	--	0	--
Fr. Canadian	2	50%	2	45%	0	--	0	--	1	35%
Italian	2	17%	1	(17%)	0	--	0	--	1	30%
Austrian	1	50%	0	--	0	--	0	--		
	312		149		28		5		67	

Total units 561   *N= Number of units

**Min.% = Minimum ethnic percentage, based on 1905 retabulation, to be included in this study.

the 1905 census and brought up-to-date by the use of impressionistic fieldwork, including interviews and correspondence with officials and long-time residents of each county.[62] Each unit used in this study had to show up on this map within its particular ethnic area. This check on persistence was more effective for townships than for villages and cities.

Additionally, church records were consulted--particularly for Lutherans. Locations and memberships of churches are available in yearbooks put out by the National Lutheran Council as well as by other denominations.[63] In addition to the Germans (Wisconsin, Missouri, and ALC Synods), this gave a sense of ethnic continuity for Norwegians (ELC), Swedes (Augustana), Danes (UELC), and Finns (Soumi). These synods remained autonomous and largely ethnically cohesive through the 1950's, beyond the termination point of this study.

In this study, religion was not treated as a separate grouping but as a subdivision of ethnic groups. This was done primarily for the Germans since most other ethnic groups fell within a single religious grouping. Germans were divided into German Catholics and German Lutherans including the few German Reformed which showed up in the study. The basis for this division was a 1946 statewide referendum on aid to parochial schools for busing pupils. Research in newspapers and other sources for the period indicated that almost all the German Catholics supported parochial school aid, and almost all German Lutherans opposed aid.[64] All German voting units which cast 65% or more yes votes were labelled German Catholic and all German voting units which cast 35% or less yes votes were labelled German Lutheran. German voting units falling between 35% and 65% were labelled German Mixed. This initial list was verified by checking church lists. All of the German Catholic areas contained or were near Catholic churches; all of the German Lutheran areas contained or were near German Lutheran churches of the Wisconsin, Missouri, or American Lutheran Synods.[65]

This method served to divide the German voting units as follows:

Table IV   German Voting Units

	Townships	Villages and Cities		
	Under 2,500	2,500-10,000	Over 10,000
German Lutheran	85	28	3	0
German Mixed	50	39	15	5
German Catholic	30	19	4	0
Total	165	86	22	5

Among other ethnic groups, only the Hollanders required typing by religion. Thus, three of the four Dutch townships were labelled Dutch Reformed along with two villages while one of each category was Dutch Catholic.

With the voting units selected, it was necessary to move on to the other variable--the "whom" being voted for. In addition to a variety of "whoms"--presidential, gubernatorial, and senatorial candidates in both general and primary elections--a number of "whats"--referenda on progressive issues--were also selected. Thus information was sought on both Democratic-Republican-Progressive splits and on progressive-stalwart splits within the Republican party. The elections finally selected for study were:

Table V Elections Studied at Minor Civil Division Level[66]

Presidential Elections   Senatorial Elections

   1908   1920   1932   1918
   1912   1924   1936   1934
   1916   1928   1940   1940

Presidential Primaries   Senatorial Primaries

   1912 Republican   1922 Republican
                                 1946 Republican

Gubernatorial Elections

   1898   1904
   1900   1950

Referenda

   1904 Primary election law
   1914 Initiative and referendum--Constitutional Amendment
   1926 Prohibition, Volstead Act memorial
   1946 Aid for parochial school busing--Constitutional Amendment

Before correlating the ethnic and size-of-place groupings with these election returns it is necessary to examine the nature of Wisconsin's settlement which led to the mosaic of ethnic groups existing in 1900.

NOTES

[1]Key, Politics, Parties and Pressure Groups, 5th ed. (New York, 1964), 329.

[2]Key, Southern Politics in State and Nation (New York: 1949), 18.

[3]See Benson, The Concept of Jacksonian Democracy: New York as a Test Case (Princeton, New Jersey, 1961) vii-viii, 1-2, 165, 335-336, etc.

[4]Most of the 1890 manuscripts were lost in a fire; those from 1900 are just now becoming available to scholars. See Barnes F. Lothrop, "History from the Census Returns," Southwestern Historical Quarterly, LI (April, 1948), 293-312, for a discussion of census schedules from 1820 to 1880. See also Carroll D. Wright, The History and Growth of the United States Census (Washington, D. C., 1900), and Henry J. Dubester, Catalog of United States Census Publications, 1790-1945 (Washington, D. C., 1950).

[5]Curti, The Making of an American Community: A Case Study of Democracy in a Frontier County (Stanford, California, 1959), 65-77.

[6]Bogue, From Prairie to Corn Belt: Farming on the Illinois and Iowa Prairies in the Nineteenth Century (Chicago, 1963), 27.

[7]Davis, "Prairie Emporium: Clarence, Iowa 1860-1880: A Study of Population Trends," Mid-America, LI (April, 1969),

130-139. The quote is from pages 137-138.

[8]Thernstrom, Poverty and Progress: Social Mobility in a Nineteenth Century City (Cambridge, Massachusetts, 1964), 168. Emphasis added.

[9]Malin, "The Turnover of Farm Population in Kansas," Kansas Historical Quarterly, IV (November, 1935), 352-353, 358. See also Malin, The Grasslands of North America: Prolegomena to its History (Gloucester, Massachusetts, 1967), 278-291, 312-315, and "Local Historical Studies and Population Problems" in Caroline F. Ware, ed., The Cultural Approach to History (New York, 1940), 300-307.

[10]Coleman, "Restless Grant County: Americans on the Move," Wisconsin Magazine of History, XLVI (Autumn, 1962), 16-20. The quote is from page 20. In the same article Coleman pointed out that, "only a modest amount of land changed hands in the eighties and nineties." Ibid.

[11]See Chapter III for details of Norwegian settlement.

[12]Munch, "Segregation and Assimilation of Norwegian Settlements in Wisconsin," Norwegian-American Studies and Records, XVIII (1954), 114. The use of the term "alien" provides a nice bit of irony as the alien element in this case consisted primarily of Yankees.

[13]Ibid., 132-134. The actual figure was 343 out of 358.

[14]Joseph Schafer, "Documenting Local History," Wisconsin Magazine of History, V (December, 1921), 152-153. Reprinted in Schafer, Wisconsin Domesday Book: Town Studies,

Vol I (Madison, 1924), 87. In another volume of his
Domesday Book series, Schafer noted that "of the purchasers of farms sold in Fredonia [township in Ozaukee
County] between 1880 and 1910 a large proportion were
'neighbors' and some are described as 'owning land adjoining'." Four Wisconsin Counties: Prairie and Forest,
General Studies, Vol. II (Madison, 1927), 282.

Dieter Brunnschweiler details a similar pattern in
New Glarus township in Green County, "Tradition and Environment as Counter-Influences in the History of New
Glarus," in Leo Schelbert, ed., New Glarus, 1845-1970: The
Making of a Swiss-American Town (Glarus, Switzerland, 1970),
160-189.

C. Luther Fry, in his 1920 comparative study of Sheboygan and Price Counties, reached the following conclusions
for Sheboygan County, "The population, at least the rural
part of it, has remained stationary for decades" and,
for Price County, "There is a tendency toward clannishness,
especially among the Norwegians, Swedes and Bohemians, so
that as yet the races have not mingled to any extent."
The New and Old Immigrant on the Land: A Study of Americanization and the Rural Church (New York, 1922), 38 and 42.

[15]John H. Kolb, Trends of Country Neighborhoods: A
Re-study of Rural Primary Groups, 1921-1931, Agricultural
Experiment Station of the University of Wisconsin, Research
Bulletin 120 (Madison, November, 1933), 3. See also Kolb,

Rural Primary Groups: A Study of Agricultural Neighborhoods, Research Bulletin 51 (Madison, 1921), 192. Hereinafter, all references to Research Bulletins will omit the Agricultural Experiment Station information.

[16]Kolb, Trends of Country Neighborhoods, 4; Kolb and Douglas G. Marshall, Neighborhood-Community Relationships in Rural Society, Research Bulletin 154 (Madison, November, 1944), 3; Kolb, Neighborhood-Family Relationships in Rural Society, Research Bulletin 201 (Madison, May, 1957).

[17]Kolb and Marshall, Neighborhood-Community Relationships, 3.

[18]Hill, "The use of the Culture-Area Concept in Social Research," The American Journal of Sociology, XLVII (July, 1941), 44. The data was charted on a map entitled "The Peoples of Wisconsin According to Ethnic Stocks, 1940," in Wisconsin's Changing Population. Science inquiry Publication IX. Bulletin of the University of Madison (Madison, October, 1942). The retabulation is still available in manuscript form: "A Retabulation of Population Schedules from the Wisconsin State Census of 1905." Departments of Rural Sociology and Agricultural economics, Wisconsin Agricultural Experiment Station, University of Wisconsin Cooperating with the Works Progress Administration. Directed by George W. Hill. July 30, 1940, 11 vols. Now in the archives of the Wisconsin State Historical Society. George A. Boeck, "A Historical Note on the Uses of Census

Returns," <u>Mid-America</u>, XLIV (January, 1962), 46-50, calls for retabulating the Nineteenth Century censuses omitting children to get a more accurate picture of ethnic groups for voting studies without apparent awareness of the Wisconsin retabulation.

[19]Karl B. Raitz and Cotton Mather, "Norwegians and Tobacco in Western Wisconsin." <u>Annals of the Association of American Geographers</u>, LXI (December, 1971), 684-696. This study found a very high correlation between tobacco-growing areas and Norwegian areas in Wisconsin.

[20]Donald Whiteside, "The Use of Historical Data in a Sociological Study of Lafayette County, Wisconsin," (University of Wisconsin M.S. Thesis, 1960), 39-40.

[21]The only major changes after 1898 were the creation of Rusk (Gates) County from Chippewa County in 1901 and changes in the boundaries of Forest, Oneida, and Vilas Counties in 1901 and 1905. See Louise Kellog, "Organization, Boundaries and Names of Wisconsin Counties," <u>Proceedings of the Wisconsin State Historical Society</u>, LVII (Madison, 1909), 184-231; and Wisconsin Historical Records Survey, <u>Origin and Legislative History of County Boundaries in Wisconsin</u> (Mimeograph) (Madison, 1942). An additional county was created in 1959 beyond the limits of this study. Menomonie County consists of the former Menomonie Indian reservation and was organized from Oconto and Shawano Counties. See Paxton Hart, "The Making of Menomonie County,"

Wisconsin Magazine of History, XLIII (Spring, 1960), 181-189.

[22] The U. S. Census reports all boundary changes in political units during the previous ten years. Consulting the census for each decade from 1890 to 1950 gave a complete listing of boundary changes from 1898 to 1950. A number of townships which underwent boundary or demographic changes early or late in the period covered by this study were retained and used only for their period of population stability. See James R. Donoghue, "The Local Government System of Wisconsin," The Wisconsin Blue Book, 1969, 89, for the number of townships, villages, and cities for each decade since 1900.

[23] See Robert F. Fries, Empire in Pine: The Study of Lumbering in Wisconsin 1830-1900 (Madison, 1951), for a description of this industry.

[24] See Arlan Helgeson, Farms in the Cutover (Madison, 1962), and George W. Hill and Ronald A. Smith, Man in the "Cut-over": A Study of Family-Farm Resources in Northern Wisconsin. Research Bulletin 139 (Madison, April, 1941). The Hill-Smith delineation of eighteen cutover counties has been used in this study.

[25] La Crosse's single change between 1891, when ten wards were split to form twenty wards, and 1956, when a major ward realignment occurred, was in 1904 when ward twenty-one was split off from ward eight. Albert H. Sanford and H. J. Hirscheimer, A History of La Crosse, Wisconsin,

1841-1900 (La Crosse, 1951), 109-110. For ward changes in Milwaukee see Bayrd Still, Milwaukee: The History of a City (Madison, 1965, Reprint of 1948 edition), 595-599, and various biennial and occasional publications of the Milwaukee Board of Election Commissioners which include maps and descriptions of ward boundaries.

[26]Still, Milwaukee, 454-455.

[27]Rural-farm was defined by the census during most of the period under consideration as "all persons living on farms without regard to occupation." Department of Commerce, Bureau of the Census, United States Census of Population, 1950, Vol. II, Characteristics of the Population. The category rural-nonfarm included essentially all other residents of political units under 2,500 in size, including villages and small cities. The 70% figure was determined as reasonable to ensure that the units were primarily agricultural. Leon Epstein in the two studies referred to below used 50% as the dividing line for rural-farm townships. David Adamany, a student of Epstein's, used a 75% figure in his follow-through on Epstein's study. See "The Size-of-Place Analysis Reconsidered," Western Political Quarterly, XVIII (September, 1964), 477. A township had to meet the 70% test in 1905, 1930, 1940, and 1950 to be included in this study. The 1905 percentages were obtained using the data on "Occupations by Towns, Cities and Villages," Secretary of State, Tabular Statements of the 1905 Census

Enumeration of Wisconsin (Madison, 1906), 276-601. The 1930, 1940, and 1950 percentages were obtained using the data in Wisconsin Crop and Livestock Reporting Service, Agricultural Statistics, Research Bulletin 202, Nos. 1 to 71 (Madison, 1939-1942), and County Agricultural Statistics Series, Third Series (Madison, 1952-1955).

[28]See Epstein's Politics in Wisconsin (Madison, University of Wisconsin Press, 1958), 56-76, and "Size-of-Place and the Division of the Two-Party Vote in Wisconsin," Western Political Quarterly, IX (March, 1956), 138-150.

[29]Epstein, Votes and Taxes (Madison, 1964), and Austin Ranney and Epstein, "The Two Electorates: Voters and Nonvoters in a Wisconsin Primary," Journal of Politics, XXVIII (August, 1966), 598-616.

[30]Angus Campbell and his cohorts from the Survey Research Center in The American Voter (New York, 1960), do provide a division in rural-farm and rural-nonfarm in discussing turn-out and split ticket voting. They do not break cities down by size-of-place, however, relying instead on an occupational breakdown in dealing with urban areas. The Gallup polls, while including farmers as an occupational group, consistently lump all communities under 2,500 (including rural areas) into a single category. See for example New York Herald Tribune, September 16, 1962; Milwaukee Journal, September 27, 1967, December 31, 1967; Des Moines Register, April 11, 1968. The Gallup Opinion

Index (formerly Gallup Political Index) reprints the most important Gallup polls with a single category for "under 2,500, rural." Other Gallup subdivisions by size are 2,500-49,999; 50,000-499,999; and 500,000 and over. Robert S. Friedman, "The Urban-Rural Conflict Revisited," Western Political Quarterly, XIV (June, 1961), 481-495, uses an "under 15,000" category to type legislative districts as rural, totally ignoring the small town vs. farm split. Howard W. Beers, "Rural-Urban Differences: Some Evidence from Public Opinion Polls," Rural Sociology, XVIII (March, 1953), 1-14, used only those polls with a rural category specifically designated "farmer." John L. Haer, "Conservatism-Radicalism and the Rural-Urban Continuum," Rural Sociology, XVII (December, 1952), 343-347, distinguished between incorporated and unincorporated areas under 2,500.

[31] Samuel Lubell, The Future of American Politics, 3rd ed. (New York, 1965), 165.

[32] Table from Ibid., 166.

[33] Ibid., 170.

[34] Dykstra, "Town-Country Conflict: A Hidden Dimension in American Social History," Agricultural History, XXXVIII (October, 1964), 195-204. The quote is from 195. Dykstra's article is weakened by his example--Kansas cattle towns in the 1870's. More to the point would be a study of agricultural service center towns in the Nineteenth and Twentieth Centuries. The author knows by the personal ex-

perience of growing up in a rural area of the continuance of the attitude reflected in the folksong growing out of the Granger movement:

> The farmer is the man, the farmer is the man,
> He lives on credit 'til the fall.
> Then they take him by the hand,
>   and they lead him from the land,
> And the merchant is the man who gets it all.

See Edith Fowke and Joe Glazer, Songs of Work and Freedom, (Garden City, New York, 1961), 213 for the complete words.

[35]Vidich and Bensman, Smalltown and Mass Society: Power and Religion in a Rural Community (Princeton, New Jersey, 1958). See especially 207-211.

[36]In Wisconsin, a village may shift to being classified as a city of the fourth class when the population reaches 1,000. However, it is not required to do so. For example, in 1950, sixty-one villages had populations of more than 1,000. See George S. Wehrwein "Village Government in Wisconsin," The Wisconsin Blue Book, 1940, 161-170; "City and Village Government in Wisconsin," The Wisconsin Blue Book, 1952, 136-146.

[37]Nicholas A. Masters and Deil S. Wright, "Trends and Variations in the Two-Party Vote: The Case of Michigan," American Political Science Review, LII (December, 1958), 1078-1090. The quote is from 1090. A study of Iowa cities by Robert Harmel, "Size-of-Place Analysis: The Case of Iowa," Comment, II (Decorah, Iowa, Luther College, Spring, 1972), 15-26, bears out the Epstein-Adamany conclusions for one more state.

[38] These divisions at 10,000 and 50,000 match Epstein's greatest breaks in the two-party vote, with a sharp Democratic upswing at both points.

[39] See Appendix E for a complete listing of voting units and the years for which they were used.

[40] Campbell, et al., The American Voter (New York, 1960) and Elections and the Political Order (New York, 1966). In the Survey Research Center's earlier studies of the 1952 election, Angus Campbell and his associates paid much closer attention to ethnic groups in tables which make clear the variation between the groups. See Campbell and H. C. Cooper, Group Differences in Attitudes and Voting (Ann Arbor, 1956), and Campbell, Gerald Gurin and Warren E. Miller, The Voter Decides (Ann Arbor, 1954).

[41] Key, "A Theory of Critical Elections," Journal of Politics, XVII (February, 1955), 7-8. Key also stressed ethnic and religious considerations in his article written with Frank Munger "Social Determinism and Electoral Decision: The Case of Indiana," in Eugene Burdick and Arthur J. Brodbeck, eds., American Voting Behavior (Glencoe, Illinois, 1959), 281-299.

[42] Key, Politics, Parties and Pressure Groups, 5th ed., 537-538.

[43] Key, The Responsible Electorate: Rationality in Presidential Voting, 1936-1960 (Cambridge, Massachusetts, 1966).

⁴⁴Glazer and Moynihan, Beyond the Melting Pot: The Negroes, Puerto Ricans, Jews, Italians, and Irish of New York City (Cambridge, Massachusetts, 1963). Duane Lockard, New England State Politics (Princeton, 1959) and Edgar Litt, The Political Cultures of Massachusetts (Cambridge, Massachusetts, 1965) also stress ethnicity.

⁴⁵Rischin, "Our Own Kind": Voting by Race, Creed or National Origin (Santa Barbara, California, 1960).

⁴⁶Dawidowicz and Goldstein, Politics in a Pluralist Democracy; Studies of Voting in the 1960 Election (New York, 1963), 95.

⁴⁷Wolfinger, "The Development and Persistence of Ethnic Voting," American Political Science Review, LIX (December, 1965), 896-908. The quote is from page 908. See also Elmer E. Cornwell, "Party Absorption of Ethnic Groups: The Case of Providence, Rhode Island," Social Forces, XXXVIII (March, 1960), 205-210, and Michael Parenti, "Ethnic Politics and the Persistence of Ethnic Identification," American Political Science Review, LXI (September, 1967), 717-726. The Wolfinger article along with several others on politics and ethnic groups and a very good bibliography and bibliographic essay is reprinted in Lawrence O. Fuchs, ed., American Ethnic Politics (New York, 1968).

⁴⁸Herberg, Protestant, Catholic, Jew (Garden City, New York, 1955).

⁴⁹Lipset, "Religion and Politics in American History,"

in Earl Rabb, ed., Religious Conflict in America (Garden City, New York, 1964), 60-89, "Religion and Politics in the American Past and Present," in Robert Lee and Martin Marty, eds., Religion and Social Conflict (New York, 1964), 69-126, and "How Big is the Bloc Vote?" New York Times Magazine, October 25, 1954, 32, 124-127. See also Gerhard Lenski, The Religious Factor, Chapter IV, "Religion and Politics," (Garden City, New York, 1961), 120-191; Wesley and Beverly Allinsmith, "Religious Affiliation and Politico-Economic Attitudes: A Study of Eight Major U. S. Religious Groups," Public Opinion Quarterly, XII (Fall, 1948), 377-389; and Scott Greer, "Catholic Voters and the Democratic Party," Public Opinion Quarterly, XXV (Winter, 1961), 611-625.

[50]Benson, Jacksonian Democracy, 165. The emphasis is his. Benson discusses each ethno-cultural group and arrives at a percentage break-down for each group (See Chapter VIII, especially page 185). David Hackett Fischer has criticized Benson's use of statistical evidence as "statistical impressionism" and indeed one of the failings of Benson's book is a lack of explanation of the quantitative method used. No one can readily check his data to see if it supports the generalizations he makes. See Fischer, Historians' Fallacies: Toward a Logic of Historical Thought (New York, 1970), 113-116. See also Michael A. Lebowitz, "The Significance of Claptrap in American History," Studies on the Left,

III (Winter, 1963), 79-95, and Edward Pessen, "Jacksonian Quantification," in Herbert J. Bass, ed., The State of American History (Chicago, 1970), 362-372.

[51]Hays, "Political Parties and the Community-Society Continuum," in William Nisbet Chambers and Walter Dean Burnham, eds., The American Party Systems: Stages of Political Development (New York, 1967), 158-159. Hays goes on to point out that this ethnic orientation persisted into the 1930's when socio-economic divisions replaced ethno-cultural community voting patterns.

[52]Swierenga, "Ethno-cultural Political Analysis: A New Approach to American Ethnic Studies," Journal of American Studies, V (April, 1971), 59-79; McSeveney, "Ethnic Groups, Ethnic Conflicts, and Recent Quantitative Research in American Political History," International Migration Review, VII (Spring, 1973), 14-33. See also Oscar and Mary F. Handlin, "The New History and the Ethnic Factor in American Life," Perspectives in American History, IV (1970), 5-24; Timothy L. Smith, "New Approaches to the History of Immigration in Twentieth-Century America," American Historical Review, LXXI (July, 1966), 1265-1279; and Rudolph J. Vecoli, "Ethnicity: A Neglected Dimension of American History," in Bass, ed., State of American History, 70-88.

[53]See Joel Silbey, "The Civil War Synthesis in American Political History," Civil War History, X (June, 1964), 130-140,

and Michael Holt, Forging a Majority: The Formation of the Republican Party in Pittsburgh, 1848-1860 (New Haven, 1969).

[54] In addition to the studies by Hays cited earlier, see Stanley Parsons, "Who were the Nebraska Populists?" Nebraska History, XLIV (June, 1963), 83-99; Frederick Luebke, Immigrants and Politics: The Germans of Nebraska, 1880-1900 (Lincoln, Nebraska, 1969), and "German Immigrants and Churches in Nebraska, 1889-1915," Mid-America, L (April, 1968), 116-130.

[55] Paul Kleppner, The Cross of Culture: A Social Analysis of Midwestern Politics, 1850-1900 (New York, 1970); Richard Jensen, The Winning of the Midwest: 1888-1896 (Chicago, 1971), and "The Religious and Occupational Roots of Party Identification: Illinois and Indiana in the 1890's," Civil War History, XVI (December, 1970), 325-342; and Roger Wyman, "Wisconsin Ethnic Groups and the Election of 1890," Wisconsin Magazine of History, LI (Summer, 1968), 269-293.

[56] John Allswang, A House for All People: Ethnic Politics in Chicago, 1890-1936 (Lexington, Kentucky, 1971); Dorothy Homer, "The Rockford Swedish Community," Journal of the Illinois State Historical Society, LVII (Summer, 1964), 149-155; and John L. Shover, "Ethnicity and Religion in Philadelphia Politics, 1924-1940," American Quarterly, XXV (December, 1973), 499-515.

[57] Huthmacher, *Massachusetts: People and Politics, 1919-1933* (Cambridge, 1959); Rogin and Shover, *Political Change in California: Critical Elections and Social Movements, 1890-1966* (Westport, Connecticut, 1970); Rogin, *The Intellectuals and McCarthy: The Radical Specter* (Cambridge, 1967).

[58] Weibull, "The Wisconsin Progressives, 1900-1914," *Mid-America*, XLVII (July, 1965), 191-221.

[59] This data is contained in "A Retabulation of Population Schedules From the Wisconsin State Census of 1905," Vols. I and VI.

[60] See Schafer, "Documenting Local History," 142-159, and *Wisconsin Domesday Book: Town Studies*, Vol. I, 84-89.

[61] This data is contained in *Tabular Statements of the 1905 Census of the State of Wisconsin*, 64-274. State censuses often gave minor civil division breakdowns by ethnic groups; the Federal census never went below the county and major city level in this category.

[62] See footnote 18 for the location of the map. The working maps from which the overall map is taken are preserved in the Rural Sociology Department of the University of Wisconsin.

[63] See for example National Lutheran Council, *Lutheran Directory and Statistical Handbook* (New York, 1953), 133-145. An excellent source for Norwegian Lutherans is Olaf M. Norlie, *Norsk Lutherske Menigheter i Amerika, 1843-1916*

(Minneapolis, 1918), Vol. I, 91-320. Norlie gives a history of every Lutheran congregation in the United States and Canada. For the Wisconsin Synod, data was obtained from the Statistical Report of the Wisconsin Evangelical Lutheran Synod for 1965 (Beaver Dam, n.d.).

[64] See Chapter III for a more complete discussion of the 1946 parochial school referendum vote, including sources.

[65] In addition to the sources on the Lutheran Church, cited above, Harry H. Heming, The Catholic Church in Wisconsin (Milwaukee, 1895-1898), gives a history of each Catholic parrish often including the ethnic background of families in the parish.

[66] See Appendices A and C for complete information on each election as well as the location of the data on a minor civil division level. This varied from the biennial Wisconsin Blue Book, a mine of information especially in the 1890's and early 1900's, to the records of the Secretary of State's office in the archives of the State Historical Society of Wisconsin. Strikingly, almost no electoral records at the local level are retained by county or city clerks in Wisconsin.

CHAPTER III   SETTLEMENT OF WISCONSIN

The limits of this study, 1900 to 1950, also define the period of greatest stability for Wisconsin's population. Starting with a population of 30,945 in 1840, the beginning of large scale immigration from eastern United States and Europe, Wisconsin grew by 900% in the 1840's and by 150% during the 1850's. The state's growth then varied from 22.2% to 35.9% between 1860 and 1900. However, from 1900 to 1950, Wisconsin's growth rate was never higher than 12.8%, reaching a low of 6.8% in the depression decade of the 1930's.

Most of this post-1900 growth was in urban areas, as Table I in Appendix B clearly shows. During this period, the city of Milwaukee reached almost 20% of the state's population; the next fifteen largest cities in the state were about equal in size to the state's largest city. In Wisconsin as in the nation, the urban population surpassed the rural population during the decade of the 1920's. Already in that decade rural-farm areas were declining in population; after 1940 rural population decreased by almost 20% every ten years. By the 1960's even urbanization was displaced by suburbanization as the primary cause of population growth.[1]

Thus it is the pre-1900 movement of people into the state which determined the basic composition of the state's population. Wisconsin settlement began around trading centers and forts at Green Bay and Prairie du Chien. Then, in the 1820's, lead was discovered in the region surrounding Galena, Illinois, and soon thereafter Wisconsin received its first large influx of people into the southwestern lead mining region of Grant, Lafayette, and Iowa Counties.[2] With the surveying of the southern and eastern part of the state from 1833 to 1837 and the opening of land offices in Mineral Point, Green Bay, and Milwaukee, settlement began in earnest.[3]

By 1850, southeastern Wisconsin was settled, first by American settlers, then by an ever increasing tide of European immigrants dominated in numbers by Germans. The lead mining region of southwestern Wisconsin rapidly changed over to agriculture in the 1840's, and in the period from 1850 to 1880, settlement pushed on into the Western Uplands north of the Wisconsin River, along the Mississippi River. During this same period, northeastern Wisconsin was also occupied. The sandy Central Plains around Adams and Juneau Counties was slower to fill up, though by 1880 it, too, had reached its peak.[4]

Thus by 1880, well before the beginning date of this study, most of Wisconsin had been settled and the frontier had passed further west.* There remained only the northern

---

*See Map I on the next page for the date at which population stabilized.

MAP I   DATE OF POPULATION STABILITY

The date indicates the census year in which the
population reached a point of stability.

part of the state, covered by pine forests, the bête noir
of the settler. The eighteen counties lying north of the
line from Clark to Shawano Counties--many of them not yet
created in 1880--included only 31,000 people in 1880. Ten
years later this figure had increased to over 130,000, and
by 1900 to 215,000.

Central to this increase was the development of the
lumber industry in northern Wisconsin. At its high point
in 1892, four billion board feet of lumber were harvested.
By 1909 the state forester estimated that between 40 and
45% of the area in each of the ten northernmost counties
had been cutover. Whatever its effect on the ecology of
the region, the removal of the pine forests did clear the
way for settling in the area, as agriculture then became
possible, if still difficult.[5]

In 1885 there were about 4,400 farms in the eighteen
counties of the soon-to-be cutover area; by 1905 that figure
had risen to 15,368 and by 1920, to 26,115. This figure
remained constant until the 1950's. By 1960 the number of
farms in the cutover area had dropped to 15,987.[6] Even in
1920, only one-twentieth of the fourteen northernmost cutover counties was under cultivation.[7]

Perhaps more important than the change in land use
was the major shift in the type of agriculture. Wisconsin
first developed as a wheat growing area when the world mar-
ket for that product opened up in the 1850's and 1860's.

By the 1880's wheat was on the way out, though it was still raised in the northwestern counties of the state. In 1850 Wisconsin's wheat production was about 5,000,000 bushels. At its high point in 1860, production approached 29,000,000 bushels. By 1895 this figure had dropped to 8,500,000 bushels, and by 1905 to 2,700,000.[8] Wheat was replaced by dairying and by 1900 the dairy cow could justly be called the symbol of Wisconsin.[9]

Along with dairying came a diversification of farming interest. Tobacco was grown by the Norwegians of south central and western Wisconsin;[10] livestock raising was most prevalent in the old lead mining region in the southwest; cherry and apple orchards began to appear in Door County, and so on.

In addition to diversification by area, there was considerable diversification by farm. Few farmers depended on a single cash crop. Wisconsin farmers were thus less affected by world markets and less prone to turn to agrarian protest movements such as Populism in the 1890's or the Non-partisan League in the 1910's and 1920's. The degree to which agriculture had shifted and become more diversified is revealed by Table II in Appendix B based on the 1885 and 1905 state censuses. The continued centrality of dairying can be seen in the 1950 agricultural census in which 69.1% of all farms in Wisconsin were listed as dairy farms and 84.8% of the state's farms reported having milk cows.[11]

A corollary of the growth of Wisconsin's urban areas has been the growth in the proportion of the population involved in urban-oriented occupations. By the early 1900's, Wisconsin was beginning to move into the ranks of industrializing states. Its early industries were connected with local raw materials. Flour milling was the leading industry to 1880; lumber and timber products in 1890 and 1900. By 1910, foundry and machine shop products were challenging lumber products for the lead. By 1920, the manufacture of butter, cheese, and condensed milk had moved to the fore, to be displaced in turn by motor vehicle manufacture as of 1930. Paper and wood pulp, malt liquors (except during Prohibition), slaughtering and meat packing, round out Wisconsin's leading manufacturing ventures during this period.[12] The number of people involved in the "manufacturing and mechanical industries" surpassed those in agricultural pursuits as of 1920. Table III in Appendix B gives a picture of Wisconsin's occupational distribution from 1900 to 1950.

The bulk of the state's manufacturing has always been located in southeastern Wisconsin, with the remainder of the Lake Michigan shore, the Fox and Rock River valleys, also contributing heavily to the state's industrial output. These areas also contain the counties of greatest population growth. The western, central, and especially the northern counties, have actually declined in population in recent years.

The story of Wisconsin's settlement is best told not as the sum of individuals or even individual families moving into the state, but as the tale of the different nationality groups which populated the state during the Nineteenth and early Twentieth Centuries. It is necessary to describe briefly each of these groups in order to gain a better understanding of the actors in the political field of the Twentieth Century. Table I on the following page[13] and Tables IV, V, and VI in Appendix B give an indication of the main immigrant groups which settled the state. The retabulated state census of 1905 gives perhaps the best picture of the ethnic composition of Wisconsin's population.

Major groups to be included in this study are the Germans, Norwegians, and Native-stock. Groups of secondary importance (in numbers) are the Swedes, Danes, Poles, and Bohemians. Studied in much smaller numbers are the French and French Canadians, English, Irish, Belgians, Hollanders, Swiss, Finns, and Italians. Of these, the English and Irish are most underrepresented due to the dispersal of their settlement pattern.

Before turning to the first important group of settlers in Wisconsin, the Native-stock, it is necessary to define more clearly the terms native-stock and foreign-stock. In referring to the retabulated census of 1905 or to any other census, foreign-stock refers specifically

Table I Wisconsin 1905 State Census Retabulation

Ethnic Group	Total Population Foreign-born	Heads - of - Household			
		Foreign-born	Native-born Foreign Parents	Total Foreign-stock	Percent of Total
German	226,154	102,047	77,185	179,232	39.4%
Norwegian	62,329	24,642	9,072	33,714	7.4%
Irish	18,327	8,252	18,139	26,391	5.8%
Canadian	30,202	13,172	6,833	20,005	4.4%
English	15,253	7,347	12,254	19,601	4.3%
Polish	36,285	13,131	1,635	14,766	3.2%
Swedish	26,950	10,191	550	10,741	2.4%
Danish	16,686	6,898	808	7,706	1.7%
Bohemian	14,026	5,461	2,032	7,493	1.6%
Hollander	6,675	2,585	1,785	4,370	1.0%
Swiss	7,626	2,922	1,382	4,304	.9%
Scots	3,974	1,302	2,521	3,823	.9%
Belgian	4,160	1,580	1,291	2,871	.6%
Welsh	2,811	1,085	1,590	2,675	.6%
Austrian	8,729	2,319	161	2,430	.5%
Finnish	4,608	1,129		1,129	.2%
Italian	4,221	887		887	.2%
French	1,487	195	471	666	.1%
Others	14,412	9,705	8,381	15,565	3.5%
Total	504,942	214,850	143,569	358,419	78.8%
Native-born	1,724,007				
Native-born of Native Parents				96,174	21.2%
Total	2,228,949			454,593	100.00%

to the first and second generation of an immigrant group,
usually labelled foreign-born and native-born of foreign-
born parent(s). Native-stock then refers to native-born
of native-born parents. When used in a general sense these
two terms refer to all descendants of a particular group,
including third and fourth generations. Thus many in the
native-stock--by census definition--belong more accurately
in one of the foreign-stock groups. Joseph Schafer points
to this problem in discussing the "Peopling of the Midwest":

> The population movement into Wisconsin from
> New York and New England carried along
> numbers of Irish and others who had settled
> first in those states. In 1850 New York
> natives were living in Wisconsin to the
> number of 68,595, a considerable proportion
> being children of Irish and German families.[14]

This study, by using the 1905 retabulation of nativity
of heads-of-household, avoids this problem for most ethnic
groups. The native-stock category in the 1905 retabulation
is reduced to only 96,174 or 21.16% of the state's 454,593
heads-of-household. Even this figure no doubt includes a
fair number of third and fourth generation foreign-stock
whose parents were born in New York, Ohio, Pennsylvania,
Indiana, Illinois, or Wisconsin itself. Thus, almost always,
data on foreign-stock underrepresents the actual numbers
of the group while data on native-stock overrepresents the
presence of Yankees and New Yorkers.

YANKEES

With this caution in mind, it is possible to turn to the first non-Indian group to settle in Wisconsin in large numbers--the Native-stock. This group was primarily of New England origin, hence the term "Yankee" is appropriate as a general label, although only a small portion of the family heads in 1905 listed a New England parent.[15]

Table II   Native-stock Heads-of-Household - 1905 Census[16]

Place of Birth	Number	Percent of Total Population	Percent of Native-stock
Wisconsin	47,562	10.5%	49.5%
Neighboring States*	7,358	1.6%	7.7%
Middle States**	25,322	5.6%	26.3%
New England	6,209	1.4%	6.5%
South	1,214	.3%	1.3%
Others	8,509	1.9%	8.8%
Total Native-stock	96,174	21.3%	100.1%
Total Population	454,593		

New Englanders and New Yorkers began moving into Wisconsin with the first opening for settlement of the land south and east of the Fox and Wisconsin Rivers. Most of this area was settled by 1860--at first only by Yankees

*Illinois, Michigan, Iowa, and Minnesota.
**New York, Pennsylvania, Ohio, and Indiana.

but increasingly by foreign-born. In this area, only parts
of Walworth County were able to retain their Yankee character
into the Twentieth Century. The lead mining area of Grant,
Iowa, and Lafayette Counties, settled first by miners in
the 1820's, shifted to agriculture and had a few Yankees
mixed with Southerners and settlers direct from England and
Ireland.

Richland and Vernon Counties also show up with a high
proportion of native-stock, though their location just north
of the lead mining region indicates that a disproportion-
ate share of the native-stock in this case may have had
English or Irish grandparents. Adams County in the sandy
Central Plains area was settled later by New Englanders
moving out of southeastern Wisconsin.[17]

Eagle, located in Richland County, had a large number
of settlers from the South and from Indiana,[18] but this
pattern was very much an exception, as Table II on place-of-
birth indicates. Few residents of the South settled in
the state after the lead mining era of the 1820's and
1830's, and most of those listing place-of-birth as Ohio,
Indiana, and Illinois were born in passage to Wisconsin
from other places of origin.

Even with these exceptions in mind one can conclude
that the native-born townships were Yankee-dominated by
noting the predominance of the old-line Yankee Protestant
churches they contained. The most important of these

churches in Wisconsin were the Methodist, Congregational, Presbyterian, Episcopal, and Northern Baptist. Southern-oriented denominations such as the Disciples of Christ are present only in small numbers. Table VII in Appendix B indicates the breakdown of church membership for the state in 1906, 1926, and 1952.[19] Each of the Yankee townships and villages included in this study contained or was near one or more mainline Protestant churches.[20]

Native-stock tended to be more prominent in Wisconsin villages than almost any of the foreign-stock. In 1905, 17.4% of native-stock heads-of-household lived in villages compared to 9.9% for all foreign-stock heads-of-household. Thus in 1905 only thirty-nine townships show 60% or more native-stock while twenty-five villages and cities met this base line. Of these, twenty-two townships, twenty villages and cities under 2,500, and two cities over 2,500, were included in this study. In addition, five urban wards--Beloit's second and fourth, Janesville's third, Madison's tenth, and Oshkosh's seventh--can be used for the early part of the study, sufficient, at least to give a partial picture of Yankee urban response to progressivism. The Oshkosh ward can be used throughout the entire study.*

Despite its lack of size, this group dominated Nineteenth Century Wisconsin politics completely out of proportion to

*See Map II on the next page for the location of Yankee voting units.

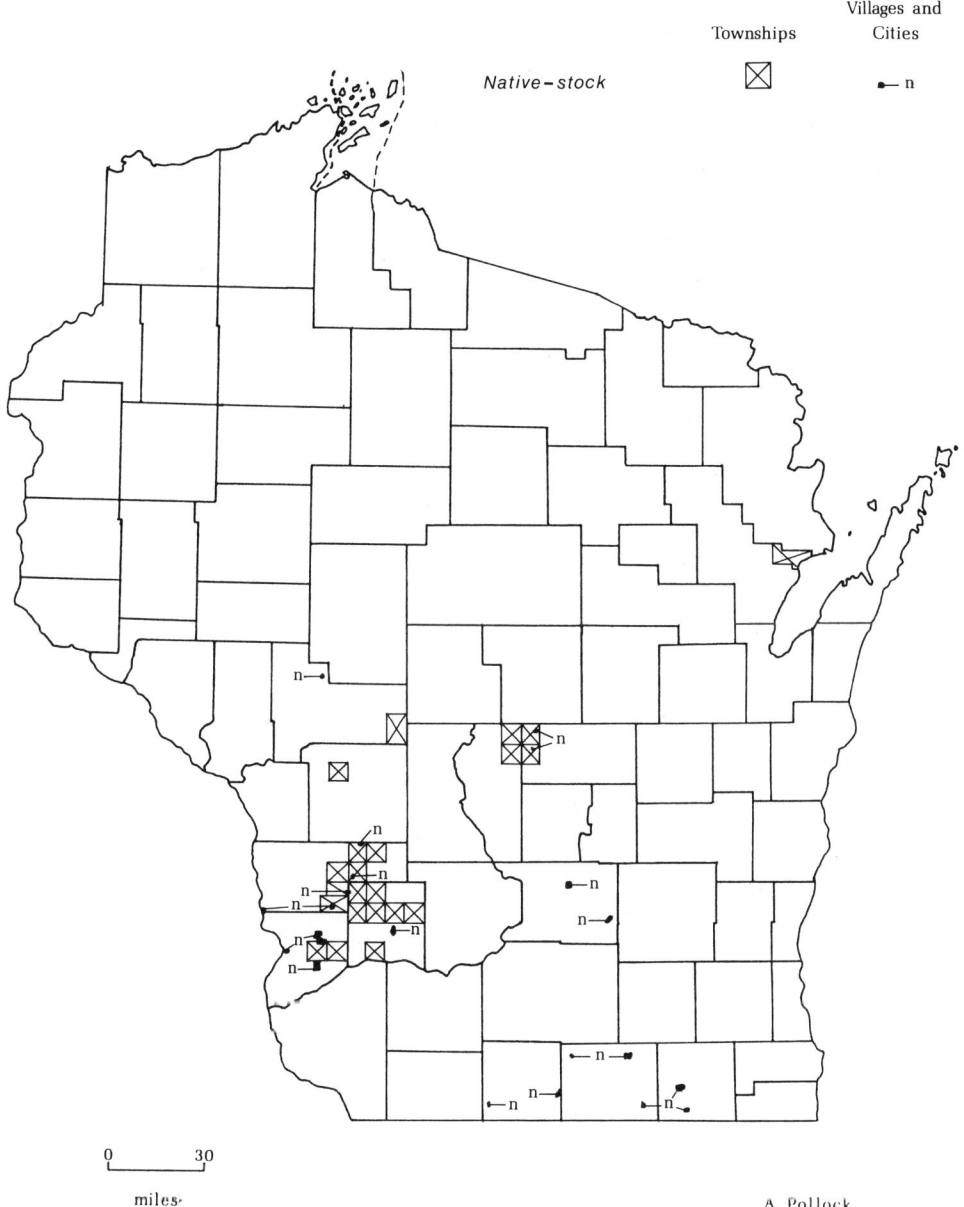

MAP II NATIVE-STOCK VOTING UNITS

its numbers. Not only were its members prominent in terms of political leadership but they also determined the issues over which Wisconsin politics divided in the Nineteenth Century.[21]

The remaining ethnic groups will be considered roughly in order of settlement. Perhaps the best index of that order can be gained from reordering the table drawn from the 1905 census retabulation so that it is in reverse order of proportion of foreign-born to total foreign-stock for each group. This process yields the following results and roughly determines the order in which the groups will be discussed.

Table III   Foreign-born Heads-of-Household - 1905 Census[22]

	Foreign-born	Total foreign-stock	Percent Foreign-born
French	195	666	29.3%
Irish	8,252	26,391	31.3%
Scottish	1,302	3,823	34.1%
English	7,347	19,601	37.5%
Welsh	1,085	2,675	40.6%
Belgian	1,580	2,871	55.0%
German	102,047	179,232	56.9%
Hollander	2,585	4,370	59.2%
Canadian	13,172	20,005	65.8%
Swiss	2,922	4,304	67.9%
Bohemian	5,461	7,493	72.9%

Table III   Continued

Norwegian	24,642	33,714	73.1%
Polish	13,137	14,766	88.9%
Danish	6,898	7,706	89.5%
Austrian	2,319	2,480	93.5%
Swedish	10,191	10,741	94.9%

FRENCH AND FRENCH CANADIANS

The French are present in Wisconsin in such small numbers that it is difficult to locate communities which have any preponderance of French stock. They either came over prior to the 1830's, settling in the Green Bay and Prairie du Chien areas, or came via Quebec.[23] French Canadians, much more prevalent, began coming to Wisconsin in the pre-Civil War logging days. As a result of this, most French Canadian communities are clustered along the lower edge of the cutover in Brown, Marinette, Oconto, Chippewa, and St. Croix Counties. Unfortunately, Wisconsin's 1905 census did not distiguish between British and French Canadians, but four communities can be labelled the latter by using church records. They are Somerset and Somerset village in St. Croix County, Saxon in Iron County; and Coleman village in Marinette County.[24] Ward seven in Ashland has a substantial Canadian minority in its midst. The city of Marinette has a large French

Catholic church but its French Canadian population is too dispersed to allow for study at the ward level.*

British Canadians, usually labelled "other Canadians" in censuses, are more widely dispersed throughout Wisconsin. This group, though largely British in background, would also include large numbers of other foreign-stock who were born in Canada in transit to Wisconsin, or who came from foreign settlements in Canada, particularly the prairie provinces. Thus one of the larger ethnic groupings in Wisconsin, "other Canadians," cannot be pinpointed in sufficient numbers to allow generalizations about voting. In fact, their varied background makes it difficult to discuss them as a group at all.[25]

BRITONS

Closely allied to the Yankees in outlook and settlement were immigrants from the British Isles--the English, Scots, and Welsh. English settlers, especially from Cornwall, were prominent in the lead mining region, but by 1905 only one township in the state showed over 60% family heads of English stock and only seven showed over 40%. In addition, five villages and cities showed 40% or better English stock. All eleven of these units were in Grant, Iowa, and Lafayette Counties. Like the Native-stock, the English were dispro-

---

*See Map III on page 102 for the location of French Canadian voting units.

portionately represented in villages with 16.9% of their number located there in 1905.

Most discussions of the English as well as of the Scots in Wisconsin stress the degree to which they assimilated into the New England population group:

> Except in the three lead producing counties . . . there was little tendency on the part of the English and the Scotch when they came to Wisconsin to form separate and distinct settlements.[26]

In fact, the Scots are nowhere to be found in numbers above 21% in the 1905 population retabulation.[27]

The exceptions to the general pattern of dispersal for British settlers are the Cornish and the Welsh. Most of the Cornish immigrated from Cornwall to Wisconsin in the 1830's and 1840's to work in the lead mines. With the end of lead mining in the 1840's, they either went to California in the gold rush or settled down in the villages or farms of Iowa, Lafayette, and Grant Counties. Most of them carried over their allegiance to the Methodist church, joining either the Primitive Methodist or Methodist Episcopal churches.

An estimate of the 1890's placed the number of pure-blooded Cornish in the lead region at 10,000. Of this number, Linden and Hazel Green (villages and townships) were listed as half Cornish in population. All of the townships and villages which show up as 40% or more English in 1905 are Cornish. Usually these communities had significant

Irish minorities, and, if near the German area of settlement, were gradually being encroached upon by German settlers.[28]

Little Grant township and Hazel Green village in Grant County; Linden township and village in Iowa County; and White Oak Springs township in Lafayette County are used in this study to represent English settlements.*

The Welsh are more easily traced than the Cornish for they are recorded as a separate group in census data. The Welsh immigrated in the 1840's and 1850's, settling primarily in southeastern Wisconsin. No township lists over 35% of Welsh stock in 1905. However, two townships in Columbia County, Courtland and Springvale; and two villages, Cambria and Randolph, are sufficiently Welsh to allow some conclusions on voting patterns.**

The Welsh were the most village oriented of all the immigrant groups. In 1905, 20.3% of their number lived in villages. The Welsh came over as dissenters from the Anglican church and formed their own churches here, affiliating with the Presbyterians as an independent synod in 1920.[29]

---

*See Map III on page 102 for the location of English voting units.

**See Map III on page 102 for the location of Welsh voting units.

IRISH

Although the Irish probably rank second only to the Germans in numbers of foreign-stock in Wisconsin, they are almost as difficult as the Scots and English to locate in concentrated settlements. Immigration of the Irish came at the same time Wisconsin was going through its heaviest population growth, from 1847 to 1854. Many of the Irish worked first in urban areas of the East before continuing West.

> That numerous groups of foreign immigrants disembarking at eastern ports continued their journey by proceding westward immediately is particularly true of German and Scandinavian elements, but not true of the Irish. These latter usually remained at least for some time in the East as laborers and artisans, crowding the cities and laboring in public works; or they gradually worked their way westward while employed in building railroads and canals or performing farm labor.[30]

Nevertheless, by 1850 there were 21,043 Irish-born in Wisconsin and by 1860 this figure had risen to 49,961. After 1860, Irish immigration to Wisconsin declined, and by 1870 it had almost ceased.[31]

The Irish were quite closely tied to Wisconsin's non-agricultural growth. The lead mining region proved to be the first major attraction, though it was displaced by railroad building as of 1850. With the completion of the railroads across southern Wisconsin, the Irish either stayed on as laborers--often on the railroads they had built--or moved westward and northward. A surprisingly large number joined those Irish who had gone into farming. Consequently by 1905, 45.2% of the Irish heads-of-household lived in rural areas.[32]

The most well known rural Irish community was that of Erin Prairie in St. Croix County.[33] By 1905 this township alone recorded above 50% of Irish stock. No villages recorded over 35%. This illustrates well the dispersal of the Irish. Like the non-Cornish English and the Scots, the Irish of Wisconsin did not maintain concentrated settlements. This was true even in urban areas like Milwaukee, where the old Irish third ward shifted almost entirely to Italian in the late Nineteenth Century.

Further evidence of the general Irish dispersal comes from looking at the 1905 retabulated census for five counties scattered throughout the state: Adams in central Wisconsin, Washburn in the north, Brown in the northeast, Grant in the southwestern Wisconsin, and Walworth County in southeastern Wisconsin. In these five counties, eighty-six out of 103 townships and twenty-two out of twenty-three villages and cities had 2% or more Irish stock. However, only twenty townships and seven villages and cities had over 10% Irish, and only three townships topped 20%.

Nine townships, with 37% as the minimum Irish stock, and no villages, will be used in this study to determine the Irish vote. In each case these are areas settled by

Catholic Irish, as the existence of Catholic churches and a high vote on the 1946 parochial school busing issue indicates.[34] One ward--Janesville's fifth--shows up with a sufficient Irish population to be used, though with much caution, for the first twenty years of this study. Milwaukee's ward three--the premier Irish ward of the Nineteenth Century--had been "Italianized" by 1900.*

GERMANS

In 1905 German-stock made up 39.4% of Wisconsin's population. Wisconsin may not have been the German state some of its early German settlers hoped for, but at least two out of every five residents were of German descent. Other foreign-stock groupings could not top 7.4% of the population, and the 21.2% native-stock--which included third and fourth generation foreign-stock among its members-- was only half the size of the German group.

Beginning in 1839, German migration into the state followed hard on the heels of the Yankees, English, and Irish.[35] The 1840's and 1850's were the flood tide years of their migration. Germans settled in the wooded areas which the Yankees by-passed in their search for prairie land. Then, gradually, the Germans displaced other groups as their settlements spread. They dominated the city of

---

*See Map III on page 102 for the location of Irish voting units.

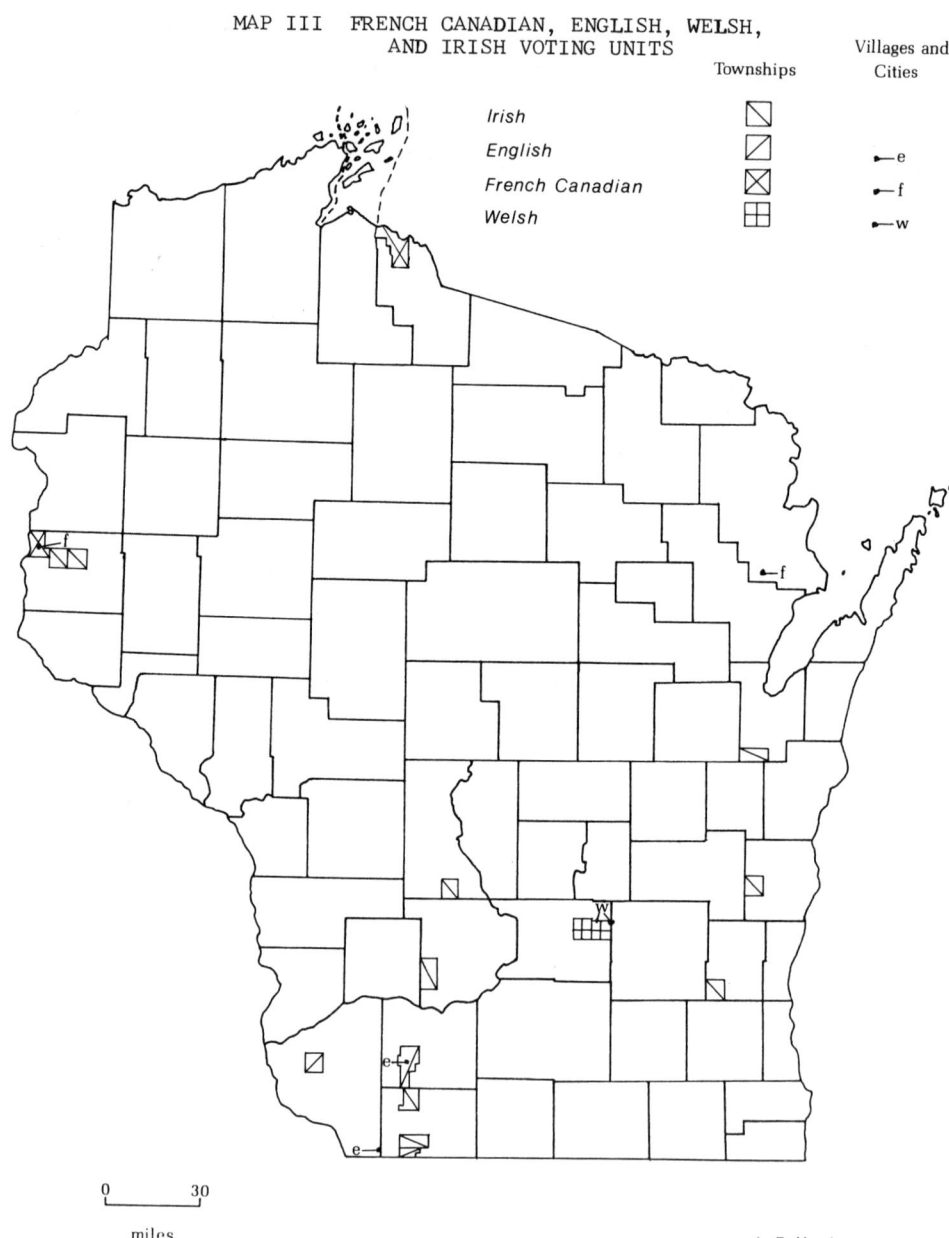

Milwaukee and also many of Wisconsin's other cities.

After its beginning in 1839 and a follow through in 1843-1844, migration from North Germany dropped off until the period from 1854 to 1857, and again until 1866. After 1870 most German migration again came from North Germany. The bulk of this migration came from Prussia, especially the providences of Pomerania and Brandenberg.[36] Most of these settlers were Lutheran, which aids in pinpointing religious differences.

The primary areas of settlement for North Germans in Wisconsin were:

1. Milwaukee, Ozaukee, and Washington Counties. Settled first by Old Lutherans from Pomerania, these counties continued to draw North Germans. The city of Milwaukee became a major German center with most settling on the north side of the city.

2. Dodge and Jefferson Counties. Centering in Watertown, this area was first entered by Old Lutherans in 1843-1844. Between 1850 and 1865 these counties filled up with Prussians and Mecklenbergers.

3. Manitowoc and Sheboygan Counties. These counties were settled in the post-1854 movement primarily by North Germans, but with a strong mixture from other parts of Germany.

4. Northern Winnebago County, north of Oshkosh, along with parts of nearby counties. These areas were settled

at the same time as the Manitowoc-Sheboygan area.

5. South-central Shawano County, north-central Marathon County, and the adjoining townships of Lincoln County. This region was settled from 1855 through the 1870's, with the western cutover filling up in the 1870's.[37]

One of the few cohesive settlements of non-Prussian North Germans came from Lippe-Detmold beginning in 1847. They came for the purpose of preserving their form of the reformed religion as well as for the usual economic reasons. Their most concentrated settlements were in Manitowoc and Sheboygan Counties.

South Germans were predominantly Catholic. This was particularly true of those who came from Bavaria, Baden, and Luxemburg. Rhenish Prussia also sent a large Catholic contingent along with Lutherans and Reformed. Saxony served primarily as a source of Lutheran migration. Despite a later start, South Germans, as a group, came earlier than the bulk of their northern compatriots, with 1848 to 1854 serving as the years of their heaviest settlement in Wisconsin. Concentrated in eastern counties and in urban areas, they spread throughout the state. Primary areas of settlement, outside the urban areas, included Fond du Lac County, with the largest concentration of Rhenish Prussians, Outagamie, Manitowoc, and Sheboygan Counties. Bavarians are found in Jefferson, Dane, Sauk, and Outagamie Counties, but their heaviest concentration was along the Wisconsin

Central Railroad line in north-central Wisconsin, settled from 1879 to 1889. An estimated 1,100 families settled in this area of Clark, Taylor, Price, and Ashland Counties.[38] Baden contributed one of the more unusual German settlements--a Catholic communitarian group which settled at St. Nazianz in the town of Eaton in Manitowoc County.[39] Luxemburgers formed a separate ethnic group usually discussed with the Germans. They came first in the 1840's, then in large numbers from 1854 to 1857, filling the area around Port Washington and Fredonia in Ozaukee County.[40]

Germans provide the one ethnic group which can be looked at extensively on the urban level. Based on the 1905 census retabulation, eighty-six villages and cities with a population under 2,500; twenty-two cities with a population from 2,500 to 10,000; and five cities of over 10,000 can be classified as German. Port Washington in Ozaukee County is the banner Catholic city but most German-dominated cities are too diversified in religious background to permit a division along Lutheran-Catholic lines. The five cities of over 10,000 which could be classified as German were led by Sheboygan with a 1905 reading of 75%. The other large cities, varying from 53% to 61% in Germanness, were Wausau in Marathon County, Manitowoc in Manitowoc County, Appleton in Outagamie County, and Oshkosh in Winnebago County.

For Appleton, an 1898 church survey serves further to

identify the city as German. In that year 1,526 of 2,731 church families in the city were German. The second largest foreign group was the Irish with 212 families. No other group topped one hundred. American families reached almost one-fourth of the total--742 out of 2,731. In addition to four large Catholic churches, the city also contained one of the largest Congregational churches in the state and served as a center of Methodism. In fact, "Appleton came to be known as such a Methodist center that it was said no one could get ahead there unless he were Methodist."[41] Nonetheless, its voting population was basically German.

The retabulation of the 1905 census contained ward data for eighteen cities. This list includes the following:

Table IV Urban Wards in 1905 Retabulation

City	County	Total Wards in 1905	60% German Wards 1905	German % Entire City
Ashland	Ashland	10	0	16.1%
Green Bay	Brown	8	0	24.5%
Madison	Dane	10	0	31.0%
Superior	Douglas	10	0	8.6%
Eau Claire	Eau Claire	10	0	19.6%
Fond du Lac	Fond du Lac	16	2	41.3%
Kenosha	Kenosha	8	2	38.5%
La Crosse	La Crosse	21	1	38.0%
Manitowoc	Manitowoc	7	3	55.3%
Wausau	Marathon	9	5	61.3%

Table IV   Continued

Marinette	Marinette	5	8	21.0%
Milwaukee	Milwaukee	23	11	57.9%
Appleton	Outagamie	6	3	56.6%
Racine	Racine	11	0	30.9%
Beloit	Rock	5	0	14.0%
Janesville	Rock	5	0	19.5%
Sheboygan	Sheboygan	8	7	74.6%
Oshkosh	Winnebago	13	6	52.5%

Using a base of 60% German, a potential of fifty German wards was yielded by the 1905 census. Nine of the eleven wards in Milwaukee were usable--nine, ten, thirteen, fifteen, nineteen, twenty, twenty-one, twenty-two, and twenty-three. Boundary changes and a growing Polish population led to the dropping of ward thirteen after the 1912 ward reapportionment. Inmigration of Russian Jews, Hungarians, Yugoslavs, and Negroes removed ward nine. These two wards were replaced by new ward seven, in the heart of Kleine Deutschland on Milwaukee's north side, and ward twenty-five on the city's far northwest. The next reapportionment, twenty years later, left these nine wards, though wards nine and twenty-three were newly created in recently annexed areas of the city. Ward nine was the former North Milwaukee village--some 65% German in 1905.[42] In addition to the Milwaukee wards, thirty other urban German wards will be used in this study, as long as they are unchanged by a reshuffling of boundaries or a shift in ethnic domination. These wards were located in nine cities, the most prominent being Manitowoc, Wausau, Appleton, Sheboygan, and Oshkosh. Manitowoc's German population was centered in three of the city's five wards, while in Sheboygan Germans dominated all of the city's eight wards in 1905.

These, then, were the main German areas of concentration, although almost every part of the state received its injection of Germans. German voting units also have been divided for this study according to religion. There is no aggregate data on religion below the county level. For this reason, a 1946 referendum vote on aid to parochial schools was used as the preliminary religious dividing line.

In 1945 the Wisconsin legislature gave its final approval to an amendment to the state constitution adding the following words to Article X, Section 3 of the constitution, which barred aid for sectarian instruction "except that such prohibition shall not ban the legislature from providing for the transportation of children to and from any school or institution of learning."[43] The amendment was submitted to the voters of the state in the November, 1946 election. After a most bitter battle, the amendment was defeated 437,817 to 545,475. The struggle divided along religious lines with Protestants charging that the

Catholic church was using the referendum as an opening wedge to gain recognition as a state church,[44] and with Catholics calling on Protestant churches to fight communism not children.[45]

Support for the amendment came almost entirely from Catholic clergy and lay leaders. On Sunday, October 13, 1946, parish announcements in Catholic churches throughout the state urged members to support the amendment.[46] State committees formed to support the amendment included primarily Catholic laymen, with the Knights of Columbus being particularly active.[47] Almost no Catholics spoke in public opposition to the amendment.[48]

On the other side, the fight against adoption was led by the Wisconsin Council of Churches representing eleven denominations and 1,500 churches.[49] Their "front" organization, the Wisconsin Committee for Religious Liberty, was chaired by the Reverend Ellis H. Dana, Executive Vice-President of the Council.[50] In addition, the Madison Ministerial Association, Milwaukee Ministerial Association, Wisconsin Congregational Conference, Methodists of Western and Southern Wisconsin, and Presbyterians of Southern Wisconsin all announced opposition to the amendment.[51]

All of this was somewhat predictable. However, the key group for the purpose of this study are the German Lutherans. Although their parochial schools enrolled only 18,000 students in 1946 compared to 126,000 Catholic students,[52] these schools were an important feature of the Joint Synod of Wisconsin, and, to a lesser degree, of the Missouri Synod. While Lutheran pastors were scarce among the early opponents of the busing amendment, they gradually took stands. On April 15, 1946, for example, a letter calling on legislators to defeat Joint Resolution 19-S rather than submit it to the people in referendum form was signed by twenty-eight religious leaders, mainly from Madison. The signers included only one Lutheran pastor.[53] However, by June, the newly organized Madison-area National Lutheran Council Pastoral Conference announced its opposition to the referendum.[54] This organization included the Scandinavian Lutheran churches along with the German-based American Lutheran Church and United Lutheran Church of America. The Lutheran pastors of the A. L. C. of Northwestern Wisconsin and the Lutheran Brotherhoods of the A. L. C. publicly opposed the referendum.[55] Although the Missouri Synod did not take a public position and that of the Wisconsin Synod was given little publicity, individual pastors from both Synods wrote letters indicating their positions.[56] Only one reference could be located of any Lutheran support for the amendment.[57]

The best argument for use of the referendum as an indicator of German Catholic and German Lutheran areas of concentration comes from the data itself. Of the 165 German townships, 113 German villages and cities, and thirty-three wards the vote breaks down as follows:

Table V   German Vote 1946 Parochial School Bus Referendum

	Under 35% Yes	35% to 65% Yes	Over 65% Yes
Townships	85	50	30
Villages and cities to 2,500	28	39	19
Cities 2,500 to 10,000	3	15	4
Cities over 10,000	0	5	0
City Wards-Milwaukee	0	10	0
City Wards-Other	4	18	1

Clearly, German areas varied in their response to the amendment. A look at the voting of other ethnic groups in the table below underscores the religious factor in the split:

Table VI   Other Ethnic Vote
1946 Parochial School Bus Referendum, Yes Vote

	Townships		Villages and Cities		Wards	
	N=*	Median	N=	Median	N=	Median
Catholic Ethnic Areas						
Polish	11	78%	2	77%	8	73%
Bohemian	11	68%	2	89%	-	-
Belgian	7	79%	-	-	-	-

*N= number of units.

Table VI Continued

Irish	9	71%	-	-	-	-
French Canadian	2	78%	2	80%	1	70%
Italian	2	62%	1	73%	1	51%
Catholic Hollander	1	94%	1	94%	-	-
Austrian	1	94%	-	-	-	-
Protestant Ethnic Areas							
Yankee	22	21%	22	20%	1	31%
English	3	35%	2	26%	-	-
Welsh	2	15%	2	10%	-	-
Norwegian	35	9%	20	10%	4	32%
Swedish	13	14%	5	24%	1	38%
Danish	8	22%	4	28%	4	28%
Finnish	10	40%	-	-	-	-
Reformed Hollander	3	14%	2	8%	-	-
Swiss	3	23%	3	14%	-	-

If all other ethnic groups split along religious lines, the split among the Germans also must have a religious explanation. Those German voting units which cast a "yes" vote of 65% or more have been labelled "Catholic"; those which cast a "yes" vote of less than 35% have been labelled Lutheran. The remaining units were labelled "Mixed" or, more accurately, "Mixed and Uncertain."

All of these German townships, villages, and cities were checked for Lutheran and Catholic churches. The location of the churches matched the designation based on the referendum vote. Finally, the discussions of German migration by Joseph Schafer and Kate Everest Levi, when they clearly indicated an area was settled by German Catholics or German Lutherans, matched with this division.

Andrew Baggaley, in an article entitled "Religious Influence on Wisconsin Voting, 1928-1960," also found a close relationship between Catholic percentage and vote on the parochial school referendum, concluding that "the 1946 referendum can be used as a rather valid indicator of the percent of Roman Catholics in the smaller political units."[58]

The division in terms of numbers of voting units in each category, comes quite close to representing the German Lutheran-German Catholic split as reported in 1893, toward the end of the period of German migration. At that time Wisconsin was reported to have 225,000 German Lutherans and 105,000 German Catholics.[59] Most German Protestants were Lutherans; in the 1952 religious census, 552,569 belong to German Lutheran synods, 77,007 to the Reformed and Evangelical denominations. Almost all of the Protestant voting units used had clear Lutheran majorities; very few might be labelled German Reformed, German Evangelical, or German Methodist.[60]

The German Mixed category serves as a control group. This group, which varied from 35% to 65% in its vote on the school bus aid issue, was adjudged to be either a mixture of German Catholic and German Protestant groupings, or one in which voting along religious lines did not take place, at least in 1946. Interestingly enough, on almost every issue from 1900 to 1952 the median vote for this group fell between the Lutheran and Catholic voting units.*

Almost coterminous with the great German migration was that of several smaller central and northern European groups--the Swiss, Hollanders, Bohemians, and Belgians.

SWISS

The primary Swiss settlement in Wisconsin was in Green County, surrounding the community of New Glarus. Settled in 1845, the New Glarus area soon became a center of Swiss immigration in the United States. In addition, major Swiss settlements developed along the Mississippi River in Buffalo County and the Prairie du Sac area of Sauk County. While the Green County settlement continued to grow and expand in the Twentieth Century and Swiss continued to come to the city of Milwaukee, the other areas remained stagnant or declined after 1860. Most Swiss affiliated with the Reformed Church, though a number joined the Evangelical Association

---

*See Map IV on the next page for the location of German Catholic, Lutheran, and Mixed voting units.

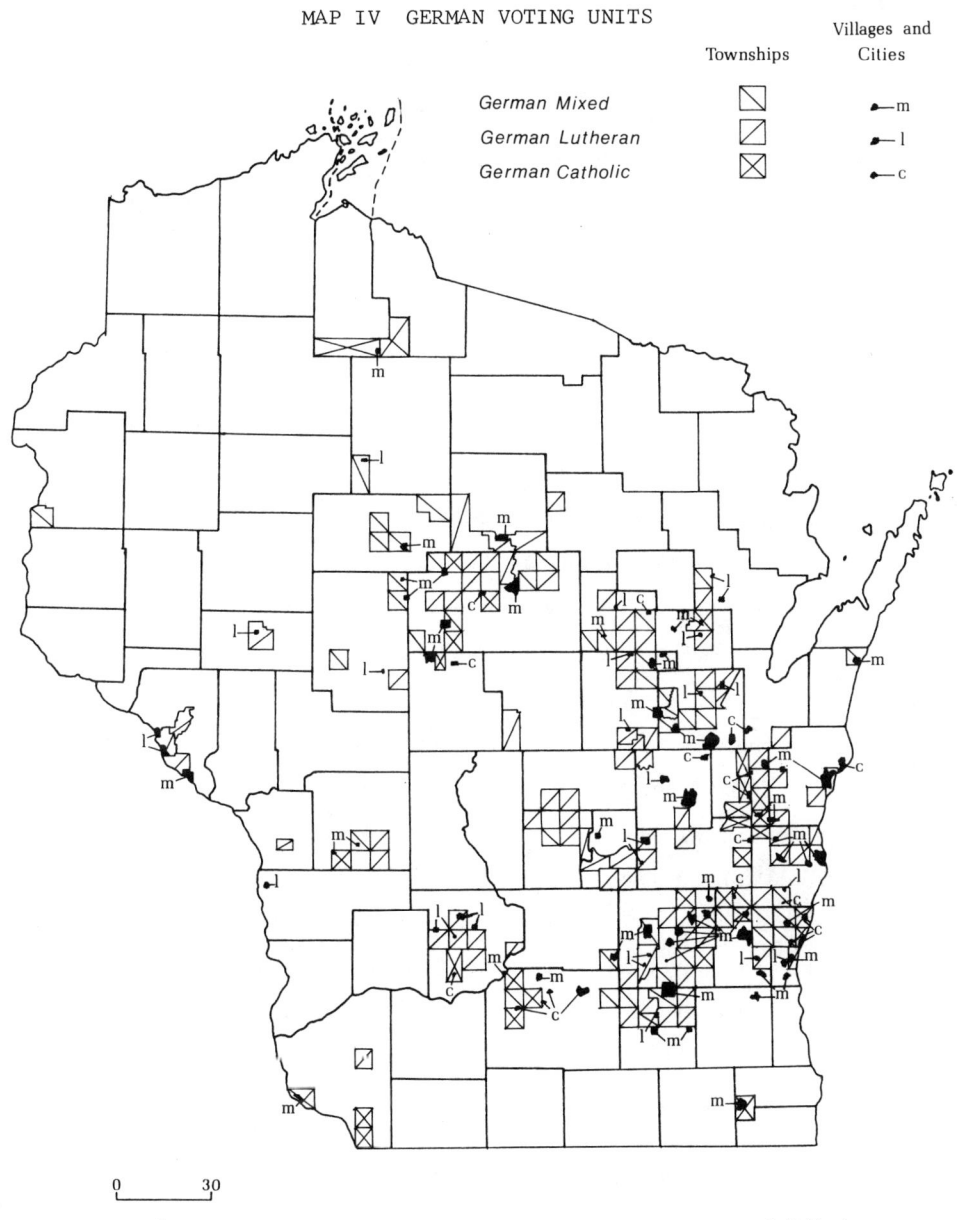

or Methodist church. The Green County Swiss settlement has been one of the centers of dairy industry. From its origin, it has specialized in the manufacture of Swiss cheese.[61] Three townships above 47% Swiss, one village and one city under 2,500, and one city over 2,500 are used in this study. All of these voting units are in Green County.*

HOLLANDERS

The Dutch also began coming to Wisconsin in the late 1840's. They, too, maintained tightly-knit communities. Almost alone among the non-German groups, the Dutch must be split into Protestant and Catholic segments. Dutch Reformed communities were established at Alto in Fond du Lac County and in the Cedar Grove-Oostburg area of Sheboygan County. Most of the Dutch Protestants organized Dutch Reformed churches, now called the Reformed Church in America; a few in Cedar Grove affiliated with the Presbyterian church.

In 1848, a Dutch Catholic priest began a Catholic community at Little Chute in Sheboygan County, with an extension fifteen miles east in Hollandtown in Brown County. Almost an anomaly in Dutch migration, this community remained extremely close-knit and very Catholic.[62]

Three Dutch Reformed townships and one Catholic township are used in this study; two Dutch Reformed villages,

*See Map V on page 120 for the location of Dutch voting units.

Cedar Grove and Oostburg, and one Dutch Catholic city under 2,500, Little Chute, are also used.*

BOHEMIANS

Bohemians, from the area of Europe that was to become Czechoslovakia after World War I, came in larger numbers than did either the Swiss or Hollanders. Beginning in 1848 when the Hapsburgs first allowed emigration, Bohemian movement into Wisconsin continued until about 1880. The largest rural settlement was that of northern Manitowoc and southern Kewaunee Counties beginning in 1851, with close to 8,000 Bohemians in the two counties by the turn of the century. Other Czech settlements were at Castle Rock in northern Grant County, Yuba City in Richland County, the city of La Crosse with over 500 Bohemians, and the Prairie du Chien area in Crawford County. In the early 1900's the northern cutover area received an influx of Bohemians, many of whom had worked first in Chicago or Milwaukee. Phillips in Price County, northern Barron County, and Neva township in Langlade County received large influxes of Bohemians at this time.[63] Wisconsin Bohemians tended to settle in areas which also contained Germans. Of the 17 townships which were more than 40% Bohemian in 1905, only six were less than 20% German. Three villages and cities--Kewaunee, Muscoda, and Prairie du Chien--had almost equal numbers of Bohemians

*See Map V on page 120 for the location of Dutch voting units.

and Germans.

Bohemians were split by traditional Catholic vs. freethinking attitudes far more than the Germans. An estimated 50% to 70% of the Bohemian immigrants left the church.[64] Most of the leaders of the Wisconsin Czech community were freethinkers, but in rural areas the Catholic church predominated. This was especially true of the settlements in Kewaunee, Manitowoc, and Wood Counties. However, settlements in Barron, Langlade, and Vernon Counties lacked active Catholic churches, while Muscoda and Castle Rock, in Grant County, had sizable non-Catholic Bohemian minorities.[65] This split does explain the great variation on the parochial school issue among the eleven Bohemian townships and two villages used in this study. The solidly Catholic communities all report in at over 65%; the others vary from 27% to 68%.*

BELGIANS

The Belgians of Wisconsin are unusual in that almost all of them are located in one large community extending from Green Bay in Brown County, through Kewaunee County and into Door County. Only some 400 out of 2,871 Belgian heads-of-household lived outside of these three counties in 1905. Except for Green Bay's 900 families and the forty families in Superior's tenth ward, Wisconsin's Belgians were

*See Map V on page 120 for the location of Bohemian voting units.

a rural people. Settled by some 15,000 Belgian Walloon
immigrants between 1853 and 1857, this area in northeastern
Wisconsin has remained overwhelmingly Belgian. Though
devoutly Catholic--there are fourteen Catholic churches to
serve the area--the Belgians never supported a parochial
school system, no doubt due to their familiarity with a
publicly supported school system in Belgium.[66] Nevertheless,
they voted for aid to parochial schools in the 1946 referendum by votes ranging from 72% to 93%. Seven townships from
this area are included in this study. Ward four of Green
Bay is also used from 1898 to 1920.*

NORWEGIANS

Norwegians replaced the Irish in the middle of the
Nineteenth Century as the second largest ethnic group in
Wisconsin, to be displaced in turn by the Poles in the early
Twentieth Century. Although the first Norwegian settlements
in southwestern Wisconsin came in 1839 and 1840, Norwegian
immigration did not begin in large numbers until the 1850's.
By 1870, "the general areas of Norwegian settlement in
Wisconsin were fairly well marked out along lines that have
persisted until today."[67]

Most Wisconsin Norwegians came directly to the state,
so very few show up as born in other states. Retabulations

*See Map V on the next page for the location of Belgian
voting units.

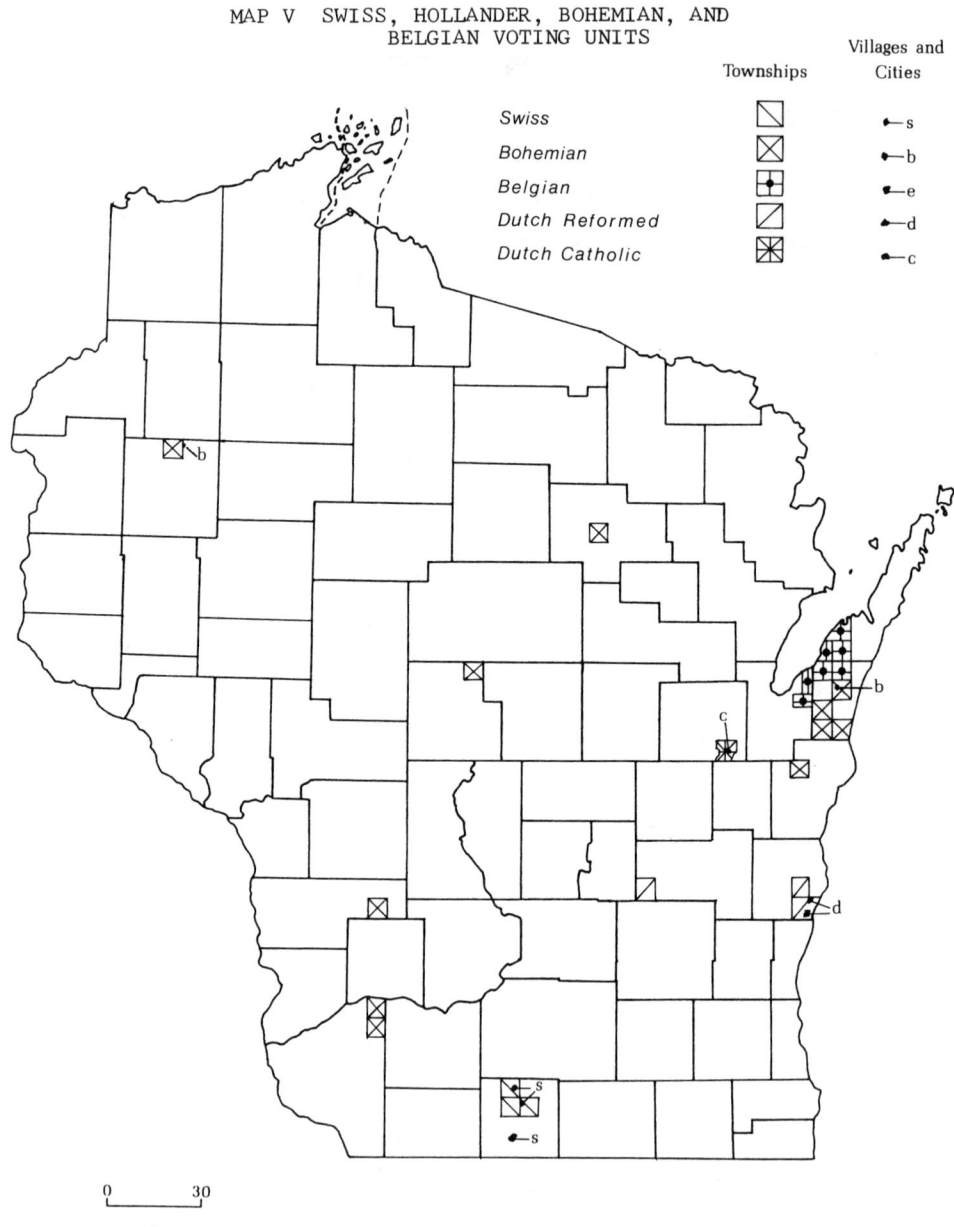

of the first three censuses in which nationality is listed
yields the following results:

Table VII Birthplace of Norwegian Stock[68]

Birthplace	1850	1860	1870
Norway	8,011	19,758	37,574
Wisconsin	1,413	9,598	21,686
Elsewhere	43	201	359
Total Norwegian Stock	9,467	29,557	59,619

Many of the early Norwegian settlements were just beyond the area of German settlement or interspersed with those areas. Earliest settlements included the Muskego area in Waukesha and Racine Counties; the Rock Prairie and Jefferson Prairie areas of Rock County; and the large Koshkonong settlement in Dane and Jefferson Counties centering at Stoughton. These three areas served as staging grounds for settling the remainder of Wisconsin. Two other areas of Dane County, one extending north into Columbia County, the other southward into eastern Iowa and LaFayette Counties, along with Manitowoc County were settled in the late 1840's.

By 1850, Norwegian settlement was beginning in northern Winnebago County and the bordering area of Portage and Waupaca Counties. However, the largest Norwegian settlement in Wisconsin was the Coon Prairie-Coon Valley area of

Vernon County, extending north into La Crosse County and south into Crawford County.[69] Jackson, Trempealeau, and Buffalo Counties also received heavy influxes of Norwegians in the 1850's and 1860's. Many Norwegians worked in the logging operations along the Black River in these counties to earn sufficient money to buy farms farther south.[70] As lumbering moved northward, so did the Norwegians along the St. Croix and Chippewa Rivers, into Eau Claire, Dunn, Pierce, St. Croix, Chippewa, and Barron Counties.

The Norwegians were essentially a rural people. In 1905, 64.1% of Norwegian family heads lived in rural areas; 10.1% in villages, and 25.2% in cities. The proportion engaged in farming was so great that Carleton Qualey, in his retabulation of the 1850, 1860, and 1870 censuses mentioned occupation only in the rare occasions when it was not farming. Most of those engaged in agriculture turned to dairying, though tobacco was also raised in the Vernon and Dane County areas.

Most Norwegians remained in the Lutheran Church of their homeland, with the Norwegian Synod, founded in 1853, closest to the old State Church. The Hauge Synod, founded in 1876, represented the Inner Mission, pietistic low-church emphasis, and the United Church, begun in 1890, served as a middle way. In 1917 these three groups united as the Norwegian (later Evangelical) Lutheran Church. A few smaller Lutheran groups, led by the Lutheran Free

Church, retained separate identities and some Norwegians joined the Norwegian Baptist, Methodist, and Moravian churches.[71]

For this study, thirty-five townships, nineteen villages and cities to 2,500, and one city of over 2,500--Stoughton, in Dane County--were sufficiently Norwegian to be included. Wards seven, eight, and ten in Eau Claire, and ward nine in La Crosse were all over 35% Norwegian in 1905. However, the last three had sizable German minorities and must be used with caution. Both Madison and Milwaukee had Norwegian communities but in neither city were they sufficiently concentrated to allow for voting analysis.*

SWEDES

Swedish settlement in Wisconsin came both later and in lesser numbers than that of the Norwegians. Despite efforts to set up a Utopian society, New Upsala, in 1841 at Pine Lake in Waukesha County, and to develop a community of scholars at Lake Koshkonong in 1843, only some 600 Swedes were present in Wisconsin by the time of the Civil War. The big period of Swedish settlement began in 1868 along the St. Croix River in Burnett and Polk Counties, with smaller settlements in Pierce, Pepin, St. Croix, and Price

---
*See Map VI on the next page for the location of Norwegian voting units.

MAP VI   NORWEGIAN VOTING UNITS

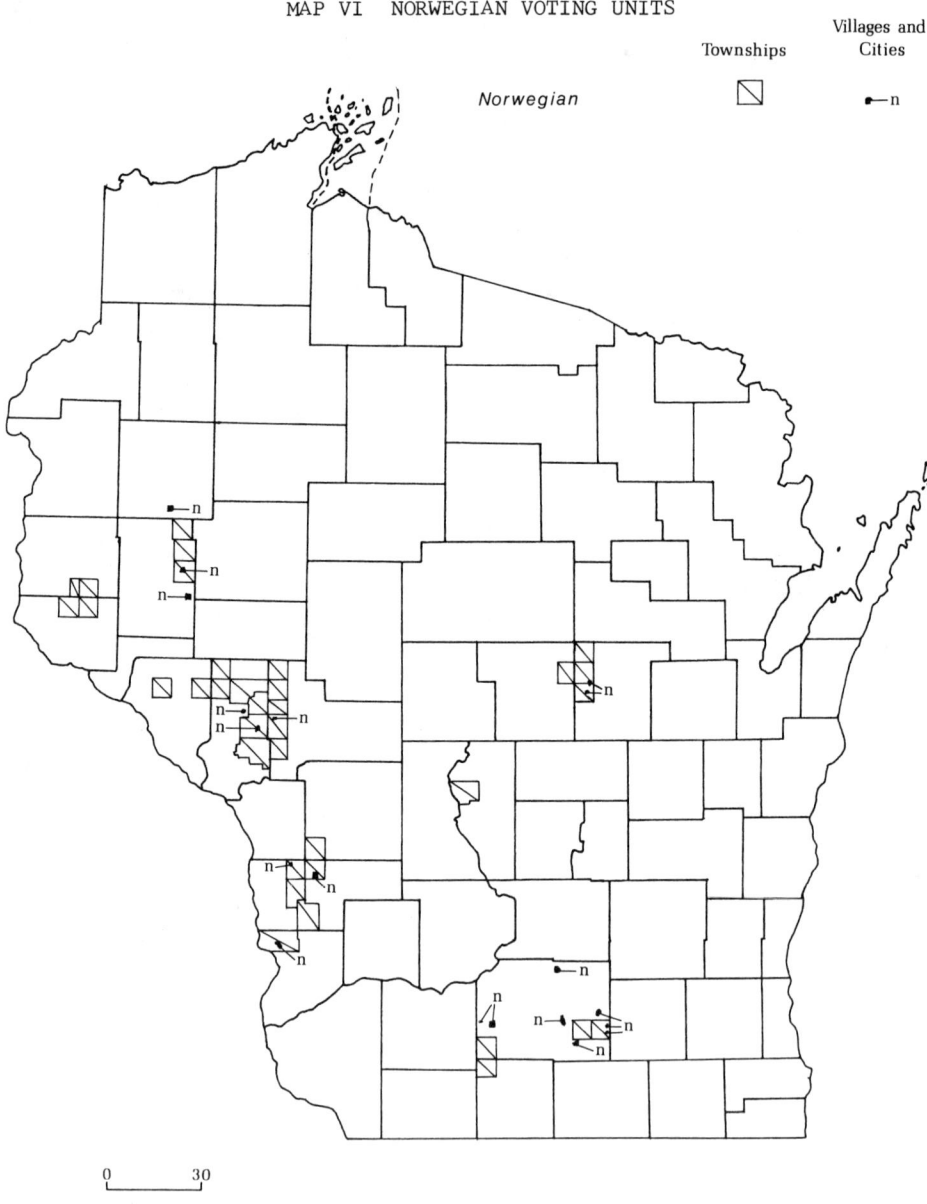

Counties. Swedish immigration peaked in the 1880's and 1890's.[72] Most of this movement by-passed Wisconsin, concentrating in Minnesota. In a way, the Wisconsin Swedish settlements in the northwestern part of the state may be regarded as an extension of the Minnesota Swedish community. In 1900, 64% of the foreign-born Swedes in Wisconsin lived in that area. By the early 1900's, Swedes were occupying other areas of the cutover as they came to be involved in lumbering and sawmill operations, mining, shipping on the Great Lakes, and farming. Thus, the city of Superior in Douglas County, the city of Ashland in Ashland County, Bayfield County, and Florence County all had significant Swedish settlements. The Swedes were one of the most rural people in the state in 1905 with 60.0% of heads-of-household living in rural areas and 30.0% living in cities. Only the Finns and Norwegians topped the rural figure.[73]

Most Swedes were Lutheran, the Augustana Synod representing their brand of Lutheranism. The Augustana Synod was part of the General Council until 1918, when it split from that predominantly German group. A second church among Swedes, the Swedish Mission Convenant, was formally organized in 1885.[74] In 1926, the first year the Augustana Synod reported separately from the General Council, there were 10,942 Swedish Lutherans and 1,181 Swedish Covenanters in Wisconsin. By 1952 these figures had risen to 13,906 and 1,466 respectively.[75]

For this study, fourteen townships, five villages, and the city of Park Falls in Price County, are sufficiently Swedish to be used. In addition, Ashland's second ward was 31% Swedish in 1905 and can be used, with caution, for the entire fifty years.*

DANES

Danish settlement in Wisconsin began in the late 1840's. More spread out and more urban than their fellow Scandinavians, the Danes did form a few compact communities. The city of Racine served as the first magnet and to this day has a sizable Danish minority and the largest number of Danes in Wisconsin. Some Racine industries, such as the Mitchell Wagon Works and J. I. Case Company, employed mainly Danes as late as the mid-1940's. However, many Danes tarried only briefly in Racine before leaving for western and northern Wisconsin. By 1900 some 3,000 Danish stock could be found in the northern and western townships of Polk County. Danish urban areas of concentration, in addition to Racine, were Waupaca, Neenah, and Oshkosh in Winnebago County, and the city of Kenosha. Rural concentrations other than Polk County developed in New Denmark in Brown County, beginning in 1848, Orange township in Juneau County, the Maple Valley area of Oconto County, and,

---

*See Map VII on page 130 for the location of Swedish voting units.

in 1893, the Withee area of Clark County. The Withee settlement, drawing mainly from Danes already present in urban areas of the U. S., continued to grow until the 1910-1920 period. It remains one of the most compact rural Danish settlements in Wisconsin.[76]

Although Lutheran in background, the Danes were slower to organize churches than their fellow Scandinavians. Ultimately, two Danish churches were established: the Danish Evangelical Lutheran Church in America, later called the American Evangelical Lutheran Church, established in 1872 by the Gruntvigians; and the United Danish Evangelical Lutheran Church of America (Danish was later dropped from the title), established in 1872 by the Inner Mission people. By 1952 the former had 1,280 members, the latter, 11,946.[77]

Eight townships, three villages, and the city of Waupaca in Waupaca County represent Danish voting patterns in this study. In addition, wards eight and eleven in Racine, respectively 38% and 44% Danish in 1905, can be used for the early part of the study. A reapportionment after 1910 yields wards eight, eleven, twelve, and thirteen as primarily Danish.[78] These wards can be used, with caution, through the 1952 election.*

FINNS

The Finns were the last of the Scandinavian groups to

---

*See Map VII on page 130 for the location of Danish voting units.

engage in large scale immigration. Coming over primarily from 1880 to 1920 to work in mines, logging camps, and on the docks of the Great Lakes, the Finns later turned to farming, concentrating their settlement in the eighteen northernmost counties of Wisconsin. In 1905, 86.9% of the state's 4,608 foreign-born Finns lived in these counties; in 1930 the figure was still high at 79.8%. Emigrating at first primarily for economic reasons from Finland's rural areas, the movement reached its high point in 1902. By that date, an increasing number of the Finns were dissidents from the Russian authoritarian government and often from the church, as well.

In 1888, the Oulu settlement in Bayfield County and the adjoining Maple area of Douglas County were settled by Finnish farmers. By 1906, forty-one farms were occupied by Finns; by 1924, ninety additional farms had been settled by Finnish families.[79] The same pattern was repeated in the rural Finnish settlements of Ashland and White River in Ashland County; Hoard in Clark County; Kimball, Knight, Oma, and Carey in Iron County; the Knox area of Price, Oneida, and Lincoln Counties; and Phelps in Vilas County. Each of these areas reached its peak of settlement after the 1905 census. Thus, while only three townships (increasing to five in later subdivisions) show up with over 40% Finns in 1905, use of the excellent history of the Finns in Wisconsin by John Kohlemainen and George Hill yields seven additional usable Finnish townships. Moreover, there were good-sized Finnish contingents in the cities of Superior and Ashland, and growing communities in Kenosha and Milwaukee.*

The Finns concentrated more in developing cooperative and temperance societies than they did on the church, though the Finnish Lutheran churches had a combined membership of 1,035 in 1906 and 2,312 in 1926.[80]

POLES

The remaining group with significant settlements outside the urban areas of the state was from Poland. Most Polish immigration occurred after the Civil War, with its peak coming in the early Twentieth Century. The Poles were by far the most urban of the major ethnic groups, 65.2% in cities compared with 46.2% for the Germans and 25.2% for the Norwegians in 1905.

Poles began settling on Milwaukee's south side by 1865, near the factories in which they found employment. By 1905 this area was predominantly Polish, as were the adjoining communities of South Milwaukee and parts of Cudahy and West Allis.[81] Large numbers of Poles also settled in Ashland, Kenosha, Racine, Superior in Douglas County, and Stevens Point in Portage County.

*See Map VII on the next page for the location of Finnish voting units.

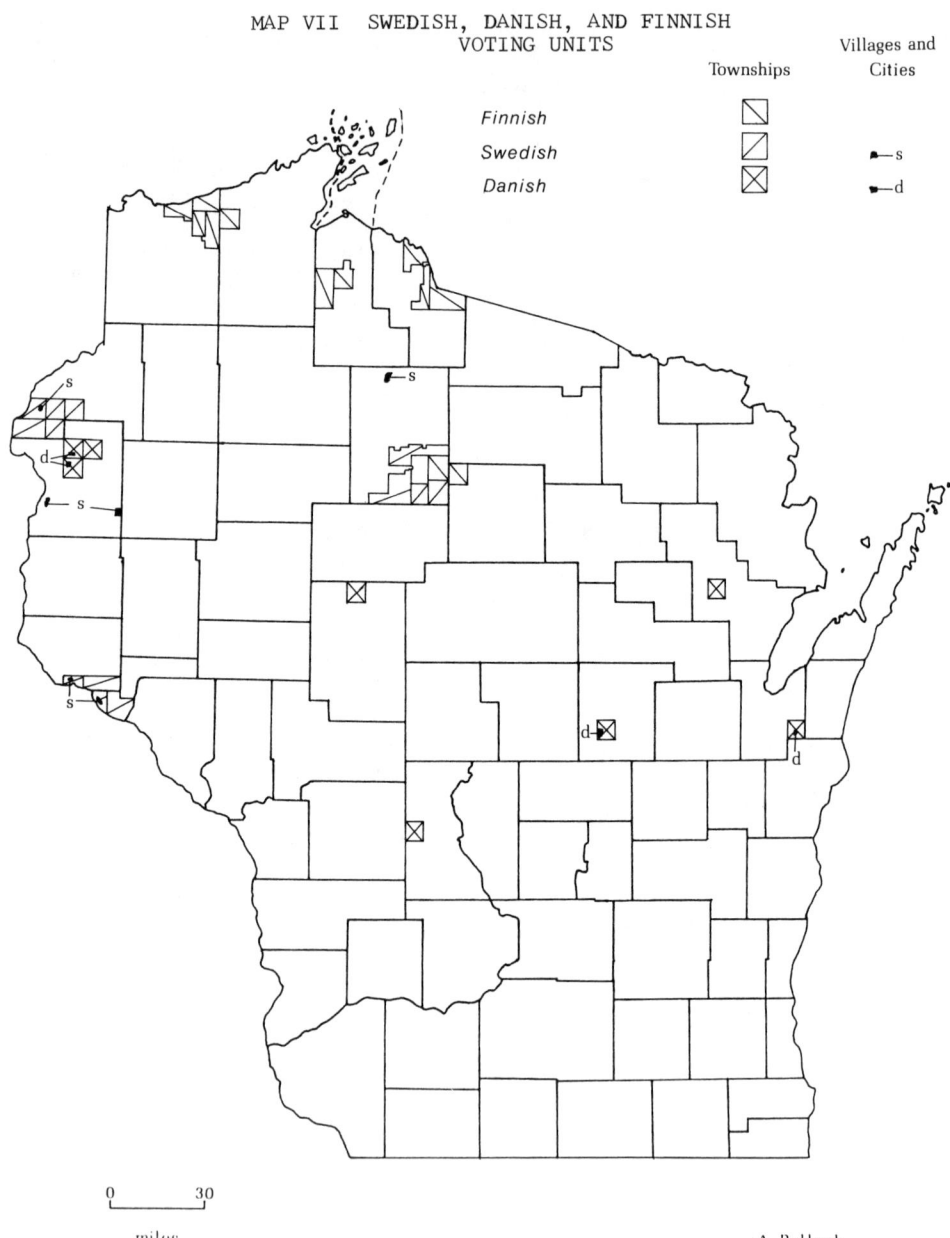

MAP VII SWEDISH, DANISH, AND FINNISH VOTING UNITS

Portage County was also the center of the largest rural Polish community in Wisconsin. Begun in 1858 at Polonia in Sharon township, the Polish settlement was almost complete by 1905. The heaviest influx of settlers came in the decade after 1871, in response to European economic conditions and Bismark's multiple efforts to gain government control over Polish parochial schools; to force the use of the German language on the Poles; and to draft Poles for service in the German army. The Poles in Portage County tended to avoid intermarriage with other ethnic groups and to expand the boundaries of their settlements, rather than to disperse.[82]

A Polish settlement was begun in Trempealeau County around Pine Creek and Arcadia during the Civil War.[83] Settlements were also begun around Berlin in Green Lake County, Pulaski in Brown, Oconto, and Shawano Counties, and near Wild Rose in Waushara County.[84] Settlements in the cutover area included the Withee area of Clark County, beginning in 1891,[85] Weyerhauser in Rusk County, Lublin in Taylor County, and other scattered townships throughout the northern counties. These formed and grew as land companies were able to attract Polish settlers from the urban areas of the state as well as from other Great Lakes industrial areas.[86]

The Poles, in addition to being very clannish, were also church oriented. Almost all cities with a sizable

Polish population had separate Catholic parishes. In 1903 one estimate placed the number of Polish Catholic parishes in Wisconsin at seventy-six, with a membership of 150,000. In all there were 708 Catholic parishes in Wisconsin and 467,000 Catholics in that year.[87] Polish Catholics stressed parochial school education and other efforts to retain their cultural identity.

Twelve townships, four of them in Portage County, and two villages are used in this study. Five wards in Milwaukee; ward seven in Manitowoc; and wards four and seven in Stevens Point, the center of the Portage County Polish settlement, give a good picture of the urban Polish vote. In Milwaukee, wards twelve and fourteen were quite Polish by 1900 and remained so through the redrawing of ward boundaries in 1912 and 1931. New wards eight and twenty-four and ward eleven can be added in 1912. These continued to be Polish through 1950. An indication of the clannishness of the Poles is that while all five of these wards contained sizable German minorities, none of them provided a home for other ethnic groups, and all except one totally excluded blacks as late as 1920. A history of Milwaukee's Polish community, compiled in 1946, labels these wards as follows:[88]

Ward eight	majority Polish
Ward eleven	about 65% Polish
Ward twelve	89% Polish--oldest Polish area

Ward fourteen   original Polish area

Ward twenty-four   about 70% Polish

High votes on the parochial school bus issue in 1946 and small percentage declines in Franklin Roosevelt's vote from 1932 to 1940 further identify these areas as Catholic and non-German.*

ITALIANS

Few Italians came to Wisconsin before the 1880's when a major influx began to the state's urban centers. The earliest settlement and one of the oldest Italian farming colonies in the United States was Genoa in Vernon County, the destination of eight families from Italy's Piedmont in 1863. In 1911 this settlement numbered forty-four families out of a total of 207 families in Genoa township and the unincorporated village therein. Later rural settlements were in the Cumberland area of Barron County and around Hurley and Montreal in Iron County.

However, the main areas of concentration of Italians were the industrial cities of the state--84% of Wisconsin's Italian foreign-stock were classified as urban by the 1930 census. Already by the turn of the century, Beloit, Kenosha, Madison, and Racine had their "little Italies" or "little Sicilies." Milwaukee had the only sizable Italian com-

---

*See Map VIII on page 135 for the location of Polish voting units.

munity, centered in the third ward east of the Milwaukee
River. Beginning in the 1880's with a nucleus of
Sicilians, by 1900 the Italians had displaced the Irish
in that area of Milwaukee. In 1905, 32% of the heads-of-
household and 52% of the foreign-born in the third ward
were Italian compared to figures of 29% and 10% for the
Irish. In 1915 the Detroit Street School at the heart of
the third ward was reported to be 98% Italian.[89] Ward
three underwent few changes in the boundary rearrangements
of 1912 and 1931 and thus can be used throughout the
period of this study as a barometer of the Italian urban
vote. Crystal Lake in Barron County and Genoa, including
the village of Genoa, incorporated in 1935, indicate the
Italian rural-small town vote. Both of these communities
are listed by Heming as having Catholic churches populated
mainly by Italian families[90] and both show up on the 1940
ethnic map as Italian.*

OTHER ETHNIC GROUPS

Several ethnic groups are completely omitted from this
study because of the lateness, smallness, and/or dispersal
of their settlements in the state. In addition to the
British Canadians and Scots already referred to, this listing includes the Russians, Yugoslavs, Hungarians, and

---

*See Map VIII on page 135 for location of the Italian voting
units.

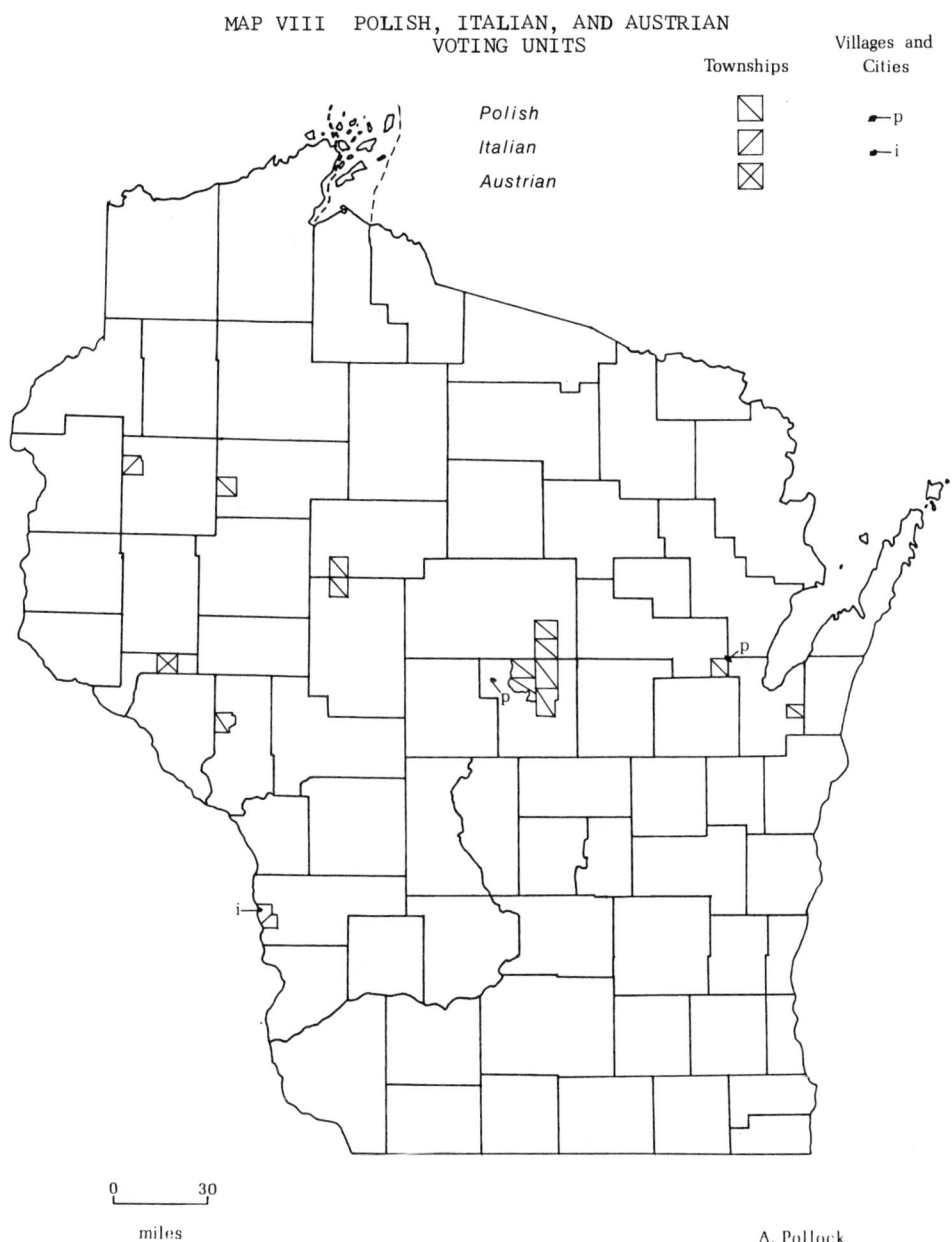

Greeks.[91] These groups are centered in Wisconsin's urban areas, especially the city of Milwaukee, as Table VIII in Appendix B makes clear. A lone Austrian township, Lima in Pepin County, will be used as an illustration of how one small segment of immigrants from Austria voted.*

Perhaps the group most difficult to sort out is the Jewish immigrant. One way of locating this group is through censuses which ask for mother tongue of the foreign-born and foreign-stock. Thus, in 1930, 44% of the Russian immigrants to the United States in the Twentieth Century spoke Yiddish, while 80% of the immigrants from Rumania did.

Applying this analysis to Wisconsin: most of those listed as Russian or Rumanian in Twentieth Century censuses were in fact Jewish. Settling largely in cities, Jewish population concentrations appeared in Kenosha, Madison, Oshkosh, Racine, and Sheboygan. The largest settlement was Milwaukee, centering in the second and sixth wards. An estimated 25,000 Jews lived in that city by 1929. A rare exception to the non-rural character of Jewish settlement was the agricultural community of Arpin in Wood County begun in 1904. Reaching a high point of seventy to eighty individuals in 1913, the community was dying out by 1920.[92]

*See Map VIII on page 135 for location of the Austrian voting unit.

BLACKS

Blacks have also been omitted from this study. The Black population of Wisconsin has always been almost entirely urban-centered and is of relatively recent origin. Table IX in Appendix B makes this clear.

World War I gave the first boost to Wisconsin's Black population. However, as of 1930, Milwaukee was the only city in the state to top 1,000. Even this city's big climb began after 1945. By 1950, ward six had close to a Black majority, wards two, seventeen, and thirteen bordered the Black community and contained sizable Black minorities. Other than Milwaukee, only Beloit, Racine, Madison, Kenosha, and Granville township in Milwaukee topped the 100 mark in 1930. Most of the rest of the state's 10,606 Blacks in that year lived scattered in urban communities, with a handful on farms. The largest rural group was the settlement in Forest township in Vernon County with 113 Blacks in 1930. By the early 1950's this settlement had virtually died out. By that date, urban Black voting patterns could readily be studied--just beyond the limits of this work.[93]

INDIANS

A different set of problems faces the would-be student of the Indian vote. Until the Citizenship Act was passed in 1924, most Indians living on reservations were denied the right to vote. Even after that date local white resistance and disinterest on the part of the Indians kept the Indian vote at a minimum. Coupled with this was the relative smallness of Wisconsin's Indian population. The total number of Indians in the state had reached 8,372 in 1900, 11,548 in 1930, and 12,196 in 1950. In the latter year only 1,189 Indians were classified as urban and 1,589 as rural-farm. The remaining 9,418 were listed as rural-non-farm, primarily living on Indian Reservations throughout the northern part of the state. Several townships can be identified as basically Indian reservations: the Menomonie Reservation in Oconto and Shawano Counties (this area became Menomonie County in 1961); the smaller Stockbridge Reservation located in Bartleme township in Shawano County; Flambeau in Vilas County; Lac Court Oreilles, covering parts of several townships in Sawyer; Hobart in Brown and Oneida in Outagamie, comprising the Oneida Reservation. The subtleties of Indian participation in United States and state politics and government involves an understanding of tribal differences, the nature of Bureau of Indian Affairs contact, and the degree of organization of tribal councils well beyond the range of this study.[94]

This then is the mosaic of people on which national and Wisconsin politics made its imprint. The pattern that developed from that contact through the first half of the Twentieth Century will be the subject of the remaining chapters of this study.

NOTES

[1] Douglas G. Marshall, Wisconsin's Population: Changes and Prospects, 1900-1963, Agricultural Experiment Station of the University of Wisconsin, Research Bulletin 241 (Madison, March, 1963). Hereinafter, all references to Research Bulletins will omit the Agricultural Experiment Station information. The Rural Sociology Department at the University of Wisconsin continuously studies population change in the state. In addition to publications in the Agricultural Experiment Station Series, the Department publishes Population Series, Population Notes, and pamphlets on individual counties. Many of these are cited in John H. Kolb, Emerging Rural Communities: Group Relations in Rural Society, A Review of Wisconsin Research in Action (Madison, 1959).

[2] See O. G. Libby, et al., "An Economic and Social Study of the Lead Region of Wisconsin, Illinois, and Iowa," Transactions of the Wisconsin Academy of Science, Arts, and Letters, Vol. XIII (1900), 188-281, and Joseph Schafer, The Wisconsin Lead Region, Wisconsin Domesday Book, General Studies, Vol. III (Madison, 1932), for extensive discussions of the lead mining region. See also the first issue of Prologue: The Journal of the National Archives, I (Spring, 1969) for two articles on the area: Herman R. Friis, "The David Dale Owen Map of Southwestern Wisconsin," 9-28, and Jane F. Smith, "The Use of Federal Records in Writing

Local History: A Case Study," 29-51. The latter is a study of Linden township, Iowa County, one of the English townships used in this study.

[3] Paul W. Gates, "Frontier Land Business in Wisconsin," Wisconsin Magazine of History, LII (Summer, 1969), 306-327.

[4] On settlement in general, see especially Guy-Harold Smith, "The Populating of Wisconsin," Geographical Review, XVIII (July, 1928), 401-421, and "The Settlement and the Distribution of the Population in Wisconsin," Wisconsin Academy of Science, Arts, and Letters Transactions, XXIV (1929), 53-107. See also the Domesday Book Series authored by Joseph Schafer: Four Wisconsin Counties: Prairie and Forest, Wisconsin Domesday Book, General Studies, Vol. II (Madison, 1927); The Wisconsin Lead Region; The Winnebago-Horicon Basin: A Type Study in Western History, General Studies, Vol. IV (Madison, 1937); and Town Studies, Vol. I (Madison, 1924). Schafer describes his plans for a detailed study of Wisconsin at the local level in "The Wisconsin Domesday Book," Wisconsin Magazine of History, IV (September, 1920), 61-74. On Twentieth Century developments see the series by Edwin E. Witte: "Statistics relating to Wisconsin from the 1920 Census," Wisconsin Blue Book, 1923, 17-40; "Wisconsin in the 1930 Census," Wisconsin Blue Book, 1933, 103-132; and "Some Trends Revealed by the 1940 Census," Wisconsin Blue Book, 1942, 129-150. On the state in general see Robert C. Nesbit, Wisconsin: A

History (Madison, 1973), and William F. Raney, Wisconsin: A Story of Progress (New York, 1940; Reprint 1963). A definitive six volume history of the state sponsored by the State Historical Society of Wisconsin is in the process of being written. The first volume, by Alice E. Smith, The History of Wisconsin: From Exploration to Statehood, was published in 1973.

[5] Robert Fries, Empire in Pine: The Story of Lumbering in Wisconsin, 1830-1900 (Madison, 1951), 239 and 251.

[6] The 1885 data is from the Tabular Statements of the (1885) Census Enumeration and the Agricultural, Mineral, and Manufacturing Interests of the State of Wisconsin, 788. Rusk County figures are extrapolated from those for Chippewa County. Douglas County is omitted from the 1885 agricultural census and data for it is also estimated using 1895 and 1905 data. See Tabular Statements of the (1895) Census Enumeration and the Agricultural, Mineral, and Manufacturing Interests of the State of Wisconsin, 1021; Tabular Statements of the (1905) Census and the Agricultural, Dairying, and Manufacturing Interests of the State of Wisconsin, 328. The data for 1920 is from Fourteenth Census of the United States: 1920, Vol. VI, Part I, Agriculture, 460-466. For 1950 and 1960 data see Economic Research Service, U. S. Department of Agriculture, An Economic Survey of the Northern Lake States Region. Agricultural Economic Report No. 108, 131. This report contains much information on the northern

cutover in Wisconsin as well as in Michigan and Minnesota.

[7]C. Luther Fry, The New and Old Immigrant on the Land: A Study of Americanization and the Rural Church (New York, 1922), 16. See Walter A. Rowlands, "The Great Lakes Cutover Region," in Merrill Jensen, ed., Regionalism in America (Madison, 1951), 331-346; Arlan Helgeson, Farms in the Cutover: Agricultural Settlements in Northern Wisconsin (Madison, 1962); Lucille Kane, "Settling the Wisconsin Cutover Region," Wisconsin Magazine of History, XL (Winter, 1956-57), 91-98. A good study is needed of the actual process of settlement of the cutover. Helgeson deals with the companies and recruitment policies and almost totally ignores the recruits. Rural sociologists in the 1920's and 1930's were mainly concerned with the ability of people in the area to survive in the poor, rocky soil, to develop communities, and to integrate their lives into the broader culture. See George W. Hill and Ronald A. Smith, Man in the "Cutover": A Study of Family-Farm Resources in Northern Wisconsin, Research Bulletin 139 (Madison, April, 1941); Fry, The New and Old Immigrant on The Land; Wisconsin State Planning Board, The Cutover Region of Wisconsin: Report of Conditions and Recommendations for Rehabilitation (Madison, 1939); and Mark J. Thompson, Eighty-five Years of Farming in the Northern Coniferous Forest Areas of Minnesota, Wisconsin, and Michigan. University of Minnesota Agricultural Experiment Station Miscellaneous Report 35, June, 1959.

[8] John Griffin Thompson, The Rise and Decline of the Wheat Growing Industry in Wisconsin, Research Bulletin 292 of the University of Wisconsin Economics and Political Science Series, Vol. V (Madison, May, 1909). On agriculture in general see Joseph Schafer, A History of Agriculture In Wisconsin, General Studies, Vol. I (Madison, 1922); Oliver E. Remey, "A Half Century of Agricultural Development," in Milo Milton Quaife, Wisconsin: Its History and Its People, Vol. II (Chicago, 1924), 41-72; Walter H. Ebling, "The Development of Agriculture in Wisconsin," Wisconsin Blue Book, 1929, 51-74; and Wisconsin Crop and Livestock Reporting Service, A Century of Wisconsin Agriculture: 1848-1948. Bulletin No. 290 (Madison, 1948). A mine of information is available in the County Agricultural Statistics Series published by the Wisconsin Department of Agriculture. Series I was published from 1939 through 1942; Series II in the late 1940's; Series III from 1952 to 1955; and Series IV from 1956 to 1958. Each series included a separate report on every county in the state containing a great deal of statistical information on the township level. The third series included a five page history of each county. The first three series are described by Walter H. Ebling, head of the Statistical Division of the Wisconsin Department of Agriculture in "History and Statistics in the Counties," Wisconsin Magazine of History, XXXV (Winter, 1951), 101-105.

[9]Eric E. Lampard, The Rise of the Dairy Industry in Wisconsin: A Study in Agricultural Change, 1820-1920 (Madison, 1963). Note in footnote six above, the change in the title of the 1905 state census when "Dairying" replaced "Mineral" marking the conquest of the state's economy by the milk cow.

[10]See Karl B. Raitz and Cotton Mather, "Norwegians and Tobacco in Western Wisconsin," Annals of the Association of American Geographers, LXI (December, 1971), 684-696.

[11]Wisconsin Crop and Livestock Reporting Service, Wisconsin Dairying in Mid-Century, Bulletin Number 331 (Madison, May, 1955), 49.

[12]On industry see Margaret Walsh, The Manufacturing Frontier: Pioneering Industry in Antebellum Wisconsin, 1830-1860 (Madison, 1972); Frederick Merk, Economic History of Wisconsin During the Civil War Decade (Madison, 1916); "Distribution and Growth of Manufacturing Industries," Eleventh Biennial Report of the Bureau of Labor and Industrial Statistics: State of Wisconsin, 1903-1904, 299-408; J. H. H. Alexander, "A Short Industrial History of Wisconsin," Wisconsin Blue Book, 1929, 21-49; Wisconsin Regional Planning Committee, A Study of Wisconsin: Its Resources, Its Physical, Social and Economic Background. Wisconsin Regional Plan Report, 1934 (Madison, December, 1934); State Planning Board, A Picture of Wisconsin: Viewed from the Standpoint of Resources, Industry, and Agriculture (Madison,

August, 1945); and Economic Survey of the Northern Lake States Region.

[13]"A Retabulation of Population Schedules from the Wisconsin State Census of 1905." Departments of Rural Sociology and Agricultural Economics, Wisconsin Agricultural Experiment Station, University of Wisconsin Cooperating with the Works Progress Administration. Directed by George W. Hill, July 20, 1940, Vol. I, v. See Hill, "The Use of the Culture-Area Concept in Social Research," American Journal of Sociology, XLVII (July, 1941), 39-47; and Chapter II, pages 42 and 43 and footnote 18 for descriptions of the retabulation.

[14]Schafer, "Peopling the Midwest," Wisconsin Magazine of History, XXI (September, 1937), 96-97.

[15]Joseph Schafer consistently refers to the early American settlers as "Yankees." The Wisconsin Magazine of History of Autumn, 1952 reprinted an effort to define "Yankee":

> When a reader of the Country Gentleman encountered a story on New England sometime ago, the term "Yankees" confused him. He pleaded for a better definition of "Yankee." "In the rest of the world," he wrote, "all Americans are Yankees; in South America, all North Americans are Yankees; in the North, all New Englanders are Yankees; in New England only Vermonters are Yankees, and in Vermont only those who run a farm are Yankees, and among Vermont farmers, only those who make maple sugar are true Yankees!"

Reprinted from History News (May, 1952), in Wisconsin Magazine of History, XXXVI (Autumn, 1952), 16.

[16]"Retabulation of Wisconsin Census of 1905," Vol. I, viii.

[17]For Yankee settlement see the works by Schafer cited above, plus his "The Yankee and Teuton in Wisconsin," Wisconsin Magazine of History, VI and VIII (December, 1922 to December, 1923), a five-part series; Cardinal Goodwin, "The Movement of American Settlers into Wisconsin and Minnesota," Iowa Journal of History and Politics, XVII (July, 1919), 406-428; and Stewart H. Holbrook, The Yankee Exodus: An Account of Migration from New England (New York, 1950), 108-130.

[18]Schafer, "Eagle," in Town Studies, I, 40-44.

[19]The United States census stopped publishing data on church membership in 1936. The National Council of Churches filled the gap in 1952, basing its count on information supplied by the churches themselves. The data has been reassembled with some estimating for cross-national denominations such as the German-Dutch Reformed Church in America. The quality of the religious censuses is discussed by Wilbur Zelinsky, "An Approach to the Religious Geography of the United States: Patterns of Church Membership in 1952," Annals of the Association of American Geographers, LI (June, 1960), 139-193. See also Edwin Scott Gaustad, Historical Atlas of Religion in America (New York, 1962).

[20]The Wisconsin Historical Records Survey, Directory of Churches and Religious Organizations in Wisconsin (Mad-

ison, January, 1941), contains a list of all church organizations in the state by county. Unfortunately, membership data is not given.

[21] See Chapter IV for a fuller discussion of this domination.

[22] "Retabulation of Wisconsin Census of 1905," Vol. I, vi and vii.

[23] Glen T. Trewartha, "French settlement in the Driftless Hill Land," Annals of the Association of American Geographers, XXVIII (1938), 179-200.

[24] See Harry H. Heming, The Catholic Church in Wisconsin (Milwaukee, 1895-1898), 614-615, 820, 866-867. For example: "From the start, the population of Somerset may be said to be composed of French Canadian Catholics." Heming, 866. All of these communities are discussed by Fred L. Holmes in his chapter on the French, "Romantic Days are Fading," in Old World Wisconsin: Around Europe in the Badger State (Eau Claire, Wisconsin, 1944), 21-34, and all except Coleman show up on the 1940 map of Wisconsin labelled "French Canadian."

[25] On Canadian immigration in general, see Leon E. Truesdell, The Canadian Born in the United States: An Analysis of the Statistics of the Canadian Element in the Population of the United States, 1850 to 1930 (New Haven 1943); and Marcus Lee Hansen, The Mingling of the Canadian and American Peoples (New York, Russell and Russell, 1970.

Reprint of 1940 edition).

[26] William F. Whyte, "The British Elements in Wisconsin," in Quaife, Wisconsin, II, 225-226.

[27] Anna Adams Dickie, "Scotch-Irish Presbyterian Settlers in Southern Wisconsin," Wisconsin Magazine of History, XXXI (March, 1948), 291-304, has a discussion of one group of Scottish settlers.

[28] Louis Albert Copeland, "The Cornish in Southwest Wisconsin," Collections of the State Historical Society of Wisconsin, XIV (1898), 301-334; Holmes, "Come, Let's Touch the Pipes a Bit," in Old World Wisconsin, 39-50. Note also the books on the lead mining region, listed in footnote two.

[29] Whyte, in Quaife, Wisconsin, II, 213-217; Sadie Rowlands Price, "The Welsh of Waukesha County," Wisconsin Magazine of History, XXVI (March, 1943), 323-332; Daniel Jenkins Williams, The Welsh Community of Waukesha County (Columbus, Ohio, 1926); Holmes, "Songs from the Heath and Heather," in Old World Wisconsin, 195-210; and Laura J. Phillips, "The Colonization of Wisconsin by the Welsh," (University of Wisconsin Ph. B. Thesis, 1910). Commenting on their clannishness, Williams says that 90% of the Welsh in Waukesha County live within a $4\frac{1}{2}$ mile radius of the intersections of Highways 41 and 83. Unfortunately this community includes parts of five townships rather than being centered in one.

[30] Sister M. Justille McDonald, History of the Irish in

Wisconsin in the 19th Century (Washington, D. C., 1954), 9-10.

[31] Ibid., 26-29.

[32] McDonald gives the following data on Irish occupations for 1850 and 1860:

	1850	1860
Farm owners	4,400	10,500
Farm laborers		2,400
Common laborers	3,200	6,200
Miners	670	360
Other	?	2,940
Total	?	22,400

Ibid., 118-123.

[33] In addition to the comprehensive study by McDonald, see McDonald "The Irish of the North Country," Wisconsin Magazine of History, XL (Winter, 1956-57), 126-132; Reverend Lincoln F. Whelan, "'Them's They': The Story of Monches, Wisconsin," Wisconsin Magazine of History, XXIV (September, 1940), 39-55; and Holmes, "Saint Patrick's Sons Don the Green," in Old World Wisconsin, 173-190. For examples of Irish settlers being displaced by the more numerous Germans see William F. Whyte, "Chronicles of Early Watertown," Wisconsin Magazine of History, IV (March, 1921), 311; Samuel Pedrick, Ripon Commonwealth, January 27, 1939, quoted in Pedrick, Ripon (Ripon, Wisconsin, 1954), 343; and Joseph Schafer, "Church Records in Migration Studies," Wisconsin Magazine of History, X (March, 1927), 329-330.

[34] See Heming, Catholic Church in Wisconsin, for loca-

tions of Catholic churches with Irish congregations and/or priests for each of these areas.

³⁵Much has been written on German settlement in Wisconsin. In addition to the works by Joseph Schafer in the Domesday series cited above, see Kate A. [Everest] Levi, "How Wisconsin Came by Its Large German Element," *Collections of the State Historical Society of Wisconsin*, XII (1892), 299-334, "Geographical Origin of German Immigration to Wisconsin," *Collections*, XIV (1898), 341-393, "Early Lutheran Immigration to Wisconsin," *Transactions of the Wisconsin Academy of Science, Arts, and Letters*, VIII (1892), 289-298; Guy-Harold Smith, "Notes on the Distribution of the German-Born in Wisconsin in 1905," *Wisconsin Magazine of History*, XIII (December, 1929), 107-120; Hildegard B. Johnson, "The Location of German Immigrants in the Middle West," *Annals of the Association of American Geographers*, XLI (March, 1951), 1-41; John H. A. Lacher, "The German Element in Wisconsin," in Quaife, ed., *Wisconsin*, Vol. II, 153-206; and Holmes, "Freiheit Ist Meine," in *Old World Wisconsin*, 51-74. For a useful discussion of geographical and religious differences among Germans in another state see Frederick C. Luebke, *Immigrants and Politics: The Germans of Nebraska, 1880-1900* (Lincoln, Nebraska, 1969), and "German Immigrants and Churches in Nebraska, 1889-1915," *Mid-America*, L (April, 1968), 116-130.

³⁶In his retabulation of the 1870 census, Schafer found

in Racine, Kenosha, Milwaukee (excluding the city of Milwaukee), and Ozaukee Counties the following breakdown of the German-born heads-of-household:

Prussia	3,359	Hanover	185
Mecklenburg	617	Würtenburg	140
Saxony	434	Hamburg and	
Bavaria	397	Brunswick	48
Hesse	251	Luxemburg	594
Baden	229	Total	6,561

Data from "Appendix," Prairie and Forest, 388-398.

37Johnson, "German Immigrants in the Middle West," Annals, 33-39.

38Levi, "Geographical Origins," Collections, XIV, 381-383.

39Ibid., 385-387; W. A. Titus, "St. Nazianz: A Unique Religious Colony," Wisconsin Magazine of History, V (December, 1921), 160-165.

40Levi, "Geographical Origins," Collections, XIV, 374-379; Holmes, "Spire Guides Luxemburgers," in Old World Wisconsin, 79-88.

41Land of the Fox: Saga of Outagamie County (Appleton, Wisconsin, 1949), 171.

42See Still, Milwaukee, chapters six and eleven; Gerd Korman, Industrialization, Immigrants, and Americanizers: The View from Milwaukee, 1866-1921 (Madison, 1967); and Korman, "A Social History of Industrial Growth and Immigrants, A Study with Particular Reference to Milwaukee, 1880-1920," (University of Wisconsin Ph. D. Dissertation, 1950). The United States Census from 1900 to 1930 included ward level data on foreign-born for cities over 50,000. In 1900 and 1910, this meant Milwaukee, in 1920, Milwaukee and Racine, and in 1930, Milwaukee, Racine, and Madison. For ward data on Milwaukee, see Thirteenth Census, 1910, Vol. III, Population, 1101; and Fourteenth Census, 1920, Vol. III, Composition and Characteristics, 1137-1138. After 1930 the census divided major cities into census tracts which usually did not coincide with ward boundaries. A useful compendium of such data for Milwaukee is H. Yuan Tien, ed., Milwaukee Metropolitan Fact Book, 1940, 1950, and 1960 (Madison, 1962).

[43]Legislative Reference Bureau, State of Wisconsin, Public Transportation of Parochial and Private School Pupils: Legislation Considered by the Wisconsin Legislature, 1939-1962 (Madison, May, 1962). Mimeographed. William W. Boyer, Jr., "Public Transportation of Parochial School Pupils," Wisconsin Law Review (January, 1952), 64-90.

[44]Charles R. Bell, letter to the (Madison) Wisconsin State Journal, May 15, 1946; letter to the (Madison) Capital Times, May 16, 1946. The Reverend Mr. Bell was pastor of First Baptist Church and President of the Madison Council of Churches. All newspaper references are found in a clipping file maintained by the Wisconsin Legislative Reference Service in the State Capital at Madison.

[45]Statement of Committee Supporting the Constitutional Amendment for Transportation of School Children, Milwaukee Journal, September 27, 1946. The chairman of this committee

-153-

was August Reisweber, state chairman of the Knights of Columbus.

⁴⁶Milwaukee Journal, October 14, 1946; Milwaukee Sentinel, October 14, 1946.

⁴⁷Capital Times, October 4, 1946; Milwaukee Journal, September 27, 1946.

⁴⁸A lone exception appears to be Attorney W. H. Dougherty of Janesville who called the amendment unnecessary in a letter to the Janesville Gazette reprinted in the Capital Times of October 21, 1946.

⁴⁹Capital Times, May 12, 1946.

⁵⁰Ibid., June 1, 1946.

⁵¹Ibid., May 9, 1946; Milwaukee Journal, September 30, 1946, and April 26, 1946; Capital Times, May 6, 1946; Wisconsin State Journal, September 24, 1946; and Capital Times, April 19, 1946.

⁵²Milwaukee Journal, October 13, 1946. There were 6,000 other students in parochial and private schools.

⁵³Capital Times, April 15, 1946.

⁵⁴Ibid., June 8, 1946.

⁵⁵Milwaukee Journal, October 25, 1946.

⁵⁶See letters to the editor by Reverend Roland A. Rede and Reverend G. W. Fischer in the Milwaukee Journal, June [?], 1946, and October 16, 1946 respectively.

⁵⁷At a Knights of Columbus luncheon, State Senator Bernhard Gettleman cited the support of the Reverend Bar-

nard Schumacher, Superintendent of Lutheran Schools for the Southern Wisconsin District of the Missouri Synod. Milwaukee Journal, February 13, 1946.

[58]Andrew Baggaley, "Religious Influences on Wisconsin Voting, 1928-1960," American Political Science Review, LVI (May, 1962), 66-70.

[59]Levi, "Geographical Origins," Collections, XIV, 368.

[60]See Table VII in Appendix B for the source of this data and similar figures for 1906 and 1926. Kleppner has a very good description of the varieties of German Protestantism and the effect of this on German political behavior in The Cross of Culture: A Social Analysis of Midwestern Politics (New York, 1970), 42-51, 79-83. There were also a few German free thinkers in areas like Sauk City in Sauk County and Thiensville village in Ozaukee County. See Berenice Cooper, "Die Freien Gemeinden in Wisconsin," Transactions of the Wisconsin Academy of Science, Arts, and Letters, LIII (Fall, 1914), 53-65; N. T. Demerath III and Victor Thiessen, "On Spitting Against the Wind: Organizational Precariousness and American Irreligion," American Journal of Sociology, LXXI (May, 1966), 674-687; and Holmes Old World Wisconsin, 60-62.

[61]John Luchsinger, "The Swiss Colony of New Glarus, Wisconsin," Collections of the State Historical Society of Wisconsin, VIII (1879), 411-439, and "The Planting of the Swiss Colony at New Glarus, Wisconsin," Collections, XII

(1892), 335-382; Levi, "Geographical Origins," Collections, XIV, 387-390; Holmes, "Swiss Yodel Cares Away," Old World Wisconsin, 129-148; John Paul von Greuningen, ed., The Swiss in the United States (Madison, 1940), 31-34; Joseph Schafer, "New Glarus," in Town Studies, I, 78-82; and Leo Schelbert, ed., New Glarus, 1845-1970: The Making of a Swiss-American Town (Glarus, Switzerland, 1970).

[62]Henry S. Lucas, Netherlanders in America: Dutch Immigration to the United States and Canada, 1789-1950 (Ann Arbor, Michigan, 1955), 196-225, 358-361; Arnold Mulder, Americans From Holland (Philadelphia, 1947), 119-121, 172-180; Sipko F. Rederus, "The Dutch Settlement of Sheboygan County," Wisconsin Magazine of History, I (March, 1918), 256-265; Holmes, "Holland's Puritan Ways," Old World Wisconsin, 109-130; Saga of Outagamie County.

[63]Karel D. Bicha, "The Czechs in Wisconsin History," Wisconsin Magazine of History, LIII (Spring, 1970), 194-203; Glen L. Taggart, "The Czechs of Wisconsin as a Culture Type," (University of Wisconsin, Ph. D. Thesis, 1948), 13-17.

[64]Thomas Capek, The Czechs (Bohemians) in America (New York, 1920), 119; Robert I. Kutak, The Story of a Bohemian-American Village: A Study of Social Persistence and Change (Louisville, Kentucky, 1933; Arno Press Reprint, 1970), 41-52.

[65]See Heming, Catholic Church in Wisconsin, for the location of Bohemian Catholic congregations.

[66] Hjalmar Rued Holand, Wisconsin's Belgian Community (Sturgeon Bay, Wisconsin, 1933); Xavier Martin, "The Belgians of Northeast Wisconsin," Collections of the State Historical Society of Wisconsin, XIII (1895), 375-396; Lee W. Metzner, "The Belgians in the North Country," Wisconsin Magazine of History, XXVI (March, 1943), 280-288; and Holmes, "Belgian Dust Dancers Celebrate," in Old World Wisconsin, 149-174.

[67] Carleton Qualey, Norwegian Settlement in the United States (Northfield, Minnesota, 1938), 41. For Norwegian settlement, in addition to Qualey, 40-75, see Theodore C. Blegen, Norwegian Migration to America: 1825-1860 (Northfield, 1931), and Norwegian Migration to America: The American Transition (Northfield, 1940); Olaf Morgan Norlie, History of the Norwegian People in America (Minneapolis, 1925); and Guy-Harold Smith, "Notes on the Distribution of the Foreign-Born Scandinavian in Wisconsin in 1905," Wisconsin Magazine of History, XIV (June, 1931), 419-436.

[68] Qualey, Norwegian Settlement in the United States, Appended, 221-225.

[69] Hjalmar Rued Holand, Coon Prairie (Minneapolis, 1927), and Coon Valley (Minneapolis, 1928). See also the works by Peter A. Munch, "Social Adjustment Among Wisconsin Norwegians," American Sociological Review, XIV (December, 1949), 780-787, and "Segregation and Assimilation of Norwegian Settlements in Wisconsin," Norwegian-American Studies and Records, XVIII (1954), 102-140.

[70] Among these was the great-grandfather of the author who came to the Black River Falls area in 1849 and, in 1852, with his brother and cousin, settled in the Coon Valley community. On Trempealeau County, see Merle Curti, The Making of an American Community: A Case Study of Democracy in a Frontier County (Stanford, California, 1959, 1969 paperback).

[71] E. Clifford Nelson and Eugene L. Fevold, The Lutheran Church Among Norwegian-Americans: A History of the Evangelical Lutheran Church (Minneapolis, 1960), two vols., and J. C. K. Preus, ed., Norsemen Found a Church: An Old Heritage in a New Land (Minneapolis, 1953); Fevold, The Lutheran Free Church: A Fellowship of American Lutheran Congregations, 1897-1963 (Minneapolis, 1969); and E. Clifford Nelson, Lutheranism in North America (Minneapolis, 1972).

[72] See the table in Adolph B. Benson and Naboth Hedin, Americans From Sweden (Philadelphia, 1950), 121.

[73] In addition to the Benson and Hedin book, for Swedish immigration to Wisconsin, see Helge Nelson, The Swedes and the Swedish Settlements in North America (New York, 1943), two vols.; Guy-Harold Smith, "Foreign-Born Scandinavians in Wisconsin in 1905"; Erik Ehn, "The Swedes in Wisconsin: Immigration to Wisconsin," Swedish Pioneer Historical Quarterly, XIX (April, 1968), 116-129; Holmes, "Swedes Make Happy the Yuletide," in Old World Wisconsin, 233-246; and Fry, The New

and Old Immigrant on the Land, 39-46; and O. Fritiof Ander, The Cultural Heritage of the Swedish Immigrant: Selected References (Rock Island, Illinois, 1956).

[74] On religion see Benson and Hedin, Americans From Sweden, 126-139, George M. Stephenson, The Religious Aspect of Swedish Immigration (Minneapolis, 1932), and G. Everett Arden, Augustana Heritage: A History of the Augustana Lutheran Church (Rock Island, Illinois, 1963).

[75] Census of Religious Bodies: 1926, I, 270-273; Churches and Church Membership in the United States, Series B, Bulletin No. 8.

[76] John H. Bille, "A History of the Danes in America," Transactions of the Wisconsin Academy of Science, Arts, and Letters, XI (1896-97), 1-48; Thomas Christiansen," Danish Settlement in Wisconsin," Wisconsin Magazine of History, XII (September, 1928), 19-40; Holmes, "Most Danish City in America," in Old World Wisconsin, 299-318; Harald A. Pedersen, "Acculturation among Danish and Polish Ethnic Groups in Wisconsin," (University of Wisconsin Ph.D. Dissertation, 1949).

[77] See Table VII in Appendix B for the data on religion. See also John M. Jensen, The United Evangelical Lutheran Church: An Interpretation (Minneapolis, 1963).

[78] For the Racine ward data see Fourteenth Census, 1920, Vol. III, Composition and Characteristics, 1139.

[79] Thorpe M. Langley, "Geography of the Maple Area, Douglas County, Wisconsin," (University of Wisconsin M.A. Thesis, 1932), 13-22.

[80] Arthur Hoglund, Finnish Immigrants in America, 1880-1920 (Madison, 1960); John Kolehmainen and George W. Hill, Haven in the Woods: The Story of the Finns in Wisconsin (Madison, 1951); Kolehmainen, "The Finns of Wisconsin," Wisconsin Magazine of History, XXVII (June, 1944), 391-399; Holmes, "Children of the Midnight Sun," Old World Wisconsin, 247-266; and Ralph T. Jalkanen, ed., The Faith of the Finns: Historical Perspectives on the Finnish Lutheran Church in America (Lansing, Michigan, 1972). For religious data see Table VII in Appendix B.

[81] Still, Milwaukee, especially chapter eleven; Korman, Industrialization, Immigrants, and Americanizers; Frank H. Miller, The Polanders in Wisconsin (Milwaukee, 1896); John Tomkiewicz, "Poles in Wisconsin," Proceedings of the State Historical Society of Wisconsin (1901), 148-152; Thaddeus Borun, Comp., We the Milwaukee Poles: 1846-1946 (Milwaukee, 1946); and Holmes, "Poles Rejoice in New Freedom," in Old World Wisconsin, 337-353.

[82] Albert Hart Sanford, "The Polish People of Portage County," Proceedings of the State Historical Society of Wisconsin (1907), 259-288, see especially 280-281.

[83] The interrelationships of this community with the dominant Yankee and Norwegian communities of Trempealeau County has been ably described by Merle Curti in The Making of an American Community.

[84] See Douglas Marshall, "Nationality and the Emerging

Culture," *Rural Sociology*, XIII (March, 1948), 40-47, on Wild Rose.

[85]See Pedersen, "Acculturation among Danish and Polish Ethnic Groups," on the Withee settlement.

[86]Hill and Smith, *Man in the "Cutover"*, 48-49. Ladislas J. Siekaniec, "The Poles of Upper North Wisconsin," *Wisconsin Magazine of History*, XXXIX (Spring, 1956), 195-198, and "Poles in Ashland, Wisconsin, 1884-1888," *Polish American Studies* (January-June, 1949), discusses primarily the Polish settlements of Ashland, Bayfield, and Douglas Counties centered in the cities of Ashland and Superior.

[87]Sister Mary Adele Dabrowska, "A History and Survey of the Polish Community in Brooklyn," (Fordham University M. A. Thesis, 1946), 75, cited in Joseph A. Wyrtwal, *America's Polish Heritage: A Social History of the Poles in America* (Detroit, 1961), 321.

[88]*We the Milwaukee Poles*, 154-158. The ward information for 1920 is from *Fourteenth Census, 1920*, Vol. III, *Composition and Characteristics*, 1137-1138.

[89]On Genoa, see A. E. Cance, "Piedmontese on the Mississippi," *The Survey*, XXVI (September 2, 1911), 779-785; on Milwaukee, see George La Piana, *The Italian Colony in Milwaukee* (Milwaukee, 1915); on Wisconsin in general see Holmes, "Sarsa Time and Spaghetti," in *Old World Wisconsin*, 319-336.

[90]Heming, *Catholic Church in Wisconsin*, 803-804, 858.

[91] For these and other smaller ethnic groups in Wisconsin, see Theodore Saloutos, "The Greeks of Milwaukee," Wisconsin Magazine of History, LIII (Spring, 1970), 175-193; Marie Prisland, "The Slovenians, Most Recent American Immigrants," Wisconsin Magazine of History, XXXIII (March, 1950), 265-280; Juris Veidemanis, "Latvian Settlers in Wisconsin: A Comparative View," Wisconsin Magazine of History, XLV (Summer, 1962), 251-255, and "Two Generations of Mental Isolation: Latvians in Northern Wisconsin," The Wisconsin Sociologist, I (June, 1960), 1-23; and Holmes, "Iceland Fishermen go Seafaring," "Russians Bow to the Eastern Cross," and "Voices of Little Nations," in Old World Wisconsin, 215-228, 267-280, and 281-298.

[92] An excellent study of the Milwaukee Jewish community is Louis J. Swichow and Lloyd P. Gartner, The History of the Jews of Milwaukee (Philadelphia, 1963). Swichow has also written on "The Jewish Agricultural Colony of Arpin, Wisconsin," American Jewish Historical Quarterly, LIV (September, 1964), 82-91. A useful treatment of the problem of identifying Jewish immigrants can be found in Maurice Davie, World Immigration with Special Reference to the United States (New York, 1936), 135-146.

[93] Emmett J. Scott, Negro Migration During the War (New York, 1969. Reprint of 1920 book), 110-118; Charles T. O'Reilly, The Inner Core-North: A Study of Milwaukee's Negro Community (Milwaukee, 1963), and The People of the

Inner Core-North: A Study of Milwaukee's Negro Community (New York, 1965); Robert W. Wells, "The Negro in Wisconsin," Milwaukee Journal, November 3-13, 1967.

[94] A basic study dealing with Indian involvement in politics is Helen L. Peterson, "American Indian Political Participations," The Annals of the American Academy of Political and Social Science, CCCXI (May, 1957), 116-126. On Wisconsin Indians see the excellent study by Nancy Ostreich Lurie, "Wisconsin: A Natural Laboratory for North American Indian Studies," Wisconsin Magazine of History, Liii (Autumn, 1969), 3-20; as well as Joyce Erdman, Handbook on Wisconsin Indians (Madison, 1961); John M. Douglass, The Indians in Wisconsin History, Milwaukee Public Museum Popular Science Handbook Series, No. 6 (Milwaukee, 1954); and Harvey A. Uber, Environmental Factors in the Development of Wisconsin (Milwaukee, 1937), 57-65.

CHAPTER IV   THE WISCONSIN POLITICAL SCENE IN 1900

The Wisconsin political scene in 1900 mirrored closely the national scene. Along with the rest of the United States, Wisconsin had gone through a series of realigning elections in the 1890's culminating in the McKinley-Bryan tilt of 1896. On the national level, this period has been well-delineated by V. O. Key, Walter Dean Burnham, Charles Sellers, Samuel Hays, and Carl Degler. Hays writes:

> The years from 1893 to 1896 witnessed the first major voting realignment in American politics since the 1850's. This realignment seems to have been a product of the depression of 1893 and of the shifting attractiveness of parties and candidates to ethno-cultural groups. Many voters turned Republican in the elections of 1893 and 1894 and remained so in 1896.[1]

Hays sees Bryan drawing evangelical Protestants away from their normal adherence to the Republican party while McKinley drew to his cause the growing industrial immigrant vote.

Degler also stresses the urban basis of the Republican dominance which began in the 1890's: "Taken together, the elections of 1894 and 1896 mark the emergence of the Republican party as the party of the rising cities."[2] It is difficult to measure which is the more important factor in this realignment--the economic impact of the depression and the inability of the Democratic party under the conservative, old-guard leadership of Grover Cleveland to deal with it, or the failure of a rural-oriented Bryan platform and campaign to meet the needs of a growing industrial populace. The suggestion that Bryan's Protestant fundamentalism realigned the two major parties along different ethno-cultural lines has found popularity recently among historians. Burnham lists both of these factors as reasons for the shift; Key implicitly accepts the first for New England at least:

> Perhaps the significant feature of the 1896 election was that, at least in New England, it did not form a new division in which partisan lines became more nearly congruent with lines separating classes, religions, or other such social groups. Instead the Republicans succeeded in drawing new support, in about the same degrees, from all sorts of economic and social classes.[3]

Key, in fact, suggests that the Republican dominance is tied more to the entrance of an industrial working class with immigrant roots into the political arena than to changes among groups already present.[4]

The two studies which deal with Wisconsin in the 1890's as part of an overall view of Midwestern politics--Paul Kleppner's Cross of Culture and Richard Jensen's Winning of the Midwest--follow Hays in placing great stress on the ethno-cultural factors let loose by the coming to power of Bryan-style leaders in the Democratic party:

> The elections of 1893 and 1894 saw a shift away from the Democrats that cut across all social groups. Voting units differed not in the direction of their movement, but only its extent, as all units moved to a lower level of Democratic strength. . . .
> In 1896 a different pattern of voter movement

occurred. Not all social groups moved in the
same direction. Instead, a polarization of
social groups took place. This movement,
combined with that of 1894, created a new
political configuration, one in which the
Democracy was reduced to the status of a minority party.[5]

Kleppner and Jensen both attribute this shift to the nature of William Jenning Bryan's appeal and the Republican response. The moralistic crusade Bryan led in 1896 attracted pietistic voters from the normally Republican ranks of the native-born Yankee-Yorkers and also among the more pietistically-oriented English, Swedish, and Norwegian voters. Opposition to this moralistic crusade, combined with a well-financed pluralistic Republican campaign under the umbrella issue of "a return to prosperity" centered not in monetary panaceas but in a protective tariff, brought normally Democratic Catholic and German Lutheran voters into the ranks of the GOP. This reversal of roles by the two parties helped transform the Democrats into a minority party throughout the Midwest for a generation.

The Democratic party in Wisconsin matched the national Democratic party in its decline beginning in 1894 and 1896, lending apparent support to the portrait drawn by Jensen and Kleppner of the impact of the depression and the Bryan-McKinley contest in 1896. However, when one turns from gross changes in partisan strength to an investigation of the extent of realignment of groups, Key's suggestion of a general shift involving all groups in the electorate with an underlying continuity of partisan alignments matches the data more closely.[6]

In fact, the distribution of ethnic groups among the two parties does not change that much between 1892 and 1900. At the beginning of the period, Kleppner sees the following distribution of partisan strength emerge by the 1890's from a fifty year period of ethno-cultural conflict beginning with the first large scale immigration of Irish and Germans in the 1840's:[7]

Table I   Estimated Partisan Division
Ethno-Cultural Groups

Solidly Democratic (80% to 100%)

Irish Catholics	German Catholics
Polish Catholics	Dutch Catholics

Bohemian Catholics

Strongly Democratic (60% to 80%)

French Canadians	Old French

Marginal (40% to 60%)

German Lutherans	Disciples of Christ
German Reformed	Southern Baptist
Danish Lutherans	Southern Presbyterians
Dutch True Reformed	New York Baptists

Strongly Republican (60% to 80%)

German Sectarians	Norwegian Lutherans
Dutch Reformed	Cornish Methodists

Presbyterians

Table I   Continued

Solidly Republican (80% to 100%)

English Canadians	Quakers
Swedish Lutherans	Congregationalists
Irish Protestants	New York Methodists
Welsh Methodists	Free Will Baptists
Haugean Norwegians	

From these data and other evidence, Kleppner suggests that "religious groups offering strong support to the Republican party were more pietistic, or evangelical, in their orientation than those offering similar support to the Democrats."[8] The key to this division lay in the cultural issues which arose with the entrance of immigrants into American social and political life. Central to this emergence was the effort of the dominant Yankee Protestant society to exercise social control over the newcomers through the instrumentality of the Republican party. The greatest arenas of conflict came in the areas of prohibition, Sunday blue laws, parochial education, and efforts to restrict immigration or voting on the part of the immigrant.[9]

Jensen draws a similar picture of pietistic religious groups lining up on the side of the Republican party and liturgical (ritualistic for Kleppner) groups in the Democratic column. In the 1890's, Republican political professionals displaced the more amateurish moralistic leaders of the party and broadened its appeal by curtailing its nativistic, prohibitionist side. Triumphant behind this approach in 1896, the Republican party continued to dominate United States politics until the 1920's.

However, both Jensen and Kleppner, while detailing the shifts of ethno-cultural groups through 1896, fail to follow through to determine whether the apparent realignment in that year persisted for later elections. This study does exactly that, using the elections of 1898 and 1900 in Wisconsin. Before viewing that distribution, it is necessary to do a retrospective on Wisconsin politics as they had developed to 1900.

After a brief period of Democratic dominance following statehood in 1848, Wisconsin emerged as a Republican-oriented state by the Civil War period.[10] From 1855 to 1888 the Republican percentage of the two-party vote for governor varied from 50% to 54% with only three exceptions. Republican candidates in 1863 and 1879 drew 56% and 57% respectively. And, in the 1873 election, the Granger-backed Democrat, William R. Taylor, received 55% of the vote. In that year, the Democrats also gained control of the state legislature. This victory was tied to a nationwide Democratic trend resulting from the depression which began in 1873 and to state issues--the passage of the Graham Law, a stringent liquor licensing act, and pressure for railroad regulation spearheaded by the Wisconsin Grange. The legislature of 1874 responded by weakening the Graham Law and passing legislation to regulate the railroads. Much dispute has arisen over whether the latter act was passed by the Granger-oriented rural legislators or by railroad-oriented legislators to stave off further reform efforts. In any case, it was repealed four years later.[11]

Except for this brief period of eclipse, Republicans maintained comfortable control of the state legislature during this period. They also dominated the Congressional delegation, except for the 1883 session. Presidential elections went to the Republicans from their first effort in 1856 to 1888 by votes varying from 51% to 56%. The charts on the next page indicate the consistency of this support--as well as the continued strength of the minority Democratic party. By the general definition used today, a variation between 50% and 55% of the electorate, Wisconsin was a marginal Republican state.

In the 1890's this condition changed and Wisconsin passed into the ranks of one-party Republicanism. Before that change took place, the Democrats enjoyed again a brief period of dominance growing out of the election of 1890 and continuing through that of 1892. In the former year, Democrats captured the governorship with 55% of the vote, the State Assembly with a sixty-six to thirty-three margin, and eight out of nine Congressional seats. In

Chart I   Partisan Division 1848 to 1900*

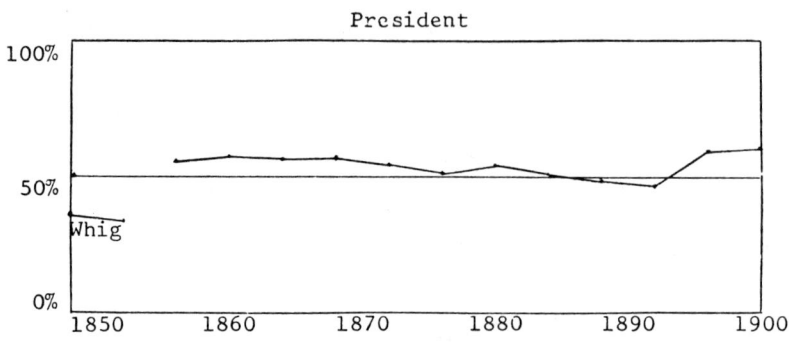
President

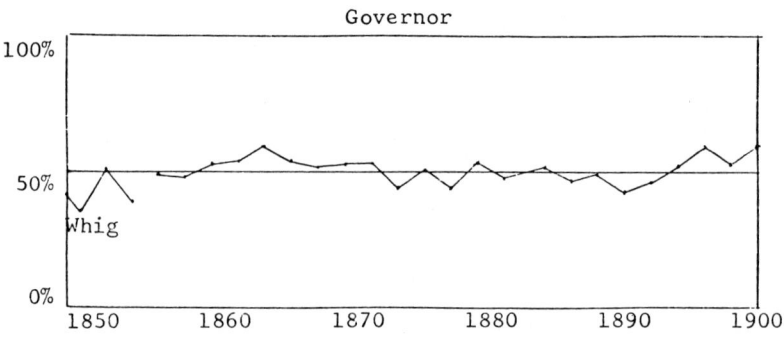
Governor

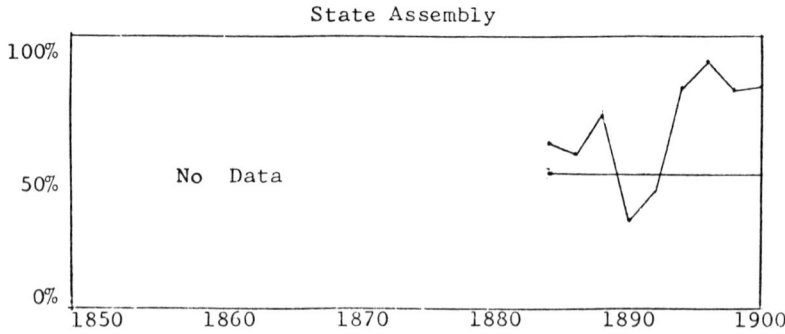
State Assembly

Sources of data: See Appendix C   *Republican Percentage

1892 they narrowly retained their control of the Assembly, fifty-five to forty-four, barely carried the governorship, delivered Wisconsin's eleven electoral votes to Grover Cleveland by a vote of 47.7% to 46.1%, and continued to hold six of the state's Congressional seats. The temporariness of this rosy picture for the Democracy becomes clear when one looks at 1894. In that year Republicans captured eighty-one Assembly seats, 58% of the vote for governor, and all ten positions in the state's Congressional delegation.

The 1890 election deserves special attention because of the impact of cultural issues on the electorate in that year. The Republican-controlled legislature of 1889 had passed a compulsory education law aimed in part at more rapid assimilation of immigrant children into the American way-of-life via the state's public school system. In order to qualify as a legitimate educational institution under this act, called the Bennett law after its author, a parochial school had to meet the following provision:

> No school shall be regarded as a school, under this act, unless there shall be taught therein, as part of the elementary education of children, reading, writing, arithmetic and United States history, in the English language.[12]

Since most parochial school instruction was in the language of the immigrant group, the law was perceived as a threat to the schools themselves. Approximately 70,000 children attended parochial schools in Wisconsin. Of this number some 40,000 attended Catholic schools. Most of these were German or Polish. The remaining parochial schools were primarily German Lutheran. Among Catholics, the Irish, Italians, Bohemians, and Belgians seldom sent their children to parochial schools. Few Scandinavian Lutherans attended parochial schools though a lively controversy over use of the English language made the language issue a sensitive one for Wisconsin's Norwegians.[13]

Because their ideology and teaching personnel dominated the public school system, Yankee Protestants had no need for separate schools and, in fact, strongly opposed an alternate educational system. Thus the path was clear for the issue to dominate the election and to divide groups along religious lines. The positions taken by the two parties in 1890 made certain that it would.

The Republican platform of that year endorsed the Bennett law; the party, led by incumbent Governor William D. Hoard, centered its campaign on preserving the common school system. Typical of the Republican appeal was the following cartoon which served as the letterhead for the party in Jackson County.[14] The message was clear:

STAND BY IT!

Haugen Papers, SHSW

The 1890 campaign slogan, used as a letterhead by the Jackson County Republican Committee.

Democrats, on the other hand, condemned the law as a "local manifestation of the settled republican policy of paternalism."[15]

The election resulted in a resounding victory for the Democrats. In part this victory represented general Democratic gains that year--overall the Democrats gained eighty seats in Congress, including eighteen others in the Midwest. But the key issue in Wisconsin was the Bennett law, and the voting of ethnic groups reflected that issue. German Catholic Democrats became even more firm in their allegiance to the Democracy; German Lutherans increased their normally Democratic margin; Norwegians and Swedes, concerned about

language use but unable to bring themselves to vote for
the "Catholic party", stayed at home. Among Wisconsin's
other ethnic groups, Bohemians, Belgians, and Swiss Reformed increased their support of the Democrats while the
Irish, Polish, and Dutch remained staunchly Democratic.
English, Welsh, and Yankee precincts stayed Republican
though without increasing their support for Hoard over
his 1888 percentage.[16] The Bennett law controversy retained sufficient saliency to return most Democrats to
office two years later while Grover Cleveland narrowly
carried the state that year.

By 1894, however, the depression had displaced cultural issues in importance despite the efforts of the
American Protective Association to challenge what were
felt to be Catholic inroads in the fields of education and
politics. In Wisconsin, as in most other states, the APA
was close to the Republican party during the brief period
of the organization's ascendency from 1892 to 1896. APA
support generally went to the conservative Republican
leadership, apparently contributing to William H. Upham's
nomination for the governorship over insurgent Nils P.
Haugen in 1894. The <u>Wisconsin Patriot</u>, main spokesman for
the APA in the state, consistently opposed Robert La Follette
in the early stages of his rise to power within the Republican party.[17]

Both Jensen and Kleppner detail the general movement

toward the Republican party growing out of the depression. They also delineate the greater impetus in the Republican direction on the part of ritualistic-liturgical groupings as a result of the Bryan take-over of the Democratic party. Suffice is it for now to point out the dominance of Wisconsin politics by the Republican party beginning in 1894. As Chart I indicates, all electoral indices moved in the Republican direction beginning in that year. From 1894 to 1932, Republicans won the governorship with percentages varying from 56% to 88%, with the exceptions of 1912 and 1914, when they were held to 52% and 53% respectively.* The general Republican strength shown by this voting is indicated by the fact that the 1912 Republican candidate, who drew 52% of the vote, was progressive Francis McGovern; the 1914 winner with 53% of the vote was stalwart Emmanuel Philipps. Even more striking are the 1920 and 1922 elections--the high water mark of Republican dominance. In 1920 Warren Harding, more nonentity than conservative, received 71% of the vote in Wisconsin, while only two years later liberal progressive John Blaine, running for governor, garnered 76% of the vote.

During these years the Republicans also gained complete control of the State Assembly, falling below seventy-five of the hundred seats only in the years from 1910 to

---

*See Chart II on the next page for Presidential, Gubernatorial, and State Assembly divisions, 1900-1952.

Chart II Partisan Division 1900 to 1952*

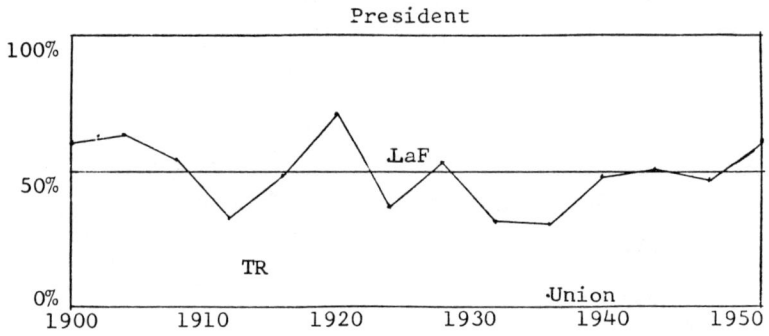

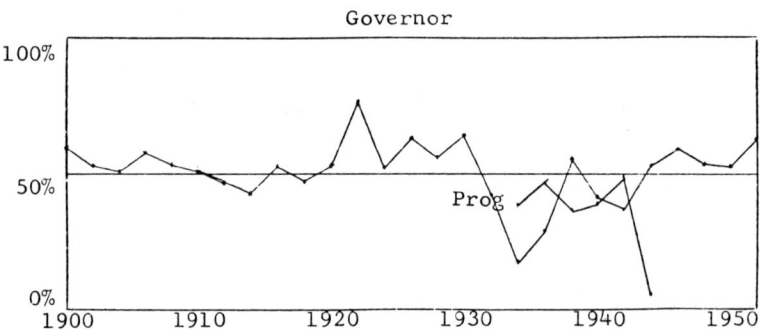

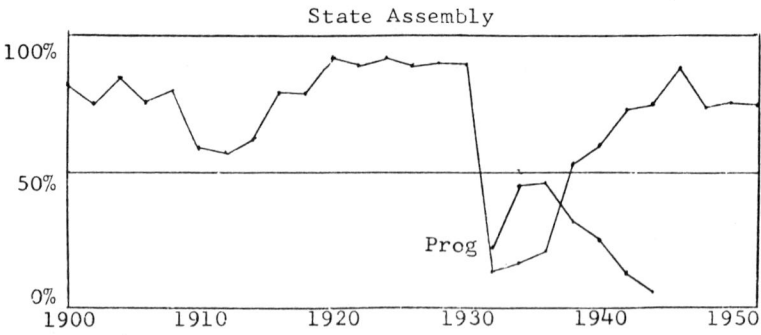

Sources of data: See Appendix G   *Republican Percentage

1914, their nadir being a comfortable total of fifty-seven seats. On the Congressional level, Republicans held at least eight and frequently ten of the state seats during this thirty-eight year period.[18]

Of course, this single-party dominance masks the very real conflict going on within the state for control of the Republican party between the La Follette progressives and GOP stalwarts. This struggle had its beginning in the 1890's. Traditionally described as one between reformers and special interests, the definition of the struggle has been shifted by recent historians to one between moralistic amateurs such as Hoard, Haugen, and La Follette, and professional pluralistic political leaders of the stripe of Henry Payne, Philetus Sawyer, and John Spooner. Thus, Richard Jensen describes the struggle between the two groups as follows:

> In Wisconsin, the leading moralist, ex-governor Hoard, attempted a comeback by promoting first Nils Haugen and later Robert La Follette for governor. La Follette, formerly as regular a professional as the GOP could boast, had broken sharply with the party leadership in 1891 and was becoming more and more the crusading moralist. In a hard-fought series of contests the professionals defeated Haugen and La Follette, and eliminated crusading from the Republican stylebook.[19]

This judgment, of course, ignores the great successes enjoyed by Robert La Follette, beginning in 1900 when he handily captured both the gubernatorial nomination and election and embarked on a lengthy political career built on a most moralistic appeal. The shift in the moralistic emphasis by La Follette and other progressives from cultural issues to purity in business and government was an important factor in broadening their appeal.

Equally important in the rise to power of La Follette and the reform coalition was a widening of their political base of support to include the rising ethnic groups long courted by the major parties but shut out from the real exercise of power. The triumph of the progressives over the stalwarts in Wisconsin marked not a return to amateurism or culturally-ordered moralism but the entrance into power of a new generation of political leaders, predominantly from the immigrant groups of the mid-Nineteenth Century.

The stranglehold of Yankees on the political leadership of a state in which they formed only a small proportion of the electorate has been inadequately explored. In fact, the best treatments of this situation appeared in 1898 and 1900 in two articles by Ellis Usher, former state Democratic chairman. The articles aimed at showing that "Wisconsin institutions were formed and have been dominated by Americans of New England lineage from the beginning." Between 1848 and 1900, sixteen of Wisconsin's nineteen governors and eleven of her twelve senators had Yankee-New York backgrounds. Three of the exceptions were Scottish by birth or background, and one lone governor, Edward Salomen, came from Prussia.

Salomen, however, was not an elected governor but the
lieutenant governor who succeeded Governor Louis Harvey
at his death in 1862.

Not only did the Yankees dominate the state executive branch and Senatorial delegations, but men of New England birth or background also controlled state party leadership. Eight of thirteen Republican chairmen from 1854 to 1900, and, even more strikingly, ten of fifteen Democratic state chairmen from 1860 to 1900, were Yankees.[20]

The same patterns held for such quasi-political organizations as the Wisconsin State Agricultural Society, the Wisconsin Dairymen's Association, and the Wisconsin State Grange. A study of 137 officers and 296 rank-and-file members of these organizations between 1873 and 1900 revealed only thirteen who came from non-English-speaking countries. Two-thirds of the 433 were of native-stock, the remainder were from Canada, Great Britain, or Ireland.[21]

Beginning in 1894, however, this dominance was challenged by an upwardly mobile group of political leaders largely outside the political power structure, representing the second generation of non-Yankee ethnic groups which had filled the state from 1840 to 1880. Robert M. La Follette early assumed leadership of these elements. Of French Huguenot and Scotch-Irish background, La Follette had grown up in the Norwegian community of Primrose in Dane County, Wisconsin. He had fought with the Dane County

postmaster, served three terms in congress, and then
found his upward political progress apparently thwarted
in the 1890's.[22] The reform coalition candidate for
governor at each of the Republican state conventions
from 1894 to 1898 was Nils O. Haugen, born in Norway.
Closely allied with La Follette and Haugen were John M.
Nelson, Herman Ekern, and James O. Davidson among Norwegians; Irving Lenroot representing the Swedes; and Theodore Kronshage and Henry Cochems, still "under-representing"
Wisconsin's Germans. Also in the reform coalition were a
number of Yankees shut out of power by the dominant Payne-Sawyer-Spooner faction. These men included Isaac Stephenson,
millionaire lumberman from Marinette; William Dempster
Hoard, governor from 1889 to 1891 and leader of Wisconsin's
dairymen; and General George E. Bryant, former Madison
postmaster. By 1900, these insurgents within the Republican party had gained enough strength to obtain the nomination for governor--the honor falling to La Follette.[23]

Thus, in Wisconsin, the rise to power of the progressive movement appears to represent the mid-Nineteenth
Century immigrant groups coming into their own in the
political arena. This "status revolution" and the coming
to power of upwardly mobile ethnic groups, rather than
the resurgence to power of a displaced Yankee elite, more
nearly describes Wisconsin progressivism than the model
set forth by Richard Hofstadter and George Mowry.[24] A de-

tailed look at voting patterns in Chapter V will bear this out.

Before examining the political sources of support for Wisconsin progressivism, it is necessary to examine the state's political alignment at the beginning of the period. The elections of 1898 and 1900 have been chosen as the benchmark of political support prior to the progressive movement. The election of 1898 pitted stalwart Edward Scofield against the Democratic candidate, while 1900 yields the first race between a representative of the new force in the Wisconsin Republican party and the Democratic standard bearer.

In fact, 1900 represents more nearly the political situation after the realignment of the Nineties. In 1898, La Follette and his supporters had called for boycotting the stalwart Republican gubernatorial candidate. As a result the head of the ticket ran 7,000 votes and almost three percentage points behind the rest of the ticket.[25]

In 1900 the Republican machine in yielding to La-Follette, also gave him its full support. With this aid he ran even with both President McKinley and the Republican candidates for minor state offices. La Follette gave little evidence of his future insurgency in this campaign. A study of his speeches in 1900, for example, found him very close to the national ticket on foreign policy issues.[26]

A detailed look at country-level data also bears out the "normalcy" of the vote for governor in 1900. In only eight of the state's seventy counties did the vote for governor in that year vary by more than 1.0% from that for president or lieutenant-governor. A similar pattern held true for 1896, but in 1898 only fourteen counties found the vote for governor and lieutenant-governor within 1.0% of each other.[27]

Two years later, as the outlines of the La Follette progressive program became clearer, stalwarts began defecting. However, 1900 represented one of the last cases of Republican party unity and thus serves as the best election to use in determining the "normal" vote after the shifts of the 1890's but before the effect of a Republican party controlled by progressives had made its impact on the electorate.

Table I in Appendix D shows the distribution of the vote according to ethnic groups and size-of-place for the elections of 1898 and 1900. Republicans drew very strongly in both years from voters of Yankee, English, Welsh, Scandinavian, Dutch Reformed, and Belgian background. Democrats drew very solidly from Polish and Irish voters and did almost as well among Bohemian and German Catholic voters. Single examples of Austrian and Dutch Catholic townships and a Dutch Catholic city suggest that these two groups also voted solidly Democratic. Returns from French Canadian and Italian communities are too sparse and varied

to allow for firm conclusions. Italians appear to have
been quite strongly Democratic in the city of Milwaukee
and much less so in rural areas. Swiss Reformed townships
and villages were fairly evenly divided between the two
parties with the exception of the village of Monticello,
a bastion of Green County Republicanism. German Lutherans
and urban Germans in general tended to divide fairly
evenly between the two parties. The German Mixed category
need not be discussed on its own since it represents
interminglings of Lutheran, Reformed, and Catholic Germans rather than a grouping of its own. As such a mixture, however, its vote should tend to fall somewhere
between the other two German categories. In 1898, this
pattern was true only of the rural units; in 1900 it was
generally true.

Taken together, these two elections indicate the lack
of variation in voting from year to year. The boycott of
the stalwart candidate in 1898 by the La Follette forces
clearly affected some groups more than others. La Follette's
greatest gains over Scofield came in Norwegian areas where
he picked up an average of 13% to 18% across the board, topped by an astounding jump of 53% in Harrison township in
Waupaca County. The two Finnish townships also registered
large gains for La Follette. Smaller increases among non-
rural Yankees, English, German Lutheran, and Milwaukee
voters matched La Follette's overall gains among the voters

of the state. La Follette's 59.8% of the vote was a gain of 7.2% over Scofield's 52.6% in 1898. Thus those groups among which there was no Republican gain or even a slight loss must be rated as negative to La Follette's appeal. German Catholics, urban Germans outside Milwaukee, rural Yankees, Welsh, Swedish, and Irish voters fit into this category.

One inescapable conclusion which an examination of the vote in these two years reveals is that the description by Hays, Jensen, and Kleppner of 1896 as a realigning election is not borne out by the data at the turn of the century. Comparison of Table I in Appendix D based on the 1898 and 1900 elections with Table I showing the distribution of the ethnic groups prior to the 1890's indicates the same basic spread. Both sets of data match for the following groups.

    Solidly and Strongly Republican

Swedish	Norwegians
Welsh	English (Cornish)
Native-stock	Dutch Reformed

    Solidly and Strongly Democratic

Polish	Dutch Catholics
Irish	German Catholics
Bohemians	French Canadian

  Marginal

    German Lutherans

Omitted from the Kleppner list are the strongly Republican Belgians, an anomaly among Catholic groups, and the Swiss Reformed with a slight leaning in the Democratic direction, an anomaly among pietistic groups. Finns, Italians, and Austrians are also omitted from his list--data for this study which labels these groups strongly Republican, varied, and solidly Democratic, respectively, must be used with caution for reasons already suggested. The data do indicate some movement in the direction of the Republican party on the part of Danish, German Lutheran, and Bohemian voters but hardly sufficient in its size to justify the label "realignment".

Thus the 1896 election appears to have been more of a deviating election than a realigning election bearing out V. O. Key's conclusion that all groups moved uniformly away from the Democratic party in the direction of Republicanism. The depression of the 1890's and the failure of the Democratic party to respond adequately to the problems it caused was probably more basic to this shift than the moralism of the Bryan campaign. The politics of the 1890's resulted in a solid Republican majority both in the nation and in Wisconsin; it did not reshuffle the groups within each party's constellation at least on an ethnic basis. Before proceeding to Twentieth Century events which did lead to such a realignment, each ethnic group must be examined in some detail.[28]

Yankees*

	Rural	Villages and Cities To 2,500	Over 2,500	City wards
1898 Election	73%	73%	63%	79%
1900 Election	74%	80%	71%	80%
Number of units	18	11	2	4

Most of Wisconsin's Native-stock voters came from New England and New York with backgrounds in the mainline Yankee Protestant churches--Methodist, Congregational, Presbyterian, Northern Baptist, and Episcopalian. All of these groups but especially the Methodists and Congregationalists were solidly in the Republican camp. Kleppner and Jensen suggest that this was because of the emphasis of these denominations on right behavior and moralism and a willingness to use the state to bring about these ends. Thus early Republican connections with abolitionism and with the prohibition movement and Sunday blue laws throughout its career was determined by a Native-stock, Yankee constituency. Also related to this orientation was a nativist-tinged stress on "Americanizing" the immigrant--exemplified by the Bennett law effort to use the school system for this purpose. Anti-immigrant legislation and anti-Catholic rhetoric also found a more receptive audience among Republicans.

*Each ethnic section will be headed by a table giving the median Republican vote of the units for each size-of-place category.

While this attraction to Republicanism was a part of
the New England heritage of the party's adherents, it was
reinforced by the influx into the Democratic party of most
Catholic immigrant groups entering Wisconsin in the Nineteenth Century. The double negative operates in reference
group theory even if not in sentence structure. Thus
Catholic immigrants rejected the Republican party and
joined the Democracy because the former was dominated by
a Yankee willingness to interfere with one's personal
liberty. This led the Yankees in turn to become even firmer
in their opposition to the party of "Rum, Romanism, and
Rebellion".[29]

In 1898, the eighteen Native-stock townships averaged
73% Republican varying from a low of 48% to a full 100%
of the votes cast in Leola in Adams County. Eleven villages
and cities under 2,500 also averaged 73% Republican. Of
the two cities over 2,500, Richland Center cast only 52%
of its vote for the Republican candidate while Delavan in
Walworth County went 73% for the GOP. The four wards which
were most solidly Native-stock, wards two and four in
Beloit, three in Janesville, and seven in Oshkosh weighed
in at a solid 79% for the Republicans.

In 1900, the picture is unchanged for the rural townships and the four city wards, while only six of the thirteen
villages and cities bettered the jump for the GOP in the
state as a whole. This suggests a pattern which will be-

come clearer in the next chapter of Yankee lack of enthusiasm for the rising progressive leadership in its take-over of their party.

English and Welsh

	English		Welsh	
	Rural	Villages	Rural	Villages
1898 Election	70%	76%	79%	79%
1900 Election	79%	79%	80%	77%
Number of units	3	2	2	2

The Cornish settlements in the old lead-mining region of Grant, Iowa, and LaFayette Counties and the Welsh areas of Columbia and Dodge Counties show up with even more impressive Republican credentials than the more diverse Native-stock voting units. Except for Hazel Green village and Little Grant township, both in Grant County and affected by sizable German minorities, the nine units in these two categories cast Republican votes varying from 70% to 87% in 1898. The 1900 pattern is very similar. In fact, the votes of the Cornish and Welsh taken alone probably approached 100% in their loyalty to the Republican party. The reasons for their Republicanism are similar to those of the Yankee, Native-stock, accounted for by close affiliation with the latter in social contacts and by membership in churches affiliated with the mainline Yankee denominations.

Norwegians

	Rural	Villages and Cities		City wards
		To 2,500	Over 2,500	
1898 Election	75%	68%	71%	57%
1900 Election	89%	86%	86%	70%
Number of units	29	7	1	4

Settled in compact communities, Norwegians rapidly overcame the barriers of isolation and language to seek an active role in Wisconsin politics.[30] Merle Curti attributed this involvement at the local level to contact with Yankee neighbors long familiar with democratic institutions. Necessity no doubt also had its effect--a community which was 100% Norwegian had to provide its own leadership both for reasons of internal needs and, even more so, to represent the community to the outside world.[31]

In any case, Norwegians participated early in politics-- and very early moved into the ranks of the Republican party. The high point of Norwegian migration, the 1850's and 1860's, corresponded with the rise of that party. The traditional suggestion that the allegiance to the GOP was due to an abhorence of slavery and to a desire to prove oneself a good citizen by rallying to the party of the Union,[32] is probably less important than a Norwegian response to the Democratic party in negative reference terms. It was, after all, the party of the Irish, Germans, and other Catholics. Both Jensen and Kleppner stress the

pietism of Norwegians, especially those from the Hauge
Synod of the Lutheran Church, as a major factor leading
to their support of the moralistic Republican party:

> Haugeans, imbued with an intense spirit of
> evangelical pietism and disdain for litur-
> gical forms, were much stronger in their
> opposition to the Democrats than the litur-
> gically oriented members of the Norwegian
> Synod.[33]

The strength of this Republicanism was severely tested
in the 1890 Bennett law controversy which appeared to those
Norwegians defensive about retaining language and culture
to be a general attack on foreign language usage. Rather
than vote for the opposition Democrats, the Norwegians
seem to have responded to the cross pressures by staying
home from the polls on election day.[34] Whatever waver-
ings there may have been in the 1890's, Norwegians showed
a strong Republican face by the end of the decade. They
were even unmoved by the pietistic appeal of Bryan in
1896. Laurence Larson, then a young principal of a strug-
gling Lutheran academy in Scandinavia, in Waupaca County,
reported being ostracized for speaking to a Democratic
meeting that year in such a closely-knit Norwegian community.[35]

In 1898, the twenty-nine Norwegian townships cast a
median Republican vote of 75%; seven villages and cities
under 2,500, a median of 68%; Stoughton in Dane County,
the lone entry in the 2,500 to 10,000 category, a 71% Republican vote; and four city wards, three in Eau Claire

and one in La Crosse, a median of 57%. That this balloting represented a depressed Republican vote because the La Follette forces found Norwegians most receptive to their boycott efforts, becomes clear when one examines the results two years later. In 1900, the Republican vote jumped an average of 14% in the rural precincts, 18% among the villages and cities, and 13% in the four Norwegian wards. Clearly the favorable Norwegian response to La Follette is already apparent in 1900 even before the issues of progressivism have been fully defined.

Swedes

	Rural	Villages and Cities To 2,500	Over 2,500	City ward
1898 Election	88%	85%		60%
1900 Election	87%	84%		76%
1902 Election			57%	
Number of units	9	1	1	1

Swedes were the banner Republican group in 1898. The nine Swedish townships present on the voting lists in that year had a median Republican vote of 88%--Wood Lake and Trade Lake in Burnett County topping the list with 98% and 97% respectively. Grantsburg, also in Burnett, the lone Swedish village as of 1898, shows up with an 85% Republican vote. The single Swedish ward in Ashland, a port city on Lake Superior, ranks lowest in its Republicanism at 60%.

In 1900, Swedish Republicanism actually declines while the rest of the state rises in its allegiance to the GOP and the Norwegians, Finns, and Belgians actually surpass the Swedes in their rush to cast votes for the Republican La Follette. Again the Swedish ward in Ashland operates differently from the other Swedish voting units--moving in the progressive Republican direction to cast 76% of its vote for La Follette. The city of Park Falls in Price County, incorporated in 1901, cast a 57% Republican vote in its maiden political venture the following year.

Kleppner suggests that the intensity of Republicanism on the part of the Swedes was due to the high level of pietism among those Swedes who came to the country. This Republicanism received continual reinforcement from two sides. George Stephenson stresses the general conservatism of Swedish immigrants, tracing part of this emphasis to the fact that the Swedish-American pastor was "undoubtedly one of the most orthodox conservative Protestant ministers in the country." The editors of Swedish language newspapers were also, almost without exception, conservative and Republican, identifying the Democratic party with slavery, corruption, and Catholics: "However much the newspapers disagreed with one another on other points, they maintained allegiance to the Republican party and upheld conservative political principles."[36]

Danes

	Rural	Rural units with villages	City over 2,500	City wards
1898 Election	64%	70%	79%	
1900 Election	69%	74%	83%	
1904 Election				57%
Number of units	4	4	1	2

The Danes were much less pietistic--and less Republican--than other Scandinavians. In 1898, they must be rated as generally Republican with a median in four Danish townships of 64%. However, the variance was so great--from 51% in Orange township in Juneau County to a high of 77% in Waupaca township in Waupaca County--that an overall explanation of Danish voting is difficult. Four townships with embryo villages were somewhat more Republican with a median of 70%. The city of Waupaca topped the list with a 79% GOP ranking. By 1900 the pattern had tightened considerably: the four purely rural townships varying from 65% to 79%, with a 69% median; the four other townships varying from 73% to 75%. The city of Waupaca again headed the list at 83% Republican.

The two wards in Racine cannot be used before the election of 1904--in that year they cast votes of 53% and 61% for the GOP with significant minorities going for the Social Democratic candidate in that year. This was a strictly urban Danish phenomenon as the rural townships cast only scattered votes for Socialist candidates in that election.

Finns

	Rural
1898 Election	72%
1900 Election	90%
Number of units	2

Finns, the last of the Scandinavian groups to immigrate to Wisconsin, were just beginning to appear in sufficient numbers in 1898 to allow for measuring their response to the state's politics. The two Finnish townships, Brule in Douglas County and Knox in Price County, cast Republican votes of 67% and 77% respectively giving the Finns a decidedly Republican complexion. However, the unsettled nature of the cutover region of northern Wisconsin and the recentness of Finnish immigration make this a figure to be treated with caution. In 1900 the electorate of the two townships shot up in its Republicanism to 87% and 92%.

The radicalism which was to mark Finnish involvement in politics in the later years did not show up as of 1900--in fact the Prohibition candidate did better among Finns than either the People's party or the two Socialist candidates in that election.

Kleppner found a positive correlation of Finnish voters in Dickinson County in Michigan with Democratic

party support but wisely did not generalize from this as
the pattern clearly does not hold for Wisconsin. In fact,
the main historian of America's Finnish immigrants suggests that before 1920, Democratic votes and editorial support from Finnish journals were the exception rather than
the rule.[37]

Dutch Reformed

	Rural	Villages
1898 Election	69%	
1900 Election	74%	93%
Number of units	2	1

The Dutch Reformed communities in Fond du Lac and
Sheboygan Counties also delivered substantial Republican
margins in 1898. In addition to the two strictly rural
townships, Holland located in the latter county and including the future villages of Cedar Grove and Oostburg
cast a 91% GOP vote. The pattern of Republican support
was the same in 1900 with newly incorporated Cedar Grove
leading the way with a Republican vote of 93%.

The basic history of Dutch migration to the United
States calls attention to this switch to Republicanism
after an early allegiance to the Democratic party, attributing it to the impact of the Civil War.[38] Kleppner
and Jensen list the Dutch Reformed as strongly Republicans,
fitting into their overall correlations between Republi-

canism and pietistic cultural groups.[39]

Belgians

	Rural	City ward
1898 Election	79%	63%
1900 Election	85%	66%
Number of units	7	1

The one remaining strongly Republican ethnic group does not fit the pietistic-liturgical dichotomy which may explain why neither Jensen nor Kleppner discuss it. The Belgians, ensconced solidly in rural northeastern Wisconsin and in the Catholic church were also firmly within the Republican party. The seven Belgian townships located in Brown, Door, and Kewaunee Counties gave a median vote to the GOP of 79% in 1898 and 85% two years later. There were no incorporated Belgian villages or cities but ward four in Green Bay cast Republican votes of 63% and 66% in the two elections under study. The actual Republican vote on the part of the Belgians probably came close to 100% as the Democratic vote in each township corresponds quite well with the presence of Catholic German, Bohemian, and Polish minorities. Wyman found Belgians shifting in the Democratic direction in 1890 over the Bennett law controversy;[40] by 1900 they had clearly returned to the ranks of the Republican party.

French Canadians

	Rural	Village	City ward
1898 Election	64%		56%
1900 Election	69%		58%
1904 Election		35%	
Number of units	2	1	1

The two French Canadian townships used in this study--Saxon in Iron County and Somerset in St. Croix County--were still in the process of settlement and their votes indicated their unsettled nature. In 1898 they voted 58% and 70% Republican respectively; two years later they reversed positions in the strength of their allegiance to the GOP with respective votes of 83% and 54%. The lone Canadian urban ward located in Ashland was more consistent, with Republican votes of 56% and 58% in the two elections. Coleman village in Marinette County cast a substantial Democratic vote of 65% in 1904. Occupational differences no doubt affected the rural townships. The 1905 state census indicates that while Somerset was clearly agricultural, Saxon had a preponderance of lumbermen and other non-agricultural laborers. Kleppner also calls attention to the probable impact of occupation on Northern Michigan's lumbermen, though for him it points in a Democratic political direction.[41]

Italians

	Rural Units		City ward
	Genoa	Crystal Lake	
1898 Election	50%		23%
1900 Election	53%		32%
1904 Election	65%	78%	
Number of units	1	1	1

The single Italian rural community in 1898, Genoa in Vernon County, divided almost evenly between the Democrats and Republicans in both elections. A large minority of Germans within the township make it impossible to generalize from this single example. In 1904 Crystal Lake in Barron County makes its appearance in the sample with a 78% Republican vote; by that date, even Genoa had climbed to 65%. Urban Italians fit the standard image of Catholic voters much more readily with votes of 77% and 68% Democratic in 1898 and 1900.[42]

Poles

	Rural	City wards
1898 Election	19%	17%
1900 Election	26%	24%
Number of units	8	3

At the head of the solidly Democratic groups, one finds the recently arrived Poles with a nearly 100% voting

record. The three most heavily Polish townships located
in Marathon and Portage Counties, gave Democratic percentages of 94%, 91%, and 86%, in 1898; two other townships
cast votes for the Democracy in excess of 80%; the remaining three Polish townships gave the Republican party
larger numbers of votes, reflecting substantial non-Polish
minorities. The most heavily Polish ward in Milwaukee,
ward fourteen in the center of the south side, cast a vote
of 70% for the Democratic party; Stevens Point's fourth
ward voted 83% Democratic; and Manitowoc's seventh ward
topped the urban list with a 90% Democratic rating. The
1900 election saw a rise in Republican support among the
Poles which reflected the general rise throughout the state.

The Poles had remained Democratic despite the depression of 1893-94 and the pietistic fallout from Bryan's
candidacy in 1896. The former apparently drove away some
unemployed urban Poles; the latter affected adversely rural
Poles--in each case the deviation was quite transient.[43]

Irish

	Rural	City ward
1898 Election	35%	42%
1900 Election	32%	42%
Number of units	8	1

The Irish were also staunch in their support of the

Democratic party. The nine Irish townships used for this study showed a median Democratic vote of 65% in 1898 and 68% in 1900. An indication that the Republican minority came from the substantial numbers of German Lutheran, English, and Native-stock voters found in most of these townships appears when one looks at the only unit over 50% Irish--Erin Prairie in St. Croix County. Over 80% Irish in 1905, Erin Prairie responded to the appeals of the Democratic party with votes of 90% and 93% in these two elections. Irish villages did not exist and among urban areas, only Janesville's third ward with a bare Irish majority gives us a clue to the Irish city vote. That ward cast identical votes of 58% Democratic in the two elections, the Republican minority no doubt coming from the substantial number of German and Native-stock voters present in the ward.

Kleppner labels the Irish as "the most consistently and persistently Democratic voting group in the Midwest." Neither the depression of 1893-94 nor Bryan's candidacy greatly affected the strength of the Democratic party among Wisconsin's Irish.[44] La Follette's candidacy apparently had a negative appeal to the Irish for they are one of the few ethnic groups actually to decline in their support of the Republican party when he was the nominee for governor.

Bohemians

	Rural
1898 Election	39%
1900 Election	45%
Number of units	9

Bohemian areas of settlement were scattered and religious sentiment more varied than among most ethnic groups. This may account for the greater variation in the Democratic vote in 1898--from a high of 83% in solidly Bohemian Franklin in Kewaunee County to only 26% in Union in Vernon County. By 1900 the latter's Democratic vote had risen considerably while everywhere else the Republican vote had increased narrowing the variance to from 42% to 77% for the nine townships in the sample.

Kleppner also calls attention to the volatility of the Bohemian vote--especially among non-Catholics. He found a movement away from the Democratic party as a result of Bryan's 1896 candidacy. Jensen found the seven Bohemian wards and townships in Iowa voting quite solidly Democratic even in 1896, though he did find a greater movement in the direction of the Republican party among Chicago's Bohemians.[45] The median Democratic votes of 61% and 55% in 1898 and 1900, indicates that Bohemians tended to be Democratic but not nearly as strongly as their more staunchly Catholic fellow-ethnics.

Dutch Catholics

	Rural	City under 2,500
1900 Election		28%
1902 Election	9%	23%
Number of units	1	1

The single Dutch Catholic settlement in the study, Vandenbroek in Outagamie County, was not organized as a separate township until 1902 when it cast a 91% Democratic vote. The city of Little Chute, created in 1899 from what was to become Vandenbroek township, voted almost as solidly Democratic in 1900 with a 72% vote, increasing this to 77% in 1902. The vast difference in voting between Dutch Reformed and Dutch Catholic is one more indication of the need to stress religion at least equally with ethnicity in studying voting behavior.

Austrian

	Rural
1898 Election	27%
1900 Election	25%
Number of units	1

The lone Austrian township, Lima in Pepin County, cast its lot with other Catholic ethnic groups in casting its ballot solidly behind the Democratic party.

German Catholics

	Rural	Villages and cities Under 2,500	2,500 to 10,000
1898 Election	32%	43%	39%
1900 Election	33%	42%	28%
Number of units	18	8	4

German Catholics responded to the same cultural pressures as did other Catholics in casting their ballots for the Democratic party. The receptivity on the part of the Democratic party to the immigrants of the 1840's and 1850's served as a positive attraction; the susceptibility on the part of the fledgling Republican party to cultural issues such as prohibition and Sunday blue laws repelled Germans in general; the identification of that party with the dominant Yankee Protestant culture brought the principle of repulsion most firmly to bear on German Catholics.

Joseph Schafer noted this in his essay demolishing the "Germans for Lincoln" myth:

> But so surely as the tally of the family heads came out as German, Irish or a combination of these two groups, the majority vote was Democratic. While some Germans, especially the Forty-eighters and some part of the Lutherans, voted the Republican ticket, that vote in 1860, while larger than in 1856, was still very light. . . . Catholics seem to have been nearly unanimous for Douglas. . . .[46]

This pattern of Democratic voting persisted at least until the 1890's. Kleppner found German Catholics voting 85% Democratic prior to the upheavals of that decade and concluded that "Wherever rural German Catholics were found, regardless of their economic prosperity, they were strong Democrats."[47] Two efforts at collective biography also place German Catholics solidly in the ranks of the Democracy. Frederick Luebke in his study of Nebraska's Germans found only two Republicans along with twenty-nine Democrats in his sample of thirty-eight from heavily Catholic Elkhorn Valley. Jensen's tabulation of the voters in Geneseo, Illinois, turned up a 75% Democratic preference among German Catholics.[48]

Most commentators suggest that German voters moved away from the Democratic party only when it flirted with inflation or easy money. When this flirtation was combined with the pietistic approach of Bryan in 1896, German Catholic defections increased.[49]

By the end of the decade, however, German Catholics appear to have returned to the Democratic banner. In a sample of fifteen Germans from Seward and York Counties in Nebraska, Luebke turned up six Democrats and no Republicans with a single Populist and six not stated. In a considerably larger sample from Platte County, drawn from a 1915 county history, fifty-four of sixty-nine German Catholics labelled themselves Democrats, only five considered themselves Republicans.[50]

The sample of eighteen townships in this study checked in at 68% Democratic in 1898 and 67% Democratic in the

La Follette election two years later. Villages and cities under 2,500, and between 2,500 and 10,000, were a bit less Democratic--57% and 61% respectively--varying by only a single percentage point two years later. Obviously, German Catholics would have no more to do with Robert La - Follette than with the stalwart candidate of 1898, Edward Scofield.

German Lutherans

	Rural units	Villages and cities Under 2,500	2,500 to 10,000
1898 Election	51%	42%	57%
1900 Election	58%	50%	62%
Number of units	70	9	3

The German Lutheran voting pattern was more varied, reflecting the cross pressures of this group's Germanness and its Protestantism. While most historians, in discussing Germans, lump together Catholics and Lutherans, Reformed and Freethinkers, Schafer perceived correctly the need to treat them differently. He saw that while both Catholics and Lutherans would respond to the pro-immigrant, anti-prohibition, "personal liberty" stress of the Democratic party during the formative years of settlement, the Catholicness of the Democratic party would in the end repel Lutheran and Reformed Germans.[51]

While Republicans wanderings in the direction of unwelcome social control--the Graham liquor law of 1872, the Bennett law of 1889--served to press German Lutherans back into the ranks of the Democratic party, by the end of the Nineteenth Century the scale was clearly tipping in the direction of the GOP. Rated 55% Democratic at the start of the 1890's by Kleppner; the German Lutherans according to the data in this study were 55% Republican by the end of the decade. Luebke's Nebraska German Lutherans showed quite a variation over both space and time. Two areas in his sample yielded Republican readings of about two to one; two yielded Democratic readings of three and four to one. The German Reformed and other German Protestants were much more likely to be Republican, a showing consistent with the model developed by Kleppner and Jensen of a pietistic-ritualistic continuum.[52]

The variation in political preference noted by Luebke and commented on by Kleppner is also borne out in this study. In 1898, the Republican percentage varied from a low of 23% in Lebanon township in Dodge County to a high of 94% in Dakota in Waushara County. Two years later the same two townships again formed the top and bottom in Republicanism at 27% and 96% respectively. Nevertheless, the bulk of the seventy German Lutheran townships grouped quite closely around the median:

Republican Vote, German Lutheran Townships

	1898	1900
0 to 25%	1	0
25% to 50%	30	23
50% to 75%	30	36
75% to 100%	9	11
Median =	51%	58%

Kleppner concludes that the movement away from the Democrats on the part of the German Lutherans was due to Bryan's moralistic candidacy in 1896.[53] The evidence suggests rather that the shift was due to a growing discomfort on the part of German Lutherans with their fellow Democrats. One bit of evidence pointing toward this explanation is that the moralistic Republican candidate for governor in 1900, Robert La Follette, made gains over his stalwart predecessor among German Lutherans consistent with his gains throughout the state; a pattern quite different from his zero appeal to German Catholics.

The nine German Lutheran villages and cities under 2,500 were considerably more Democratic, the three cities between 2,500 and 10,000, more Republican, than their rural counterparts thus reversing a pattern which held true for most other ethnic groups.

Urban Germans

	Cities over 10,000	City wards	Milwaukee wards
1898 Election	53%	46%	43%
1900 Election	54%	48%	53%
Number of units	5	26	8

One group of Germans cannot be divided so neatly into Catholic or Lutheran categories--the urban German. While there are variations, the five cities over 10,000, the twenty-six city wards (all but one of them within the five German cities over 10,000), and Milwaukee's eight German wards clustered around an even split in party preference. Only the Milwaukee wards preferred La Follette over Scofield by a significant increase, in this case a sizable 10% jump. This jump suggests that more work needs to be done on the contribution of Milwaukee to the success of La Follette. Clearly the city turned out the vote in 1900 when he headed the ticket. The Republicanism of middle-sized cities--and even of Milwaukee--bears out the observation made by Degler:

> The Republican party was more suited to the needs and character of the new urban, industrial world that was beginning to dominate America. . . . As the self-proclaimed party of prosperity and economic growth, the Republicans could expect to win support from those who manned the expanding factories and crowded into the tenements of the burgeoning cities.[54]

Degler goes on to point out that men like Robert La Follette and Theodore Roosevelt transformed this urban orientation of the Republican party into a concern for social amelioration thus increasing the identification of the Republican party with the needs of the city. The extent to which this connection was true for Wisconsin urban areas will be examined in Chapter V.

Swiss

	Rural	Villages and cities Under 2,500	2,500 to 10,000
1898 Election	48%	73%	58%
1900 Election	50%	75%	60%
Number of units	2	1	1

Swiss electoral behavior resembled that of the German Lutherans. Although an early resident historian had labelled his fellow countrymen Democratic and suggested that "for a man to change his politics is quite as rare among them as to change his religion,"[55] by the 1890's the Swiss were somewhere in limbo between the two parties. Kleppner lumped them in with the German Reformed and pegged them at 55% Democratic.[56]

The two solidly Swiss townships in Green County split down the middle in their partisan attitudes in both 1898 and 1900. The village of Monticello in Green County was solidly Republican; the city of Monroe quite Republican; and New Glarus township, including the soon-to-be-incorporated village of New Glarus more Republican than the purely rural townships. Except for Monticello, all of the voting units fell between 40% and 61% in their degree of Republicanism.

Thus the ethnic groups of Wisconsin came in contact with the political universe of the Nineteenth Century and, responding out of their group needs and attitudes, ranged themselves along a partisan and ideological continuum. How this arrangement changed in the first quarter of the Twentieth Century as the party system responded to domestic concerns and foreign involvements inevitable in an urbanizing, industrializing society is the subject of the next chapter.

NOTES

[1] Hays, "Political Parties and the Community-Society Continuum," in William Nisbet Chambers and Walter Dean Burnham, eds., The American Party Systems: Stages of Political Development (New York, 1967), 159.

[2] Degler, "American Political Parties and the Rise of the City: An Interpretation," Journal of American History, LI (June, 1964), 48.

[3] Key, "A Theory of Critical Elections," Journal of Politics, XVII (February, 1955), 12. Emphasis added.

[4] Key, "Secular Realignment and the Party System," Journal of Politics, XXI (May, 1959), 198-210. See also Walter Dean Burnham, "The Changing Shape of the American Political Universe," American Political Science Review, LIX (March, 1965), 7-28, and Critical Elections and the Mainsprings of American Politics (New York, 1970); and Charles G. Sellers, "The Equilibrium Cycle in Two-Party Politics," Public Opinion Quarterly, XXIX (Spring, 1965), 16-38.

[5] Kleppner, The Cross of Culture: A Social Analysis of Midwestern Politics, 1850-1900 (New York, 1970), 269-270. Jensen, The Winning of the Midwest: Social and Political Conflict, 1888-1896 (Chicago, 1971), arrives at a very similar conclusion.

[6] This lack of variation is also borne out by Key's comparison of partisan alignments in Indiana from 1868 to

1900 and from 1920 to 1948. Key and Frank Munger, "Social Determinism and Electoral Decision: The Case of Indiana," in Eugene Burdick and Arthur Brodbeck, eds., American Voting Behavior (New York, 1959), 281-299. See especially the maps and scatter diagrams.

[7] Based on the table in Kleppner, Cross of Culture, 70.

[8] Ibid., 71.

[9] See Joseph Gusfield, Symbolic Crusade: Status Politics and the American Temperance Movement (Urbana, Illinois, 1963), for an effort to deal with prohibition as an exercise in social control.

[10] For early politics in Wisconsin, in addition to the general works by Alice Smith, Robert Nesbit, and William Raney, see the following studies: Joseph Schafer, "Sectional and Personal Politics in Early Wisconsin," Wisconsin Magazine of History, XVIII (June, 1935), 442-465, "Know-Nothingism in Wisconsin," Ibid., VIII (September, 1924), 3-21, "Prohibition in Early Wisconsin," Ibid., VIII (March, 1925), 281-299, and "Who Elected Lincoln?" American Historical Review, XLVII (October, 1941), 51-63; Theodore C. Smith, "The Free Soil Party in Wisconsin," Proceedings of the State Historical Society of Wisconsin (1894), 97-161; Frank L. Byrne, "Maine Law Versus Lager Beer: A Dilemma of Wisconsin's Young Republican Party," Wisconsin Magazine of History, XLII (Winter, 1958-59), 115-120; Frank L. Klement, "Copperheads and Copperheadism in Wisconsin: Democratic Opposition

to the Lincoln Administration," Ibid., XLII (Spring, 1959), 182-192, and "Wisconsin and the Civil War," Wisconsin Blue Book, 1962, 72-180; and Helen J. and Harry Williams, "Wisconsin Republicans and Reconstruction, 1865-70," Wisconsin Magazine of History, XXIII (September, 1939), 17-39.

¹¹On Wisconsin politics in the 1870's see Herman J. Deutsch, "Yankee-Teuton Rivalry in Wisconsin Politics of the Seventies," Wisconsin Magazine of History, XIV (March and June, 1931), 262-282, 403-418; and "Disintegrating Forces in Wisconsin Politics of the Early Seventies," Ibid., XV (December, 1931, March and June, 1932), 168-181, 282-296, 391-411; Robert T. Doland, "Enactment of the Potter Law," Ibid., XXXIII (September, 1949), 45-54; Graham A. Cosmas, "The Democracy in Search of Issues: The Wisconsin Reform Party, 1873-1877," Ibid., XLVI (Winter, 1962-63), 93-108; William L. Burton, "Wisconsin's First Railroad Commission: A Case Study in Apostasy," Ibid., XLV (Spring, 1962), 190-198; George H. Miller, Railroads and the Granger Laws (Madison, 1971); and Ellis B. Usher, The Greenback Movement of 1875-1884 and Wisconsin's Part in It (Milwaukee, 1911).

¹²Laws of Wisconsin, 1889, 729-733. The Bennett law campaign of 1890 has been well-covered in Rogert E. Wyman, "Wisconsin Ethnic Groups and the Election of 1890," Wisconsin Magazine of History, LI (Summer, 1968), 269-293; Kleppner, Cross of Culture, 158-171; Jensen, Winning of the

Midwest, 122-153; and Robert J. Ulrich, "The Bennett Law of 1889: Education and Politics in Wisconsin," (University of Wisconsin Ph. D. Dissertation, 1965). Earlier sources on the election are Louise Phelps Kellogg, "The Bennett Law in Wisconsin," Wisconsin Magazine of History, II (September, 1918), 3-25, and William I. Whyte, "The Bennett Law Campaign," Ibid., X (June, 1927), 363-390, with an editorial comment by Joseph Schafer on 455-461.

[13]On the English language controversy among Norwegian-Americans, see Laurence M. Larson, "Skandinaven, Professor Anderson, and the Yankee School," in The Changing West and Other Essays (Northfield, Minnesota, 1937), 116-146; Theodore C. Blegen, Norwegian Migration to America: The American Transition (Northfield, 1940), 241-276; and Lloyd Hustvedt, Rasmus Bjorn Anderson: Pioneer Scholar (Northfield, 1966), 215-218.

[14]Xeroxed from Wyman, "Ethnic Groups and the Election of 1890," 275. Reprinted with permission.

[15]Wisconsin Blue Book, 1891, 394. Along with a wealth of other data and information, the biennial Blue Book also included the platforms of all state political parties.

[16]For the varying impact of the Bennett law controversy on ethnic groups see Wyman, "Ethnic Groups and the Election of 1890," 281-289; Kleppner, Cross of Culture, 138-139; and Jensen, Winning of the Midwest, 142-145.

[17]Donald L. Kinzer, Episode in Anti-Catholicism: The

American Protective Association (Seattle, Washington, 1964), and "The Political Uses of Anti-Catholicism: Michigan and Wisconsin, 1890-1894," Michigan History, XXXIX (September, 1955), 312-332. K. Gerald Marsden, "Patriotic Societies and American Labor: The American Protective Association in Wisconsin," Wisconsin Magazine of History, XLI (Summer, 1958), 287-294, deals primarily with attitudes and ignores the political aspect. Jensen dismisses the APA in Wisconsin as "a small noisy group that had threatened in a few scattered towns to engulf the regular GOP organization" until purged by John Spooner and the regular wing of the party. Winning of the Midwest, 222.

[18]Wisconsin held eleven Congressional seats from 1902 until the census of 1930 when it lost a seat. The state held its ten seats until the census of 1970 led to an additional reduction in size.

[19]Jensen, Winning of the Midwest, 176. See also pages 130-131, and Kleppner, Cross of Culture, 161-164, 256.

[20]Usher, "New England in Wisconsin," New England Magazine, XXII (June, 1900), 446-461. The quote is from page 460. See also Usher, "Puritan Influence in Wisconsin," Proceedings of the State Historical Society of Wisconsin (1898), 117-128. For a similar case on behalf of New York, see Edward P. Alexander, "Wisconsin, New York's Daughter State," Wisconsin Magazine of History, XXX (September, 1946), 11-30. Writing on the state supreme court justices in the

1880's, John B. Sanborn noted, "All were born in New York
State between the years 1817 and 1830. . . . All but one
were of English ancestry." Sanborn, "The Supreme Court of
Wisconsin in the Eighties," Wisconsin Magazine of History,
XV (September, 1931), 8. Biographical data on public of-
ficials of this period is available in Joseph Schafer,
Comp., "Our State Governors," Wisconsin Blue Book, 1927,
21-54; "Wisconsin's Former Governors, 1848-1959," Wisconsin
Blue Book, 1960, 67-206; The Law Makers of Wisconsin, 1899-
1901 (Milwaukee, 1899); and the Dictionary of Wisconsin
Biography (Madison, 1960). While all of these give place
of birth, none give ethnic background.

[21]Gerald Prescott, "Wisconsin Farm Leaders in the Gilded
Age," Agricultural History, XLIV (April, 1970), 183-199,
and "Gentlemen Farmers in the Gilded Age," Wisconsin Magazine of History, LV (Spring, 1972), 197-212. Wisconsin
lawyers in a slightly earlier period displayed similar
characteristics: Howard Feigenbaum, "The Lawyer in Wisconsin, 1836-1860: A Profile," Ibid., LV (Winter, 1971-72),
100-106. Even Wisconsinites who participated in political
and social activities beyond the boundaries of the state
had the same background: David H. Overy, Jr., "The Wisconsin Carpetbagger: A Group Portrait," Ibid., XLIV (Autumn,
1960), 15-49.

[22]On La Follette's background see David P. Thelen, "The
Boss and the Upstart: Keyes and La Follette, 1880-1884,"

Wisconsin Magazine of History, XLVII (Winter, 1963-64), 103-116, "Robert M. La Follette: Public Prosecutor," Ibid., (Spring, 1964), 214-223, "La Follette and the Temperance Crusade," Ibid., (Summer, 1964), 291-300, and The Early Life of Robert M. La Follette, 1855-1884 (Chicago, 1966); Belle Case and Fola La Follette, Robert M. La Follette, June 14, 1855-June 18, 1925 (New York, 1953), Vol. I; and Robert M. La Follette, La Follette's Autobiography (Madison, 1913, paperback, 1960).

[23]A. O. Barton, La Follette's Winning of Wisconsin, 1894-1904 (Madison, 1922); Kenneth Acrea, "The Wisconsin Reform Coalition, 1892-1900: La Follette's Rise to Power," Wisconsin Magazine of History, LII (Winter, 1968-69), 132-157, and "Wisconsin Progressivism: Legislative Response to Social Change," (University of Wisconsin Ph. D. Dissertation, 1968), two vols.; David P. Thelen, The New Citizenship: Origins of Progressivism in Wisconsin, 1885-1900 (Columbia, Missouri, 1972); and Alfred Harvey, "The Background of the Progressive Movement in Wisconsin," (University of Wisconsin Ph. M. Thesis, 1933).

[24]See Chapter I, footnotes 12 to 15 for a listing of these studies. David P. Thelen, "Social Tensions and the Origins of Progressivism," Journal of American History, LVI (September, 1969), 323-341, sees little difference between progressives and stalwarts. His failure clearly to delineate his method of labelling progressives and stalwarts raises

some questions about his conclusions. Arthur Schlesinger, Jr. develops a similar model of ethnics coming to power for the New Deal period--thirty years later than the rise of the ethnics in Wisconsin. See his The Age of Roosevelt, Vol. III, The Politics of Upheaval (Boston, 1960), 96-99, 104-110.

[25] Wisconsin Blue Book, 1899, 375-376.

[26] Padraic Colum Kennedy, "La Follette's Imperialist Flirtation," Pacific Historical Review, XXIX (May, 1960), 131-144. On the 1900 election see Robert S. Maxwell, "La Follette and the Election of 1900: A Half-Century Reappraisal," Wisconsin Magazine of History, XXXV (Autumn, 1951), 23-29, 68-71, and La Follette and the Rise of the Progressives in Wisconsin (Madison, 1956); and Robert C. Twombley, "The Reformer as Politician: Robert M. La Follette in the Election of 1900," (University of Wisconsin M. A. Thesis, 1964).

[27] Wisconsin Blue Book, 1901, 328-330. This Blue Book also includes data on the 1898 election. The 1896 data is in Wisconsin Blue Book, 1897, 364-365.

[28] In addition to Jensen's Winning of the Midwest, and Kleppner's Cross of Culture, see Frederick C. Luebke, Immigrants and Politics: The Germans of Nebraska, 1880-1900 (Lincoln, Nebraska, 1969), and John M. Allswang, A House for All Peoples: Ethnic Politics in Chicago, 1890-1936 (Lexington, Kentucky, 1971), for treatments of ethnic

voting behavior at the turn of the century.

[29]Kleppner, Cross of Culture, 88-91, and Jensen, Winning of the Midwest, 62-73, give delineations of Yankee moralism.

[30]On this involvement in Wisconsin see Bayrd Still, "Norwegian-Americans and Wisconsin Politics in the Forties," Norwegian-American Studies and Records, VIII (1934), 58-64. On Norwegians and politics in general, see Arlow W. Andersen, The Immigrant Takes His Stand: The Norwegian-American Press and Public Affairs, 1847-1872 (Northfield, Minnesota, 1953); George M. Stephenson, "The Mind of the Scandinavian Immigrant," Norwegian-American Studies and Records, IV (1929), 63-73; and Jon Wefald, A Voice of Protest: Norwegians in American Politics, 1890-1917 (Northfield, 1971).

[31]Curti, The Making of an American Community: A Case Study of Democracy in a Frontier County (Stanford, California, 1959), 296-297. The author's great-great-uncle, Peder Brye, began a political career based on this type of necessity. When the township of Coon in Vernon County was formed in 1859, he was requested to move to the edge of the Brye farm, placing his residency within the new township. He was immediately named to the posts of chairman, treasurer, assessor, and superintendent of schools, as the only English-speaking Norwegian in the community. Hjalmar R. Holand, Coon Valley (Minneapolis, 1928), 52.

[32]The Trempealeau County Record for September 18, 1868,

reflected this attitude in commenting that, in the recent elections, the Norwegians showed a "good sense of law and order by voting the Republican ticket." Quoted in Curti, American Community, 104.

33Kleppner, Cross of Culture, 52. See also Kleppner, 85-88, and Jensen, Winning of the Midwest, 81.

34Wyman, "Ethnic Groups and the Election of 1890," 286-287; Kleppner, Cross of Culture, 138; and Jensen, Winning of the Midwest, 135-137, 142-144.

35Larson, The Log Book of a Young Immigrant (Northfield, 1939), 247-248.

36Kleppner, Cross of Culture, 335. Stephenson, The Religious Aspect of Swedish Immigration (Minneapolis, 1932), 50. Stephenson's stress on Scandinavian conservatism in "The Mind of the Scandinavian Immigrant," no doubt reflects his greater familiarity with Swedish sources. On Swedish newspapers, see O. Fritiof Ander, "Swedish-American Newspapers and the Republican Party, 1855-1875," Augustana Historical Society Publications, II (1932), 64-77, and Finis Herbert Capps, From Isolationism to Involvement: The Swedish Immigrant Press in America, 1914-1945 (Chicago, 1966), 15-29. The second quote is from the latter, page 17.

37Kleppner, Cross of Culture, 53; A. William Hoglund, Finnish Immigrants in America, 1880-1920 (Madison, 1960), 116-117. John I. Kolehmainen and George W. Hill's Haven in the Woods: The Story of the Finns in Wisconsin (Madison,

1965), is weak on politics.

[38] Henry S. Lucas, Netherlanders in America: Dutch Immigration to the United States and Canada, 1789-1950 (Ann Arbor, Michigan, 1955), 541-565. Most of this appeared in Lucas, "The Political Activities of the Dutch Immigrants from 1847 to the Civil War," Iowa Journal of History and Politics, XXVI (April, 1928), 171-203. Robert P. Swierenga, "The Ethnic Voter and the First Lincoln Election," Civil War History, XI (March, 1965), 27-43, discusses the Dutch community of Pella, Iowa which became Democratic in the late 1840's behind the leadership of the Reverend Henry Peter Scholte, and has remained so until the present despite the switch to the Republican party of its leader, Scholte, in the 1850's.

[39] Kleppner, Cross of Culture, 58-61; Jensen, Winning of the Midwest, 295-298.

[40] Wyman, "Ethnic Groups and the Election of 1890," 288.

[41] Kleppner, Cross of Culture, 56-58.

[42] Humbert S. Nelli, The Italians in Chicago, 1880-1930: A Study in Ethnic Mobility (New York, 1970), 88-124, found a lower rate of naturalization and registration among Chicago's Italians. His chapter on "Ethnic Group Politics," stresses the orientation of Italians toward individuals rather than toward parties.

[43] Kleppner, Cross of Culture, 188-189, 195, 199-200, 333-336.

[44] Ibid., 55, 185-195, 328-333. The quote is from page 55. Even the well-organized Republican party of Chicago estimated the Irish vote for McKinley to be only 10% (the one group under 45%) in 1896. GOP National Committee Poll in the New York Herald, October 29, 1896, quoted in Jensen, Winning of the Midwest, 298. Sister Justille McDonald's excellent History of the Irish in Wisconsin in the Nineteenth Century (Washington, D. C., 1954), contains two very good chapters on the Irish and Wisconsin politics. William V. Shannon, The American Irish: A Political and Social Portrait (New York, 1963), paints an insightful portrait of the Irish and their ability in the political sphere.

[45] Kleppner, Cross of Culture, 67, 332-333; Jensen, Winning of the Midwest, 112, 297-300. One must treat Jensen's labelling of ethnic areas with some care--his differentiating among German Catholic and Lutheran townships in Wisconsin is most notably inaccurate. See footnote 48 of this chapter.

[46] Schafer, "Who Elected Lincoln?", 57. See also his "The Yankee and Teuton in Wisconsin: V, Social Harmonies and Discords," Wisconsin Magazine of History, VII (December, 1923), 158-162, and his editorial comments in his translation of Wilhelm Hense-Jensen and Ernest Bruncken, Wisconsin's Deutsch-Amerikaner bis zum Schluss des Neunzehnten Jahrhunderts (Milwaukee, 1900-1902), two vols. Translation in typescript, Milwaukee Public Library, 1939. The traditional view is expressed by Hense-Jensen and Bruncken and

by Bruncken in "The Political Activities of Wisconsin Germans, 1854-1860," Proceedings of the State Historical Society of Wisconsin (1901), 190-211.

⁴⁷Kleppner, Cross of Culture, 40.

⁴⁸Luebke, Immigrants and Politics, 65. The same data is contained in Luebke, "German Immigrants and Churches in Nebraska, 1889-1915," Mid-America, L (April, 1968), 116-130. Jensen, Winning of the Midwest, 61. Both of these collective biography studies are based on information contained in county histories. Jensen also has a voting behavior analysis of Wisconsin's Germans based on a sample of twenty-one Catholic and twelve Lutheran townships (pages 143 and 294). Unfortunately, this list is quite inaccurate, as the following table indicates:

	Sample used in this study			
Jensen sample	Catholic	Mixed	Lutheran	Not listed
Catholic (21 townships)	7	7	5	2
Lutheran (21 townships)	0	3	9	0

This mislabelling on Jensen's part results in a showing of almost no difference in voting between German Catholics and Lutherans, a conclusion belied by the results of this study and the work of Paul Kleppner, Frederick Luebke, and Joseph Schafer.

⁴⁹See for example the useful early studies by Deutsch, "Yankee-Teuton Rivalries in Wisconsin Politics in the Seven-

ties," 280, 416-417; Usher, The Greenback Movement, 29, 36; Jensen, Winning of the Midwest, 292-294; and Kleppner, Cross of Culture, 332-333.

[50] Luebke, Immigrants and Politics, 65.

[51] Schafer, Four Wisconsin Counties: Prairie and Forest (Madison, 1927), 140-170, and "Editorial Comment," Wisconsin Magazine of History, X (June, 1927), 455-561.

[52] Luebke, Immigrants and Politics, 65; Kleppner, Cross of Culture, 37-51; Jensen, Winning of the Midwest, 75-76, 82-85. Kleppner explains the variation in German Lutheran voting: "A painstaking analysis of the Wisconsin minor civil division data suggests that knowledge of the province in Germany from which the Lutherans came provides an important clue to their voting behavior," (pages 42-43). On the impact of the Bennett law campaign on German voters see Wyman, "Ethnic Groups and the Election of 1890," 284-285.

[53] Kleppner, Cross of Culture, 333.

[54] Degler, "American Political Parties and the Rise of the City," 44.

[55] John Luchsinger, "The Planting of the Swiss Colony at New Glarus, Wisconsin," Collections of the State Historical Society of Wisconsin, XII (1892), 375.

[56] Kleppner, Cross of Culture, 49-51.

CHAPTER V   WISCONSIN AND PROGRESSIVISM, 1900 to 1925

The first quarter of the Twentieth Century began with the entrance of Robert La Follette into the governor's office in Wisconsin; it closed with his death after an unsuccessful third party effort for the presidency in 1924. To describe La Follette's political efforts and the responses to them is to describe much of Wisconsin's politics for these twenty-five years.

After being elected and twice reelected governor, La Follette was sent to the U. S. Senate in 1905--one of the last Wisconsin senators to be elected by the state legislature. He was succeeded as governor by Lieutenant Governor James O. Davidson, though La Follette unsuccessfully backed Irvine Lenroot for the position in the 1906 gubernatorial primary. In 1910, the progressives returned to control behind Francis McGovern, leader of the Milwaukee branch of the reform coalition.

Conflicts within the progressive movement helped the new leader of the conservatives, railroad magnate Emanuel Philipp, take over the governor's office in 1914 and hold it until 1920. In that year he was replaced by progressive John J. Blaine. By 1926, the movement was again fragmenting until brought together by the pressures of Democratic resurgence in the 1930's. In 1934, the progressives finally left the Republican party to form their own third party under the leadership of La Follette's two sons, Robert Jr. and Philip.

The Republican party remained the majority party during this period--its control of the State Assembly varying from 57 to 92 of 100 seats.* This appearance of one-party dominance is deceptive--the real conflict, of course, took place within the confines of the GOP between the progressive forces led by La Follette and the stalwarts led originally be the old guard of Henry Clay Payne, John Coit Spooner, and Charles Pfister, then by Emanuel Philipp. In 1925, Republican conservatives formed the Republican party of Wisconsin, a voluntary party organization, because progressives controlled the regular party machinery, the state statutory committee. This organization took over the party in 1934 when the progressives left to form their own political party.[1]

The Democrats remained very much a minority party throughout the period under study, usually more conservative than the Republicans. After a brief period of resurgence from 1912 to 1914 during which the state went for Woodrow Wilson and elected a Democratic senator, the party was destroyed by the fallout of World War I. By 1918, it was even displaced as the minority party in the state legislature, trailing the Socialists for an entire decade, reaching a nadir of a single State Assembly seat and no Senate seats in the sessions of 1923 and 1925.

The political conflicts and legislative efforts of the

*See Chart II, in Chapter IV.

period have been well-described by Belle and Fola La Follette, Edward Doan, Robert Maxwell, Herbert Margulies, and others.[2] The subject of this study, the nature of progressive support, has been superficially described by these writers and by Jorgen Weibull, and much more thoroughly dealt with in dissertation form by Roger Wyman.[3] Weibull fails to go below county level data in his study nor is he careful to distinguish between normal Republican areas of strength and specifically progressive Republican areas; for this determination, primary elections and referenda on progressive issues must be used.

Despite the continuing contest between stalwarts and progressives, it is difficult to find clear cut primary elections to provide such a measure. The following indices have been used in this study to delineate progressive support in the pre-World I era:

I. The drop-off in support from La Follette's first race for the governorship, the unity campaign of 1900, to his third race in 1904. In that year stalwarts led by Henry Clay Payne and John Coit Spooner tried unsuccessfully to unseat La Follette at the Republican state convention. Failing in this, the die-hards among the stalwarts named ex-Governor Edward Scofield to head a ticket of "National Republicans". La Follette won handily but ran about 20,000 votes behind the rest of the Republican ticket, the Democratic candidate for governor, George Peck, running 25,000 votes ahead of his ticket. The National Republicans drew from 10,800 to 13,200 votes for their candidates. Combining this vote with Peck's additional votes yields the 37,000 votes and 9.3% separating La Follette from his 1900 total.

Table I 1900 and 1904 Elections[4]

	Republican	Democratic	Others	Total
1900 Election				
President	265,760 60.1%	159,163 36.0%	17,578 3.9%	442,501
Governor	264,419 59.8%	160,674 36.4%	16,804 3.8%	441,897
Lt. Governor	263,993 59.8%	160,044 36.3%	17,220 3.9%	443,257
1904 Election				
President	280,164 63.2%	124,107 28.0%	38,743 8.7%	443,014
Governor	227,253 50.5%	176,301 39.2% Nat. Rep.	33,860 7.5% 12,136 2.7%	449,560
Lt. Governor	247,159 55.3%	151,403 33.9% Nat. Rep.	37,516 8.4% 10,864 2.4%	446,942

This rise in split-ticket voting was a new phenomenon associated with the introduction of the Australian ballot in the 1890's and accompanied by a general decline of partisanship and of voter participation in the elections of the early Twentieth Century.[5] The conservative Democratic candidate for President, Judge Alton Parker, suffered even more from split-ticket voting than did La Follette.

In order to gain some idea of those groups most oriented toward La Follette and those most oriented toward the stalwart effort to cut La Follette in 1904, either by voting for the National Republican candidate, or for the Democratic candidate (a strategy encouraged by stalwart Republicans when they realized Scofield had no chance of winning), this study has measured the slippage in La Follette's percentage for each ethnic and size-of-place grouping.

The second and third measures of progressive support come from two state-wide referenda: the 1904 vote on establishing primary elections as the method for nominating candidates and the 1914 state constitutional amendment aimed at writing initiative and referendum methods for passing laws into the state constitution.

II. The primary election proposal was sent to the people in 1903 by conservative legislators in an effort to sidetrack it. The proposal instead carried by a vote of 130,699 (62.0%) to 80,192 (38.0%) in the November, 1904 election. The total vote of 210,891 on the proposal was far below the 449,570 ballots cast in that election. The largest drop-off came in Milwaukee County, where only 15,107 of the 72,959 voters for governor bothered to make their choice on the referendum. Other large drop-offs came in urban counties Brown, Kenosha, Racine, and Sheboygan. Nonetheless, the vote on the primary election proposal does give one measure of progressivism. No account is taken of non-voting in this study, instead the percentage of those voting on the referendum who voted yes is used.[6]

III. The vote on writing the initiative and referendum procedure into the state constitution came in a year of divisiveness in progressive ranks. In 1914, stalwart leader Emanuel Philipp defeated several progressives in the Republican primary to win the nomination for governor. In the senatorial primary, Governor Francis McGovern won despite La Follette's opposition. The two had broken over the former's support of Theodore Roosevelt in 1912.[7] In the general election, McGovern went down to defeat along with ten progressive-sponsored constitutional amendments including recall of public officials and home rule for cities and villages as well as the initiative and referendum proposal. The vote on the latter was 84,934 (36.0%) yes and 148,536 (64.0%) no. The total vote cast on the proposal was 233,470 compared to a vote of 325,430 for governor.

IV. The final measure of pre-World War I progressivism selected for use in this study was the 1912 presidential preference primary between Robert La Follette and incumbent President William Howard Taft. Run on April 12, 1912, not long after T. R. had displaced La Follette as

Taft's most serious opponent, the primary yielded the following results:

Table II 1912 Presidential Preference Primary[8]

Republican

La Follette	133,354	73.2%
Taft	47,514	26.1%
T. R. (write-in)	628	0.3%
Other	643	0.4%
Total	182,139	

Democratic

Woodrow Wilson	45,045	55.7%
Champ Clark	36,454	44.2%
Other	158	0.2%
Total	82,557	

Unfortunately, this primary proves to be the weakest index of all for measuring progressive support as the variation among voting units is not great enough to separate groups. Only seven of our ethnic size-of-place groupings fall below 63% in their support of La Follette and they contain only eleven voting units out of 504 used in the study for that year. Because the measure is based only on votes cast in the Republican primary--Woodrow Wilson, backed by the liberal forces within the Wisconsin Democracy, defeated Champ Clark in the Democratic primary held the same day--it is most valid for Republican groupings. The

Republican primary vote cast in solidly Democratic areas probably represents the small minority of other ethnic groups present in those voting units.

These votes summarized in Table II in Appendix D thus yield four separate indices to measure the degree of progressive support prior to the impact of U. S. involvement in World War I. Table III gives a rough index of progressivism using three of the indices.

The strongly progressive areas showing up well on all of the indices and reflected in the averages are not surprising. All of the Scandinavian areas lent strong support to the direct primary measure, varying from a median of 67% among Danish urban wards to 95% for the two Swedish villages. The initiative and referendum proposal in 1914 had tougher sledding but captured almost all of the Scandinavian rural units, the eleven Finnish townships topping all categories with a 71% median, followed closely by the two Danish villages and seven rural Danish units. All Scandinavian groupings, with the exception of the minimally Swedish city of Park Falls in Price County, topped the state-wide vote of 36.0%. Rural areas and villages tended to be more progressive than their urban counterparts.

The other stronghold of Republican strength responded quite differently to the new force in Wisconsin politics. Native-stock, Yankee areas were not receptive to the rise of the progressive movement led by La Follette. Native-

Table III Progressive Support, 1900 to 1914

	Referenda			Average
	1904 Prim Median	1914 I & R Median	1912 Pres Prim Median	
Scandinavian Groups				
Finnish rural	94%	71%	83%	83%
Danish villages**	--	70%	95%	83%
Swedish villages	95%	61%	89%	82%
Swedish rural	85%	61%	94%	80%
Danish rural	83%	67%	92%	81%
Norwegian rural	91%	56%	86%	78%
Norwegian wards	76%	52%	86%	71%
Norwegian villages	83%	49%	73%	68%
Scandinavian cities (3)	78%	41%	77%	65%
Danish wards	67%	45%	77%	63%
Other Progressive Groups				
Belgian rural	84%	43%	94%	74%
Italian rural**	83%	55%	82%	73%
French Canadian rural**	82%	43%	82%	69%
French Canadian ward*	89%	40%	68%	66%
Belgian ward*	76%	33%	81%	63%
Italian ward*	91%	41%	55%	62%
Milwaukee Polish wards	72%	60%	81%	71%
Milwaukee German wards	69%	55%	71%	67%
Swiss villages**	66%	48%	79%	64%
Native-stock, Anglo-Saxon Groups				
Native-stock rural	74%	31%	83%	63%
Native-stock villages	57%	53%	66%	59%
Welsh rural**	74%	37%	65%	59%
English rural	69%	21%	81%	57%
Native-stock cities**	56%	31%	63%	50%
English villages**	53%	26%	70%	50%
Native-stock wards**	42%	41%	55%	46%
Welsh villages	59%	22%	55%	45%

*Single units
**Two units

Table III Progressive Support, 1900 to 1914

	Referenda 1904 Prim Median	1914 I & R Median	1912*** Pres Prim Median	Average
Germanic Groups				
Swiss rural	48%	38%	75%	54%
Swiss city*	56%	26%	69%	50%
German Lutheran villages	56%	33%	75%	55%
German Lutheran cities	68%	34%	61%	54%
German Lutheran rural	55%	17%	72%	48%
Other German wards	60%	27%	78%	55%
Large German cities	55%	27%	64%	49%
German Mixed villages	55%	29%	67%	50%
German Mixed rural	51%	18%	74%	48%
German Mixed cities	46%	24%	63%	44%
German Catholic cities	53%	28%	67%	49%
German Catholic villages	55%	19%	67%	47%
German Catholic rural	33%	15%	77%	42%
Other Catholic Groups				
Irish rural	49%	32%	87%	56%
Dutch Catholic village*	56%	24%	74%	51%
Bohemian rural	61%	14%	75%	50%
Polish rural	38%	13%	65%	39%
Irish ward*	32%	23%	60%	38%
Austrian rural*	6%	13%	83%	34%
Other Polish wards**	16%	16%	63%	32%
Dutch Catholic rural	26%	6%	56%	29%
Wisconsin	62.0%	36.0%	73.2%	57.1%
Milwaukee city	67.4%	51.0%	72.0%	63.5%

*Single units
**Two units
***Exaggerated for Democratic areas

stock areas led the way in cutting La Follette in 1904--
the fifteen villages and cities under 2,500 dropped 29%
off their 1900 GOP vote, the two larger cities dropped 24%,
and the four urban wards experienced a phenomenal 40%
drop, from 80% Republican to only 40% for the GOP. Rural
Native-stock areas matched the state drop with 8%. English
and Welsh areas dropped in amounts varying from 9% to 19%
during the same four years. On the 1904 vote on the direct
primary, rural areas dominated by these three groups all
topped the state majority of 62% yes, while village and
urban areas fell below it. However, in 1914, rural areas
nose-dived to well below the statewide vote of 36% while
Yankee villages and cities under 2,500 turned in a striking
53% yes vote in an otherwise bleak year for progressivism.
This must be considered an anomaly for in no other election
did Yankee villager or city dweller give a high vote to
progressive candidates or measures. For example, the 1912
Presidential primary found Native-stock rural units supporting La Follette while villages and urban areas trailed
the state average of 73%.

    This voting pattern offers a strong contradiction to
Richard Hofstadter's status revolution theory. In Wisconsin,
the progressive movement did not draw from those of Yankee
background. Rather it drew most strongly from ethnic
groups on the make--particularly the Scandinavians.[9] One
historian suggests that the Norwegians, at least, must

rank as "one of the most consistently reform-bent ethnic groups in American history."[10] A study of *Scandinaven*, one of the main Norwegian language newspapers, widely read in Wisconsin though published in Chicago, found that:

> In domestic affairs it was Progressive, though it might justly be called Republican in its outlook, it was the Republicanism of La Follette and Roosevelt and not of the standpatters. Direct election of senators, direct primaries, and control of trusts were all strongly advocated.[11]

With the support of the old guard, Rasmus B. Anderson purchased *Amerika* to serve as a vehicle for opposing La Follette in Wisconsin.[12] But Anderson admitted in his autobiography that "politically I was friendless among the Norwegians because I was a stalwart Republican while they were nearly all enthusiastic admirers of La Follette."[13] These judgments are borne out by this study.

Perhaps, the lack of response to progressivism of Wisconsin's Native-stock Yankees was related to the fact that they were being ousted from their accustomed control of the Republican party. In return, they sought to protect their dominant position in the economic life of the state and return to political dominance by opposing the progressive movement. In Wisconsin, progressivism provided the threat to their status, not the vehicle for restoring it.

Germans, dominant in the state in numbers, but not in politics, are the most difficult group to type. German Catholics, along with other Catholic groups (Belgians,

Italians, and French Canadians apparently excepted), maintained their loyalty to the Democratic party and to the forces of conservatism, personal liberty, and laissez-faire which it represented.

German Lutherans are less easy to categorize. They trailed the rest of the state in support of the direct primary in 1904 and dropped in the 1914 vote to a level with their Catholic brethren. They must be rated as at least mildly anti-La Follette. In a study of positions taken on public issues by nine German-language newspapers in the state from 1909 to 1912, Gerd Korman concluded that, "Wisconsin's German-American editors did not commit themselves to progressivism. They reacted to the progressive movement on their own terms, not on Roosevelt's terms or on those of any other progressive." And that would include, most notably, Robert M. La Follette. While generally backing progressive economic reforms, the editors were lukewarm to changes in the electoral system which stressed direct democracy. Initiative and referendum could well lead to woman's suffrage, temperance legislation, anti-immigrant legislation, all measures which the German language newspapers opposed. An additional factor in their opposition to La Follette was that most of them were Democratic in their politics. However, the Republican *Germania* also opposed La Follette, and later Theodore Roosevelt, out of loyalty to the national party.[14]

Among Catholics, the observation made by Sister Justille McDonald about the Irish probably has a general truth behind it:

> Where it is possible to isolate the Irish vote in the 1900 election . . . there was no evidence of a significant defection to the La Follette branch of the Republican party. Where Irishmen had become scattered, however, the psychology of group voting was lacking, and Irishmen were more likely to break with their traditional allegiance to the Democratic party and to become independent in their voting habits.[15]

In a voting behavior study based on aggregate data, the scattered Irishman is impossible to locate. In fact, the Irish were the one ethnic group prone to scattering; those who did not, opposed La Follette and Republicans in general. Typical of Catholic rural settlement is the lone Austrian township of Lima in Pepin County. Of the ninety-four who voted on the 1904 primary election referenda, only six voted yes.

Belgians, rural Italians, and French Canadians continued to buck the trend of Democratic voting among their coreligionists. Already oriented toward the Republican party, they also formed a loyal part of the La Follette wing of that party. The seven Belgian townships turned in a 94% vote for La Follette in 1912, the single urban Belgian area, Green Bay's ward four, turned in an 81% La Follette vote.

A surprising entrant among the opponents of La Follette and progressivism was the Dutch Reformed. Quite solidly

-239-

Republican, all Dutch Reformed areas dropped in their support of La Follette between 1900 and 1904. The three Dutch units came up with a median yes vote of only 31% on the 1904 referendum; ten years later five Dutch Reformed units yielded only a 23% yes vote on initiative and referendum. Swiss Reformed areas were a bit more supportive of the two measures, particularly in urban areas.

The favorable vote for both the direct primary and for the initiative and referendum proposal in Milwaukee among German and Polish residents is striking especially when compared with the vote in other urban areas:

Table IV   Urban Vote on 1904 and 1914 Referenda

	1904 vote N=	1904 Median	1914 vote N=	1914 Median	Drop-off 1904/1914
German wards					
Milwaukee	10	69%	10	55%	14%
Other cities	30	60	30	27%	33%
Polish wards					
Milwaukee	1	72%	5	60%	12%
Other cities	2	16%	2	16%	--
Norwegian wards	4	76%	4	52%	24%
Danish wards	2	67%	4	45%	22%
Native-stock wards	5	42%	5	41%	1%
Milwaukee		67%		51%	16%
Nineteen other cities		62%		32%	30%
Wisconsin		62%		36%	26%

In a study of urban areas in Wisconsin centering on the cities of La Crosse and Milwaukee, Roger Wyman found Anglo-American (Native-stock) and middle- and upper-class wards the least progressive. Basing his analysis on the drop-off from Theodore Roosevelt's presidential vote in 1904 to La Follette's gubernatorial vote in the same year, Wyman found the following correlations:

Table V   Correlation Matrix, 1904 Election

	1904 Rep Pres	1904 Rep Gov	1904 Rep Pres - Gov
Milwaukee wards			
Upper- and middle-class	.577	.119	.674
Anglo-American	.681	.061	.556
Working class	-.782	-.046	-.745
Democratic ethnic groups (Germans, Poles, Austrians Russians, Irish, Italians, Bohemians, Hungarians)	-.669	-.036	-.689
La Crosse wards			
Upper- and middle-class	.450	-.183	.792
Anglo-American	.610	.123	.690
Working class	-.316	.187	-.626
Democratic ethnic groups	-.808	-.502	-.549

After investigating other stalwart-progressive splits, Wyman concluded that Wisconsin progressivism drew most strongly from rural areas, especially those of Scandinavian background. However:

In primary elections, the rural and Scandinavian components were aided significantly by the thousands of "fair-minded Democrats" who invaded the Republican primary to vote for progressive Republicans. In urban areas this extra measure of support came largely from German and working-class voters.16

One further possible index of progressivism must be looked at--Theodore Roosevelt's vote in the 1912 presidential election. After displacing La Follette as the progressive candidate in that year and then leaving the Republican convention when his forces lost there, T. R. found himself lacking a campaign apparatus in Wisconsin. The Milwaukee wing of the party, led by Francis McGovern, gave him support, but La Follette praised Woodrow Wilson in the pages of La Follette's Weekly though stopping short of outright endorsement of the Democrat. Wilson carried Wisconsin with 41.1% of the vote; Taft trailed in second place with 32.7%; T. R. finished a poor third with only 15.6%, much less than the 27.4% he received nationally. Table VI indicates the sources of T. R.'s greatest strength. In one way this vote measures non-regular Republican strength which La Follette could not influence, in another light it measures those groups most susceptible to the personal appeal of T. R.

Table VI T. R. Presidential Vote, 1912

	N=	Mean
Finnish rural	7	51%
Swedish rural	12	49%

Table VI Continued

Dutch Reformed villages	2	41%
Dutch Reformed rural	3	38%
Danish villages	2	38%
Danish rural	4	34%
Swedish city	1	34%
Swedish villages	2	33%
Native-stock wards	2	32%
Norwegian rural	32	28%
English rural	3	23%
Danish wards	4	21%

One fact which becomes clear in studying Table VI in conjunction with Table IV in Appendix D is that T. R.'s strength came almost entirely from Republican voters. Wilson gained votes in 1912 from every ethnic, size-of-place grouping with one exception. He lost votes to T. R. among Polish voters both in rural townships and in urban wards. Other traditionally Democratic voters may not have approached the performance of the Dutch Catholic community of Little Chute in Outagamie County where T. R. could only pull in one vote out of 256 cast, but they were far from enthusiastic about his candidacy. Even Catholic groups with a Republican past such as the Belgians, gave him scant support, seven Belgian townships averaging only 10%. German Lutheran and Swiss Reformed voters also gave only nominal support to Roosevelt.

On the other side of the picture, Dutch Reformed townships and villages, though firm in their opposition to La Follette, vied with Danish, Finnish, and Swedish rural and small town areas in support for T. R. by percentages varying from 33% to 51%. Reflecting this orientation toward T. R., the Swedish language press broke from its allegiance to the Republican party, fourteen editors backing Roosevelt, eighteen sticking with Taft, and three backing Wilson.[17] Norwegian rural areas turned in a 28% T. R. vote while other Norwegians as well as urban Danes and Swedes exercised more Scandinavian reserve varying from 11% to 21% for T. R. Native-stock and English-Welsh voters gave only nominal support to T. R., though the two urban Yankee wards averaged 32%, tops among urban areas.

Wisconsin's nineteen largest cities had a mean vote for T. R. of 19% and five German cities over 10,000 a mean of 21%, slightly topping the state-wide vote. Heading the urban list were Scandinavian Superior with 42% for T. R. and German Oshkosh with 40%.

Thus there was some correlation between those groups which backed La Follette and those which backed T. R. but the variations in support were also great. Some of the most staunchly progressive groups in the state would have little to do with T. R. On the county level, his vote correlated only .389 with La Follette's 1912 primary vote, .481 with the 1904 vote on the direct primary, and .428

with the 1914 initiative and referendum vote.

The entrance of the United States into the World War in 1917 had a number of effects on Wisconsin progressivism. In addition to redefining the issues around which campaigns were waged, it accentuated the factionalism everpresent within Wisconsin progressivism and, most relevant for purposes of this study, it brought about a shift in the groups supporting progressives and other candidates and measures.

Factionalism had been present almost from the beginning of the progressive movement. While La Follette was clearly the leader of the movement from the mid-1890's on, other individuals and groups had independent bases of support and their own reasons for backing the movement. Thus, part of the millionaire lumberman contingent--Isaac Stephenson and William D. Connor--fell by the wayside as their own ambitions ran afoul of La Follette's. Other supporters like William Dempster Hoard and James Davidson, found progressivism going too far leftward as the end of its first decade rolled around. Still others like Francis McGovern found themselves on the outs with La Follette over their support for T. R. in 1912.

However, the real watershed for Wisconsin progressives came over the issue of support for World War I, the so-called "loyalty" issue. La Follette's leadership of the forces opposed to American involvement in the war split Wisconsin progressivism wide open. Men like Irvine Lenroot, Nils P. Haugen, John R. Commons, Richard Lloyd Jones, editor of the <u>Wisconsin State Journal</u>, and Walter Goodland, all staunch La Follette men prior to 1917, found themselves condemning the senior Senator from Wisconsin for his position on the war. The State Legislature passed a resolution denouncing

> Senator Robert M. La Follette and all others who have failed to see the righteousness of our nation's cause, who have failed to support our government in matters vital to the winning of the war.[18]

Even the University of Wisconsin, long a key element in La Follette progressivism, issued a petition signed by President Charles Richard Van Hise, Richard T. Ely, John R. Commons, and 418 other members of the faculty to

> protest against those utterances and actions of Senator Robert M. La Follette which have given aid and comfort to Germany and her allies in the present war; we deplore his failure to support the government in the prosecution of the war.[19]

The war on the home front was especially bitter in Wisconsin, in part because of the prominence of Senator La Follette among the ranks of those opposing the war, in part because of the state's large German population. While the official State Council of Defense organized material support for the war, the quasi-official Loyalty Legion sought to organize people's minds. In addition to

propaganda efforts the legion undertook promotion of the
Liberty Loan campaigns in a vigilante spirit well-labeled
and described by Governor Philipp's secretary, Charles
Stewart, in an article in the Atlantic Monthly entitled
with due irony, "Prussianizing Wisconsin."[20]

A 1918 special election to fill the Senate seat left
vacant by the death of Democrat Paul Husting, saw La Follette's
man James Thompson narrowly defeated in the Republican
primary by Irvine Lenroot, the "loyalty" candidate backed
by stalwarts and by pro-war progressives.[21] In the regular
primary elections of that year, three of the state's Congressmen who had joined with La Follette in voting against the
war were defeated by pro-war Republicans.

By 1920, the electoral scales were tipping back in
La Follette's direction. His candidate for Senator, again
James Thompson, came within 20,000 votes of defeating Senator
Lenroot in the primary and, running as an independent, within
47,000 votes of unseating him in the general election. At
the same time, John Blaine, backed by La Follette and the
Nonpartisan League, won a narrow primary victory and then
the governorship with 53% of the vote. In 1922, Blaine won
re-election with an unbelievable 76.4% of the vote while
La Follette was topping the Senatorial primary with 72.2%
and the general election with 80.6%. Also in 1920, two of
the anti-war Congressmen ousted in 1918, regained their
seats and progressives replaced conservatives in three other
districts.

This strong showing in 1920 and 1922 makes it clear
that the landslide for Harding--71.1% in Wisconsin, even
greater than his 60.4% national showing--was not a repudiation of Wilsonian progressivism, but a repudiation of
Wilsonian war, internationalism, economic controls, and
trampling of civil liberties. Herbert Margulies has best
evaluated this election in a 1957 article entitled, "The
Election of 1920 in Wisconsin: The Return to 'Normalcy'
Reappraised," in which he concluded:

> The experience in [Wisconsin] suggests strongly
> that the results signified neither repudiation
> of idealism nor endorsement of reaction. In
> Wisconsin, the name "Wilson" was far from synonymous with either reform or "idealism".
> . . . Most of the protest was not against the
> war itself but rather against many of the methods
> by which the national administration and the
> Democratic party chose to conduct it. To many,
> Wilson and the Democrats seemed to have turned
> their backs on every canon of the progressive
> faith.[22]

The La Follette Senate primary victory in 1922 and
Wisconsin Presidential victory in 1924 provide the most
effective measurement of the nature of La Follette progressive support in the post-war period. Before turning
to the groups backing La Follette in these elections,
however, three other shifting electoral coalitions bear
comment: the Democratic party as of 1920; the Republican
party as of 1920; and the Socialist party as of 1920.
Data for each ethnic and size-of-place group for these
elections is found in Tables III to V in Appendix D.

The breakdown of the Wilsonian Democratic coalition is the most noticeable impact one perceives in looking at election returns in Wisconsin from 1908 to 1920. While Wilson was only able to increase his 1912 Wisconsin vote 4.4% over that which William Jennings Bryan had received four years previously (41.1% compared to 36.7%), he was able to carry the state in that divided electoral year. In 1916 he inched his vote up another 1.7% to 42.8% but narrowly lost the state to Charles Evans Hughes as most of T. R.'s 1912 third-party support returned to the Republican fold.

Wilson's gains in 1912 over the Bryan vote of 1908 had come across the electoral board, varying, for example from 2% to 5% in most German groupings, with no perceptible differences between Lutheran and Catholic, or rural, small town, or city voters. Norwegians and Danes registered the largest Democratic gains particularly in urban areas. In fact, all of Wilson's gains of 7% or more came in villages and cities from groups as varied as English and Dutch Catholic villages. Poles, on the other hand, dropped about 13% among all size-of-place groupings in their support of the Democratic party, with T. R. picking up their votes--one of his rare areas of success among Democrats.

Wilson's gains in Milwaukee were 3% and in the nineteen other large cities in Wisconsin, 5%, just above his state gain of 4.4%. Wilson lost ground in only eight of the state's fifty-four ethnic, size-of-place groupings and gained more than 7% in the same number.

By 1916, Wilson's appeal above and beyond the normal Democratic vote was no longer the same across the board. Arthur Link describes his support at the national level in that year as "a great progressive coalition" consisting of independent progressives from the social justice movement and the liberal press; labor, including both the American Federation of Labor and the Railway Brotherhoods; and farmers, especially in the Midwest and South.[23]

Pinpointing the voting responses of progressives or social workers is a task for elite analysis, not for voting behavior study based on aggregate data. One measure of progressivism, less valid in Wisconsin than elsewhere, is the T. R. Progressive party vote of 1912. As has already been noted, with the exception of the Polish vote, the T. R. vote came almost entirely from Republican ranks and returned to Republican ranks in 1916. In Wisconsin at least, T. R. did *not* serve as a transitional figure for progressives between the two parties in 1912 as La Follette was to serve in 1924. Roosevelt's denunciation of Wilson and support for Hughes may well have been a factor in returning his voters to the ranks of the Republican party.

However, other elements of the coalition can be located with greater accuracy. In the state as a whole, Wilson added only 1.7% to his 1912 vote of 41.1%. This apparent lack of change masked some very strong movements and counter-movements among the groupings which made up the electorate.

Wilson registered his greatest gains in non-German rural areas:

Table VII Democratic Gains, Non-German Rural Voters, 1912 to 1916

	N=	1912 Mean	1916 Mean	Democratic Gain
Native-stock	22	30%	37%	7%
English	3	26%	36%	10%
Welsh	2	26%	30%	4%
Norwegian	32	15%	26%	11%
Swedish	12	19%	29%	10%
Danish	4	33%	49%	16%
Finnish	7	9%	17%	8%
Dutch Reformed	3	22%	30%	8%
Belgian	7	24%	55%	31%
Italian	2	37%	42%	5%
French Canadian	2	38%	53%	15%
Bohemians	9	57%	64%	7%
Irish	9	66%	70%	4%
Polish	6	55%	85%	30%
Dutch Catholics	1	82%	86%	4%

The gains varied from 4% for Dutch Catholics, Welsh, and Irish to an astounding gain of 31% for the seven Belgian townships. Poles increased their Democratic vote by margins ranging from 21% to 30%, though approximately half of this represents a return to the Democratic party of defectors to T. R. in 1912. Danish voters were second only to the Belgians and Poles in their movement toward the Democratic party by percentages varying from 11% to 20%. Norwegian voters--especially rural ones--also turned toward Wilson, as did rural Swedes and Finns.

The state's nineteen cities over 10,000 showed an average gain of 4% for Wilson, the city of Milwaukee, 5%. In the latter city, Wilson was aided by a return to the Democratic party of T. R. defectors as Polish wards jumped 21%, up 6% over their 1908 Democratic vote. German wards held even in Milwaukee, Wilson lost only 3% in other German wards throughout the state, and he held his own in the five German cities over 10,000.

Outside the large urban areas, the German voting pattern was a disaster for the Democrats:

Table VIII Democratic Losses, German Voters
1912 to 1916

Rural areas	N=	1912 Mean	1916 Mean	Democratic Loss
Lutherans	76	45%	27%	-18%
Mixed	44	48%	32%	-16%
Catholics	25	60%	44%	-16%

Table VIII Continued

Swiss	3	60%	42%	-18%
Austrians	1	75%	68%	- 7%
Villages and Cities under 2,500				
Lutheran	17	50%	42%	- 8%
Mixed	15	53%	40%	-13%
Catholic	11	63%	48%	-15%
Swiss	2	57%	48%	- 9%
Urban areas, 2,500-10,000				
Lutheran	3	48%	41%	- 7%
Mixed	15	55%	48%	- 7%
Catholic	4	62%	58%	- 4%
Swiss	1	49%	43%	- 6%
Cities over 10,000	5	43%	42%	- 1%
Milwaukee wards	9	36%	36%	--
Other wards	30	45%	42%	- 3%

The size-of-place pattern for other ethnic groups was reversed for Germans. Among Germans, the more rural a place the greater the losses for the Democrats. In fact, German losses of 4% to 9% in most urban areas matched losses in English, Welsh, and Dutch urban areas.

This analysis is borne out by a study of county level coefficients of correlation:

Table IX Correlation Matrix: 1908 to 1920 Elections

	1905 Retabulated State Census		
	Ger %	Scan %	Native-stock %
1908 Democratic %	.691	-.678	-.337
1912 Democratic %	.622	-.661	-.270
1916 Democratic %	.090	-.277	-.177
1920 Democratic %	-.010	-.327	.028
1908 to 1912 Dem gain	.175	.072	-.196
1912 to 1916 Dem loss	.707	-.596	-.188
1916 to 1920 Dem loss	.134	-.044	-.271

The initial strong rapport with the Democratic party on the part of Germans as indicated in the 1908 and 1912 correlations had vanished by 1916. While no significant variation in the ethnic pattern shows up in changes in the Democratic vote between 1908 and 1912, a very high correlation of .707 appears between the German proportion in each county and Wilson's losses between 1912 and 1916. Scandinavians correlate at .596 with Wilson's gains bearing out the minor civil division analysis.[24]

Thus it appears that only the urban labor side of a farmer-labor coalition was able to hold firm against German ethnic fears in 1916. For non-German farmers, economic considerations had moved to the fore; for their German counterparts, the impending war over-shadowed all other considerations.

Oddly enough, this pattern of German defection has been greatly underrated in the literature on the subject. Link concluded that despite the fact that Hughes had

> the open support of organized German-American groups and practically the entire German language press . . . the vaunted German-American bloc had been so riddled by the Democratic peace appeal and Roosevelt's campaign blasts that the so-called hyphen vote almost vanished.[25]

David Burner and Thomas Kerr follow Link in their interpretations of the election, the latter suggesting that, "Wilson's appeal as the president who 'kept us out of war' may have had more impact among rank and file Germans especially in the Mid-West and Far West."[26]

These conclusions are all based primarily on the post-election analysis of the New York Times, which headlined its interpretations of the results, "Hyphen Shot to Pieces," "The Hyphen Vote was Practically a Myth," and "With the Possible Exception of Oregon, the German-American Vote was not an Election Factor Anywhere in the U. S." While admitting that Hughes had gained over 12,000 votes in twelve German counties in Wisconsin (presumably above the combined Taft-T. R. vote of 1912), the *Times* analyst concluded:

> Thousands of German-Americans of both the Socialists and Republican parties, abandoned their own tickets to vote for President Wilson, not because of any issue closely or remotely connected with a foreign war but because of the record of the Administration at Washington for the last four years.[27]

The German voting bloc, normally Democratic, was in fact riddled, though not by the Democratic peace appeal. Rather, it was riddled by the association of the Democratic party with a hard line toward Germany and preparedness for war. In this case the elite leaders of Germanic organizations and editors and publishers of German language publications, accurately reflected their constituency in their preference for Hughes. The fact that this movement toward the Republicans was most pronounced in rural German areas and barely existent in urban areas over 10,000 probably indicates that the opinion makers were not responsible for it. The presence of an organized counter-pressure to Republican inroads in the form of the labor movement may explain the urban vote. In Milwaukee, for example, the Democratic vote declined in five of the nine German wards, the Republican vote increased by an average 15% in these nine wards, while the Social Democratic vote was declining by 7%. Compare this to Wilson's performance in the five Milwaukee Polish wards where his vote increased by an average of 21% while both the Social Democrats and Republicans were declining in strength. The erroneous conclusions drawn by the New York Times and subsequent historians who have relied on its interpretations need little additional comment.

In the face of this pattern, the fact that Democrats made greater inroads among other ethnic groups in rural areas, indicates the salience of the farm issue with ethnicity removed as a major consideration. The one non-German group for whom ethnicity might well have been important was the normally Republican Belgian rural contingent which turned in an amazing majority of 53% for Wilson in 1916.

One other ethnic group, assumed to be susceptible to ethnic appeals in 1916 was the Irish. Efforts of the British to suppress the Irish independence movement came to a head in 1916 with the crushing of the Easter rebellion and the execution of its leadership. Supporters of Irish independence in the United States and pro-German publicists sought to use this event against Wilson in the 1916 campaign.

However, the Irish were too staunch in their support of the Democratic party to be moved by this appeal. In Wisconsin, the nine rural Irish townships actually increased their Democratic vote from the 66% mean of 1908 and 1912 to a mean of 70% in 1916. Erin Prairie in St. Croix County, the most solidly Irish township in the state, declined slightly from 89% to 84% while Irish ward five in Janesville declined only 2% from 58% to 56%. In this case, the leadership of Irish organizations and press clearly did not reflect their constituency in their opposition to Wilson.

In analyzing the Irish vote, students of voting behavior have done a far more thorough and accurate piece of work than they have for the Germans. As William Leary concluded:

> The weight of evidence, then, indicates that Irish Americans, despite the exhortations of their leaders, voted for Wilson in as great or greater numbers than they had ever voted for a Democratic presidential candidate in the immediate past.[28]

The Wisconsin Irish vote, while less important in numbers than its Eastern counterpart, bears out this conclusion.

One further observation, though peripheral to the main interests of this study, bears mentioning. Though Wilson increased slightly his vote both in absolute and in percentage terms in 1916, he still failed to carry the state, losing to Hughes by fewer than 30,000 votes. The proportion of Germans in the electorate, probably around 40%, and the size of the declines in strength among German voters for the Democratic party when it was making gains every--where else, point to the conclusion that the war issue lost the state for Wilson in 1916.

Table X   Presidential Vote, 1912 and 1916[29]

	1912 Vote		1916 Vote	
Woodrow Wilson (Dem)	164,230	41.1%	191,363	42.8%
William H. Taft (Rep)	130,596	32.7%		
Charles E. Hughes (Rep)			220,822	49.4%
Theodore Roosevelt (Prog)	62,448	15.6%		
(Social Democratic)	33,476	8.4%	27,631	6.1%

Table X Continued

Others	9,216	2.3%	7,318	1.6%
Total	399,966		447,134	

While Wilson increased both his overall vote and his percentage of the total vote in Wisconsin, he suffered vote losses in fourteen counties and percentage declines in twenty-five counties. Nineteen of these counties were among the state's twenty-five top German counties. Had these nineteen voted Democratic in 1916 by the same percentage they did in 1912 Wilson would have received over 8,300 additional votes, and Hughes would have had his total reduced by the same 8,300 votes. This 8,300 far underrates the actual loss to Wilson in German areas as additional losses among Germans in these and other counties were cancelled out by Wilson's gains among non-Germans. For example, closer examination of the results for Marathon County, a heavily German area, reveals that Wilson lost votes in all but five of the thirty voting precincts that had a German percentage of 55% or more according to the 1905 census retabulation. In the remaining twenty-eight voting precincts, he lost votes in only nine while gaining votes in nineteen. From this, it is but a short step to interpolate an additional loss among German voters of more than the 7,000 votes Wilson needed to hold in order to retain Wisconsin in his column in 1916.

Democratic losses in 1916 were mild compared to the avalanche which developed in 1920. In that year the Democratic party could capture only 16.2% of the vote in the face of Warren G. Harding's 71.1% and Eugene Debs 11.5%. The Democrats dropped to two seats in the hundred man State Assembly and did not rise above six for the entire decade of the twenties, ranking as the third party in the state legislature, behind the Social Democrats.

With a vote this small, it is difficult to locate any solidly Democratic groups as of 1920. The following table indicates those groups which still retained some loyalty to the Democratic party:

Table XI Democratic Groups 1920

	1920 Democratic Mean
Dutch Catholic village	60%
Polish rural	56%
Polish wards	45%
Dutch Catholic rural	45%
Irish rural	42%
German Catholic cities over 2,500	33%
French Canadian villages	31%
French Canadian ward	30%
Polish villages	30%
Italian ward	29%
Irish ward	26%

Dutch Catholics, Polish, Irish, and French Canadians along with urban German Catholics retained the greatest loyalty for the Democratic party, though few units gave even as much as a majority to the Democracy.

A reverse table, indicating areas of greatest Democratic weakness in 1920, reveals some new entrants. Even setting an upper limit of 10% gives a sizable listing:

Table XII   Non-Democratic Groups 1920
Democratic Mean

Norwegian rural	5%	Welsh villages	8%
Swiss rural	5%	Italian rural	8%
Swiss villages	5%	German Mixed rural	9%
German Lutheran rural	6%	German Catholic rural	9%
Dutch Reformed rural	6%	Norwegian city	9%
Dutch Reformed rural	7%	Swedish villages	10%
Finnish rural	7%	English villages	10%
Swedish rural	7%	Welsh rural	10%
Belgian rural	8%	Swiss city	10%
Norwegian villages	8%		

In addition to normally "un-Democratic" Scandinavian, Yankee, British, Belgian, Dutch Reformed, and Italian rural voters, this listing includes all the Swiss groupings and all German rural groups.

A whole literature has developed around the interpretation of the 1920 election varying from Frank Freidel's oft-cited observation that "there is nothing to indicate that anti-League Irish and Germans deserted the Democratic party in any greater proportion than the population as a whole,"[30] to Samuel Lubell's conclusion:

> The worst Democratic setbacks in 1920 came in areas of Swedish, German, Norwegian, and Irish backgrounds, with a smaller drop among Italo-Americans. In large part it was a vote of revenge. The war had precipitated a hysterical movement to eradicate everything German. With the war's end the German-Americans proceeded to settle old scores.[31]

A statistical study by R. A. Burchell based on Irish and German voting patterns in seven states which concluded that there was a "lack of significant correlations between the fall in turnout and the Democratic vote and the presence of Irish and German voters,"[32] would seem to bear out the Freidel thesis.

However, all of these studies and especially the last one, suffer from major methodological weaknesses. Either they use county level data which does not allow for fine enough location of ethnic areas or they begin their time series in 1916. As this study has already shown, the German movement away from the Democratic party was already in full swing by that election. Correlation analysis is insufficient unless carefully used.[33]

The problem of testing the thesis that there was no connection between Democratic losses and German or Irish voters in 1920 is not easy to resolve, especially for a

state like Wisconsin in which the Democratic vote dropped
so precipitously in 1920. A table showing size of loss
from 1908 to 1920 would be valid only for largely Democratic groups. Norwegian rural Democrats, for example,
formed such a small proportion of the Norwegian rural vote
in 1908 (12% at most) that even their entrance en masse
into the Republican party in 1920 would leave a Democratic
decline of only 12%, well below the statewide drop of 20.5%
The last column in Table III in Appendix D indicates the
percentage decline in Democratic support for the different
ethnic and size-of-place groupings from 1908, selected as
the most "normal" year, to 1920. In order to determine
whether there is a differential in vote loss between the
groupings, the key word in Freidel's observation is
"proportion". The following table indicates those groups
which suffered the greatest proportionate Democratic loss
from 1908 to 1920.

Table XIII Greatest Democratic Losses, 1908 to 1920

	1908 Mean	1920 Mean	Loss 1908 to 1920 Absolute	Proportion
Swiss rural	54%	5%	49%	93%
Swiss villages	50%	5%	45%	90%
German Lutheran rural	41%	6%	35%	85%
German Catholic rural	60%	9%	51%	85%
Austrian rural	75%	15%	60%	80%
German Mixed rural	45%	9%	36%	80%

Table XIII   Continued

Italian rural	34%	8%	26%	77%
Swiss Reformed cities	42%	10%	32%	76%
Dutch Reformed villages	27%	7%	20%	74%
German Mixed villages	48%	13%	35%	73%
Welsh villages	28%	8%	20%	71%
Dutch Reformed rural	21%	6%	15%	71%
German Lutheran villages	45%	14%	31%	69%
Other German wards	45%	15%	30%	67%
German Lutheran cities	42%	14%	28%	67%
German Mixed cities	50%	18%	32%	64%
Milwaukee German wards	30%	11%	19%	63%
Bohemian rural	52%	20%	32%	62%
Swedish villages	26%	10%	16%	62%
Belgian rural	21%	8%	13%	62%
German Catholic villages	54%	21%	33%	61%
German cities over 10,000	43%	17%	26%	61%
Norwegian villages	20%	8%	12%	60%
Wisconsin	36.7%	16.2%	20.5%	56%

Clearly, there is a variation not only in absolute loss but also in proportion lost. Heading the list of Democratic losses is a surprising entrant--the Swiss. German and Austrian rural areas follow closely behind. The only non-Germanic groupings in the top fifteen are the Dutch Reformed townships and villages, Italian rural areas, and

Welsh villages. Losses among these four groups may be due primarily to German minorities present in each one.

At the other end of the scale, groups where the proportionate loss to the Democrats was less than half, one finds Yankee villages and cities, Swedish and Norwegian cities, Danes in general, French Canadians, Poles in general (Stevens Point's fourth ward turned in a banner 70% Democratic vote in 1920), Irish townships, and the single Dutch Catholic village.

Thus the answer to the question "Did the Irish and German voters desert the Democrats in 1920?" in greater numbers than other voters, must be answered in the affirmative for the Germans. The movement of this group away from the Democratic party which had begun in 1916 was almost total by 1920. Even for the Irish voter, attachment to the Democratic party was severely shaken. Erin Prairie in St. Croix, the only totally Irish township in the sample, dropped over half in its Democratic vote, from 82% to 38%, while the lone Irish ward in Janesville dropped just half, from 52% to 26%. Lubell is most correct in typing the German vote, despite his misuse of the colorful term "politics of revenge," he is erroneous in stressing Democratic losses among Swedes and Norwegians, for Wisconsin at any rate.

To examine the constituent elements of the Republican party as of 1920 is almost to stand this table on its head--after first subtracting the socialist vote. Almost all groups registered 70% or better Republican votes in 1920. Every group was more Republican than it had been in 1908, the variation came only in the extent of the gains.

Before turning to the impact of the war on progressivism, one additional factor remains to be discussed--the socialist vote. While this vote varied from 6.1% to 8.4% in the three presidential elections prior to the war, it jumped to 26.1% in a special senatorial election in 1918 and to 11.5% in the 1920 presidential election.

Before the war the socialist vote was primarily an urban phenomenon with only one ethnic grouping under cities of 10,000 topping 5%--rural Finns averaging about 20% in each of the three prewar elections. (See Table V in Appendix D.) In the special senatorial election of April 12, 1918 to fill the seat left vacant by the death of Democrat Paul Husting, Victor Berger received 26.1% (110,487 votes) of the ballots cast, compared to 38.7% (163,983 votes) for the winning candidate, pro-war Republican Irvine Lenroot, and 35.1% (148,923 votes) for the Democratic candidate, Joseph E. Davies. In the November election, Berger was elected to Congress from the fifth Congressional district on Milwaukee's heavily German north side.[34] Some of these gains carried over into the 1920 presidential race especially in rural German areas.

The best way to evaluate areas of socialist strength during these years is to take the voting units in this sample for these four presidential elections and one senatorial election, listing those units outside Milwaukee County in which the socialists pulled the highest vote. Tables VI A to E in Appendix D contain the lists. Several conclusions can be drawn from them. While a few voting units are repeaters, most appear only once or twice on the lists indicating perhaps a brief flurry of organization related to one person or a local issue, followed by a quiescent socialist movement. Secondly, most units are German or Finnish, with an occasional Swedish, Danish, or Native-stock unit making the list. Finally, the socialist vote was largely an urban phenomenon except in 1918 and 1920 when it can be typed more accurately as a German protest vote.

In 1918 Victor Berger, in addition to drawing 42% of the vote in the city of Milwaukee, gained over 80% in twenty-one of the units used in this study. All but three of these were German Lutheran including sixteen rural townships and two villages. The other three units among the top twenty-one were German Catholic, German Mixed, and Swedish rural townships. The second set of twenty-four units, all over 75% for Berger, was solidly German including nineteen rural townships (twelve of them Lutheran), one Lutheran village and three urban wards. Swiss Reformed,

Swedish and Finnish rural, the lone Austrian township, and five Milwaukee Polish wards were the only non-German units giving significant percentages to the Social Democratic candidate.

In 1920 the top twenty-one Social Democratic voting units outside Milwaukee County included nineteen German units, one Finnish township, and one Polish ward. Of the German units, eight were Lutheran townships, compared to two Catholic townships, and six were urban wards.[35]

Milwaukee socialism deserves at least a brief mention since that city not only gave sizable votes to Social Democratic presidential candidates during the period but also sent socialists to the state legislature and to Congress, and elected a socialist city administration beginning in 1910. Emil Seidel was elected the city's first Social Democratic mayor in that year along with twenty-one socialist aldermen and Victor Berger for his first term in Congress. Ousted in 1912 by a Democratic-Republican coalition, the Social Democrats returned to power behind Daniel Hoan in 1916. Hoan remained mayor of the city until 1940. Temporarily displaced in 1940, the Social Democrats returned to power in 1948 with Frank P. Zeidler who remained as mayor until his retirement in 1960.[36]

The highest total of socialist legislators was sixteen Assemblymen and four State Senators in 1918. Fourteen

of these were from Milwaukee, the remaining six from
Calumet, Marathon, Manitowoc, and Sheboygan Counties, all
heavily German. Victor Berger sent to Congress in 1918
by voters of Milwaukee's fifth Congressional district,
then defeated in the Republican landslide of 1920, was
returned in 1924, 1926, and 1928 despite efforts to keep
him from being seated because of the Social Democratic
party's position on the war.

The leading historian of Milwaukee socialism concluded
that, "socialist votes were concentrated in working class
districts, more obviously when these districts were German rather than Polish, and less clearly whenever Catholics
predominated."[37]

Data for this study indicate that the difference between Polish and German wards was not that great:

Table XIV Milwaukee and Manitowoc Socialist Vote,
1908 to 1920

	Presidential				Sen
	1908	1912	1916	1920	1918
Milwaukee	25%	28%	22%	31%	42%
Nine German wards (seven in 1908)	30%	33%	26%	38%	51%
Five Polish wards (two in 1908)	29%	41%	30%	38%	39%
One Italian ward	9%	10%	6%	11%	16%
Manitowoc	17%	20%	7%	28%	40%
German ward five	29%	32%	12%	43%	58%
Polish ward seven	26%	36%	5%	43%	36%

Polish voters in Milwaukee were more inclined to vote Social
Democratic than Germans in 1912 and 1916; in 1908 and 1920,
average votes for the two groups were even. The two wards
in Manitowoc bear out the similarity in voting for the Poles
and Germans. The immediacy of the wartime experience probably explains the 1918 differences.

Finnish socialism has been dealt with at some length
in the histories by Hoglund and by Kolehmainen and Hill.[38]
Suffice is to say that this study indicates its existence.
During the years from 1908 to 1920 the seven Finnish townships in this study increased from 19% to 25% Social Democratic.

The final impact of the war to be investigated is the
effect it had on the support given Robert La Follette.
Two postwar elections have been selected for measurement
of that effect.

I. The 1922 Senate primary election pitted La Follette
against William Ganfield, a relatively unknown Presbyterian
minister and the president of Carroll College. Despite an
intense effort on the part of the stalwarts, La Follette
won overwhelmingly and went on to do the same in the general
election. The Democrats did so badly in the primary election
that they were forced to go on the ballot in the November
general election as Independents. Mrs. Jessie Jack Hooper,
the Democratic candidate, a liberal and an active suffra-

gist,[39] received only 3.2% of the total vote in the
primary and 16.6% of the vote in the general election.
The Social Democrats did not oppose La Follette in this
election. The results for the primary and general elections were as follows:

Table XV   1922 Senatorial Vote[40]

	September Primary			General Election	
Republicans					
Robert La Follette	362,445	69.7%	(72.2%)	379,494	80.6%
William Ganfield	139,327	26.8%	(27.8%)		
Democrats			(100.0%)		
Jessie Jack Hooper	16,663	3.2%		78,029	16.6%
Others	1,282	0.2%		13,296	2.8%
Total Vote	519,717			470,819	

More votes were cast in the primary election than in
the general election, a not uncommon pattern for Wisconsin
during this period. Since so few people voted in the Democratic primary, the results in the Republican primary can
be studied for normally Democratic ethnic groups as well
as for Republicans. One-fifth or 3,273 of Hooper's primary
votes came from Milwaukee County.

As an indication that La Follette's vote was not completely a personal vote or, at the very least, that it was
transferable, a brief look at the governor's race is instructive.

Table XVI 1922 Gubernatorial Election[41]

	September Primary		General Election	
Republican				
John J. Blaine	336,453	62.5%	367,929	76.4%
William Morgan	147,379	27.4%		
A. C. McHenry	16,716	3.1%		
Democratic				
Arthur Bentley	10,313	1.9%	51,061	10.6%
Karl Mathie	8,584	1.6%		
Social Democratic	17,375	3.2%	39,570	8.2%
Others	1,520	0.3%	23,268	4.8%
Total Vote	538,340		481,828	

Incumbent Governor John Blaine did almost as well as La Follette in the primary election against stalwart William Morgan. The remainder of the progressive state ticket also won in the primary though by smaller margins.

II. The 1924 Presidential election is more important for pinpointing La Follette's sources of support than is the primary election. In 1924 La Follette ran as a third party candidate requiring voters to leave their own party's columns to vote for him. While this action is easier to take than crossing the two-party line, it is still not an easy matter for voters with solid past party loyalties. For most Democrats, these had already been broken by the 1920 election, for many Republicans, the way had been pre-

pared by a third of a century of factional strife within
the Republican party.

La Follette was aided in his efforts in 1924 by support from a number of sources. Organized labor was solidly behind him with endorsements from the American Federation of Labor and the Railway Brotherhoods. Farm groups, especially the Nonpartisan League and other groups centered in the Midwest and West, gave him their backing. The Social Democrats endorsed La Follette as did independent liberal journals like the Nation and New Republic. Midwestern progressive Senators giving him vocal support included Magnus Johnson and Henrik Shipstead of Minnesota and Lynn Frazier and Edwin Ladd of North Dakota. Senators Smith Brookhart of Iowa, Hiram Johnson of California, and George Norris of Nebraska, while not openly backing La Follette, pointedly ignored the Coolidge-Dawes ticket.[42]

In terms of votes, this support gave La Follette 4,822,856 or 16.6% of a total nationwide vote of 28,933,458. On the Wisconsin level the results were:

Robert M. La Follette (Prog)	453,678	54.4%
Calvin Coolidge (Rep)	311,614	37.4%
John W. Davis (Dem)	69,096	8.2%

This election permits the investigation of a number of questions relative to La Follette's support. What were the partisan origins--and ultimate resting place--of the La Follette votes? Were those votes from discontented Democrats or Republicans? Did the same voters ultimately back the New Deal of F. D. R. or was La Follette's effort the dying gasp of a backward looking rural progressivism as Richard Hofstadter and others have suggested?[43] Which ethnic size-of-place groupings were supporting La Follette in these elections? What new groups had been added to the La Follette coalition? Had La Follette lost support among any groups as a result of his position on World War I? The two primaries of 1912 and 1922 with their respective La Follette shares of the Republican party vote of 73.2% and 72.2% will give a good indication of the changes.

Before turning to specific groupings, the use of coefficient of correlation analysis based on county level data will provide some preliminary answers to the above questions:

Table XVII Correlation Matrix: La Follette Elections 1900 to 1924

	1912 Pres Primary	1916 Sen Primary	1922 Sen Primary	1924 Pres
1900 Governor (Rep)	.401	.358	-.283	-.071
1912 President (T. R.)	.389	.380	.007	-.116
1914 I. and R.	.595	.608	-.060	.096
1918 Senate (Soc)	-.312	.030	.435	.379
1932 President (Dem)	-.141	-.136	.691	.558
1912 La Follette-Pres Prim	1.000	.659	.064	.290

Table XVII Continued

1916 La Follette-Sen Prim	1.000	.164	.341
1922 La Follette-Sen Prim		1.000	.748
1924 La Follette-Pres			1.000

La Follette's 1912 and 1916 primary races correlate at .659; his 1922 and 1924 races at .748, both quite high. However, the 1922 race correlates not at all with the earlier races and 1924 minimally correlates. The two elections also fail to correlate with T. R.'s 1912 support, a judgment borne out in a study by Alan Havig of Bull Moose response to La Follette which concluded that it was largely negative.[44] Finally, the elections correlate negatively with 1900 Republican strength implying a slight positive correlation with traditional Democratic areas. More striking is the correlation of La Follette's 1922 and 1924 votes with F. D. R.'s vote in 1932, at .691 and .558 respectively. Combining La Follette's 1924 vote with the miniscule Democratic vote in that year boosts the latter correlation to .732.

The ultimate lodging of La Follette's backing as a part of the New Deal Democratic coalition is a subject for Chapter VI. The origin of those backers must be looked at in more detail than coefficients of correlation based on county level data allow. Table VII in Appendix D gives the La Follette median vote in 1922 and 1924 by ethnic and

size-of-place groupings and the changes by grouping for
La Follette from 1912 to 1922. Combining this measurement
with the 1924 results allows us to determine both traditional
areas of La Follette support, carried with him into the
1920's, and new sources of support picked up because of
his war time position.

A breakdown of the ethnic size-of-place groupings
according to those which tended to support La Follette and
progressive measures before the war and also after the
war yields the following results:

Table XVIII

Prewar Supporters of La Follette Progressivism

	1912 to 1922 change	1924 vote
Norwegian rural	4%	78%
French Canadian ward	18%	75%
Belgian rural	- 1%	72%
Italian rural	- 9%	69%
French Canadian rural	4%	64%
Danish rural	- 8%	64%
Swedish city	- 2%	59%
Norwegian villages	- 4%	58%
Norwegian wards	- 3%	57%
Finnish rural	3%	54%
Swedish rural	- 8%	53%
Norwegian city	-22%	52%

Table XVIII Continued

Swedish ward	7%	50%
Danish city	-32%	45%
Swedish villages	-22%	44%
Danish wards	-11%	33%
Danish villages	-33%	25%

Norwegians clearly remained loyal to La Follette through the war experience except for the always volatile city of Stoughton in Dane County which dropped to just below the state average in both 1922 and 1924. Belgian rural areas remained solidly progressive as did the pairs of French Canadian and Italian townships and the solitary French Canadian ward in Ashland. Danish townships voted strongly for La Follette, while Finnish and Swedish rural areas voted at about the state average of 54%. However, all other Danish voting units and the five Swedish villages dropped in La Follette support by percentages varying from 11% to 33% between 1912 and 1922 and, in 1924, found themselves at the bottom of the list of prewar La Follette voters.

Groups on Table XIX were even more firmly committed to La Follette in the postwar period--and had been almost as opposed to the Senator in the period before the war. It is this change in their behavior which largely explains the lack of correlation between La Follette's pre- and postwar areas of support.

Table XIX Prewar Non-supporters, Postwar Supporters of
La Follette

	1912 to 1922 change	1924 vote
Swiss rural	19%	84%
German Catholic rural	18%	83%
German Lutheran rural	21%	82%
Swiss villages	12%	82%
German Mixed rural	17%	80%
Austrian rural	(- 8%)*	70%
Milwaukee German wards	6%	68%
Bohemian rural	18%	67%
Dutch Catholic rural	(41%)*	64%
German Mixed villages	15%	62%
German Catholic villages	15%	60%
German Lutheran villages	- 6%	60%
Dutch Catholic village	(20%)*	60%
German Catholic cities	19%	59%
Other German wards	9%	59%
Other Polish wards	27%	58%
Milwaukee Polish wards	2%	58%

*Single voting units

Clearly La Follette gained large increments of strength from Germanic areas formerly hostile to progressivism. All German rural groups ranked above even the Norwegian farmers in their devotion to Wisconsin's senior Senator in

the 1920's, turning in phenomonal third party votes in
excess of 80%. While the Scandinavians, other than Danes,
Belgians, rural Italians, and French Canadians had registered little change from 1912 to 1922, all of the groups
on this table registered gains of more than 14% except for
the most urban areas and the inexplicable 6% drop among
German Lutheran villages. In addition to Germans; Swiss,
Austrian, Bohemian, Dutch Catholic, and urban Poles cast
solid 58% or better third party votes. The urban German
and Polish votes undoubtedly include a goodly percentage
which would have gone to a Social Democratic Presidential
candidate had there been one. For example, Louis Arnold,
the Social Democratic candidate for Governor received
over 33,000 votes in Milwaukee County.

Almost all of these voting groups had been Democratic,
many by very solid margins prior to World War I. Wrenched
from their Democratic moorings by the war, their refuge
with La Follette was only temporary, the question of their
final partisan resting place remained open. These groups
were also, of course, the same ones which had shifted most
massively toward the Republican party in 1920.

Table XX is equally striking in illustrating those
groups which were hostile to La Follette before the war
and even more so after the war.

Table XX Prewar and Postwar Opponents of La Follette

	1912 to 1922 change	1924 vote
Republican		
Yankee rural	-15%	54%
English rural	-12%	50%
Welsh rural	-6%	48%
English villages	-18%	48%
Yankee villages	-16%	45%
Dutch Reformed rural	-27%	37%
Yankee cities	-30%	23%
Dutch Reformed villages	-25%	22%
Yankee wards	-24%	14%
Welsh villages	-37%	14%
Democratic or Mixed Democratic-Republican Groups		
Swiss city	-1%	52%
Polish villages	-6%	52%
German cities over 10,000	14%	51%
German Mixed cities	8%	51%
Irish rural	-2%	48%
French Canadian villages	--	43%
German Lutheran cities	-7%	41%
Italian ward	3%	39%

Welsh were the least likely group in the state to vote for La Follette in the 1920's; the small La Follette vote

in the two Welsh townships almost certainly came from the
German minorities present. Urban Yankees and Dutch Reformed
in general, found their already small La Follette vote
dropping by from 24% to 30%. Slightly less virulent in
their opposition to La Follette were Yankee and English
rural areas and villages, dropping in primary support for
La Follette by margins varying from 12% to 18% and nestling
between 45% and 54% in 1924, just under the state average.

Normally Democratic groups which changed little as a
result of the war but still gave La Follette sizable votes
in 1924 included German Lutheran and Mixed cities, the five
German cities over 10,000, Irish rural areas, and Polish
villages. Individual examples of a Swiss city, a French
Canadian village, and an Italian ward also fit in this
category. Erin Prairie in St. Croix County, as Irish as
its name, broke ranks with its fellow Irishmen to record
a 1924 vote of 86% for La Follette.

Thus progressivism in 1924 stood on two legs--one
firmly rooted in the Scandinavian and Belgian support pre-
dating the war; the other in Teutonic groups clearly affected by their wartime experiences. Samuel Lubell has
suggested that La Follette progressivism in Wisconsin in
the inter-war period served as a

> halfway station for two distinct streams
> of insurgents--those who were leaving the
> Republican party in protest against big-
> business domination, and those who had
> forsaken the Democratic party in vengeful
> memory of "Wilson's War."[45]

The final lodging of these two groups is the subject of the concluding chapter. Basic to this examination will be the impact of the Depression and New Deal, and of a second war with Germany, followed by Cold War with the Soviet Union, on the fortunes of the major political parties and the third party Progressives. The chapter will end with an investigation of the distribution across the political spectrum of the ethnic size-of-place groupings as the half-century under examination came to a close in 1950.

NOTES

¹Liberal Democrats formed a similar organization in 1948. See Frank J. Sorauf, "Extra-Legal Parties in Wisconsin," American Political Science Review, XLVIII (September, 1954), 692-704, and "The Voluntary Committee System in Wisconsin: An Effort to Achieve Party Responsibility," (University of Wisconsin Ph. D. Dissertation, 1953).

²Belle Case and Fola La Follette, Robert M. La Follette, June 14, 1855--June 18, 1925 (New York, 1953), two vols.; Robert M. La Follette, La Follette's Autobiography (Madison, 1913); Edward N. Doan, The La Follettes and the Wisconsin Idea (New York, 1947); A. O. Barton, La Follette's Winning of Wisconsin, 1894-1904 (Madison, 1924); Robert S. Maxwell, La Follette and the Rise of the Progressives in Wisconsin (Madison, 1956), and Emanuel L. Philipp, Wisconsin Stalwart (Madison, 1959); Herbert Margulies, The Decline of the Progressive Movement in Wisconsin, 1890-1920 (Madison, 1968); Stanley P. Caine, The Myth of a Progressive Reform: Railroad Legislation in Wisconsin, 1903-1910 (Madison, 1970); David P. Thelen, "Robert La Follette's Leadership, 1891-1906: The Old and New Politics and the Dilemma of the Progressive Politician," Pacific Northwest Quarterly, LXII (July, 1981), 97-109; Padraic Kennedy, "Lenroot, La Follette, and the Campaign of 1906," Wisconsin Magazine

of History, XLII (Spring, 1959), 163-174; and Robert Griffith, "Prelude to Insurgency: Irvine L. Lenroot and the Republican Primary of 1908," Ibid., XLIX (Autumn, 1965), 16-28. For a very negative view of La Follette, matched by that of the paper he worked for, The Milwaukee Journal, see Craig Ralston, "The La Follette Dynasty," (unpublished manuscript, State Historical Society of Wisconsin, c. 1939).

[3]Weibull, "The Wisconsin Progressives, 1900-1914," Mid-America, XLVII (July, 1965), 191-221. Wyman, "Voting Behavior in the Progressive Era: Wisconsin as a Case Study," (University of Wisconsin Ph.D. Dissertation, 1970), three vols. Weibull also fails to separate Germans and Poles, since the census he uses--that of 1910--failed to do so.

[4]For the 1900 data, see the Wisconsin Blue Book, 1901, 327-336, 382-383; for 1904, see Wisconsin Blue Book, 1905, 366-382, 560.

[5]See Walter Dean Burnham, "The Changing Shape of the American Political Universe," American Political Science Review, LIX (March, 1965), 7-28, and Critical Elections and the Mainsprings of American Politics (New York, 1970), 71-90; Jerrold G. Rusk, "The Effect of the Australian Ballot Reform on Split Ticket Voting: 1876-1908," American Political Science Review, LXIV (December, 1970), 1220-1238; and Angus Campbell, "Surge and Decline: A Study of Electoral Change," Public Opinion Quarterly, XXIV (Fall, 1960), 397-418.

⁶In addition to the above, see Allen F. Lovejoy, La Follette and the Establishment of the Direct Primary in Wisconsin (New Haven, Connecticut, 1941); Ruth F. Robinson, "The Control of the Republican Party in Wisconsin, 1904," (University of Wisconsin M. A. Thesis, 1930); and Waldo Schumacher, "The Direct Primary in Wisconsin," (University of Wisconsin Ph. D. Dissertation, 1923). None of these sources gives an adequate explanation for the drop-off in vote for the direct primary election.

⁷Herbert Margulies, "The Background of the La Follette-McGovern Schism," Wisconsin Magazine of History, XL (Autumn, 1956), 21-29. On the 1912 struggle between La Follette and T. R. see also George E. Mowry, Theodore Roosevelt and the Progressive Movement (Madison, 1946).

⁸Wisconsin Legislative Reference Bureau, The Presidential Preference Primary in Wisconsin. Research Bulletin 128 (Madison, April, 1960), 31.

⁹David Thelen, The New Citizenship: Origins of Progressivism in Wisconsin, 1885-1900 (Columbia, Missouri, 1972), 300-301, presents a similar interpretation.

¹⁰Jon Wefald, A Voice of Protest: Norwegians in American Politics, 1890-1917 (Northfield, Minnesota, 1971), 3.

¹¹Agnes M. Larson, "The Editorial Policy of Skandinaven, 1900-1903," Norwegian-American Studies and Records, VIII (1934), 126.

¹²See Lloyd Hustvedt, Rasmus Bjorn Anderson: Pioneer

Scholar (Northfield, Minnesota, 1966), 234-237; Paul Knaplund, "Rasmus B. Anderson, Pioneer and Crusader," *Norwegian-American Studies and Records*, XVIII (1954), 23-43.

[13] Rasmus B. Anderson, *Life Story of Rasmus B. Anderson* (Madison, 1917), 649. Anderson also noted that, "In every Norwegian community in the state, there was the greatest enthusiasm for 'Bob' La Follette," *Life Story*, 616.

[14] Gerd Korman, "Political Loyalties, Immigrant Traditions, and Reform: The Wisconsin German-American Press and Progressivism, 1909-1912," *Wisconsin Magazine of History*, XL (Spring, 1957), 161-168. The quote is from page 161. For an unsuccessful effort to prove that German Catholics were reform-oriented, see Philip Gleason, "An Immigrant Group's Interest in Progressive Reform: The Case of the German-American Catholics," *American Historical Review*, LXXIII (December, 1967), 367-379, and *The Conservative Reformers: German-American Catholics and the Social Order* (Notre Dame, Indiana, 1968). An article which tries to make a case for a growing sense of German nationalism during this period is G. A. Dobbert, "German-Americans Between New and Old Fatherland, 1870-1914," *American Quarterly*, XIX (Winter, 1967), 663-680.

[15] McDonald, *History of the Irish in Wisconsin in the Nineteenth Century* (Washington, D. C., 1954), 187-188.

[16] Wyman, "Middle-Class Voters and Progressive Reform: The Conflict of Class and Culture," *American Political*

Science Review, LXVIII (June, 1974), 488-504. The table is from page 497, the quote from pages 503-504. Wyman did not use referenda on progressive issues in his analysis.

[17]Paul E. Johnson, "The Swedish-American Press in the Election of 1912," (University of Iowa M. A. Thesis, 1940), 116, as cited in Finis Herbert Capps, From Isolation to Involvement: The Swedish Immigrant Press in America, 1914-1945 (Chicago, 1966), 20. See also O. Fritiof Ander, "The Swedish-American Press in the Election of 1912," The Swedish Pioneer Historical Quarterly, XIV (July, 1963), 103-126.

[18]Belle and Fola La Follette, La Follette, II, 860.

[19]Ibid., II, 847. One of the most thorough descriptions of these two events is contained in this work, II, 842-853, 859-865, even if written with the somewhat pardonable bias of La Follette's daughter, Fola. Padraic Kennedy, "La Follette's Foreign Policy: From Imperialism to Anti-Imperialism," Wisconsin Magazine of History, XLVI (Summer, 1963), 287-293, is on La Follette's earlier change in attitude.

[20]Stewart, "Prussianizing Wisconsin," Atlantic Monthly, CXXIII (January, 1919), 99-105. See also Karen Falk, "Public Opinion in Wisconsin During World War I," Wisconsin Magazine of History, XXV (June, 1942), 389-407; Lorin Lee Carey, "The Wisconsin Loyalty Legion, 1917-1918," Ibid., LIII (Autumn, 1969), 33-50; Henry Huber, "War Hysteria," (unpublished manuscript, State Historical Society of Wisconsin, 1928); "Wisconsin's War Activities," Wisconsin Blue

Book, 1919, 301-438; Fred L. Holmes, Wisconsin's War Record (Madison, 1919); R. B. Pixley, Wisconsin in the World War (Milwaukee, 1919); Gerd Korman, Industrialization, Immigrants, and Americanizers: The View from Milwaukee, 1866-1921 (Madison, 1967), 167-175; Margulies, Decline of the Progressive Movement, 193-243; Maxwell, Emanuel Philipp, 111-180; James E. Jackson, "Wisconsin Attitudes toward American Foreign Policy since 1910," (University of Wisconsin Ph. D. Dissertation, 1934); Charles A. Nelson, "Progressivism and Loyalty in Wisconsin Politics, 1912-1918," (University of Wisconsin M. S. Thesis, 1961); Alan Edmond Kent, "Portrait in Isolationism: The La Follettes and Foreign Policy," (University of Wisconsin Ph. D. Dissertation, 1957); Lawrence J. Martin, "Opposition to Conscription in Wisconsin, 1917-1918," (University of Wisconsin M. A. Thesis, 1952).

[21]On the 1918 election, see Herbert Margulies, "The La Follette-Philipp Alliance of 1918," Wisconsin Magazine of History, XXXVIII (Summer, 1955), 248-249; Seward Livermore, Politics is Adjourned: Woodrow Wilson and the War Congress, 1916-1918 (Middleton, Connecticutt, 1966; paperback edition, Washington University Press, 1968), 115-122; and Karl E. Meyer, "The Politics of Loyalty from La Follette to McCarthy in Wisconsin, 1918-52," (Princeton University Ph. D. Dissertation, 1956), 27-73, in addition to the Wisconsin sources cited above.

[22]Margulies, "The Election of 1920 in Wisconsin: The

Return to 'Normalcy' Reappraised," Wisconsin Magazine of History, XLI (Autumn, 1957), 15-22. The quote is from page 15.

[23]Link, Woodrow Wilson and the Progressive Era, 1910-1917 (New York, 1954), 239-251, and Wilson: Campaigns for Progressivism and Peace, 1916-1917 (Princeton, New Jersey, 1965), 160-163. See David Burner, The Politics of Provincialism: The Democratic Party in Transition, 1918-1932 (New York, 1968), 3-33, for a similar view which also stresses an isolationist component of the vote for Wilson.

[24]Ralph Kloske, "Ecological Correlations and German Americans: A Research Note," (Luther College, May, 1974) has a comparison of county level and minor civil division level correlation analysis.

[25]Link, Woodrow Wilson and the Progressive Era, 245 and 249. See also H. C. Petersen and Gilbert Fite, Opponents of War, 1917-1918 (Madison, 1957); Carl Wittke, German-Americans and the World War, Ohio Historical Collections, Vol. V (Columbus, Ohio, 1936); Clifton Child, The German-Americans in Politics, 1914-1917 (Madison, 1939); Felice A. Bonadio, "The Failure of German Propaganda in the United States, 1914-1917," Mid-America, XLI (January, 1959), 40-58; Howard W. Allen, "Isolationism and German-Americans," Journal of the Illinois State Historical Society, LVI (Summer, 1964), 321-339; and Dean R. Esslinger, "American-German and Irish Attitudes Toward Neutrality, 1914-1917:

A Study of Catholic Minorities," Catholic Historical Review, LIII (July, 1967), 194-216. Clifford L. Nelson, German-American Political Behavior in Nebraska and Wisconsin, 1916-1920, University of Nebraska-Lincoln Publication No. 217 (Lincoln, Nebraska, 1972), reaches conclusions similar to those reached in this study for both 1916 and and 1920. The definitive study of German-Americans and World War I, Frederick C. Luebke's, Bonds of Loyalty: German-Americans During World War I (Dekalb, Illinois, 1974), was published too late to be used in this study.

26Thomas J. Kerr, "German-Americans and Neutrality in the 1916 Election," Mid-America, XLIII (April, 1961), 103.

27New York Times, November 12, 1916, 6, and New York Times Magazine, November 19, 1916, 3. The quote is from the latter source. The entire Times analysis though labelled "superb" by Link bears reevaluation in light of its inaccuracy for Wisconsin.

28Leary, "Woodrow Wilson, Irish-Americans, and the Election of 1916," Journal of American History, LIV (June, 1967), 71. For similar conclusions, see Edward Cuddy, "Irish-American Propagandists and American Neutrality, 1914-1917," Mid-America, XLIX (October, 1967), 252-275, and "Irish-Americans and the 1916 Election: An Episode in Immigrant Adjustment," American Quarterly, XXI (Summer, 1969), 228-243.

29County level data is contained in the Wisconsin Blue

Book, 1913, 214, and Wisconsin Blue Book, 1917, 238. See
also James R. Donoghue, How Wisconsin Voted, 1848-1960
(Madison, 1962), for county level data for all Presidential,
Gubernatorial, and Senatorial races.

[30]Freidel, Franklin D. Roosevelt, Vol. II, The Ordeal
(Boston, 1954), 88. Freidel has since indicated that he
did not intent to establish a "thesis" but was merely re-
porting the results of a study done at the University of
Illinois by one of his students. Freidel, letter to author,
February 2, 1973.

[31]Lubell, The Future of American Politics (New York,
1952; paperback third edition, 1965), 136. Lubell's chapter
on "The Myth of Isolationism" is most perceptive though he
accepts the general assumption that isolationism is not a
rational precept and that the norm is American involvement
and intervention abroad. Wesley M. Bagby, The Road to
Normalcy: The Presidential Campaign and Election of 1920
(Baltimore, 1962), is of little use in interpreting the
election results. On the effort of affected ethnic groups
to influence the Treaty of Versailles and their subsequent
reactions to the Treaty, Woodrow Wilson, and the Democratic
party see the series of articles on individual groups in
Joseph P. O'Grady, ed., The Immigrant's Influence on Wilson's
Peace Policies (Lexington, Kentucky, 1967). In addition
to his essay on the Italians in this book, John B. Duff
has also authored "The Versailles Treaty and the Irish-

Americans," Journal of American History, LV (December, 1968), 582-598, and "German-Americans and the Peace, 1918-1920," American-Jewish Historical Quarterly, LIX (June, 1970), 424-444. Another article on the Irish is by Kenneth R. Maxwell, "Irish-Americans and the Fight for Treaty Ratification," Public Opinion Quarterly, XXXI (Winter, 1967-1968), 620-641. On the Germans, see also Carl Wittke, "Ohio's German Language Press in the Campaign of 1920," Proceedings of the Mississippi Valley Historical Association, X (1921), 468-480.

[32]Burchell, "Did the Irish and German Voters Desert the Democrats in 1920? A Tentative Statistical Answer," Journal of American Studies, VI (August, 1972), 153-164. The reference is to page 160.

[33]The example given by Burchell for Massachusetts which yields a -.736 coefficient of correlation for Democratic losses and German percentage of the electorate looks impressive until one realizes that the German percentage of the electorate being correlated with the losses varies from 0.2% to 4.0%. The independent variable being tested must range at a far higher level before causality (or lack of causality) can even be implied.

[34]On Berger, see Roderick Nash, "Victor L. Berger: Making Marx Respectable," Wisconsin Magazine of History, XLVII (Summer, 1964), 301-308; Edward J. Muzik, "Victor L. Berger: Congress and the Red Scare," Ibid., 309-318; Sally M. Miller, Victor Berger and the Promise of Constructive

Socialism, 1910-1920 (Westport, Connecticut, 1973); Henry F. Bedford, "A Case Study in Hysteria: Victor L. Berger, 1917-1921," (University of Wisconsin M. A. Thesis, 1953); Max Gordon, "Victor Berger: Socialist Persuader in Congress," (University of Wisconsin M. A. Thesis, 1941).

[35]Frederick Luebke has pointed out that the Social Democratic gains were all in a northern and western direction from Milwaukee, while the southern counties, including heavily German Dodge and Jefferson Counties, did not contribute significantly to the socialist vote. Conversation with Frederick Luebke, Upper Midwest Ethnic Studies Association Meeting, Minnesota, April 6, 1974.

[36]On socialism in Milwaukee, see Marvin Wachman, History of the Social-Democratic Party of Milwaukee, 1897-1910 (Urbana, Illinois, 1945); Henry M. Pelling, "The Rise and Decline of Socialism in Milwaukee," Bulletin of the International Institute of Social History, X (1955), 91-103; Frederick I. Olson, "The Socialist Party and the Union in Milwaukee, 1900-1912," Wisconsin Magazine of History, XLV (Winter, 1960-61), 110-116, "Milwaukee's First Socialist Administration, 1910-1912: A Political Evaluation," Mid-America, XLIII (July, 1961), 197-217, and "The Milwaukee Socialists, 1897-1941," (Harvard University Ph. D. Dissertation, 1952), two vols.; Bayrd Still, Milwaukee: The History of a City (Madison, 1948), 279-320, 515-568; Edward S. Kerstein, Milwaukee's All-American Mayor: Portrait

of Daniel Webster Hoan (Englewood Cliffs, New Jersey, 1966); and Lindsay Hoben, "Dan Hoan, Mayor of Milwaukee," in J. T. Salter, ed., The American Politician (Chapel Hill, North Carolina, 1938), 261-281. On Mayor Hoan's difficulties during the War, see Robert C. Reinders, "Daniel W. Hoan and the Milwaukee Socialist Party During the First World War," Wisconsin Magazine of History, XXXVI (Autumn, 1952), 48-55. See also John M. Work, "The First World War," Ibid., XLI (Autumn, 1957), 32-44, and James Weinstein, "Anti-War Sentiment and the Socialist Party, 1917-1918," Political Science Quarterly, LXXIV (June, 1959), 215-239.

37Olson, "Socialist Party and the Union," 114. See also Olson, "Milwaukee Socialists," 121-126 and Appendix.

38A.William Hoglund, Finnish Immigrants in America, 1880-1920 (Madison, 1960), 104-120; John Kolehmainen and George W. Hill, Haven in the Woods: The Story of the Finns in Wisconsin (Madison, 1951), 118-150.

39Lawrence L. Graves, "Two Noteworthy Wisconsin Women: Mrs. Ben Hooper and Ada James," Wisconsin Magazine of History, XLI (Spring, 1958), 174-180, and James Howell Smith, "Mrs. Ben Hooper of Oshkosh: Peace Worker and Politician," Ibid., XLVI (Winter, 1962-63), 124-135.

40Wisconsin Blue Book, 1923, 500-501, 564-565.

41Ibid.

42On the 1924 election and the Progressive party see James H. Shideler, "The La Follette Progressive Party

Campaign of 1924," Wisconsin Magazine of History, XXXIII (June, 1950), 444-457, and "The Disintegration of the Progressive Party Movement of 1924," Historian, XIII (Spring, 1951), 189-201; Scott D. Johnston, "The Socialists and La Follette Progressivism," Institute of Social Studies Bulletin (Winter, 1952), 87 and 94, and "Wisconsin Socialists and the Conference for Political Progressive Action," Wisconsin Magazine of History, XXXVII (Winter, 1953-54), 96-100; James Weinstein, "Radicalism in the Midst of Normalcy," Journal of American History, LII (March, 1966), 773-790; Kenneth C. MacKay, The Progressive Movement of 1924 (New York, 1947); and David B. Burner, "The Democratic Party in the Election of 1924," Mid-America, XLVI (April, 1964), 92-113.

[43]Hofstadter, The Age of Reform: From Bryan to F. D. R. (New York, 1955; paperback edition, 1960), 283-284.

[44]Havig, "A Disputed Legacy: Roosevelt Progressives and the La Follette Campaign of 1924," Mid-America, LIII (January, 1971), 44-64.

[45]Lubell, Future of American Politics, 142.

CHAPTER VI WISCONSIN VOTES, 1925 TO 1950

Before the Roosevelt revolution, there was an Al Smith revolution, and before the Al Smith revolution there was a La Follette revolution. Or was there? The Roosevelt revolution clearly existed in Wisconsin as elsewhere. F. D. R. swept the state with 63.5% of the vote in 1932, bringing into office with him a Democratic Senator, F. Ryan Duffy, and a Democratic Governor, Albert G. Schmedeman, as well as the first Democratic State Assembly in forty years. Fifty-nine Democrats in the Assembly and eight in the State Senate marked quite an increase from the grand total of three Democrats in the previous legislature.

While F. D. R. managed to gain the same margin in 1936, and to carry the state, though barely, in 1940, the state Democratic party was soon eclipsed, first by the third party Progressives, then by a resurgent Republican party. Ultimately the groundwork laid in the 1930's bore fruit in the founding of the liberal Democratic Organizing Committee in 1948 and in the arrival of Wisconsin at full two-party status in the 1960's just beyond the mid-century endpoint of this study.[1]

Samuel Lubell has best described the make-up of the New Deal coalition as it evolved from 1932 to 1936 with a stress on both its ethnic and its class composition. This study will concentrate on the ethnic side of the Democratic party of F. D. R. as well as on an investigation of its roots in the La Follette movement of 1924 and the Al Smith vote of 1928.

Lubell himself called attention to the importance of the latter in the resurgence of the Democratic party in urban areas among the new immigrants, their wives, and sons and daughters who were coming of age in the late 1920's.[2] Smith's 44.2% of the vote in Wisconsin indicates that he also did well outside the major urban areas of the country.

Four years earlier, the Democratic candidate had received only 8.2% of the vote in the state while La Follette was receiving 54.4% and the state's thirteen electoral votes. Lubell has referred to the third party Progressive movement of 1924 and of the period from 1934 to 1946 in Wisconsin as providing a half-way house for groups in transit between the two major parties. V. O. Key, Duncan Macrae and James Neldrum, and Bruce Stave have also stressed the transitional nature of the La Follette Progressive vote in 1924, Macrae and Neldrum observing as follows:

> Analysis of the 1924 La Follette vote suggests that it came in part from elements of the population that might have voted for Al Smith had he been nominated by the Democrats in the 1924 convention. Contrary to the image some entertain of La Follette--that of an agrarian reformer-- he obtained stronger support in Illinois from urban counties with heavy foreign-born population than from rural counties of native-born population. The La Follette vote was correlated at +.68, for example, with pro-wet sentiment on a 1922 referendum, and +.54 with per cent Catholic.[3]

Key's analysis of the New England vote and Bruce Stave's work on the vote in Pittsburgh led them to make similar conclusions.[4] Richard Hofstadter, on the other hand, concluded that, "Four years later most of La Follette's supporters seem to have voted for Hoover."[5]

Wisconsin, as the home state of La Follette and the only one carried by him in 1924, is obviously not a typical state to study in this connection but it does provide one arena in which the Hofstadter thesis can be tested. The latter downplays the progressive nature of the La Follette campaign and vote, stressing its agrarian protest and anti-war, ethnic backlash elements. In Wisconsin, as Chapter V makes clear, it was precisely the farmers, mainly Scandinavian and Belgian, who made up progressivism's most loyal locus of support in the early 1900's. The same farmers continued to give progressivism support in the 1920's even as it became more radical. La Follette did indeed pull in new ethnic groups in the 1920's--Germans, Swiss, Bohemians, Austrians, and Dutch Catholics--most of whom were attracted by his opposition to the recent war.

However, the latter groups did not vote for the Republican party in 1928 or in 1932. They had been good ethnic Democrats before the war and they returned to the party of their fathers and grandfathers with Al Smith, if they were Catholic ethnics, **or** with F. D. R. if they were Protestant ethnics, until a new war with Germany once again raised issues which invalidated the Democratic party for them.

The prewar Scandinavian supporters of La Follette progressivism, though coming from solidly Republican antecedents, also voted solidly Democratic in 1932. However, as staunch Protestants they found themselves unable to accept Al Smith in 1928. While full verification for this requires the use of minor civil division data, the following correlation matrix based on county level data gives at least a tentative indication of the antecedents of the New Deal vote:

Table I Correlation Matrix: Democratic Vote, 1928 to 1936

	Presidential Elections		
	1928 Dem	1932 Dem	1936 Dem
1900 Gov Dem	.713	.468	.309
1912 Pres Prim: La F.	-.408	-.141	-.089
1922 Sen Prim: La F.	.504	.691	.559
1924 Pres Prog	.137	.558	.286
1924 Pres Dem	.423	.249	-.011
1924 Pres Dem & Prog	.337	.732	.304
1928 Pres Dem	1.000	.720	.615
1932 Pres Dem		1.000	.578

The votes received by Robert La Follette prior to World War I were from voters with Republican antecedents. However, his postwar elections correlate positively with the Al Smith vote and even more so with the vote received by F. D. R. in 1932. In fact, La Follette's vote correlates more closely with the latter than does the vote for John Davis in 1924.

Further verification for this relationship comes in a study of the 105 old progressives for whom Otis Graham was able to establish a position on the New Deal.[6] Investigation of secondary accounts, autobiographies, and the New York Times yielded the following spread for forty-nine of the 105 old progressives on the 1924 presidential race:

Table II Progressives, the 1924 Election, and the New Deal

	1924 Position		
Graham list	La Follette	Davis	Coolidge
More radical than the New Deal	3	0	0
Supporter of the New Deal	11	5	1
Opposed to the New Deal	3	12	14

The surest bridge between progressivism and the New Deal appears to have been support for La Follette and his third party movement in 1924, only three of his supporters opposed the New Deal. Despite the fact that most were staunch Democrats, only five of the seventeen Davis backers could bring themselves to support the New Deal. Predictably only a single Coolidge backer found himself in F. D. R.'s camp.

The Wisconsin vote for T. R. in 1912, discussed in

Chapter V, shows that the same pattern did not emerge after that election. Most of T. R.'s 1912 backers returned to the Republican party and remained there after the folding of that Progressive party. Alan Havig's study of the response of T. R.'s more prominent backers to the La Follette movement in 1924--most saw it as too radical, class-oriented, and pro-labor--bears out this observation.[7]

Table VIII in Appendix D provides the background for a discussion of the response of Wisconsin's ethnic groups to Al Smith in 1928 and to F. D. R. in 1932. The table also helps pin down the final resting place of La Follette's 1924 vote.

The 1924 Democratic plus Progressive vote in Wisconsin comes very close to equalling F. D. R.'s 1932 vote no matter on what level one examines it. On the state level, La Follette's 54.4% plus Davis' 8.2% total 62.6% just under F. D. R.'s 63.5%. At the county level, the combined vote for Davis and La Follette in 1924 came within 7% of F. D. R.'s for all but thirteen of Wisconsin's seventy-one counties. This seems like a bit of a spread until one compares it with the difference between F. D. R.'s 1932 and 1936 votes. In the period between these two elections, despite a state-wide change of only 0.3%, thirty-five of the state's seventy-one counties changed by more than 7% toward or away from F. D. R.

At the minor civil division level, the 1924 combined

vote came within 5% of F. D. R.'s 1932 vote for twenty-one of the state's fifty-three ethnic, size-of-place groupings, and within 10% for an additional twelve. Groupings among which F. D. R. did noticeably better than the 1924 combined vote included all Polish, Irish, Belgian, Dutch Catholic, Austrian, French Canadian, and Welsh; as well as Danish, Bohemian, and German Catholic villages. All other German units changed by less than 10% as did all Yankee, Norwegian, and Swedish units. The state's twenty largest cities jumped 9% and Milwaukee 12%. Correlation analysis adds further verification to the closeness of fit between the two elections: the 1924 combined Progressive and Democratic vote correlates at .732 with F. D. R.'s 1932 vote. For Wisconsin, at any rate, the vote for La Follette in 1924 presaged the greater share of the vote for F. D. R. in 1932.

Al Smith's vote in 1928 also pointed toward a part of F. D. R.'s 1932 vote--the traditional Democratic vote with its primary base in Catholic ethnic groups. The Smith vote, correlates at a level of .720 with the 1932 F. D. R. vote, at .713 with the 1900 Democratic vote for governor, and at a very high .839 with the 1946 parochial school busing referendum. This last vote can be used as a very close approximation of the Catholic-Protestant split for reasons discussed in Chapter III.

Andrew Baggaley also found a close correlation between the votes for Smith and for the parochial school busing referendum in his study of "Religious Influences on Wisconsin Voting, 1928-1960."[8] However, other studies of the 1928 election have downplayed the impact of religion, and have stressed instead the effect of the wet-dry split, foreign-birth, and the rural-urban split. William Ogburn and Neil Talbot, using county level correlation analysis, placed greatest stress on the first factor while downplaying urbanness. Ruth Silva concluded that neither religion nor prohibition were important but rather the fact that Smith was a Democrat. Paul Carter in a 1963 essay also underplayed Smith's Catholicism as a factor in 1928. Gilbert Fite stressed the rural protest component of Smith's vote, a useful addendum to the Lubell stress on the urban vote.[9]

On the other hand, Robert Moats Miller, Kenneth Bailey, and Edmund Moore have all suggested that the issues of foreignness, prohibition, and the city may well have served as code words for the underlying issue of Smith's religion, discussion of which was "limited by a widespread sense of delicacy and shame."[10]

The following table indicates the degree of correlation between the vote for Smith and the other four factors under discussion for Wisconsin's seventy-one counties:

Table III Correlation Matrix: 1928 Vote

	1900 Gov Dem	1928 Gov Dem	1928 Pres Dem
1946 Par. School Ref.	.388	.457	.839
1926 Proh. Ref.	.555	.547	.796
1930 Urban (2,500 +)	.076	.063	.178
1900 Gov. Dem.	1.000	.807	.713
1928 Gov. Dem.		1.000	.810

The 1946 parochial school bus referendum has already been mentioned. The 1926 vote on prohibition was on a proposal to memorialize Congress to amend the Volstead Act to allow for the manufacture and sale of beer. This referendum passed by a vote of 349,443 (66.3%) to 177,602 (33.7%).[12]

Since this table seems to indicate that religion, the wet-dry split, and normal Democratic vote all correlate about equally with the Smith vote, it is necessary to dig deeper to determine the relative importance of each factor. One method of doing this is to use multiple regression analysis.[11] This analysis yields the following results for the Al Smith vote of 1928:

	Beta (Standardized regression coefficient)
1928 Dem. Gov	.493
1946 Par. Sch. Ref.	.490
1926 Proh. Ref.	.170
Multiple coefficient of correlation	.972

Thus it appears that the regular Democratic vote and Catholic proportion of the population contributed about equally to the Smith vote, with the wet-dry split explaining a lesser amount. Urbanness added almost nothing when thrown into the equation. The multiple correlation coefficient of .972 (yielding a coefficient of variance of .945) indicates that almost all of the variation in Smith's vote is explained by these three factors.

The data for this study contained in Table VIII in Appendix D provide an even better testing ground for the various explanations of the Smith vote. In addition to the Presidential election data for 1924, 1928, and 1932, returns for the two referenda are given. Table VIII has been set up with Native-stock and British groups first, followed by Scandinavians, Reformed Dutch and Swiss, and German Lutherans. The German Mixed category forms the midpoint with Catholic groups listed in the second part of the table.

The vote on prohibition in 1926 drew a favorable response from all of the Catholic ethnic groups in addition to German Lutherans, German Mixed, Swiss, and Scandinavian city dwellers. It drew solid opposition from most Native-stock, British, and Dutch Reformed units. Non-urban Scandinavians voted against prohibition with somewhat less unanimity, Finnish rural units even giving it a bare majority.

Comparison of the vote for Al Smith in 1928 with support for the prohibition referendum indicates some correlation with some major discrepancies--German Lutheran units most noticeably favoring prohibition but not the Governor from New York. The much larger yes vote on prohibition--twenty percentage points above the Smith vote--gives further emphasis to the lack of a one-to-one relationship between the two votes.

However, comparison of Al Smith's vote with the 1946 parochial school busing referendum yields a much closer connection, suggesting beyond any question the religious nature of the vote in 1928. Almost no Yankee, British, Dutch Reformed, or Scandinavian unit topped 30% in its vote for Smith, or in its vote for parochial school busing in 1946. German Lutherans barely topped the 30% figure in 1928--a vote probably reflecting in part the presence of German Catholic and other Catholic minorities within the boundaries of the units labeled German Lutheran. Only the Swiss Reformed units among Protestants gave votes of more than 50% for Smith. The German Mixed units, so categorized because they fall near the center of a Protestant-Catholic continuum, also fell near the 50% mark in their vote for Smith.

Turning to the Catholic groups, a reversal of this pattern takes place. Almost no Catholic group failed to vote for Al Smith by less than 70%. The exceptions to this rule were the Italian units. Conclusions based on the

two Italian townships and a single Milwaukee ward must be
very tenuous because of the small size of the sample and
the presence of large non-Italian minorities in all three.
Two new entrants in the ranks of the Democracy offer the
strongest proof of close correspondence between Al Smith's
vote and a Catholic constituency. Belgians and French
Canadians cast solid Democratic votes for the first time,
though the same units had given Wilson bare majorities in
1916. Thus the top fourteen Democratic ethnic, size-of-
place groupings in 1928, by median votes ranging from 73%
to 96%, were all Catholic; the sixteen least Democratic
groupings, by median votes ranging from 5% to 26%, were all
staunchly Protestant, as Table IV on the next page indicates.

Included in the latter set were the Yankee and Danish
city wards. Norwegian and Swedish city wards were not far
behind at 32% and 33% respectively. On the other hand,
the fifteen top Democratic groupings include eight rural
and five village groups. Milwaukee cast a 50% vote for Al
Smith while its ten German wards averaged only 54% Democratic. The next twenty cities in Wisconsin voted for Smith
at the state level of 44%.

A study by Thomas Schlereth of efforts on the part
of Wisconsin progressive leaders, including Senator John
Blaine, to gain support for Smith from progressive Republican voters indicates the problem the religious issue
posed. Herman Sachtjen who handled the correspondence for

Table IV 1928 Presidential Vote

	1928 Dem	1946 ParSch	1926 Proh	1932 Dem	1900 Dem
Top Fourteen					
Dutch Catholic village	96%	94%	94%	94%	72%
Dutch Catholic rural	92%	94%	81%	86%	91%
Polish rural	92%	78%	93%	97%	74%
Austrian rural	89%	94%	82%	93%	75%
Polish city wards	86%	96%	92%	91%	77%
Milwaukee Polish wards	81%	71%	93%	92%	70%
Belgian rural	81%	79%	90%	94%	15%
Irish rural	80%	79%	75%	90%	68%
Bohemian villages	78%	89%	86%	84%	--
French Canadian villages	78%	80%	88%	81%	65%
German Catholic rural	76%	80%	85%	92%	67%
Bohemian rural	75%	68%	80%	90%	55%
Polish villages	75%	77%	84%	89%	--
German Catholic villages	73%	76%	86%	85%	58%
Wisconsin*	45.3%	44.5%	66.3%	67.0%	37.8%
German Lutherans					
Villages	38%	22%	74%	67%	50%
Rural	37%	23%	80%	83%	42%
Cities	31%	29%	52%	54%	38%
Lowest Sixteen					
Native-stock ward	26%	31%	46%	28%	20%
Danish wards	26%	28%	62%	52%	18%
Danish villages	26%	38%	40%	70%	--
Norwegian villages	25%	9%	40%	51%	14%
English rural	25%	35%	62%	67%	21%
Native-stock villages	24%	20%	33%	52%	20%
Native-stock cities	24%	26%	34%	38%	29%
English villages	22%	26%	32%	43%	21%
Danish city	22%	17%	36%	46%	17%
Norwegian rural	22%	9%	47%	71%	11%
Norwegian city	21%	13%	41%	53%	14%
Swedish rural	21%	14%	42%	57%	16%
Native-stock rural	20%	21%	29%	67%	26%
Welsh villages	17%	10%	27%	35%	23%
Dutch Reformed rural	16%	14%	26%	35%	26%
Dutch Reformed villages	5%	8%	26%	27%	7%

*Percent of two-party vote

the Progressive Democratic Alliance later reported that:

> in the last two weeks the religious angle absolutely swept every thing overboard--we couldn't stop it. Out of every five letters that came in from Progressives, four of them would be on account of religion, that they would not submit to the Pope, and the fifth would be on the wet question.[13]

The conclusion is inescapable: the Al Smith vote, in Wisconsin at least, was not tied to urbanness, nor was it tied directly to the prohibition issue. It was in fact a Catholic vote, and by the same token--or rather its obverse, the Herbert Hoover vote was a Protestant one. While it is true that all of the Catholic groupings which voted for Smith had also cast large yes votes on the prohibition issue two years earlier, the behavior of the German Lutherans, the most numerous single group in the state, underscores the ethnic content of the prohibition vote and the religious content of the Smith vote. The urban and wet votes received by Smith were also Catholic votes. Urban and wet Protestant votes, both present, though in smaller numbers, went to Herbert Hoover and the Republican party in 1928.

In all fairness, it should be pointed out that this does not mark that great a change from the 1900 Democratic vote.* In that year thirteen of the top fifteen Democratic groupings were Catholic, fourteen of the top

---

*See Table XIV in this Chapter for the 1900 vote.

fifteen Republican units were Protestant. American political parties did not become ethnic in 1928, they had always been so except in the South where they were racial. However, the Al Smith-Herbert Hoover contest exacerbated the ethnic tensions already present in American politics. It remained for the pressures of depression and New Deal to displace, for a brief period at least, the ethnic pressures with economic concerns.

Franklin D. Roosevelt's victory in 1932 with 57.3% of the vote nationally and 63.5% of the vote in Wisconsin would appear at first glance to pose problems of analysis by its very magnitude. F. D. R.'s Wisconsin vote was almost 20% higher than Al Smith's 44.2%, the Democratic high point in Wisconsin in the Twentieth Century to that time. The Democratic party showed gains in all ethnic, size-of-place groupings with only a very few falling below 50% in the 1932 landslide. Nevertheless, there is enough variation in the vote to allow for verification of the members of the New Deal coalition as outlined by Samuel Lubell in The Future of American Politics.

First and most prominent were the urban ethnic groups. Milwaukee voted 78% Democratic in 1932, the five Polish wards casting 92% of their vote for F. D. R., the ten German wards equalling the citywide vote. The next twenty cities, ranging in size from 10,622 to 67,542 in the 1930 census, cast a median vote of 62%, just under that of the state as a whole with a variation from Beloit's 36% to Wauwautosa's 76%. This difference is a good indicator that size-of-place analysis by itself is not sufficient to pinpoint New Deal support.

In fact, the strongest support for the New Deal came from farmers, with all rural groupings except for the Swedes and Dutch Reformed topping the state average as Table V shows:

Table V Rural Democratic Vote, 1932

	N=	Median		N=	Median
Polish	12	97%	Italian	2	76%
Belgian	7	94%	Norwegian	35	71%
Austrian	1	93%	Danish	8	71%
German Catholic	30	92%	Welsh	2	69%
Bohemian	11	90%	Yankee	22	67%
Irish	9	90%	English	3	67%
Swiss Reformed	3	87%	Finnish	12	64%
Dutch Catholic	1	86%	Swedish	14	57%
French Canadian	2	84%	Dutch Reformed	2	35%
German Mixed	50	84%			
German Lutheran	85	83%			

This pattern does not appear to be greatly affected by the economic status of the farmer. The average value per farm for each township in the state was ascertained by use of the 1935 census of agriculture.[14] Finding the median for the smaller ethnic groups and using these data to separate out the wealthiest and poorest sets of townships for each of the larger groups yields Table VI on the next page. In almost every case, the wealthy group of townships voted _more_ Democratic than the poor units of the same nationality, not only in 1932 but also in 1928 and 1936. The only exceptions to this overwhelming pattern were the Yankee units in 1932. The wealthiest rural ethnic group was the Swiss--they were also among the top Democratic groups, leading the field in 1936. The poorest rural groups were the Swedes and Finns, who were also among the most Republican groupings in 1932, exceeded only by the Dutch Reformed.

While one cannot conclude from these data that the New Deal coalition was one of wealth as opposed to a tendency on the part of the poor to support the Republican party, one can relegate the economic factor to second place behind ethnicity even in the New Deal period, at least for Wisconsin farmers. The generally strong showing made by F. D. R. among farmers is, of course, undoubtedly related to their response to an unfavorable economic situation for agriculture.

However, the greater salience of ethnicity over economic considerations shown here for rural voters also appears in a study of Philadelphia politics from 1928 to 1940.

Table VI Rural Voting, by Wealth and Ethnic Group, 1928 to 1936

	N=	Ave value per farm	1928 Dem	1932 Dem	1936 Dem
Swiss	3	$11,205	57%	87%	83%
German Lutheran Wealthy	12	$10,502	46%	87%	72%
German Catholic Wealthy	12	$9,788	78%	92%	76%
German Mixed Wealthy	13	$8,432	58%	86%	69%
Norwegian Wealthy	6	$7,916	30%	75%	75%
Dutch Reformed	3	$7,337	16%	35%	36%
Irish	9	$7,002	80%	90%	67%
Belgian	7	$6,913	81%	94%	82%
Bohemian	11	$6,800	75%	90%	75%
Yankee Wealthy	8	$6,284	28%	67%	49%
German Catholic Poor	6	$5,593	75%	89%	67%
Danish	8	$5,228	28%	71%	63%
German Lutheran Poor	12	$4,590	36%	77%	54%
Norwegian Poor	9	$4,324	17%	71%	68%
Polish	12	$4,271	92%	97%	90%
German Mixed Poor	12	$3,851	48%	87%	66%
Yankee Poor	8	$3,568	18%	72%	48%
Swedish	14	$3,325	21%	56%	60%
Finnish	12	$2,123	28%	64%	80%

Most important are the conclusions reached on the 1936 election in Philadelphia:

> The most striking feature of the 1936 presidential vote is that in an election when the New Deal coalition, a voting combination supposedly forged from economic considerations, reached its zenith, ethnic voting patterns appeared so prominently. . . . Rather than diminishing in the 1930s, ethno-religious political consciousness flourished.[15]

These data bring to the fore the problem of the ecological fallacy in using county level data.[16] In a pathbreaking study on Wisconsin politics in the depression years, Harold Gosnell and Morris Cohen concluded that "no tendency was visible for the farmers in the areas of lowest income to give their vote to Roosevelt while those in the areas of highest farm income voted for Hoover."[17] County level data may lead to this conclusion; township level data reveals the second part of it to be false. Gosnell and Cohen further concluded that F. D. R. did better in urban, industrialized areas than in rural areas--Table IX in Appendix D makes clear that this conclusion is inaccurate when one controls for ethnicity.

Above and beyond the Milwaukee and farm vote, the following groups emerge as supporters of the New Deal by more than the statewide vote of 63.5%:

Table VII   Other Strong Democratic Areas, 1932

	N=	Median
Dutch Catholic village	1	94%
Other Polish wards	2	91%
Polish villages	2	89%
German Catholic villages	19	85%
Bohemian villages	2	84%
French Canadian villages	2	81%
Swiss villages	2	78%
(Milwaukee city)		78%
German Catholic cities	4	76%
(Wauwautosa city)		76%
(Sheboygan city)		73%
German Mixed villages	39	72%
German Mixed cities	15	71%
Other German wards	26	71%
(Manitowoc and Stevens Point cities)		71%
Danish villages	3	70%
(Green Bay city)		70%
French Canadian ward	1	69%
Italian ward	1	69%
German Lutheran villages	28	67%
(Kenosha city)		67%
Swedish city	1	66%
(Racine city)		65%
German cities over 10,000	5	63%

The surprising disclosure in this table is the fact
that most of the non-rural groupings over 63% are villages
and cities under 2,500. With only minor exceptions, the
continuum from rural township to cities over 10,000 is
also the continuum from Democratic to Republican. Urban
groups totally absent from this Democratic chart include
Yankees, English, Welsh, Norwegians, and, the most Republican ethnic group of all, the Dutch Reformed.

Among the state's twenty largest cities after Milwaukee,
only seven make the list. This set of seven, however, includes the major industrial cities of the state and the
cities with the largest concentrations of Democratic ethnic
groups.

The year 1936 marks the high point of the New Deal
nationally; for Wisconsin, Roosevelt's vote in that year
shows only a slight increase to 63.8%. This appearance
of little change masks a goodly degree of shifting around
as can be seen from Table VIII on the next page and Table
IX in Appendix D.

While holding his own in Milwaukee and making slight
gains in the twenty largest cities in the state, including
gains among all city ward groupings except for the Milwaukee
Polish wards and non-Milwaukee German wards, Roosevelt
lost ground in almost all rural areas (except for Finns,
Swedes, and Dutch Reformed) and enjoyed a mixed pattern

Table VIII F. D. R. Vote Changes 1932 to 1940

	N=	1932/1936	1936/1940	1932/1940
Greatest Gains, 1932 to 1936				
Finnish rural	12	16%	- 8%	8%
Norwegian wards	4	15%	- 2%	13%
French Canadian ward	1	14%	- 3%	11%
Norwegian city	1	12%	0%	12%
Danish wards	4	10%	- 8%	2%
Swedish ward	1	9%	- 6%	3%
Swedish city	1	7%	-18%	-11%
Native-stock ward	1	5%	- 5%	0%
Swedish villages	5	5%	- 9%	- 4%
Norwegian villages	19	4%	- 5%	- 1%
Swedish rural	14	3%	-14%	-11%
German large cities	5	2%	- 9%	- 7%
Welsh villages	2	2%	-12%	-10%
Italian ward	1	2%	-18%	-16%
Dutch Reformed rural	3	1%	-15%	-14%
Polish wards	2	0%	- 3%	- 3%
Milwaukee German wards	10	0%	-18%	-18%
Twenty Largest Cities		3%	-11%	- 8%
Wisconsin		0.3%	-13.7%	-13.4%
Milwaukee		0%	-14%	-14%
Greatest Losses, 1932 to 1940				
Swiss Reformed rural	3	- 4%	-26%	-30%
German Mixed cities	15	-12%	-18%	-30%
German Mixed villages	39	- 8%	-24%	-32%
Danish villages	3	-22%	-11%	-33%
Native-stock rural	22	-20%	-14%	-34%
Bohemian rural	11	-15%	-19%	-34%
Italian village	1	--	-37%	-37%
French Canadian rural	2	-37%	- 2%	-39%
German Catholic villages	19	-18%	-21%	-39%
Irish rural	9	-23%	-18%	-41%
Italian rural	2	-20%	-26%	-46%
French Canadian villages	2	-38%	- 9%	-47%
Belgian rural	7	-12%	-38%	-50%
German Mixed rural	50	-16%	-36%	-52%
German Catholic rural	30	-20%	-33%	-53%
Austrian rural	1	-17%	-38%	-55%
German Lutheran rural	85	-17%	-40%	-57%

of success in villages and ethnic cities. Perhaps this
mixed pattern accounts for the county level correlation
of only .578 between the 1932 and 1936 elections.

Parenthetically, it should be pointed out that
although the medians for this part of the study are calculated for only the two major parties, with the exception of the 1936 Union party vote, addition of the various
socialist and communist parties makes little difference.
The greatest difference comes with the Finnish areas
where eight of the twelve townships topped 5% in their
Socialist vote in 1932; none topped 1% in 1936; and five
topped 5% in support of the Communist party in 1940. Including these votes changes F. D. R.'s 1932 and 1936 Finnish
medians from 64% and 80% respectively to 59% and 80%.

Compare these gains, primarily in Scandinavian urban
areas, with F. D. R.'s areas of greatest decline. Roosevelt's most severe losses, all over 15%, came in French
Canadian, Dutch Catholic, German Catholic, and Bohemian
rural areas and villages as well as in Irish, Italian,
Yankee, German Lutheran, German Mixed, and Austrian rural
areas. The two Danish villages also made this list, the
only Scandinavian entrant on it.

Two types of losses appear most clearly here; most
non-Scandinavian rural areas declined in their vote for
F. D. R. by margins of from 12% to 37%. And disaffection
from F. D. R. on the part of German-Americans is already

beginning to appear as the U. S. moves toward a second war
with Germany. Of the groups which moved furthest from the
Democratic party between 1912 and 1920, only the Swiss are
absent from this list.

Gosnell and Cohen stressed the losses for F. D. R. in
rural areas and his gains in urban areas, and this time
their conclusions are borne out by minor civil division
analysis even after factoring out ethnic differences. However, they missed the impact of the approaching conflict
with Germany, no doubt in part because they were writing
in 1940, prior to the actual start of the war.

Among only a few of the smaller groupings--French
Canadians, Irish, Dutch Catholics, and Bohemian villagers--
in addition to German Catholics did William Lemke's third
party effort make any headway. For no other ethnic, size-
of-place grouping did the Union party top 5% of the vote.
Perhaps, in Wisconsin at any rate, the Lemke vote might
more accurately be labeled the Coughlin vote. Lubell also
calls attention to the German and Irish Catholic nature
of the Union party vote.[18]

Most of the Democratic losses in 1936 were in fact
tapped by the Republican party in a role that becomes even
clearer in 1940. In the latter year, F. D. R. suffered
a precipitous decline in Wisconsin, sliding 13.7% to a
bare majority of 50.1%. That the make-up of his vote was

-319-

also undergoing significant changes, becomes clear in looking at the minimal correlation this election had with the 1932 Democratic vote, a mere .129. The fact that the vote correlates at .753 with 1936 suggests that the same groups which had begun to move away from F. D. R. between 1932 and 1936 were largely responsible for his losses between 1936 and 1940. A look at Table VIII bears out this judgment. Losses of over 50% between 1932 and 1940 occur in all German rural groups and in the lone Austrian township. The 40% to 50% set of losses includes the smaller Belgian, Irish, and Italian rural groups, as well as the two French Canadian villages. The next set, with losses ranging from 30% to 40%, adds to the list German villages, Bohemian, Yankee, Swiss, and French Canadian rural areas, and Italian and Danish villages.

Germanic groupings, both rural and village, and rural areas in general seem to be the most disaffected from Roosevelt and his policies as the U. S. draws ever nearer to war with Germany. Even Scandinavian areas were unhappy with F. D. R. with the exception of the Finns where F. D. R. retained half of his 1936 gains. The President also held his own among most Polish groups and in Yankee, Scandinavian, and French Canadian wards, as well as in Norwegian villages and cities.

Again correlation analysis using county level data bears out the minor civil division results:

Table IX Correlation Matrix: 1928 to 1940 Elections

	Foreign Stock in 1930 Federal Census	
	German %	Scandinavian %
1928 Democratic %	.330	-.510
1932 Democratic %	.356	-.405
1936 Democratic %	.064	-.017
1940 Democratic %	-.424	.341
1932 to 1940 Democratic loss	.561	-.529

A comparison of this table to Table IX in Chapter V yields astonishing results--the responses to the two world wars were strikingly similar not only for Germans but also for Scandinavians. Again Germanic groups moved away from the Democratic party which appeared to be responsible for an increasingly hard line toward Germany. Lubell, though correct in stressing ethnicity, overdoes the contrast with World War I:

> Contrast the drastically altered ethnic lineup in 1940. Some lingerings of pro-German and anti-British feelings showed up in Swedish and Irish sections. Many Italo-Americans resented Roosevelt's criticism of Mussolini's attack upon France. But in the main the German-Americans were left as the hard isolationist core. Offsetting their influence was the strength Roosevelt drew from voters of Polish, Norwegian, and Jewish extraction because of Hitler's anti-semitism and his invasion of Poland and Norway.[19]

Those historians and political scientists who try to explain away the ethnic factor as the main basis for isolationism find little support for their position in the Wisconsin data.[20]

One major area of difference between the impact of World War I and World War II lies in their varying effect on progressivism in Wisconsin. The First World War greatly increased the support given La Follette and his cohorts by Germanic groups; the Second World War did not have the same effect.

The Wisconsin Progressive party was born out of the necessities of the depression and the rise of the Democratic party to a position of power in the 1932 election. Both Governor Phil La Follette and Senator John Blaine were defeated in the primary elections of that year by conservative Republicans Walter J. Kohler and John B. Chapple.[21] In the general elections, with the open support of Blaine and Senator Robert La Follette Jr., Democrats captured the Governorship, Senate seat, half the Congressional delegation, and control of the State Assembly.

Determined to retain Bob Jr.'s Senate seat and to return Phil to the Governor's chair, the La Follettes left the Republican party to form a separate Progressive party, taking with them such loyal longtime progressives as Herman Ekern and William Evjue, as well as most of the progressive constituency of the 1920's.[22] The correlation matrix on the next page illustrates this quite well.

The 1934 Progressive votes for Phil and Bob La Follette correlate at .664 and .708 respectively with the senior La Follette's 1924 Presidential vote. This continuity is

Table X Correlation Matrix, Progressive Vote,
1934 to 1946

	1934 Gov Phil LaF.	1934 Sen Bob LaF.	1938 Gov Phil LaF.	1940 Sen Bob LaF.	1946 Sen Rep Prim Bob LaF.
1912 Pres Prim Bob LaF. Sr.	.404	.418	.361	.377	.174
1916 Sen Prim Rep Bob LaF. Sr.	.423	.417	.488	.477	.424
1922 Sen Prim Rep Bob LaF. Sr.	.465	.523	.226	.362	.231
1924 Presidential Bob LaF. Sr.	.664	.708	.189	.385	.204
1932 Presidential Roosevelt	.194	.258	-.129	.019	-.168
1936 Presidential Roosevelt	.178	.248	.285	.358	.085
1936 Presidential Lemke	.126	.131	-.092	-.018	.061
1940 Presidential Roosevelt	.182	.192	.593	.595	.324
1934 Governor Phil LaF.	1.000	.959	.633	.699	.550
1934 Senator Bob LaF. Jr.		1.000	.564	.675	.491
1938 Governor Phil LaF.			1.000	.856	.721
1940 Senator Bob LaF. Jr.				1.000	.716
1946 Sen Prim Rep Bob LaF. Jr.					1.000

interesting in light of the fact that the Progressive party of the 1930's had a strong liberal, almost radical, ideological bent to it. While the personal appeal of the La Follette name was no doubt a major factor in the Progressive party's success, it was also dependent in part on a left-leaning vote mobilized by the Farmer-Labor Political Federation. Among the Federation's constituent elements were the Milwaukee based Socialists, the Wisconsin labor union movement including the American Federation of Labor and the Railroad Brotherhoods, and farm groups such as the Farm Holiday Association and Farmers Equity Union.[23]

The La Follettes frequently found themselves opposing specific New Deal measures for being too pro-business. At the same time they usually enjoyed Roosevelt's support over the conservative, anti-New Deal candidates so often fielded by the Wisconsin Democratic party.[24] Despite this cozy relationship, the votes received by the La Follettes in 1934 do not correlate well with either F. D. R.'s 1932 vote or his vote in 1936.

Surprisingly, as the La Follettes moved into open opposition to F. D. R. in 1938 with the formation of the National Progressive party[25] and with their refrain of criticism aimed at the movement of the U. S. toward a second war with Germany,[26] their constituency converged with his. The coefficient of correlation of the 1938 Phil

La Follette vote with F. D. R.'s 1940 vote was .593; running in the latter year, Bob Jr.'s vote correlated at .595 with that of Roosevelt.

This correlation reflects the fact that the ethnic isolationist segment of the progressive vote picked up in the 1920's did not stick with the Progressive party as war approached but turned instead to the more congenial blend of conservatism and isolationism found in the Wisconsin Republican party, safely regular after 1934. Table XI on the next page gives the ethnic, size-of-place breakdown for the three Senate races involving Robert La Follette, Jr.--the 1934 and 1940 general elections, and the 1946 Senate Republican primary in which La Follette was defeated by "Tailgunner Joe" McCarthy.

La Follette's greatest support in 1934 came from Scandinavian, Belgian, and Germanic rural areas. Norwegian, Swedish, and Swiss villages and cities also gave him strong support. Even Polish townships and villages turned in majority votes for the Progressives in that year. Opposition was strongest among Native-stock, English, Welsh, and Dutch Reformed voters. However, by 1940 La Follette's vote had declined among almost all groups but especially among rural groups, with Germanic groups leading the way. La Follette's greatest gains came in urban areas--especially in Milwaukee. Norwegians and Swiss across the board, along with rural Danes and Finns remained most strongly attached

Table XI Robert La Follette Jr. Vote, 1934 to 1946

	1934 Sen	1940 Sen	1946 Sen Prim	Average
Most favorable				
Norwegian rural	79%	63%	69%	70%
Finnish rural	71%	64%	71%	69%
Swiss Reformed rural	69%	59%	72%	67%
Norwegian city	66%	66%	68%	67%
French Canadian ward	60%	74%	67%	67%
Danish rural	72%	62%	61%	65%
Swiss Reformed villages	66%	57%	68%	64%
French Canadian rural	60%	53%	68%	60%
Norwegian wards	57%	60%	59%	59%
Norwegian villages	58%	55%	61%	58%
Swedish rural	67%	50%	54%	57%
Germanic groups				
Lutheran rural	68%	42%	58%	56%
Catholic rural	64%	43%	54%	54%
Milwaukee wards	49%	55%	46%	50%
Other city wards	52%	43%	53%	49%
Catholic cities	48%	50%	50%	49%
Catholic villages	54%	38%	45%	46%
Lutheran villages	50%	35%	51%	45%
Cities over 10,000	47%	38%	46%	44%
Lutheran cities	42%	31%	44%	39%
Least favorable				
Austrian rural	27%	43%	54%	41%
English villages	43%	33%	46%	41%
Native-stock villages	41%	34%	44%	40%
French Canadian villages	45%	30%	42%	39%
Dutch Reformed rural	37%	25%	52%	38%
Bohemian villages	42%	31%	39%	37%
Welsh villages	27%	29%	49%	35%
English rural	30%	33%	36%	33%
Dutch Reformed villages	32%	19%	44%	32%
Native-stock cities	25%	22%	40%	29%
Native-stock ward	17%	14%	35%	22%
Wisconsin	50.4%	45.3%	49.3%	48.3%

to his cause as World War II approached.

The movement toward war affected not only La Follette Jr. but also the Progressive party as a whole.[27] In 1938 Phil La Follette was defeated by the conservative, if congenial, Republican business man, Julius Heil, and Republicans recaptured control of the state legislature from the Progressives. Robert La Follette narrowly managed to win reelection in 1940 with 45% of the vote, and Orland Loomis gained the Governorship for the Progressives in 1942, only to die before taking office.

One factor contributing to this decline was the movement into the Democratic party of many third party progressives as the former liberalized under the impact of the New Deal and involvement in World War II. Evjue, Ekern, and other old-time progressives moved closer to the Democratic party because of their support of the Allied cause. Even the *Progressive Magazine*, the successor to *La Follette's Weekly*, broke with Bob La Follette Jr. over the war issue.[28]

Retention of the third party label became an issue as early as 1940, accompanied by a debate over which of the two parties to join.[29] Finally, in 1946, faced by a strong reelection fight in a Republican year, Bob La Follette decided the issue in favor of rejoining the Republican party. His rationale for doing so, while subject to the charge of being just that, illustrated well the condition of the Wisconsin Democratic party for most of the first half of the Twentieth

Century:

> What of the Democratic party in Wisconsin? I
> am well aware that it numbers able, sincere
> liberals in its ranks. But these liberals are
> not the Democratic party of Wisconsin. The
> Democratic party of this state is a machine-
> minded organization without principle or pro-
> gram. Look at its record in the state legis-
> lature. Most of its state senators and
> assemblymen have lined up time and time again
> with the reactionary Republicans in opposing
> Governor Goodland, just as they lined up time
> and time again with reactionary Republicans in
> opposing the liberal program of Progressive
> governors.30

This speech, given to a special convention of the Progressive party held in Portage in 1946, sealed the fate of the party. The motion to disband and to rejoin the Republican party received 286 votes--the most important one being that cast by Robert La Follette. Seventy-seven votes were cast for retaining the Progressive label and forty-seven, including most labor delegates, for joining the Democratic party.31

Leon Epstein suggests that La Follette carried with him back into the Republican ranks the older Progressive leaders, county and legislative office-holders, rural and small town progressives, and isolationist progressives, while younger leaders such as Gaylord Nelson and John W. Reynolds Jr., as well as urban and labor-oriented progressives, were joining the ranks of the Democratic party.32 Another study, based on extensive interviews of former Progressive party members, concluded that "the isolationist-internationalist schism was the best test of which became

Democrats."33 Determining this matter is a task for more
detailed elite analysis. In terms of voting behavior,
the correlation analysis indicates a much closer tie of
former Progressives from throughout the state, not just
urban areas, with the Democratic party.

Most of La Follette's former supporters, whatever
their ultimate destination, appear to have voted in the
Republican primary of 1946. However, they were too few
to bring him victory in a close race with McCarthy:

Table XII 1946 Senatorial Primary34

	State results		Milwaukee County
Republicans			
Robert M. La Follette	202,557	(46.0%)	38,437
Joseph P. McCarthy	207,935	(47.2%)	48,596
Perry J. Stearns	29,605	(6.7%)	10,497
Total Republican vote	440,097		
Democrats			
Harold J. McMurray	62,351	12.3%	31,816
Socialists	3,673	0.7%	
Total Primary Vote	506,131		

One area where La Follette did not do as well as usual was
Milwaukee County in which the sole Democratic entrant,
Howard J. McMurray, received over half his total vote,
31,816, while La Follette was losing to Joe McCarthy on the

Republican side of the ballot, 48,596 to 38,437, with Perry Stearns the third GOP entrant drawing 10,497 votes. McMurray also carried Kenosha County and did well in Brown (including the city of Green Bay), Racine, and Sheboygan Counties. The birth of the liberal Democratic party in Wisconsin in the late 1940's was at the expense of La Follette's Senate seat. In his previous race in 1940, Young Bob had carried Milwaukee, Racine, and Kenosha Counties by healthy margins. La Follette retained the support of the Norwegians, Swedes, Finns, Swiss, and rural Danes while regaining solid support from rural Germans. His loss of most urban German areas, urban Danes, all Yankee and English groups, and especially the city of Milwaukee, sealed his fate.[35]

The defeat of Robert La Follette Jr. may have marked the end of a forty-six year period in Wisconsin politics dominated by the La Follette name,[36] but it did not mark the end of politics for the state. F. D. R. had lost the state by less than 2% of the vote in 1944; in 1948 Harry Truman carried the state by 4.4% The latter year also marked the emergence of another third party bearing the Progressive label. However, the Wallace effort received only minimal support in Wisconsin--25,282 (2.0%) out of a total state presidential vote of 1,276,800.

The year 1950 marks an appropriate endpoint for this

study. Two years later the Eisenhower landslide and the emergence of Senator Joseph McCarthy as a controversial figure would distort voting patterns in the state. In 1950, Republican Walter Kohler Jr., son of the governor elected in 1928, defeated Democrat Carl Thompson by a vote of 605,649 (53.6%) to 525,319 (46.4%). The return of the state to two-party politics had also been marked by greater partisan cohesion as the following correlation matrix indicates:

Table XIII   Correlation Matrix: Postwar Democratic Votes

	1944 FDR	1948 Truman	1950 Gov Thompson
1900 Gov Dem	-.169	-.149	-.142
1928 Pres Dem	.135	.045	.045
1932 Pres Dem	.008	.047	.018
1936 Pres Dem	.604	.468	.485
1940 Pres Dem	.956	.793	.795
1924 Pres Prog	-.129	.046	.025
1934 Sen Prog	.124	.317	.329
1940 Sen Prog	.598	.716	.750
1946 Sen Prim LaF	.381	.577	.557
1944 Pres Dem	1.000	.851	.836
1948 Pres Dem		1.000	.928
1950 Gov Dem			1.000

Several impressions emerge from this table. The Democratic party of the postwar period is not the Democratic party of the beginning of the century nor even that of Al Smith and the early F. D. R. The first significant correlation for the postwar Democratic races is with the 1936 vote for Roosevelt. The movement of German voters out of the Democratic party which had begun in that year has already been discussed. The breakdown by ethnic groups contained in Table XIV on the next two pages indicates that this time the desertion of the party of their forebears was not reversed by postwar events.

The mid-thirties also marks the point at which the vote for the Progressive party begins to correlate significantly with the Democratic party of that time and, even more closely, with the postwar Democratic party. Robert La Follette Jr. may have returned to the Republican party in 1946; his supporters did not, other than to vote for him in the primary of that year.

Table XIV, in addition to indicating the variation between ethnic groups in four elections, bears out the conclusion that the period from 1932 to 1940 marked a realigning phase in Wisconsin politics which makes the realignment of the 1890's seem almost miniscule by comparison.[37] Although less significant than at the beginning of the Twentieth Century, ethnicity still played a major role in sorting out groups between the two major parties. A table, similar to that drawn for 1900 in Chapter IV, would yield

Table XIV A Half Century of Wisconsin Voting

	1900 Gov Dem Median	1932 Pres Dem Median	1940 Pres Dem Median	1950 Gov Dem Median	1950 N=
Native Stock					
Rural	26%	67%	33%	35%	20
Urban to 2,500	20%	52%	30%	37%	20
2,500-10,000	29%	38%	32%	29%	2
City ward	20%	28%	28%	26%	1
English					
Rural	21%	67%	38%	33%	2
Urban to 2,500	21%	43%	33%	36%	2
Welsh					
Rural	20%	69%	41%	41%	2
Urban to 2,500	23%	35%	35%	27%	2
Norwegian					
Rural	11%	71%	56%	58%	33
Urban to 2,500	14%	51%	50%	53%	19
2,500-10,000	14%	53%	57%	74%	1
City ward	30%	51%	64%	56%	1
Swedish					
Rural	16%	57%	46%	46%	13
Urban to 2,500	16%	46%	42%	37%	5
2,500-10,000	39%	66%	55%	51%	1
City ward	24%	52%	55%	45%	1
Danish					
Rural	31%	71%	49%	47%	8
Urban to 2,500		70%	37%	33%	3
2,500-10,000	17%	46%	38%	27%	1
City wards	18%	52%	53%	46%	4
Finnish					
Rural	10%	64%	72%	60%	9
Dutch Reformed					
Rural	26%	35%	21%	11%	2
Urban to 2,500	7%	27%	20%	17%	2
Belgian					
Rural	15%	94%	44%	35%	5
Italian					
Rural	47%	76%	30%	47%	2
Urban to 2,500			37%	50%	1
City ward	68%	69%	53%	47%	1
French Canadian					
Rural	31%	84%	45%	36%	2
Urban to 2,500	65%	81%	34%	48%	2
City ward	42%	69%	80%	64%	1

Table XIV A Half Century of Wisconsin Voting

	1900 Gov Dem Median	1932 Pres Dem Median	1940 Pres Dem Median	1950 Gov Dem Median	1950 N=
Swiss Reformed					
Rural	54%	87%	57%	48%	3
Urban to 2,500	25%	78%	51%	47%	2
2,500-10,000	40%	58%	40%	30%	1
German Lutheran					
Rural	42%	83%	26%	26%	68
Urban to 2,500	50%	67%	30%	27%	26
2,500-10,000	38%	54%	33%	38%	3
German Mixed					
Rural	49%	84%	32%	26%	36
Urban to 2,500	48%	72%	40%	35%	38
2,500-10,000	50%	71%	41%	37%	15
over 10,000	46%	63%	49%	46%	5
City wards	48%	71%	56%	52%	23
Milwaukee wards	35%	78%	60%	56%	10
German Catholic					
Rural	67%	92%	39%	37%	22
Urban to 2,500	58%	85%	46%	48%	19
2,500-10,000	62%	76%	61%	50%	4
Bohemians					
Rural	55%	90%	56%	46%	10
Urban to 2,500		84%	62%	44%	2
Irish					
Rural	68%	90%	49%	52%	9
Polish					
Rural	74%	97%	88%	74%	11
Urban to 2,500		89%	67%	55%	2
City wards	77%	91%	88%	73%	3
Milwaukee wards	70%	92%	84%	71%	5
Austrian					
Rural	75%	93%	38%	56%	1
Dutch Catholic					
Rural	91%	86%	59%	43%	1
Urban to 2,500	72%	94%	67%	53%	1
Twenty Cities	44%	62%	54%	50%	
Milwaukee	40%	78%	64%	58%	
Wisconsin	36.4%	63.5%	50.1%	43.7%	489

the following results based on the 1950 election:*

Table XV   Ethnic Voting Pattern, 1950

Solidly Republican	Solidly Democratic
Dutch Reformed	Polish
German Lutheran	
Native-stock	
Strongly Republican	**Strongly Democratic**
English and Welsh	Finnish
Swedish and Danish villages	Irish
German Catholic rural	
Belgian	
Mildly Republican	**Mildly Democratic**
Swedish rural	Norwegians
Danish rural	Austrians
German Catholic villages and urban	
Italians	
French Canadian rural and village	
Swiss Reformed	
Bohemians	

The table does indicate that fewer groups fall into the solidly or strongly one party category and that more groups split along size-of-place lines than in 1900. But the most striking impression one gains from it is that a major reshuffling of ethnic groups has taken place in the half-century that has passed since 1900. German Lutherans

*See Chapter IV, pages 184 and 185 for the 1900 patterns.

have moved from a 50-50 status to a position second only
to the Dutch Reformed in their devotion to the Republican
party. German Catholics have moved from being among the
staunchest of Democrats to a moderately Republican position,
and, for rural German Catholics, a strongly Republican
position. On the other hand, Finnish voters have joined
the Irish and Poles as staunch Democrats, and Norwegians
are at least mildly Democratic, quite a switch from the
strong Republicanism of these two groups in 1900.

Thus, Wisconsin politics aligned the ethnic, size-
of-place groupings in 1950. New issues, the emergence of
the Democratic party to equality with the Republican party,
and the gradual dissolution of ethnic areas after 1950
would bring about changes in the nature and degree of
ethnic response. As of 1950, however, ethnicity still
carried a good deal of salience in determining the location of individuals along the electoral spectrum.

NOTES

[1]A number of good studies have been written on recent Wisconsin politics including Leon Epstein, Politics in Wisconsin (Madison, 1958); John H. Fenton, "Programmatic Politics in Wisconsin," in Midwest Politics (New York, 1966), 44-74; and Michael Paul Rogin, "Wisconsin: McCarthy and the Progressive Tradition," in The Intellectuals and McCarthy: The Radical Specter (Cambridge, Massachusetts, 1967), 59-103.

[2]Lubell, The Future of American Politics (New York, 1952; paperback third edition, 1965). Lubell follows up on this interpretation in Revolt of the Moderates (New York, 1956). On the 1928 election and the cities see also Carl Degler, "American Political Parties and the Rise of the City: An Interpretation," Journal of American History, LI (June, 1964), 41-59; Charles E. Gilbert, "National Political Alignments and the Politics of Large Cities," Political Science Quarterly, LXXIV (March, 1964), 25-51; and Jerome M. Clubb and Howard W. Allen, "The Cities and the Election of 1928: Partisan Realignment?" American Historical Review, LXXIV (April, 1969), 1205-1220.

[3]Macrae and Neldrum, "Critical Elections in Illinois: 1888-1958," American Political Science Review, LIV (September, 1960), 669-683. The quote is from page 677.

[4]Key, "A Theory of Critical Elections," Journal of Politics, XVII (February, 1955), 3-18; Stave, "The

'La Follette Revolution' and the Pittsburgh Vote, 1932," Mid-America, XLIX (October, 1967), 244-251, and The New Deal and the Last Hurrah: Pittsburgh Machine Politics (Pittsburgh, 1970).

[5]Hofstadter, Age of Reform: From Bryan to F. D. R. (New York, 1955; paperback edition, 1960), 284.

[6]Graham, An Encore for Reform: The Old Progressives and the New Deal (New York, 1967), especially Appendices I to III, 187-217.

[7]Havig, "A Disputed Legacy: Roosevelt Progressives and the La Follette Campaign of 1924," Mid-America, LIII (January, 1971), 44-64.

[8]Baggaley, "Religious Influences on Wisconsin Voting, 1928-1960," American Political Science Review, LVI (May, 1962), 66-70. David Adamany also used the parochial school bus referendum as a measure of religious difference in "The 1960 Election in Wisconsin," (University of Wisconsin M. A. Thesis, 1963).

[9]Ogburn and Talbot, "A Measurement of the Factors in the Presidential Election of 1928," Social Forces, VIII (December, 1929), 175-183; Silva, Rum, Religion, and Votes: 1928 Re-examined (University Park, Pennsylvania, 1962); Carter, "The Campaign of 1928 Re-examined: A Study in Political Folklore," Wisconsin Magazine of History, XLVI (Summer, 1963), 263-272; Fite, "The Agricultural Issue in the Presidential Campaign of 1928," Mississippi Valley

Historical Review, XXXVI (March, 1951), 653-672.

¹⁰Miller, "A Footnote to the Role of the Protestant Churches in the Election of 1928," Church History, XXV (June, 1956), 145-159, and American Protestantism and Social Issues, 1919-1939 (Chapel Hill, North Carolina, 1958), 48-62; Bailey, "The Campaign of 1928," in Southern White Protestantism in the Twentieth Century (New York, 1964), 92-110; Moore, A Catholic Runs for President: The Campaign of 1928 (New York, 1956). The quote is from Moore, page 41. An excellent survey of these works along with his own analysis is contained in David Burner, The Politics of Provincialism: The Democratic Party in Transition, 1918-1932 (New York, 1968), 217-243. John Shover's chapter on "Was 1928 a Critical Election in California?" in Michael P. Rogin and Shover, Political Change in California: Critical Elections and Social Movements, 1890-1966 (Westport, Connecticut, 1970), 90-111, manages to avoid mentioning religion altogether.

¹¹See Charles M. Dollar and Richard J. Jensen, Historian's Guide to Statistics: Quantitative Analysis and Historical Research (New York, 1971), chapter 3, for an explanation of regression analysis.

¹²Wisconsin Blue Book, 1927, 592-593. One of the few discussions of prohibition votes in Wisconsin is William F. Raney, Wisconsin: A Story of Progress (New York, 1940; reprinted, 1963), 316-324.

¹³Testimony before Wisconsin Legislative Interim Committee on Campaign Expenditures, Hearings, III Madison, July 30, 1930, 328-329, quoted in Schlereth, "The Progressive-Democratic Alliance in the Wisconsin Presidential Election of 1928," (University of Wisconsin M. A. Thesis, 1965), 179.

¹⁴Wisconsin Crop and Livestock Reporting Service, [Adams-Wood County] Agricultural Statistics. Research Bulletin 202, Nos. 1-71 (Madison, 1939-1942). Mimeographed. This series is described in Chapter III, footnote 8.

¹⁵John L. Shover, "Ethnicity and Religion in Philadelphia Politics, 1924-1940," American Quarterly, XXV (December, 1973), 509 and 513.

¹⁶See the discussion of the problem in Chapter I and in W. S. Robinson, "Ecological Correlations and Behavior of Individuals," American Sociological Review, XV (June, 1950), 351-357.

¹⁷Gosnell and Cohen, "Progressive Politics: Wisconsin an Example," American Political Science Review, XXXIV (October, 1940), 920-935, reprinted and brought up-to-date to include the 1940 election in Gosnell, Grass Roots Politics: National Voting Behavior of Typical States (Washington, D. C., 1942), 38-57. The quote is from pages 921-922 in the former. More sophisticated county level correlation analysis can be found in Ralph Kloske, "The

New Deal in the Badger State: A Look at Some County Level Data," (Decorah, Iowa, Luther College Senior Thesis, 1974).

[18]Lubell, Future of American Politics, 142-144. Edward C. Blackorby, Prairie Rebel: The Public Life of William Lemke (Lincoln, Nebraska, 1963), does not go beyond Lubell in explaining the Lemke vote except for North Dakota. David O. Powell, "The Union Party of 1936: Campaign Tactics and Issues," Mid-America, XLVI (April, 1964), 126-141, stresses the Coughlinite, anti-New Deal emphasis in the Union party campaign.

[19]Lubell, Future of American Politics, 137. Louis Bean, How to Predict Elections (New York, 1968), 94-99, also points out the German defections.

[20]See Manfred Jonas, Isolation in America, 1935-1941 (Ithaca, New York, 1966); Leroy N. Rieselbach, "The Basis of Isolationist Behavior," Public Opinion Quarterly, XXIV (Winter, 1960), 645-657, and The Roots of Isolationism: Congressional Voting and Presidential Leadership in Foreign Policy (Indianapolis, Indiana, 1966); Ralph H. Smuckler, "The Region of Isolationism," American Political Science Review, XLVII (June, 1953), 386-401; and Bruce M. Russett, "Demography, Salience, and Isolationist Behavior," Public Opinion Quarterly, XXIV (Winter, 1960), 658-664. These studies suffer from the use of gross statistics, poor definition of urban-rural, and, most of all, from an in-

adequate conceptual framework within which to define isolationism and internationalism. Generally they assume that a position in favor of United States involvement abroad is equal to internationalism. An example of observations based on survey data which totally ignore the ethnic factor is Hadley Cantril, "America Faces the War," Public Opinion Quarterly, IV (September, 1940), 387-407.

[21] Chapple's campaign presaged Joe McCarthy's use of the Communist issue. See, for example, Chapple, La Follette Socialism (Ashland, Wisconsin, 1931), and La Follette Road to Communism--Must We Go Further Along That Road (Ashland, Wisconsin, 1936), complete with horror stories and pictures of sons and daughters debauched at the University of Wisconsin under pro-La Follette policies and ideas. The 1932 campaign is discussed in Karl E. Meyer, "The Politics of Loyalty from La Follette to McCarthy in Wisconsin, 1918-1952," (Princeton University Ph. D. Dissertation, 1956), 74-126, and Leland C. DeVinney, "The Rise of a Political Leader: A Study of Modern Political Methods and of Newspaper Reactions," (University of Wisconsin M. A. Thesis, 1933). On the Democratic party during this period see Robert E. Long, "Wisconsin State Politics, 1932-1934: The Democratic Interlude," (University of Wisconsin M. S. Thesis, 1962).

[22] On the Progressive party of the 1930's see Edward N. Doan, The La Follettes and the Wisconsin Idea (New

York, 1947); Roger T. Johnson, <u>Robert M. La Follette, Jr. and the Decline of the Progressive Party in Wisconsin</u> (Madison, 1964); Wallace S. Sayre, "Robert M. La Follette, Jr.," in J. T. Salter, ed., <u>The American Politician</u> (Chapel Hill, North Carolina, 1938), 138-149; Theodore Rosenof, "'Young Bob' La Follette on American Capitalism," <u>Wisconsin Magazine of History</u>, LV (Winter, 1971-72), 130-139; Donald Young, ed., <u>Adventures in Politics: The Memoirs of Philip La Follette</u> (New York, 1970); Donald R. McCoy, "The Formation of the Wisconsin Progressive Party in 1934," <u>The Historian</u>, XIV (Autumn, 1951), 70-90, <u>Angry Voices: Left of Center Politics in the New Deal Era</u> (Lawrence, Kansas, 1958), and "The Development of the Wisconsin Progressive Party of 1934-1946," (University of Chicago M. A. Thesis, 1949); and Charles H. Backstrom, "The Progressive Party of Wisconsin, 1934-1946," (University of Wisconsin Ph. D. Dissertation, 1956).

[23]John W. Wyngaard, "A Popular Front in Wisconsin: An Examination of the Farmer-Labor-Progressive Federation," (Madison, January, 1937), Mimeographed; and Lester F. Schmidt, "The Farmer-Labor-Progressive Federation: The Study of a 'United Front' among Wisconsin Liberals, 1934-1941," (University of Wisconsin Ph. D. Dissertation, 1955).

[24]Arthur M. Schlesinger, Jr., <u>The Age of Roosevelt</u>, Vol. III, <u>The Politics of Upheaval</u> (Boston, 1960), 104-108, and James T. Patterson, <u>The New Deal and the States:</u>

Federalism in Transition (Princeton, New Jersey, 1969), 177-180.

[25] Donald R. McCoy, "The National Progressives of America, 1938," Mississippi Valley Historical Review, XLIV (June, 1957), 75-93, and Angry Voices, 163-181.

[26] See Alan Edmond Kent, "Portrait in Isolationism: The La Follettes and Foreign Policy," (University of Wisconsin Ph. D. Dissertation, 1957).

[27] Hugh A. Bone, "Small Political Parties, Casualties of War?" National Municipal Review, XXXII (November, 1943), 524-538.

[28] Douglas A. Zischke, "La Follettes and the Progressive: The Case Study of a Liberal Magazine," (University of Wisconsin M. A. Thesis, 1952). The Capital Times edited by Evjue, also split with the La Follettes on the foreign policy issue. Kenneth C. Wagner, "William T. Evjue and the Capital Times," (University of Wisconsin M. A. Thesis, 1949).

[29] For examples of the debate, see Capital Times, November 11, 12, and 16, 1940; Wisconsin State Journal, January 31 and June 7, 1941; Capital Times, April 2, 12, 16, 1942, November 10, 1944; Wisconsin State Journal, January 11, 21, 1945. John Wyngard reported in his column, October 11, 1945, "The vast majority of the articulate spokesmen for the Progressive party, men who have run for office, county chairmen, precinct committeemen, etc., want to

return to the Republican column on the ballot." Appleton Post-Crescent, October 11, 1945.

30Capital Times, March 18, 1946, page 5.

31Meyer, "Politics of Loyalty," 129. Phil La Follette, privately opposed to the dissolution of the party, later wrote, "I was not invited to attend . . . . If I [had] appeared and spoke[n] my convictions, I was reasonably sure the convention would not vote for disbandment." Memoirs of Philip La Follette, 275.

32Epstein, Wisconsin Politics, 51-53. Reynolds father, Attorney-General from 1927 to 1933, and a longtime activist in the progressive movement in Wisconsin, had urged La Follette to return to the Republican party as the only practical alternative. Capital Times, November 16, 1945.

33Backstrom, "Progressive Party of Wisconsin," 451.

34Wisconsin Blue Book, 1948, 604.

35On McCarthy vs. La Follette in 1946, see Meyer, "Politics of Loyalty," 127-158; Reinhard Luthin, "Joseph R. McCarthy: Wisconsin's Briefcase Demagogue," in American Demagogues: Twentieth Century (Boston, 1954), 272-301; and John P. Steinke, "The Rise of McCarthyism," (University of Wisconsin M. A. Thesis, 1960). The idea that Communist opposition to La Follette because of his critical attitude toward the Soviet Union in the postwar period was responsible for his defeat adds an ironic, if unproven, grace note to McCarthy's entrance into the political scene. McCarthy had not yet discovered the Communist issue. On this question, see John Steinke and James Weinstein, "McCarthy and the Liberals," Studies on the Left, II (Summer, 1962), 43-50; James Rorty and Moshe Dector, McCarthy and the Communists (Boston, 1954), and William T. Evjue, A Fighting Editor (Madison, 1968), 606-612. A good recent study of McCarthy is Robert Griffith, The Politics of Fear: Joseph R. McCarthy and the Senate (Lexington, Kentucky, 1970).

[36] In 1964, Robert La Follette's son Bronson, then only 28 years old, was elected Attorney-General of Wisconsin as a Democrat. In 1968, he was narrowly defeated in an effort to wrest the governorship from the Republican party. The author was a Democratic candidate for the Wisconsin State Senate from the La Crosse area district in the latter year and can testify from campaigning with him that "Young Bronson" inherited the La Follette name attraction along with the nonmagnetism of his father.

[37] For definitions of "critical" and "realigning" elections, in addition to Key, "Critical Elections," and Macrae and Neldrum, "Critical Elections in Illinois," see Walter Dean Burnham, "The Changing Shape of the American Political Universe," American Political Science Review, LIX (March, 1965), 7-28, and Critical Elections and the Mainsprings of American Politics (New York, 1970); and Charles G. Sellers, "The Equilibrium Cycle in Two-

Party Politics," *Public Opinion Quarterly*, XXXIX (Spring, 1965), 16-38.

CONCLUSION

At the end of the first half of the Twentieth Century, Wisconsin found itself on the verge of returning to two-party status. Full arrival at that status would not come until 1957 with the election of Democrat William Proxmire to fill out the term of the expired Joseph McCarthy, and 1958 with the election of Gaylord Nelson as the second Democratic Governor in the Twentieth Century.

The continued importance of ethnicity into the second half of the Century is a matter for further investigation. This study, by using minor civil division electoral and demographic data, has probed the import of ethnic background for Wisconsin voting during the period from 1900 to 1950. In this period, at least, ethnicity remained an important factor even as the second- and third-generations of immigrant groups took their places in the ranks of voters.

Wisconsin proved to be a good laboratory in which to test the importance of ethnicity because of the size of the non-Native-stock population--only 20% of the state fit the Native-born of Native-born parents category in the retabulation of the 1905 state census--and because of the availability of demographic data at the minor civil division level.

The division of the electorate in 1900 largely along ethno-religious lines grew out of the political socialization process by which immigrant groups entered into the American political arena. Yankees and their allies among the recent Scottish, British, and Welsh immigrants controlled the Republican party from its inception. Germans, both Catholic and Lutheran, Bohemian, Dutch Catholic, Austrian, and Swiss voters entering the state in the mid-Nineteenth Century also entered the Democratic party in reaction to the domination of the Republican party by Yankees--and worse yet--by Yankee ideals of Sabbatarianism, prohibition, and nativism. Scandinavians and Dutch Reformed, entering the state hard on the heels of the Germanic groups, responded to the appeal of the Republican party in part at least because they perceived the Democratic party as the home of Catholic domination. Belgians, as staunch in their Catholic loyalties as in their devotion to the GOP, prove the major exception to this pattern. Later arriving Poles and urban Italians joined the ranks of their coreligionists in the Democratic party.

By 1900, the inherent tension between their Protestantism and their Democratic allegiance was moving German Lutherans and Swiss Reformed into the ranks of the Republicans.

More important than this gradual shift was the growing pressure of the emergent Scandinavians on the Yankee domination of the Republican party. Thoroughly loyal to the GOP, the Scandinavians found their rising economic and social status unrecognized. The man who tapped this pressure and turned it into a political movement was Robert M. La Follette. Progressivism in Wisconsin did not represent the Yankee ethos or vote--in fact the Native-stock voter remained the most loyal element in the declining stalwart ranks. Richard Hofstadter described the wrong status revolution in attributing the rise of progressivism to its workings.

The Democratic party, led at the national level by Woodrow Wilson, and by Paul Husting at the state level, made inroads into the Republican majority in 1912 and 1914, only to have its base of support in the German community totally destroyed by the impact of World War I. Historians have been uncertain of the differential impact of World War I on ethnic groups--in part because the gains made by Wilson in 1916 seemed to indicate that he was not hurt by the war issue in that election, in part because the massive Harding landslide in 1920 seemed to show a movement away from the Democratic party among all groups. For Wisconsin, however, 1916 found almost all non-Germanic ethnic groups, especially farmers, becoming more Democratic, while Germanic groups--including the Swiss--began to slide away from the Democratic party, a movement which approached totality in the 1920 election.

In addition to turning to the Republican party, the German voting groups began to support La Follette in numbers

unthinkable prior to the war when La Follette and his
programs had enjoyed only minimal backing from traditionally
Democratic ethnic voters. Even in his third-party effort
in 1924, La Follette received massive votes from German-
Americans.

Use of minor civil division ethnic data as well as
county level statistics allows one to deal with two questions about electoral behavior in the 1920's. Did the
vote for La Follette in 1924 represent a retrogressive
looking backward attitude as Richard Hofstadter indicates
or an action presaging the New Deal as V. O. Key and
others have suggested? In Wisconsin the latter proves
to be the case as the vote for La Follette added to the
more traditional Democratic vote received by John Davis
almost exactly equals the vote received by F. D. R. in
1932 whether looked at on the county level or on the
minor civil division level.

The ethno-religious data combined with size-of-place
analysis and a vote on a 1926 prohibition referendum
also settles quite conclusively the issue of the sources
of the vote for and against Al Smith in 1928. It was
primarily a religious vote--Catholic for, Protestant
against. Urban Protestants voted for Hoover; Protestant
wets--most prominently the German Lutherans--also voted
for Hoover; rural and small town Catholics, whatever their
backgrounds, returned overwhelmingly to the Democratic

party to vote for Smith. Even Catholic Belgians, long
a mainstay of the Republican party, moved into the ranks
of the Democracy in 1928.

La Follette in his third-party effort in 1924 and
Al Smith in his restoration of Catholic Democrats to the
Democratic party paved the way for the victories of F. D. R.
in the 1930's. Normally considered as representing the
displacement of traditional ethnic politics with class
politics, the elections of 1932 and 1936 prove more amenable to continued ethnic analysis than to a dividing
along economic lines. Rural areas cast the heaviest Democratic votes--contrary to the conclusions reached by
political scientists like Harold Gosnell using county
level data and correlation analysis. And when one sorts
out the rural ethnic groupings according to wealth as
measured by average value per farm, one finds the wealthiest
set of townships casting the greater Democratic vote in
almost every case for both 1932 and 1936.

The Democratic victory of 1932 forced La Follette's
two sons into a third-party effort--the Progressive party,
existent from 1934 to 1946. Analysis of their 1934 support indicates a close relationship to Robert La Follette
Sr.'s 1922 and 1924 support as well as to the support
F. D. R. was receiving.

However, with war again emerging on the horizon, the
support for both Roosevelt and the La Follettes began to

shift in 1936 as German voters found the Republican party more congenial both in its economic conservatism and in its isolationism. This time the opposition to the war on the part of the younger La Follettes did not win them the support of Wisconsin's German voters as opposition to an earlier war had done for their father. In fact, as they moved further away from F. D. R. over the war issue, their base of political support converged with his--Scandinavian and Belgian votes served to buttress each, German voters deserted both the Democrats and the Progressives.

This basic pattern, confirmed by actual participation in the war, remained the pattern for Wisconsin, at least until 1950, the closing date for this study. Ethnicity continued to divide Wisconsin voters between the two parties but in quite different groupings from the beginning of the fifty-year period covered in this study.

APPENDICES

APPENDIX A **SOURCES OF** DATA

The basic source of demographic data for this study is the retabulation of the 1905 state census done in the late 1930's by the University of Wisconsin Department of Rural Sociology under the Works Progress Administration: "A Retabulation of Population Schedules from the Wisconsin State Census of 1905," (Madison, July 30, 1940), typescript, 11 vols. The retabulation was done for heads-of-household only, thus approximating the male voting population of 1905. Along with ethnic data by country or state of birth and country or state of birth of parents, the retabulation includes data at both the county and minor civil division level for occupation, farm tenancy, age distribution, size-of-family, and other indices. The ethnic data, brought up-to-date by the use of field surveys, was charted on a map entitled "The Peoples of Wisconsin According to Ethnic Stock, 1940," in Wisconsin's Changing Population, Science Inquiry Publication IX, Bulletin of the University of Wisconsin (Madison, October, 1942). The project was described by its director, George W. Hill, in "The Use of the Culture Area in Social Research," American Journal of Sociology, XLVII (July, 1941), 39-47.

The 1905 state census was the last undertaken by the state of Wisconsin. In addition to a population count for each township, village, city, and ward, these censuses also include place of birth, occupation, and agricultural production data at the minor civil division level.

The U. S. census reports are much less comprehensive at the minor civil division level. Most demographic and economic data in the federal census is given either at the county level or at the state level. The 1910 and 1930 censuses are the only two which give country of birth for both foreign-born and for native-born of foreign parents at the county and major city level. Unfortunately, the 1910 census does not include Bohemians and Poles as separate groups. Until 1930, the federal census also gave a ward breakdown of ethnic groups for cities over 50,000; since that date the breakdown for large cities has been by census tracts. A very complete compilation of the latter for Milwaukee County is H. Yuan Tien, ed., Milwaukee Metropolitan Fact Book, 1940, 1950, and 1960 (Madison, 1962).

The Wisconsin Blue Book reprints the number of inhabitants section of the federal census, occasional other data from the census, and analyses of the census such as Edwin E. Witte, "Wisconsin in the 1930 Census," Blue Book, 1933, 103-132.

A mine of agricultural data, including rural-farm proportion and value per farm at the township level, is contained in the Wisconsin Crop and Livestock Reporting Service, County Agricultural Statistics Series: Research Bulletin 202 (1939-1942); Second Series (late 1940's); Third Series

(1952-1955); and Fourth Series (1956-1958). The first three of these were described by Walter H. Ebling in "Statistics in the Counties," Wisconsin Magazine of History, XXXV (Winter, 1951), 101-105. A county level compilation which uses value per acre rather than value per farm is Thomas Pressley and William Scofield, Farm Real Estate Values in the United States by Counties, 1850-1959 (Seattle, Washington, 1965).

The Historical Records Survey, another WPA project provided additional useful information in its mimeographed reports: Origin and Legislative History of County Boundaries in Wisconsin (Madison, 1942); Directory of Churches and Religious Organizations in Wisconsin (Madison, 1941), A Directory of Catholic Churches in Wisconsin (Madison, 1942); and Development of Town Boundaries in Wisconsin, No. 9: Chippewa County (Madison, 1942).

The last named was helpful in separating out the townships which were to become Rusk (Gates) County in 1901 for the 1898 and 1900 elections. In general for boundary changes the footnotes to the U. S. census, either in the census itself or reproduced in the Wisconsin Blue Book reprints of the number of inhabitants by minor civil division, provide the most comprehensive source.

The Directories of Churches included a list of every church with location. Unfortunately, the locations were not always given precisely nor was membership data included.

For more precise location of churches and membership data, see Harry H. Heming's The Catholic Church in Wisconsin (Milwaukee, 1895-1898), and Olaf M. Norlie's Norsk Lutherske Menigheter i Amerika, 1843-1916 (Minneapolis, 1918). Later data, including information on German Lutheran Synods, can be found in the publications of the synods themselves as well as the National Lutheran Council's annual Lutheran Directory and Statistical Handbook.

The basic source for sorting out Protestant and Catholic areas within ethnic groups such as the Germans and Dutch was the vote on the effort to amend the constitution to allow Parochial School Busing Aid in 1946. The results of this referendum are contained in a mimeographed publication put out by Wisconsin's Legislative Reference Bureau. The rationale and method for determination of Catholic and Protestant areas from this vote can be found in Chapters II and III.

The Census of Religious Bodies for 1906, 1916, 1926, and 1936 gives data only on the county level and is of questionable accuracy. The effort by the National Council of Churches, Churches and Church Membership in the United States (New York, 1956-1958), suffers from similar problems. A critique of the religious censuses can be found in Wilbur Zelinsky, "An Approach to the Religious Geography of the United States," Annals of the Association of American Geographers, LI (June, 1960), 139-193.

Additional data on Wisconsin population can be found in several series published by the University of Wisconsin Agricultural Experiment Station including Douglas G. Marshall, Wisconsin Population: Changes and Prospects, 1900-1963 (Madison, March, 1963). The biennial reports of the Wisconsin Bureau of Labor and Industrial Statistics for 1883 to 1910 often included useful demographic and economic data. The Wisconsin Regional Planning Committee's bulletin also contained much information for the 1930's, sometimes in usable form.

Individuals whose work proved especially useful for studying demographic changes were Joseph Schafer, Guy-Harold Smith, and Kate Everest Levi. The footnotes in Chapters II and III contain many additional sources for individual ethnic groups as well as for the state as a whole.

The major source of electoral data at both the county level and minor civil division level, including wards, is the Wisconsin Blue Book published biennially from 1885 to 1937, and from 1940 to the present. A treasure trove of data from the 1890's through 1909, the Wisconsin Blue Book became a bit more sparse after 1911.

For this study, the Wisconsin Blue Book was the source for minor civil division level data for all Presidential elections since 1900, except 1924 and 1928; for all Gubernatorial elections since 1898; for the Gubernatorial primaries of 1906, 1912, and since 1916; for the Senatorial primary of 1922; and for the vote on the Direct Primary referendum in 1904. For Milwaukee County, see also the Annual Reports of the Milwaukee County Board of Election Commissioners.

An additional published source of information for elections used in this study was the Industrial Commission of Wisconsin, The Primary Election of 1910 and the Presidential Primary of 1912 (Madison, 1912), 90-191.

Data for the remaining elections are to be found in the election returns filed with the Secretary of State, now located in the Archives Division, State Historical Society of Wisconsin in Madison. For this study, the elections in the archives include the Presidential races of 1924 and 1928, the Senate races of 1918, 1934, and 1940, the Senate Republican primary of 1946, and the referenda results on Initiative and Referendum in 1914 and on memorializing Congress to amend the Volstead Act in 1926. County level data for almost all elections including referenda are contained in the Wisconsin Blue Books and in James R. Donoghue, How Wisconsin Voted, 1848-1960 (Madison, 1962).

APPENDIX B WISCONSIN SOCIAL AND ECONOMIC DATA

Table I Wisconsin Population Distribution, 1900 to 1950

	1900	1910	1920	1930	1940	1950
Milwaukee	285,315	373,857	457,147	578,249	589,472	637,392
%	13.8%	16.0%	17.4%	19.7%	18.7%	18.6%
Next 15 cities	285,361	352,887	451,654	538,167	573,205	653,166
%	13.8%	15.1%	17.2%	18.3%	18.3%	19.0%
Other urban	219,637	277,576	336,057	437,427	518,467	615,805
%	10.6%	11.9%	12.8%	14.9%	16.5%	17.9%
Total urban (2,500 +)	790,213	1,004,320	1,244,858	1,553,843	1,679,144	1,906,363
%	38.2%	43.0%	47.3%	52.9%	53.5%	55.5%
Rural non-farm	-	-	471,972	512,155	586,254	802,337
%			17.9%	17.4%	18.7%	23.4%
Rural farm	-	-	915,237	873,008	872,189	725,875
%			34.8%	29.7%	27.8%	21.1%
Total rural	1,278,829	1,329,540	1,387,209	1,385,163	1,458,443	1,528,212
%	61.8%	57.0%	52.7%	47.1%	46.5%	44.5%
Total	2,069,042	2,333,860	2,631,839	2,939,006	3,137,587	3,434,575
Growth by decade	-	12.8%	12.8%	11.7%	6.8%	9.5%

Source: Douglas G. Marshall, Wisconsin's Population Changes and Prospects, 1900-1963 (Madison, 1963), and U. S. census publications.

Table II Wisconsin Agricultural Production in 1885 and 1905

	1885		1905	
Crop	Amount*	Value**	Amount*	Value**
Wheat	21,033 bu.	$13,928	2,701 bu.	$ 2,264
Oats	43,047 bu.	$11,009	72,494 bu.	$20,061
Corn	37,718 bu.	$12,577	41,767 bu.	$16,917
Potatoes	11,692 bu.	$ 3,232	29,848 bu.	$ 5,744
Hay	2,306 tons	$13,218	3,933 tons	$24,777
Tobacco	29,595 lbs.	$ 2,951	37,651 lbs.	$ 2,527
Wool	6,175 lbs.	$ 1,337	3,736 lbs.	$ 1,016
Butter	36,240 lbs.	$ 5,850	34,620 lbs.	$ 6,556
Milk	No data		100,419 gals.	$ 9,586
Hogs	1,047,000	$10,324	1,780,000	$16,099
Cattle and calves	221,000	$ 5,981	792,000	$12,618
Sheep and lambs	297,000	$ 793	428,000	$ 1,348
Eggs	No data		45,098,000	$ 6,633

* Given in thousands of bushels, tons, pounds, gallons.
**Given in thousands of dollars.

Sources: Tabular Statements of the [Wisconsin 1885] Census, 760-778; "Agricultural Statistics," in Tabular Statements of the [Wisconsin 1905] Census, Part II, 328-360.

Sources for Table III: Twelfth Census of the United States, 1900, Vol. II, Population, Part II "Occupations," 540-544; Thirteenth Census of the United States, 1910, Vol. IV, Population, "Occupation Statistics," 138-151; Edwin E. Witte, "Wisconsin in the 1930 Census," Wisconsin Blue Book, 1933, 110-111; and United States Census of Population: 1950, Vol. II, Characteristics of the Population, Part 49, "Wisconsin," 48-49.

Table III Wisconsin Occupations, 1900 to 1950

	1900	1910	1920	1930	1940	1950
Agriculture	263,053	297,121	308,050	289,989	274,007	251,930
Forestry and Fishing	7,201	8,823	14,851	7,242	2,052	2,256
Mining	2,915	5,994	3,901	3,235	2,504	3,035
Manufacturing, Mechanical Industries	172,352	279,519	339,811	364,511	270,021	414,643
Construction					39,863	66,543
Transportation and Communication	105,260	58,454	60,643	78,911	60,666	85,386
Trade		78,697	96,028	131,519	167,661	233,789
Financial, Insurance Real Estate					24,769	32,881
Clerical (not stores)		32,971	61,084	79,729		
Public Service		7,338	10,561	14,114	28,820	40,938
Professional Services	32,266	42,285	52,036	73,328	78,769	106,090
Entertainment and Recreation					7,226	11,112
Domestic and Personal Service	72,434	81,210	68,435	86,883	68,990	56,424
Laborers not specified	76,057					
Business and Repair Services					19,956	32,115
Industries not reporting					15,104	18,136
Total Employed	133,538	892,412	995,549	1,129,461	1,060,408	1,255,283

Table IV Wisconsin Foreign-born Population, 1860 to 1940

	1860	1880	1900	1920	1940
Germany	116,798	184,328	242,777	151,250	88,808
Poland	407	5,263	31,789	50,558	31,487
Norway	21,442	49,349	61,575	45,433	23,211
Canada	18,146	28,965			
Other Canadian			23,860	14,497	9,332
French Canadian			10,091	4,917	2,363
Sweden	673	8,138	26,196	22,896	13,697
Austria	7,081	4,601	7,319	19,641	14,880
Czechoslovakia (Bohemia)		13,848	14,145	19,811	12,654
Russia	95	312	4,243	21,447	15,114
Italy	113	253	2,172	11,187	11,086
Denmark	1,150	8,797	16,171	15,420	9,507
England	30,567	25,028	17,995	10,834	6,259
Ireland	49,961	41,907	23,544	7,809	
Irish Free State					2,236
Northern Ireland					508
Netherlands (Holland)	4,906	5,698	6,496	7,473	4,956
Switzerland	4,722	6,283	7,666	7,797	6,080
Yugoslavia				8,784	8,463
Hungary			447	1,123	10,016
Finland			2,198	6,757	4,715
Belgium		4,647	5,267	4,412	3,444	1,691

Table IV Continued

Lithuania				2,934	3,629
Scotland	6,902	5,770	4,569	3,022	2,049
France	2,634	2,412	1,637	2,142	961
Greece		13	63	3,833	2,636
Wales	6,454	5,352	3,356	1,750	675
Rumania			53	970	909
Others	219	3,394	2,521	5,506	4,424
Total	276,927	405,425	515,971	460,128	288,774
Total Population	775,881	1,315,497	2,069,042	2,632,067	3,137,587
Percent Foreign-born	35.7%	30.8%	24.9%	17.5%	9.2%

Source of data: Mainly from U. S. Census of Population: 1950, Vol. II, Characteristics of the Population, Part 49, "Wisconsin," 43.

Table V Wisconsin Foreign Stock, 1910 and 1930

	1910 Census			1930 Census		
	Foreign-born	Native-born Foreign Parents	Total	Foreign-born	Native-born Foreign Parents	Total
Germany	233,384	561,559	794,943	128,269	479,931	608,200
Poland				42,359	96,896	139,255
Norway	56,999	100,701	157,700	34,391	101,562	135,953
Canada				15,572	49,146	64,718
Other	16,929	33,367	50,296			
French	7,992	20,413	28,405			
Sweden	25,739	29,647	55,386	18,808	38,107	56,915
Austria	38,691	43,035	81,726	12,709	22,194	34,903
Czechoslovakia				19,580	39,570	59,150
Russia	29,644	15,763	45,407	16,418	21,419	37,837
Italy	9,273	3,967	13,240	12,599	19,538	32,137
Denmark	16,454	21,861	38,315	13,094	27,829	40,923
England	13,959	38,529	52,488	8,477	35,504	43,981
Ireland	14,049	60,786	74,835			
Free State				3,473	36,944	40,417
Northern Ireland				1,057	7,441	8,498
Netherlands	7,379	14,441	21,820	6,260	19,239	25,499
Switzerland	8,036	12,840	20,876	7,669	19,071	26,740
Yugoslavia				12,266	12,835	25,101
Hungary	10,554	2,612	13,166	6,490	6,382	12,872
Finland	5,705	3,991	9,696	5,724	8,872	14,596
Belgium	4,020	9,939	13,959	2,458	10,499	12,957
Lithuania				4,109	4,523	8,632
Scotland	3,885	9,122	13,007	2,723	9,549	12,272
France	1,396	3,661	5,057	1,459	7,402	8,861
Greece	2,764	226	2,990	2,900	2,446	5,346
Wales	2,507	6,250	8,757	1,241	5,304	6,545
Rumania	446	104	550	1,345	1,330	2,675
Other	2,764	51,953	54,717	4,763	7,621	12,384
Total	512,569	1,044,761	1,557,330	386,213	1,091,154	1,477,367
Total Population			2,333,860			2,939,006

Source: <u>Thirteenth Census, 1910</u>, Vol. III, <u>Population</u>, "Wisconsin," 1075; <u>Fifteenth Census of the United States, 1930</u>, Vol. III, <u>Population Reports by State</u>, Part II, "Wisconsin," 1312.

Table VI Wisconsin Foreign Stock, 1950

	1950 Census			Milwaukee		
	Foreign-born	Native-born Foreign Parents	Total	Foreign-born	Native-born Foreign Parents	Total
Germany	58,526	346,200	404,726	18,259	80,865	90,124
Poland	24,446	78,510	102,956	16,989	36,035	47,024
Norway	14,663	76,440	91,103	1,036	4,755	5,791
Canada						
Other	8,035	29,145	37,180	1,596	4,510	6,105
French	1,642	7,300	8,942	249	1,045	1,294
Sweden	9,285	32,325	41,610	680	3,165	3,845
Austria	12,262	28,145	40,407	5,183	9,260	14,443
Czechoslovakia	9,682	30,430	40,112	2,290	6,370	8,660
Russia	11,941	21,510	33,451	5,011	7,740	12,751
Italy	9,663	22,805	32,468	3,701	8,710	12,411
Denmark	6,537	23,155	29,692	472	1,655	2,128
England	6,325	24,835	31,160	1,436	3,640	5,076
Ireland	1,808	19,915	21,723	451	3,950	4,401
Northern Ireland	79	220	299	8	15	23
Netherlands	4,152	16,745	20,897	275	1,290	1,465
Switzerland	4,695	15,880	20,575	636	1,925	2,561
Yugoslavia	7,597	11,475	19,072	3,185	4,290	7,475
Hungary	6,006	8,535	14,541	3,082	3,565	1,209
Finland	3,282	7,835	11,117	164	1,045	1,209
Belgium	1,331	7,460	8,791	113	430	543
Lithuania	3,136	5,020	8,156	465	940	1,405
Scotland	1,750	6,165	7,915	368	1,035	1,403
France	1,044	5,175	6,219	279	1,145	1,424
Greece	2,476	3,175	5,651	1,203	1,525	2,728
Wales						
Rumania	620	870	1,490	359	420	779
Other	725	11,844	19,095	2,359	3,170	5,529
Total	218,234	841,115	1,059,349	63,450	192,495	255,94

Source: *U. S. Census, 1950*, Vol. IV, Special Reports: Nativity and Parentage, Part 3, Chapter A, 74, 78, and 79.

Table VII Wisconsin Church Membership 1906 to 1952

Denomination	1906	1926	1952
Yankee Protestant			
Methodist Episcopal	54,817	73,143	98,735
Congregational	26,163	35,031	48,323
Presbyterian	18,077	34,932	48,602
Protestant Episcopal	16,527	30,273	37,896
Northern Baptist	19,474	20,096	26,700
Christian Scientist	1,704	4,035	
Other U. S. Protestant			
Disciples of Christ	1,707	3,769	4,894
Seventh Day Adventist	3,194	3,185	4,507
Germans			
Lutheran	c.190,919	351,577	552,569
Evangelical and Reformed	c.29,403	c.39,744	c.51,962
Evangelical-United Brethren	15,316	19,431	25,049
Scandinavians			
Norwegian Lutheran	81,986	108,144	169,135
Swedish Lutheran	c.5,000	10,942	13,906
Danish Lutheran	5,043	8,191	13,226
Finnish Lutheran	1,035	2,312	521
Other Ethnic			
Dutch Reformed	1,917	c.5,000	c.8,100
Moravian (mixed)	2,713	4,648	6,263

Table VII Continued

	1906	1926	1952
Polish National Catholic	100	2,379	
Greek Orthodox	1,156	1,519	
Russian Orthodox		936	
Presbyterian-Welsh Calvinist-Methodist	2,579		
Roman Catholic	505,264	657,511	1,016,724
Jewish	1,199	31,839	37,295
Other	6,915	24,253	28,521
Total	1,000,903	1,472,890	2,192,928

Sources: Religious Bodies: 1906, Part I Summary and General Tables, 288-291, 371-373; Religious Bodies: 1926, Part I Summary and Detailed Tables, 270-273, 701-704; National Council of Churches, Churches and Church Membership in the United States: An Enumeration and Analysis by Counties, States and Regions [80 parts] (New York, 1956-1958).

Table VIII Other Ethnic Groups--Urban Foreign-born

	Wisconsin	Milwaukee	Next six cities*	Other urban	Rural	Urban %
Non-French Canadians						
(1910)**	16,989	1,650	2,453	4,816	8,070	52.1
1930	11,358	2,206	1,765	3,320	4,067	63.9
1950	8,035	1,596	1,281	2,600	2,558	68.2
Scots						
1905	3,974	618	476	871	2,009	49.4
1930	2,723	622	590	765	746	72.6
1950	1,750	368	344	537	501	71.4
Russians						
1905	8,125	2,209	2,269	1,582	2,065	74.6
1930	16,418	7,443	4,244	1,858	2,873	82.5
1950	11,941	5,011	2,932	1,834	2,164	81.9
Austrians						
1905	8,724	2,397	1,334	1,093	3,900	55.3
1930	12,709	5,827	878	2,319	3,685	71.0
1950	12,262	5,183	1,098	2,794	3,187	74.0
Yugoslavs**						
1930	12,266	5,647	1,553	2,583	2,483	79.8
1950	7,597	3,185	1,036	1,790	1,586	79.1
Hungarians						
1905	3,072	1,317	394	395	966	68.6
1930	6,490	3,789	555	825	1,321	79.6
1950	6,006	3,082	448	1,164	1,312	78.2
Greeks						
1905	873	404	243	174	52	94.0
1930	2,900	1,455		1,286	159	94.5
1950	2,476	1,203	379	657	237	90.4
Lithuanians**						
1930	4,109	543		2,365	1,201	70.8
1950	3,136	465	1,387	376	908	71.6
Rumanians						
(1910)**	446	267				
1930	1,345	787		300	258	80.8
1950	620	359		33	112	81.3

* Kenosha, Madison, Oshkosh, Racine, Sheboygan, Superior.
** No data for 1905.

Table IX Black Population of Wisconsin, 1900 to 1960

Year	Wisconsin	Milwaukee	Racine	Beloit	Madison	Other urban	Rural
1900	2,542	862	87	66	69	775	683
1905	2,120	649	57	82	89	1,243	
1910	2,900	980	112	94	143	812	759
1920	5,201	2,229	294	834	259	735	850
1930	10,739	7,501	477	836	348	711	866
1940	12,158	8,821	432	990	365	738	812
1950	28,182	21,772	1,489	1,376	648	1,464	1,433
1960	74,546	62,458	4,738	2,098	1,489	2,882	886

Sources for Tables VIII and IX: U. S. census publications, 1900 to 1960; Wisconsin state census of 1905.

APPENDIX C WISCONSIN ELECTIONS, 1888 to 1952

I. Presidential Elections

	Rep	Dem	Soc	Third Party		Other	Total Vote
1888	49.7%	43.7%		Un Lab	2.4%	4.2%	354,614
1892	46.0%	47.7%		Pop	2.7%	3.6%	371,581
1896	59.9%	37.0%				3.1%	447,409
1900	60.1%	36.0%	1.6%			2.3%	442,501
1904	63.2%	28.0%	6.4%			2.4%	443,014
1908	54.5%	36.7%	6.1%			2.6%	454,421
1912	32.7%	41.1%	8.4%	Prog	15.6%	2.2%	399,966
1916	49.4%	42.8%	6.1%			1.6%	447,134
1920	71.1%	16.2%	11.5%			1.2%	701,280
1924	37.4%	8.2%		Prog	54.4%		833,388
1928	53.5%	44.2%	1.8%			.4%	1,016,831
1932	31.1%	63.5%	4.8%			.5%	1,114,808
1936	30.3%	63.8%	.8%	Union	4.8%	.3%	1,258,560
1940	48.3%	50.1%	1.1%			.5%	1,405,522
1944	50.4%	48.6%	1.0%			.1%	**1,339,152**
1948	46.3%	50.7%	1.0%	Prog	2.0%		1,276,800
1952	61.0%	38.7%				.3%	1,607,370

Source: <u>Wisconsin Blue Book, 1954</u>, 535-537.

II. Gubernatorial Elections

	Rep	Dem	Soc	Third Party		Other	Total Vote
1888	49.5%	43.8%				6.7%	354,714
1890	42.7%	51.9%				5.4%	309,254
1892	45.9%	47.9%		Pop	2.6%	3.6%	371,559
1894	52.5%	37.9%		Pop	6.8%	3.1%	375,449
1896	59.7%	38.1%				2.2%	444,110
1898	52.6%	41.1%	.8%	Pop	2.6%	2.9%	329,430
1900	59.8%	36.4%	1.5%			2.3%	441,900
1902	52.9%	39.9%	4.4%			2.8%	365,676
1904	50.5%	38.5%	5.5%			5.5%	449,570
1906	57.4%	32.3%	7.6%			2.7%	320,003
1908	54.0%	36.9%	6.4%			2.7%	449,656
1910	50.6%	34.6%	12.4%			2.4%	319,522
1912	45.5%	42.5%	8.8%			3.2%	393,849
1914	43.3%	36.7%	8.0%	Prog	10.0%	2.0%	325,430
1916	52.9%	37.9%	7.1%			2.1%	434,340
1918	47.0%	34.0%	17.3%			1.7%	331,582
1920	53.0%	35.8%	10.3%			.9%	691,294
1922	76.4%	(10.6%)	8.2%			4.8%	481,828
1924	51.8%	39.9%	5.7%			2.6%	796,432
1926	63.5%	13.1%	7.3%	Ind	13.8%	2.3%	552,912
1928	55.4%	39.9%	3.7%			1.0%	989,143
1930	64.8%	28.0%	4.2%			3.0%	606,825
1932	41.9%	52.5%	5.1%			.5%	1,124,502
1934	18.1%	37.7%	4.7%	Prog	39.1%	.4%	953,797

II. Continued

Year	Rep	Dem		Third Party	Other	Total Vote
1936	29.4%	21.7%		Prog 46.4%	2.5%	1,237,095
1938	55.4%	8.0%		Prog 36.0%	.6%	981,560
1940	40.7%	19.3%		Prog 39.8%	.2%	1,373,754
1942	36.4%	12.3%	1.4%	Prog 49.6%	.3%	800,985
1944	52.8%	40.6%	.7%	Prog 5.8%	.1%	1,320,483
1946	59.8%	39.1%	.9%		.2%	1,040,444
1948	54.1%	44.1%	.7%	Prog 1.0%	.1%	1,266,139
1950	53.2%	46.2%	.3%	Prog .3%		1,138,148
1952	62.5%	37.3%			.2%	1,615,214

Source: <u>Wisconsin Blue Book, 1968</u>, 589-590.

III. Senatorial Elections

	Rep	Dem	Soc	Third Party	Other	Total Vote
1914	43.5%	43.8%	9.7%		3.0%	308,413
1916	59.3%	31.9%	6.9%		1.9%	421,953
1918sp	38.7%	35.1%	26.1%		.1%	423,997
1920	41.6%	13.2%	9.8%	Prog 34.7%	.8%	677,149
1922	80.6%	(16.6%)			2.8%	470,819
1925sp	67.5%	(3.1%)	3.2%	(Rep) 26.0%	.2%	351,705
1926	55.0%	12.2%	5.7%	Prog 20.4%	6.7%	545,638
1928	85.6%			(Rep) 10.9%	3.5%	742,553
1932	36.2%	57.0%	6.1%		.7%	1,070,996
1934	22.8%	24.2%	4.8%	Prog 47.8%	.3%	921,926
1938	47.7%	24.7%		Prog 26.6%	1.0%	937,503

III. Continued

1940	41.4%	13.2%		Prog	45.3%	.2%	1,338,135
1944	50.5%	42.8%	.8%	Prog	5.8%	.1%	1,256,374
1946	61.3%	37.4%	1.2%			.2%	1,012,504
1950	53.3%	46.2%	.4%			.1%	1,116,077
1952	54.2%	45.6%				.2%	1,605,167

Sources: Paul T. David, Party Strength in the United States, 1872-1970 (Charlottesville, Virginia, 1972), 280.

James R. Donoghue, How Wisconsin Voted, 1848-1960 (Madison, 1962), 89-98.

IV. Selected Referenda and Constitutional Amendments

	Yes	No	Total Vote
Nov. 1904 Direct Primary	62.0%	38.0%	210,468
Nov. 1908* State Income Tax	69.4%	30.6%	123,425
Nov. 1912 Women's Suffrage	37.4%	62.6%	362,569
Nov. 1914* Initiative and Ref.	36.0%	64.0%	233,470
Nov. 1926 Amend Volstead Act	66.3%	33.7%	527,045
Apr. 1932 Blue Law Repeal	59.3%	40.7%	668,222
Nov. 1946* Parochial School Aid	44.5%	55.5%	983,292
Apr. 1947 Daylight Savings Time	45.2%	54.8%	692,831

*Constitutional Amendment

Source: Wisconsin Blue Book, 1968, 318-324.

V. Wisconsin State Legislature--Partisan Division

	State Assembly					State Senate				
	Rep	Dem	Soc	Third Party		Rep	Dem	Soc	Third Party	
1888	71	29				24	6			3
1890	33	66		Un Lab	1	14	19			
1892	44	55				7	26			
1894	81	19				20	13			
1896	91	8		Fusion	1	29	4			
1898	81	19				31	2			
1900	82	18				31	2			
1902	75	25				30	3			
1904	85	11	4			28	4	1		
1906	76	19	5			27	5	1		
1908	80	17	3			28	4	1		
1910	59	29	12			27	4	2		
1912	57	37	6			23	9	1		
1914	62	29	8	Prog	1	21	11	1		
1916	79	14	7			24	6	3		
1918	79	5	16			27	2	4		
1920	92	2	6			27	2	4		
1922	89	1	10			30	0	3		
1924	92	1	7			30	0	3		
1926	89	3	8			31	0	2		
1928	90	6	3	Ind	1	31	0	2		
1930	89	2	9			30	1	2		
1932	14	59	3	Prog	23	12	8	1	Prog	12
1934	17	35	3	Prog	45	7	14		Prog	11

V. Continued

1936	21	31	2	Prog	46	8	9	Prog	16
1938	53	15		Prog	32	16	6	Prog	11
1940	60	15		Prog	25	24	3	Prog	6
1942	73	14		Prog	13	23	4	Prog	6
1944	75	19		Prog	6	22	6	Prog	5
1946	88	12				27	5	Prog	1
1948	74	26				28	4		
1950	76	24				26	7		
1952	75	25				26	7		

Source: <u>Wisconsin Blue Book, 1968</u>, 329.

APPENDIX D WISCONSIN ETHNIC VOTING, 1898 TO 1952

Table I Republican Gubernatorial Vote 1898 and 1900

	Number of Units	1898 Median	1900 Median	1898 to 1900 Change
Native Stock				
Rural	18	73%	74%	1%
Urban to 2,500	11	73%	80%	7%
2,500-10,000	2	63%	71%	8%
City wards	4	79%	80%	1%
English				
Rural	3	70%	79%	9%
Urban to 2,500	2	76%	79%	3%
Welsh				
Rural	2	79%	80%	1%
Urban to 2,500	2	79%	77%	-2%
Norwegian				
Rural	29	75%	89%	14%
Urban to 2,500	7	68%	86%	18%
2,500-10,000	1	71%	86%	15%
City wards	4	57%	80%	23%
Swedish				
Rural	9	88%	87%	-1%
Urban to 2,500	1	85%	84%	-1%
2,500-10,000	(1)	--	57%*	--
City ward	1	60%	76%	16%
Danish				
Rural	4	64%	69%	5%
2,500-10,000	1	79%	83%	4%
City wards	(2)	--	57%**	--
Finnish				
Rural	2	72%	90%	18%
Dutch Reformed				
Rural	2	69%	74%	5%
Urban to 2,500	(1)	--	93%	--
Belgian				
Rural	7	79%	85%	6%
City ward	1	63%	66%	3%
Italian				
Rural	1	50%	53%	3%
City ward	1	23%	32%	9%
French Canadian				
Rural	2	64%	69%	5%
Urban to 2,500	(1)	--	35%**	--
City ward	1	56%	58%	2%

*1902 election   **1904 election

Table I Republican Gubernatorial Vote 1898 and 1900

	Number of Units	1898 Median	1900 Median	1898 to 1900 Change
Swiss Reformed				
Rural	2	48%	50%	2%
Urban to 2,500	1	73%	75%	2%
2,500-10,000	1	58%	60%	2%
German Lutheran				
Rural	70	51%	58%	7%
Urban to 2,500	9	42%	50%	8%
2,500-10,000	3	57%	62%	5%
German Mixed				
Rural	34	46%	51%	5%
Urban to 2,500	23	49%	52%	3%
2,500-10,000	15	38%	50%	12%
over 10,000	5	53%	54%	1%
City wards	26	46%	48%	2%
Milwaukee wards	8	43%	53%	10%
German Catholics				
Rural	18	32%	33%	1%
Urban to 2,500	8	43%	42%	-1%
2,500-10,000	4	39%	38%	-1%
Bohemians				
Rural	9	39%	45%	6%
Irish				
Rural	8	35%	32%	-3%
City ward	1	42%	42%	0
Polish				
Rural	8	19%	26%	7%
City wards	3	17%	24%	7%
Dutch Catholics				
Rural	(1)	--	9%*	--
Urban to 2,500	(1)	--	28%	--
Austrian				
Rural	1	27%	25%	-2%
Nineteen Cities		50%	56%	6%
Milwaukee		43%	51%	8%
Wisconsin	377	52.6%	58.8%	6.2%

*1902 election

Table II Progressive Support, 1900 to 1912

	1900 Number of Units	1900 to 1904 LaF Change	1904 Prim El Ref	1914 I & R Ref	1912 Pres Prim LaF	1914 Number of Units
Native Stock						
Rural	20	- 8%	74%	31%	83%	22
Urban to 2,500	15	-29%	57%	53%	66%	20
2,500-10,000	2	-24%	56%	31%	63%	2
City wards	4	-40%	42%	41%	55%	5
English						
Rural	3	-10%	69%	21%	81%	3
Urban to 2,500	2	-15%	53%	26%	70%	2
Welsh						
Rural	2	- 9%	74%	37%	65%	2
Urban to 2,500	2	-19%	59%	22%	55%	2
Norwegian						
Rural	29	- 2%	91%	56%	86%	34
Urban to 2,500	9	-13%	83%	49%	73%	17
2,500-10,000	1	-17%	79%	46%	80%	1
City wards	4	- 8%	76%	52%	86%	4
Swedish						
Rural	9	-12%	85%	61%	94%	14
Urban to 2,500	1	- 2%	95%	61%	89%	4
2,500-10,000	(1)	8%*	77%	28%	80%	1
City ward	1	1%		37%		1
Danish						
Rural	4	11%	83%	67%	92%	7
Urban to 2,500				70%	95%	2
2,500-10,000	1	-21%	78%	50%	72%	1
City wards	2		67%	45%	77%	4
Finnish						
Rural	2	- 2%	94%	71%	83%	11
Dutch Reformed						
Rural	2	-11%	30%	23%	84%	3
Urban to 2,500	1	-30%	40%	22%	70%	2
Belgian						
Rural	7	-18%	84%	43%	94%	7
City ward	1	- 1%	76%	33%	81%	1
Italian						
Rural	1	10%	83%	55%	82%	2
City ward	1	- 4%	91%	41%	52%	1
French Canadian						
Rural	2	- 2%	82%	43%	82%	2
Urban to 2,500	1		16%	10%	59%	1
City ward	1	5%	89%	40%	68%	1

*Decline from 1902

Table II Progressive Support, 1900 to 1912

	1900 Number of Units	1900 to 1904 LaF Change	1904 Prim El Ref	1914 I & R Ref	1912 Pres Prim LaF	1914 Number of Units
Swiss Reformed						
Rural	2	-17%	48%	38%	75%	3
Urban to 2,500	1	-22%	66%	48%	79%	2
2,500-10,000	1	-16%	56%	26%	69%	1
German Lutheran						
Rural	72	- 7%	55%	17%	72%	80
Urban to 2,500	11	-14%	56%	33%	75%	21
2,500-10,000	3	-12%	68%	34%	61%	3
German Mixed						
Rural	34	- 7%	51%	18%	74%	46
Urban to 2,500	23	- 7%	55%	29%	67%	34
2,500-10,000	15	-11%	46%	24%	63%	15
over 10,000	5	-11%	55%	27%	64%	5
City wards	28	.- 2%	60%	27%	78%	30
Milwaukee wards	8	-14%	69%	55%	77%	10
German Catholics						
Rural	18	2%	33%	15%	77%	26
Urban to 2,500	8	1%	55%	19%	67%	15
2,500-10,000	4	- 1%	53%	28%	67%	4
Bohemians						
Rural	9	1%	61%	14%	75%	10
Irish						
Rural	8	5%	49%	32%	87%	9
City ward	1	19%	32%	23%	60%	1
Polish						
Rural	9	1%	38%	13%	65%	10
Urban to 2,500				27%	84%	2
City wards	3	- 6%	16%	16%	63%	2
Milwaukee wards	2		72%	60%	81%	5
Dutch Catholics						
Rural	1	6%	26%	6%	56%	1
Urban to 2,500	1	- 8%	56%	24%	74%	1
Austrian						
Rural	1	-13%	6%	13%	83%	1
Nineteen Cities		-12%	55%	32%	64%	
Milwaukee		- 9%	67.4%	51.0%	72%	
Wisconsin	389	-9.3%	62.0%	36.0%	73.2%	511

Table III Democratic Presidential Vote 1908 to 1920

	Number of Units	1908 Mean	1912 Mean	1916 Mean	1920 Mean	1908 to 1920 Decline
Native Stock						
Rural	22	28%	30%	37%	12%	-16%
Urban to 2,500	20	25%	32%	33%	13%	-12%
2,500-10,000	2	34%	37%	36%	17%	-17%
City wards	2	24%	30%	33%	13%	-11%
English						
Rural	3	26%	26%	36%	14%	-12%
Urban to 2,500	2	21%	34%	27%	10%	-11%
Welsh						
Rural	2	20%	26%	30%	10%	-10%
Urban to 2,500	2	28%	33%	23%	8%	-20%
Norwegian						
Rural	32	12%	15%	26%	5%	- 7%
Urban to 2,500	14	20%	28%	33%	8%	-12%
2,500-10,000	1	14%	23%	32%	9%	- 5%
City wards	4	31%	38%	46%	15%	-16%
Swedish						
Rural	12	14%	19%	29%	7%	- 7%
Urban to 2,500	2	26%	27%	24%	10%	-16%
2,500-10,000	1	24%	29%	34%	16%	- 8%
City ward	1	32%	34%	31%	19%	-13%
Danish						
Rural	4	31%	33%	49%	20%	-11%
Urban to 2,500	2	25%	26%	46%	15%	-10%
2,500-10,000	1	17%	26%	45%	12%	- 5%
City wards	4	21%	33%	44%	16%	- 5%
Finnish						
Rural	7	14%	9%	17%	7%	- 7%
Dutch Reformed						
Rural	3	21%	22%	30%	6%	-15%
Urban to 2,500	2		31%	23%	7%	
Belgian						
Rural	7	21%	24%	55%	8%	-13%
Italian						
Rural	2	34%	37%	42%	8%	-26%
City ward	1	54%	46%	59%	29%	-25%
French Canadian						
Rural	2	38%	38%	53%	20%	-18%
Urban to 2,500	2			60%	31%	
City ward	1	51%	49%	50%	30%	-21%

Table III Democratic Presidential Vote 1908 to 1920

	Number of Units	1908 Mean	1912 Mean	1916 Mean	1920 Mean	1908 to 1920 Decline
Swiss Reformed						
Rural	3	54%	60%	42%	5%	-49%
Urban to 2,500	2	50%	57%	48%	5%	-45%
2,500-10,000	1	42%	49%	43%	10%	-32%
German Lutheran						
Rural	76	41%	45%	27%	6%	-35%
Urban to 2,500	17	45%	50%	42%	14%	-31%
2,500-10,000	3	42%	48%	41%	14%	-28%
German Mixed						
Rural	44	45%	48%	32%	9%	-36%
Urban to 2,500	35	48%	53%	40%	13%	-35%
2,500-10,000	15	50%	55%	48%	18%	-32%
over 10,000	5	43%	43%	42%	17%	-26%
City wards	30	45%	45%	42%	15%	-30%
Milwaukee wards	9	30%	36%	36%	11%	-19%
German Catholics						
Rural	25	60%	60%	44%	9%	-51%
Urban to 2,500	11	54%	63%	48%	21%	-33%
2,500-10,000	4	60%	62%	58%	33%	-27%
Bohemians						
Rural	9	52%	57%	64%	20%	-32%
Irish						
Rural	9	66%	66%	70%	42%	-24%
City ward	1	52%	58%	56%	26%	-26%
Polish						
Rural	6	68%	55%	85%	56%	-12%
Urban to 2,500	2		45%	68%	30%	
City wards	2	67%	56%	85%	45%	-22%
Milwaukee wards	5	46%	31%	52%	23%	-23%
Dutch Catholics						
Rural	1	92%	82%	86%	45%	-47%
Urban to 2,500	1	65%	86%	85%	60%	- 5%
Austrian						
Rural	1	75%	75%	68%	15%	-60%
Nineteen Cities		38%	43%	47%	19%	-19%
Milwaukee		36%	39%	44%	18%	-18%
Wisconsin	477	36.7%	41.1%	42.8%	16.2%	-20.5%

Table IV Republican Presidential Vote 1908 to 1920

	Number of Units	1908 Mean	1912 T.R.	1912 Rep.	1916 Mean	1920 Mean
Native Stock						
Rural	22	65%	9%	50%	56%	82%
Urban to 2,500	20	64%	10%	47%	61%	82%
2,500-10,000	2	60%	16%	38%	60%	79%
City wards	2	71%	32%	33%	63%	84%
English						
Rural	3	70%	23%	47%	63%	84%
Urban to 2,500	2	73%	6%	53%	70%	85%
Welsh						
Rural	2	75%	11%	56%	65%	82%
Urban to 2,500	2	66%	6%	54%	71%	84%
Norwegian						
Rural	32	86%	28%	53%	71%	92%
Urban to 2,500	14	76%	17%	49%	63%	88%
2,500-10,000	1	81%	11%	58%	64%	87%
City wards	4	63%	16%	37%	46%	75%
Swedish						
Rural	12	76%	49%	23%	61%	82%
Urban to 2,500	2	70%	33%	36%	73%	85%
2,500-10,000	1	72%	34%	28%	63%	80%
City ward	1	59%	19%	29%	59%	76%
Danish						
Rural	4	63%	34%	23%	48%	71%
Urban to 2,500	2	64%	38%	25%	48%	77%
2,500-10,000	1	64%	15%	46%	47%	83%
City wards	4	63%	21%	30%	41%	74%
Finnish						
Rural	7	65%	51%	12%	58%	64%
Dutch Reformed						
Rural	3	77%	38%	37%	68%	92%
Urban to 2,500	2	68%	41%	21%	77%	92%
Belgian						
Rural	7	77%	10%	63%	45%	90%
Italian						
Rural	2	61%	16%	41%	52%	83%
City ward	1	36%	10%	34%	35%	59%
French Canadian						
Rural	2	58%	7%	50%	47%	78%
Urban to 2,500	2	80%	11%	42%	38%	68%
City ward	1	46%	15%	27%	44%	59%

Table IV Republican Presidential Vote 1908 to 1920

	Number of Units	1908 Mean	1912 T. R. Mean	1912 Rep. Mean	1916 Mean	1920 Mean
Swiss Reformed						
Rural	3	43%	2%	32%	56%	92%
Urban to 2,500	2	47%	2%	38%	50%	90%
2,500-10,000	1	53%	10%	34%	51%	82%
German Lutheran						
Rural	76	57%	19%	33%	71%	81%
Urban to 2,500	17	51%	14%	32%	54%	79%
2,500-10,000	3	53%	11%	35%	55%	83%
German Mixed						
Rural	44	52%	17%	32%	65%	81%
Urban to 2,500	35	47%	10%	30%	56%	74%
2,500-10,000	15	46%	11%	29%	48%	75%
over 10,000	5	47%	21%	22%	49%	64%
City wards	30	45%	21%	20%	47%	63%
Milwaukee wards	9	38%	8%	23%	38%	50%
German Catholic						
Rural	25	38%	8%	28%	54%	82%
Urban to 2,500	11	43%	7%	27%	49%	73%
2,500-10,000	4	33%	8%	21%	37%	56%
Bohemians						
Rural	9	46%	10%	29%	33%	73%
Irish						
Rural	9	33%	6%	27%	27%	56%
City ward	1	40%	17%	21%	41%	71%
Polish						
Rural	6	30%	11%	32%	14%	42%
Urban to 2,500	2		12%	41%	31%	65%
City wards	2	17%	6%	19%	12%	32%
Milwaukee wards	5	22%	6%	21%	18%	38%
Dutch Catholic						
Rural	1	6%	5%	11%	12%	49%
Urban to 2,500	1	35%	0%	11%	11%	31%
Austrian						
Rural	1	23%	3%	17%	32%	84%
Nineteen Cities	5	52%	19%	27%	46%	69%
Milwaukee		37%	8%	24%	34%	51%
Wisconsin	477	54.5%	15.6%	32.7%	49.4%	71.1%

Table V Socialist Vote 1908 to 1920

	Number of Units	1908 Mean	Presidential 1912 Mean	1916 Mean	1920 Mean	Sen 1918 Mean
Native Stock						
Rural	22	1%	4%	2%	3%	6%
Urban to 2,500	20	5%	4%	2%	2%	5%
2,500-10,000	2	1%	3%	2%	1%	3%
City wards	2	1%	1%	2%	1%	6%
English						
Rural	3	1%	0%	0%	0%	0%
Urban to 2,500	2	0%	2%	1%	0%	3%
Welsh						
Rural	2	0%	1%	1%	3%	22%
Urban to 2,500	2	0%	0%	0%	0%	6%
Norwegian						
Rural	32	0%	1%	1%	2%	11%
Urban to 2,500	14	1%	2%	2%	2%	7%
2,500-10,000	1	1%	3%	2%	2%	9%
City wards	4	4%	7%	6%	8%	19%
Swedish						
Rural	12	4%	6%	6%	9%	41%
Urban to 2,500	2	6%	6%	2%	1%	3%
2,500-10,000	1	3%	6%	0%	2%	0%
City ward	1	3%	13%	6%	8%	12%
Danish						
Rural	4	4%	9%	3%	7%	10%
Urban to 2,500	2	2%	12%	5%	4%	5%
2,500-10,000	1	11%	9%	5%	4%	4%
City wards	4	12%	12%	9%	9%	13%
Finnish						
Rural	7	19%	21%	23%	25%	33%
Dutch Reformed						
Rural	3	0%	1%	1%	1%	15%
Urban to 2,500	2		1%		1%	6%
Belgian						
Rural	7	2%	1%		1%	6%
Italian						
Rural	2	0%	4%	4%	5%	12%
City ward	1	9%	10%	6%	11%	16%
French Canadian						
Rural	2	3%	4%	0%	1%	19%
Urban to 2,500	2	0%	0%	0%	0%	9%
City ward	1	3%	8%	3%	10%	11%

Table V Socialist Vote 1908 to 1920

	Number of Units	Presidential 1908 Mean	1912 Mean	1916 Mean	1920 Mean	Sen 1918 Mean
Swiss Reformed						
Rural	3	2%	3%	1%	2%	37%
Urban to 2,500	2	3%	3%	1%	3%	40%
2,500-10,000	1	1%	1%	1%	2%	16%
German Lutheran						
Rural	76	1%	1%	1%	12%	61%
Urban to 2,500	17	1%	2%	2%	5%	39%
2,500-10,000	3	1%	2%	1%	1%	17%
German Mixed						
Rural	44	1%	3%	2%	9%	56%
Urban to 2,500	35	3%	5%	3%	10%	42%
2,500-10,000	15	2%	3%	2%	6%	28%
over 10,000	5	8%	12%	8%	19%	41%
City wards	30	7%	13%	10%	22%	48%
Milwaukee wards	9	30%	33%	26%	38%	51%
German Catholic						
Rural	25	1%	2%	1%	7%	53%
Urban to 2,500	11	2%	2%	2%	5%	29%
2,500-10,000	3	1%	4%	3%	4%	18%
(Two Rivers)	1	21%	25%	13%	29%	45%
Bohemians						
Rural	9	1%	3%	2%	7%	7%
Irish						
Rural	9	0%	0%	0%	2%	5%
City ward	1	7%	3%	1%	2%	5%
Polish						
Rural	6	2%	1%	0%	2%	2%
Urban to 2,500	2		2%	0%	5%	4%
City wards	2	13%	18%	2%	23%	19%
Milwaukee wards	5	29%	41%	30%	38%	39%
Dutch Catholic						
Rural	1	1%	1%	1%	4%	10%
Urban to 2,500	1	0%	0%	4%	6%	11%
Austrian						
Rural	1	0%	2%	0%	1%	36%
Nineteen Cities		6%	8%	5%	10%	22%
Milwaukee		25%	28%	22%	31%	42%
Wisconsin	477	6.1%	8.4%	6.1%	11.5%	26.1%

Table VI A 1908 Socialist Presidential Vote
Units over 15%*

Minor Civil Division	County	Ethnic Group	S.D. Vote
Ontario village	Vernon	Native-stock	48%
Kiel city	Manitowoc	German Mixed	33%
Knox township	Price	Finnish	34%
Manitowoc ward 5	Manitowoc	German Mixed	29%
Manitowoc ward 7	Manitowoc	Polish	26%
Oulu township	Bayfield	Finnish	24%
Marengo township	Ashland	Finnish	21%
Two Rivers city	Manitowoc	German Catholic	21%
Somo township	Lincoln	Finnish	18%
Hackett township	Price	Swedish	18%
Sheboygan ward 5	Sheboygan	German Mixed	17%
Sheboygan ward 7	Sheboygan	German Mixed	17%
Manitowoc city	Manitowoc	German Mixed	17%
Manitowoc ward 3	Manitowoc	German Mixed	16%
Plainfield village	Waushara	Native-stock	16%
Brodhead city	Green	Native-stock	15%
New Holstein city	Calumet	German Mixed	15%
Racine ward 11	Racine	Danish	15%
Sheboygan ward 5	Sheboygan	German Mixed	15%

Milwaukee city	25%
Seven German wards	16% to 40%
Two Polish wards	22% to 35%
One Italian ward	9%

*Outside Milwaukee County

Table VI B 1912 Socialist Presidential Vote
Units over 18%*

Minor Civil Division	County	Ethnic Group	S.D. Vote
Knox township	Price	Finnish	46%
Reedsville village	Manitowoc	German Mixed	41%
Oulu township	Bayfield	Finnish	40%
Manitowoc ward 7	Manitowoc	Polish	36%
Manitowoc ward 6	Manitowoc	German Mixed	32%
Sheboygan ward 6	Sheboygan	German Mixed	32%
Sheboygan ward 7	Sheboygan	German Mixed	30%
Marengo township	Ashland	Finnish	27%
Wausau ward 8	Marathon	German Mixed	25%
Two Rivers city	Manitowoc	German Catholic	25%
Colburn township	Adams	Native-stock	24%
Sheboygan ward 5	Sheboygan	German Mixed	24%
Sheboygan ward 8	Sheboygan	German Mixed	24%
Sheboygan city	Sheboygan	German Mixed	21%
Somo township	Lincoln	Finnish	20%
Manitowoc ward 3	Manitowoc	German Mixed	20%
Manitowoc city	Manitowoc	German Mixed	20%
Brule township	Douglas	Finnish	19%
Maple township	Douglas	Finnish	19%
Milltown village	Polk	Danish	18%

Milwaukee city		28%
Nine German wards		12% to 47%
Five Polish wards		33% to 48%
One Italian ward		10%

*Outside Milwaukee County

Table VI C 1916 Socialist Presidential Vote
Units over 14%*

Minor Civil Division	County	Ethnic Group	S.D. Vote
Knox township	Price	Finnish	46%
Kiel city	Manitowoc	German Mixed	28%
Sheboygan ward 7	Sheboygan	German Mixed	26%
Oulu township	Bayfield	Finnish	26%
Brule township	Douglas	Finnish	25%
Marengo township	Ashland	Finnish	24%
Wausau ward 8	Marathon	German Mixed	24%
Sheboygan ward 6	Sheboygan	German Mixed	23%
Sheboygan ward 5	Sheboygan	German Mixed	21%
Sheboygan ward 8	Sheboygan	German Mixed	21%
Buffalo City	Buffalo	German Lutheran	19%
Lakeside township	Douglas	Finnish	18%
Anderson township	Burnett	Swedish	17%
Sheboygan city	Sheboygan	German Mixed	16%
Seif township	Clark	German Mixed	15%
Colburn township	Adams	Native-stock	15%
Wausau ward 9	Marathon	German Mixed	15%
Daniels township	Burnett	Swedish	15%
Scofield city	Marathon	German Mixed	14%

Milwaukee city		22%
Nine German wards		9% to 37%
Five Polish wards		23% to 42%
One Italian ward		6%

*Outside Milwaukee County

Table VI D 1920 Socialist Presidential Vote

Units over 34%*

Minor Civil Division	County	Ethnic Group	S.D. Vote
Pella township	Shawano	German Lutheran	57%
Berlin township	Marathon	German Lutheran	54%
Hamburg township	Marathon	German Lutheran	53%
Rhine township	Sheboygan	German Lutheran	50%
Maine township	Marathon	German Lutheran	48%
Knox township	Price	Finnish	48%
Wausau ward 8	Marathon	German Mixed	48%
Sheboygan ward 7	Sheboygan	German Mixed	45%
Manitowoc ward 7	Manitowoc	Polish	43%
Manitowoc ward 5	Manitowoc	German Mixed	43%
Sheboygan ward 5	Sheboygan	German Mixed	42%
Oshkosh ward 6	Winnebago	German Mixed	41%
Seneca township	Shawano	German Lutheran	39%
Washington township	Shawano	German Catholic	39%
Kiel city	Manitowoc	German Mixed	38%
Sheboygan Falls township	Sheboygan	German Lutheran	36%
Corning township	Lincoln	German Lutheran	36%
Halsey township	Lincoln	German Catholic	35%
Cecil village	Shawano	German Mixed	36%
Manitowoc township	Manitowoc	German Mixed	35%
Wausau ward 9	Marathon	German Mixed	34%
Milwaukee city			31%
Nine German wards			15% to 52%
Five Polish wards			30% to 50%
One Italian ward			11%

*Outside Milwaukee County

Table VI E 1918 Socialist Senate Vote

Units over 80%*

Minor Civil Division	County	Ethnic Group	S.D. Vote
Berlin township	Marathon	German Lutheran	93%
Mosel township	Sheboygan	German Lutheran	93%
Hamburg township	Marathon	German Lutheran	92%
Ogema township	Price	Swedish	89%
Hartland township	Shawano	German Lutheran	88%
Washington township	Shawano	German Catholic	88%
Lebanon township	Dodge	German Lutheran	87%
Rhine township	Sheboygan	German Lutheran	87%
Theresa township	Dodge	German Lutheran	86%
Lincoln township	Buffalo	German Lutheran	85%
Lincoln township	Eau Claire	German Lutheran	85%
Schleswig township	Manitowoc	German Lutheran	85%
Herman township	Shawano	German Mixed	85%
Caledonia township	Waupaca	German Lutheran	85%
Jackson township	Washington	German Lutheran	84%
Bonduel village	Shawano	German Lutheran	83%
Herman township	Dodge	German Lutheran	82%
Buffalo City village	Buffalo	German Lutheran	81%
Rantoul township	Calumet	German Lutheran	81%
DuPont township	Waupaca	German Lutheran	81%
Honey Creek township	Sauk	German Lutheran	80%

Milwaukee city			4?%
Nine German wards			31% to 69%
Five Polish wards			18% to 58%
One Italian ward			16%

*Outside Milwaukee County

Table VII Progressive Votes, 1922 and 1924

	1924 Number of Units	1922 Sen Prim LaF	1924 Pres Prog	1912 to 1922 Pres & Sen Prim Change in LaF Vote
Native Stock				
Rural	22	68%	54%	-15%
Urban to 2,500	20	50%	45%	-16%
2,500-10,000	2	33%	23%	-30%
City ward	1	31%	14%	-24%
English				
Rural	3	69%	50%	-12%
Urban to 2,500	2	18%	14%	-37%
Welsh				
Rural	2	59%	48%	- 6%
Urban to 2,500	2	18%	14%	-37%
Norwegian				
Rural	35	90%	78%	4%
Urban to 2,500	19	69%	58%	- 4%
2,500-10,000	1	68%	52%	-12%
City wards	4	83%	57%	- 3%
Swedish				
Rural	14	82%	53%	-12%
Urban to 2,500	5	67%	44%	-22%
2,500-10,000	1	78%	59%	- 2%
City ward	1	76%	50%	
Danish				
Rural	8	84%	64%	- 8%
Urban to 2,500	3	62%	25%	-33%
2,500-10,000	1	40%	45%	-32%
City wards	4	66%	33%	-11%
Finnish				
Rural	12	86%	54%	3%
Dutch Reformed				
Rural	3	57%	37%	-27%
Urban to 2,500	2	45%	22%	-25%
Belgian				
Rural	7	93%	72%	- 1%
Italian				
Rural	2	73%	69%	- 9%
City ward	1	56%		4%
French Canadian				
Rural	2	86%	64%	4%
Urban to 2,500	2	80%	43%	21%
City ward	1	87%	75%	19%

Table VII Progressive Votes, 1922 and 1924

	1924 Number of Units	1922 Sen Prim LaF	1924 Pres Prog	1912 to 1922 Pres & Sen Prim Change in LaF Vote
Swiss Reformed				
Rural	3	94%	84%	19%
Urban to 2,500	2	91%	82%	12%
2,500-10,000	1	68%	82%	- 1%
German Lutheran				
Rural	85	93%	82%	21%
Urban to 2,500	28	69%	60%	- 6%
2,500-10,000	3	54%	41%	- 7%
German Mixed				
Rural	50	91%	80%	17%
Urban to 2,500	38	82%	62%	15%
2,500-10,000	15	71%	51%	18%
over 10,000	5	78%	51%	14%
City wards	30	87%	59%	9%
Milwaukee wards	10	83%	68%	6%
German Catholics				
Rural	30	95%	83%	18%
Urban to 2,500	18	82%	60%	15%
2,500-10,000	4	86%	59%	19%
Bohemian				
Rural	11	93%	67%	18%
Urban to 2,500	2	62%	32%	
Irish				
Rural	9	85%	48%	- 2%
Polish				
Rural	12	73%	34%	8%
Urban to 2,500	2	78%	52%	- 6%
City wards	2	90%	58%	27%
Milwaukee wards	5	83%	58%	2%
Dutch Catholic				
Rural	1	97%	64%	41%
Urban to 2,500	1	94%	60%	20%
Austrian				
Rural	1	75%	70%	- 8%
Nineteen Cities		73%	45%	9%
Milwaukee		74%	56.0%	2%
Wisconsin	545	72.2%	54.4%	-10%

Table VIII Presidential Vote, 1924 to 1932

	1932 N=	1924 Prog	1924 Dem	1928 Dem	1932 Dem	1926 Proh	1946 ParSch
Native Stock							
Rural	22	54%	8%	20%	67%	29%	21%
Urban to 2,500	20	45%	6%	24%	52%	33%	20%
2,500-10,000	2	23%	13%	24%	38%	34%	26%
City ward	1	14%	7%	26%	28%	46%	31%
English							
Rural	3	50%	11%	25%	67%	62%	35%
Urban to 2,500	2	48%	7%	22%	43%	32%	26%
Welsh							
Rural	2	48%	8%	36%	69%	50%	15%
Urban to 2,500	2	14%	7%	17%	35%	27%	10%
Norwegian							
Rural	35	78%	2%	22%	71%	47%	9%
Urban to 2,500	19	58%	3%	25%	51%	40%	9%
2,500-10,000	1	57%	4%	21%	53%	41%	13%
City wards	4	57%	5%	32%	51%	66%	32%
Swedish							
Rural	14	53%	2%	21%	57%	42%	14%
Urban to 2,500	5	44%	4%	31%	46%	37%	23%
2,500-10,000	1	59%	9%	44%	66%	72%	56%
City ward	1	50%	7%	33%	52%	64%	38%
Danish							
Rural	8	64%	5%	28%	71%	43%	22%
Urban to 2,500	3	25%	12%	26%	70%	40%	38%
2,500-10,000	1	45%	6%	22%	46%	36%	17%
City wards	4	33%	3%	26%	52%	62%	28%
Finnish							
Rural	12	54%	2%	28%	64%	52%	40%
Dutch Reformed							
Rural	3	37%	5%	16%	35%	26%	14%
Urban to 2,500	2	22%	2%	5%	27%	26%	8%
Swiss Reformed							
Rural	3	84%	1%	57%	87%	73%	23%
Urban to 2,500	2	82%	2%	56%	78%	79%	12%
2,500-10,000	1	52%	7%	37%	58%	53%	31%
German Lutheran							
Rural	85	82%	3%	37%	83%	80%	23%
Urban to 2,500	28	60%	5%	38%	67%	74%	22%
2,500-10,000	3	41%	8%	31%	54%	52%	29%

Table VIII Presidential Vote, 1924 to 1932

	1932 N=	1924 Prog	1924 Dem	1928 Dem	1932 Dem	1926 Proh	1946 ParSch
German Mixed							
Rural	50	80%	5%	51%	84%	80%	44%
Urban to 2,500	39	62%	7%	48%	72%	77%	50%
2,500-10,000	15	51%	10%	46%	71%	76%	44%
over 10,000	5	51%	8%	45%	63%	75%	43%
City wards	26	59%	5%	53%	71%	86%	44%
Milwaukee wards	10	68%	7%	54%	78%	88%	43%
German Catholics							
Rural	30	83%	5%	76%	92%	85%	80%
Urban to 2,500	19	60%	9%	73%	85%	86%	76%
2,500-10,000	4	59%	11%	65%	76%	80%	69%
Bohemians							
Rural	11	67%	16%	75%	90%	80%	68%
Urban to 2,500	2	32%	24%	78%	84%	86%	89%
Irish							
Rural	9	48%	22%	80%	90%	75%	79%
Polish							
Rural	12	33%	29%	92%	97%	93%	78%
Urban to 2,500	2	52%	10%	75%	89%	84%	77%
City wards	2	58%	22%	86%	91%	92%	96%
Milwaukee wards	5	59%	14%	81%	92%	93%	71%
Austrian							
Rural	1	70%	11%	89%	93%	82%	94%
Dutch Catholic							
Rural	1	64%	9%	92%	86%	81%	94%
Urban to 2,500	1	60%	16%	96%	94%	94%	94%
Belgian							
Rural	7	72%	4%	81%	94%	90%	79%
French Canadian							
Rural	2	64%	5%	70%	84%	45%	78%
Urban to 2,500	2	43%	15%	78%	81%	88%	80%
City ward	1	75%	5%	68%	69%	76%	70%
Italian							
Rural	2	69%	6%	48%	76%	58%	62%
City ward	1	39%	16%	55%	69%	80%	51%
Twenty Cities		45%	8%	44%	62%	69%	44%
Milwaukee		56%	10%	59%	78%	87%	52%
Wisconsin	549	54.4%	8.2%	44.2%	63.5%	66.3%	44.5%

Table IX F. D. R.'s Vote, 1932 to 1940

	N=	1932 FDR	1936 FDR	1940 FDR	1936 Union	Changes: 1932/36	1932/40
Native Stock							
Rural	22	67%	47%	33%	5%	-20%	-34%
Urban to 2,500	20	52%	44%	30%	2%	- 8%	-22%
2,500-10,000	2	38%	37%	32%	3%	- 1%	- 6%
City ward	1	28%	33%	28%	3%	5%	0%
English							
Rural	3	67%	55%	38%	5%	-12%	-29%
Urban to 2,500	2	43%	42%	33%	5%	- 1%	-10%
Welsh							
Rural	2	69%	56%	41%	5%	-13%	-28%
Urban to 2,500	2	35%	37%	25%	1%	2%	-10%
Norwegian							
Rural	35	71%	65%	56%	3%	- 6%	-15%
Urban to 2,500	19	51%	55%	50%	1%	4%	- 1%
2,500-10,000	1	53%	65%	65%	0%	12%	12%
City wards	4	51%	66%	64%	1%	15%	13%
Swedish							
Rural	14	57%	60%	46%	4%	3%	-11%
Urban to 2,500	5	46%	51%	42%	4%	5%	- 4%
2,500-10,000	1	66%	73%	55%	2%	7%	-11%
City ward	1	52%	61%	55%	3%	9%	3%
Danish							
Rural	8	71%	63%	49%	4%	- 8%	-22%
Urban to 2,500	3	70%	48%	37%	3%	-22%	-33%
2,500-10,000	1	46%	42%	38%	3%	- 4%	- 8%
City wards	4	52%	62%	54%	4%	10%	2%
Finnish							
Rural	12	64%	80%	72%	1%	16%	8%
Dutch Reformed							
Rural	3	35%	36%	21%	3%	1%	-14%
Urban to 2,500	2	27%	21%	20%	3%	- 6%	- 7%
Belgian							
Rural	7	94%	82%	44%	4%	-12%	-50%
Italian							
Rural	2	76%	56%	30%	2%	-20%	-46%
Urban to 2,500	1		74%	37%	3%		-37%
City ward	1	69%	71%	53%	3%	2%	-16%
French Canadian							
Rural	2	84%	47%	45%	31%	-37%	-39%
Urban to 2,500	2	81%	43%	39%	44%	-38%	-47%
City ward	1	69%	83%	80%	0%	14%	11%

Table IX F. D. R.'s Vote, 1932 to 1940

	N=	1932 FDR	1936 FDR	1940 FDR	1936 Union	Changes: 1932/36	1932/40
Swiss Reformed							
Rural	3	87%	83%	57%	1%	- 4%	-30%
Urban to 2,500	2	78%	71%	51%	1%	- 7%	-27%
2,500-10,000	1	58%	52%	40%	2%	- 6%	-18%
German Lutheran							
Rural	85	83%	66%	26%	3%	-17%	-57%
Urban to 2,500	28	67%	57%	30%	1%	-10%	-27%
2,500-10,000	3	54%	52%	33%	2%	- 2%	-21%
German Mixed							
Rural	50	84%	68%	32%	5%	-16%	-52%
Urban to 2,500	39	72%	64%	40%	3%	- 8%	-32%
2,500-10,000	15	71%	59%	41%	4%	-12%	-30%
Over 10,000	5	63%	65%	56%	5%	2%	- 7%
City wards	26	71%	67%	56%	5%	- 4%	-15%
Milwaukee wards	10	78%	78%	60%	5%	0%	-18%
German Catholic							
Rural	30	92%	72%	39%	12%	-20%	-53%
Urban to 2,500	19	85%	67%	46%	8%	-18%	-39%
2,500-10,000	4	76%	71%	61%	6%	- 5%	-15%
Bohemians							
Rural	11	90%	75%	56%	4%	-15%	-34%
Urban to 2,500	2	84%	69%	62%	8%	-15%	-22%
Irish							
Rural	9	90%	67%	49%	12%	-23%	-41%
Polish							
Rural	12	97%	90%	88%	1%	- 7%	- 9%
Urban to 2,500	2	89%	84%	67%	2%	- 5%	-22%
City wards	2	91%	91%	88%	2%	0%	- 3%
Milwaukee wards	5	92%	88%	84%	5%	- 4%	- 8%
Austrian							
Rural	1	93%	76%	38%	4%	-17%	-55%
Dutch Catholic							
Rural	1	86%	68%	59%	25%	-18%	-27%
Urban to 2,500	1	94%	69%	67%	19%	-17%	-55%
Twenty Cities		62%	65%	54%	3%	3%	- 8%
Milwaukee		78%	78%	64%	4.5%	0%	-14%
Wisconsin	550	63.5%	63.8%	50.1%	4.8%	0.3%	-13.4%

Table X   Robert La Follette Jr. Vote, 1934 to 1946

	1934/40 N=	1934 Sen	1940 Sen	1934/40 Change	1946 Sen Prim.	1946 N=
Native Stock						
Rural	22	51%	34%	-17%	42%	20
Urban to 2,500	20	41%	34%	- 7%	44%	20
2,500-10,000	2	25%	22%	- 3%	40%	2
City ward	1	17%	14%	- 3%	35%	1
English						
Rural	3	30%	33%	3%	36%	2
Urban to 2,500	2	43%	33%	-10%	46%	2
Welsh						
Rural	2	57%	42%	-15%	60%	2
Urban to 2,500	2	27%	29%	2%	49%	2
Norwegian						
Rural	35	79%	63%	-16%	69%	33
Urban to 2,500	19	58%	55%	- 3%	61%	19
2,500-10,000	1	66%	66%	0%	68%	1
City wards	4	57%	60%	3%	59%	4
Swedish						
Rural	14	67%	50%	-17%	54%	13
Urban to 2,500	5	54%	47%	- 7%	61%	5
2,500-10,000	1	55%	39%	-16%	43%	1
City ward	1	40%	55%	15%	51%	1
Danish						
Rural	8	72%	62%	-10%	61%	8
Urban to 2,500	3	43%	43%	0%	45%	3
2,500-10,000	1	45%	40%	- 5%	40%	1
City wards	4	47%	48%	1%	46%	4
Finnish						
Rural	12	71%	64%	- 7%	71%	9
Dutch Reformed						
Rural	3	37%	25%	-12%	52%	2
Urban to 2,500	2	32%	19%	-13%	44%	2
Belgian						
Rural	7	66%	46%	-20%	52%	6
Italian						
Rural	2	56%	42%	-14%	58%	2
Urban to 2,500	(1)		34%		23%	1
City ward	1	39%	44%	5%	42%	1
French Canadian						
Rural	2	60%	53%	- 7%	68%	2
Urban to 2,500	2	45%	30%	-15%	42%	2
City ward	1	60%	74%	14%	67%	1

Table X Robert La Follette Jr. Vote, 1934 to 1946

	1934/40 N=	1934 Sen	1940 Sen	1934/40 Change	1946 Sen Prim.	1946 N=
Swiss Reformed						
Rural	3	69%	59%	-10%	72%	3
Urban to 2,500	2	66%	57%	- 9%	68%	2
2,500-10,000	1	52%	43%	- 9%	63%	1
German Lutheran						
Rural	85	68%	42%	-26%	58%	68
Urban to 2,500	28	50%	35%	-15%	51%	26
2,500-10,000	3	42%	31%	- 9%	44%	3
German Mixed						
Rural	50	67%	40%	-27%	60%	36
Urban to 2,500	39	47%	36%	-11%	47%	38
2,500-10,000	15	43%	33%	-10%	43%	15
over 10,000	5	47%	38%	- 9%	46%	5
City wards	26	52%	43%	- 9%	53%	23
Milwaukee wards	10	49%	55%	6%	46%	10
German Catholics						
Rural	30	64%	43%	-21%	54%	22
Urban to 2,500	19	54%	38%	-16%	45%	19
2,500-10,000	4	48%	50%	2%	50%	4
Bohemians						
Rural	11	59%	43%	-16%	43%	10
Urban to 2,500	2	42%	31%	-11%	39%	2
Irish						
Rural	9	47%	37%	-10%	46%	9
Polish						
Rural	12	52%	45%	- 7%	48%	11
Urban to 2,500	2	50%	40%	-10%	55%	2
City wards	2(3)	44%	56%		50%	3
Milwaukee wards	5	45%	56%	11%	41%	5
Austrian						
Rural	1	27%	43%	16%	54%	1
Dutch Catholic						
Rural	1	61%	48%	-13%	42%	1
Urban to 2,500	1	59%	55%	- 4%	30%	1
Twenty Cities		44%	44%	0%	48%	
Milwaukee		44%	52%	8%	45%	
Wisconsin	550	50.4%	45.3%	-5.1%	49.3%	492

APPENDIX E   ETHNIC VOTING UNITS

German Lutheran Townships (85)

Brown
    Morrison (-1940)
Buffalo
    Belvidere (1910-   )
    Lincoln
    Milton
Calumet
    Brillion
    Rantoul
Clark
    Lynn
Dodge
    Burnett (-1940)
    Herman
    Hubbard (1913-   )
    Lebanon
    Lowell
    Portland
    Theresa
    Williamstown
Eau Claire
    Lincoln (1906-   )

Fond du Lac
    El Dorado
    Metomen (1921-   )
    Ripon
Grant
    Liberty
Green Lake
    Green Lake
    Mackford
    Manchester
    Marquette (-1940)
Jefferson
    Concord
    Farmington (1903-   )
    Ixonia (-1940)
    Lake Mills (-1940)
    Milford (-1940)
La Crosse
    Barre
Langlade
    Summitt (1923-   )

Lincoln
- Corning
- Pine River (1902-   )
- Scott

Manitowoc
- Newton (-1940)
- Rockland
- Schleswig

Marathon
- Berlin
- Easton
- Frankfort
- Hamburg
- Maine (-1940)
- Rib Falls
- Wein (1904-   )

Marquette
- Crystal Lake
- Mecan
- Shields
- Springfield

Monroe
- Wellington
- Wilton

Oconto
- Underhill

Outagamie
- Cicero
- Greenville
- Osborn
- Seymour

Ozaukee
- Grafton (-1940)

Portage
- Grant (-1940)

Sauk
- Freedom
- Honey Creek
- Merrimac (1899-   )
- Reedsburg (-1940)
- Washington (1910-   )
- Westfield (1917-   )

Shawano
- Almon
- Grant
- Hartland (1916-   )
- Pella
- Richmond (1901-1940)
- Seneca

Sheboygan   Fremont (-1940)
   Mosel (-1940)   Union
   Plymouth (-1940)   Weyauwega
   Rhine   Waushara
   Scott (-1940)   Bloomfield
   Sheboygan Falls (-1940)   Dakota
Washington   Richford
   Jackson (1912-   )   Winnebago
Waupaca   Nekimi
   Caledonia   Wolf River
   DuPont (1899-   )

German Lutheran Cities 2,500-10,000 (3)

Fond du Lac   Jefferson
   Ripon   Fort Atkinson
      Sauk
         Reedsburg

German Lutheran Villages and Cities under 2,500 (28)

Buffalo
    Alma
    Buffalo City
    Cochrane (1910-   )

Clark
    Granton (1916-   )

Dane
    Middleton (1905-1940)

Dodge
    Iron Ridge (1913-   )
    Lowell
    Reeseville

Eau Claire
    Fall Creek (1906-   )

Fond du Lac
    Fairweather (1921-   )

Jefferson
    Johnson Creek (1903-   )

Oconto
    Gillett (1899-   )
    Suring (1915-   )

Outagamie
    Black Creek (1904-   )
    Seymour

Ozaukee
    Cedarburg (-1940)

Price
    Kennan (1903-   )

Sauk
    Lime Ridge (1910-   )
    Loganville (1917-   )
    Rock Springs (Ableman)

Shawamo
    Bonduel (1916-   )
    Bowler (1923-   )

Sheboygan
    Adell (1918-   )

Vernon
    Stoddard (1911-   )

Washington
    Jackson (1912-   )

Waupaca
    Marion
    Weyauwega

Winnebago
    Winneconne

German Mixed Townships (50)

Clark
    Colby
    Mayville (1901-   )
    Seif (1904-   )

Columbia
    Columbus

Dane
    Berry
    Medina (1905-   )

Dodge
    Beaver Dam (-1940)
    Emmet
    Hustisford

Fond du Lac
    Auburn (1902-1940)

Jefferson
    Aztalan (1903-1940)
    Waterloo
    Watertown

Kewaunee
    Ahnapee

Manitowoc
    Manitowoc (-1936)
    Meeme

Marathon
    Bern (1904-   )
    Cleveland (1910-   )
    Hewitt
    Spencer (1902-   )
    Wausau (-1940)

Marquette
    Harris (-1940)

Monroe
    Ridgeville

Oconto
    How (1915-   )

Outagamie
    Black Creek (1904-   )
    Center
    Ellington
    Hortonia (-1940)
    Liberty
    Maple Creek

Ozaukee
    Fredonia (1920-1940)
    Saukville (1915-   )

Polk
    Farmington

Price
    Kennan (1903-   )
Shawano
    Fairbanks
    Germania
    Herman (1912-   )
Sheboygan
    Sherman (1918-1940)
Taylor
    Hammel
    Medford
    Molitor
    Rib Lake (1902-   )

Washington
    Farmington (-1940)
    Hartford (-1940)
Polk
    Richfield (-1940)
    Trenton (-1940)
    Wayne
Waupaca
    Larrabee
    Bear Creek

German Mixed Villages and Cities under 2,500 (39)

Ashland
    Butternut (1903-   )
Buffalo
    Fountain City
Calumet
    Brillion
    New Holstein (1901-   )
Clark
    Colby (and Marathon Co.)
    Dorchester (1901-   )

Dane
    Dane (1899-   )
Dodge
    Clyman (1924-   )
    Horicon
    Juneau
    Lomira (1899-   )
    Theresa
Grant
    Cassville

Green Lake
- Princeton

Jefferson
- Sullivan (1918-   )

Kewaunee
- Algoma (-1940)

Manitowoc
- Kiel (and Calumet Co.)
- Reedsville

Marathon
- Athens (1901-   )
- Edgar
- Schofield (1904-   )
- Stratford (1910-   )

Monroe
- Melvina (1922-   )
- Norwalk

Outagamie
- Hortonville

Ozaukee
- Fredonia (1922-   )
- Grafton
- Thiensville (1910-   )

Sauk
- Sauk City

Shawano
- Cecil (1905-   )
- Tigerton

Sheboygan
- Elkhart Lake

Taylor
- Medford

Washington
- Germantown (1927-   )
- Kewaskum
- Slinger (Schlesingerville)

Waukesha
- Butler (1913-   )
  (New Butler)
- Menomonee Falls

Waupaca
- Embarrass

German Mixed Cities 2,500-10,000 (15)

Columbia
  Columbus
Dodge
  Beaver Dam
  Mayville
Jefferson
  Jefferson
  Watertown (and Dodge Co.)
Lincoln
  Merrill
Racine
  Burlington

Shawano
  Shawano
Sheboygan
  Plymouth
  Sheboygan Falls
Washington
  Hartford
  West Bend
Waupaca
  Clintonville
  New London (and Outagamie Co.)
Wood
  Marshfield (and Marathon Co.)

German Mixed Cities over 10,000 (5)

Manitowoc
  Manitowoc
Marathon
  Wausau
Outagamie
  Appleton

Sheboygan
  Sheboygan
Winnebago
  Oshkosh

German Catholic Townships (30)

Ashland
    Agenda (1904-   )
    Chippewa (1904-   )
        (Butternut)

Calumet
    Brothertown
    Charlestown (-1940)
    Chilton
    New Holstein (1918-   )
    Woodville

Dane
    Cross Plains (1920-   )
    Roxbury
    Springfield

Dodge
    LeRoy
    Rubicon (1902-   )

Fond du Lac
    Ashford (1902-   )
    Calumet (-1940)
    Forest

Grant
    Cassville
    Jamestown (-1940)
    Paris (-1940)

Marathon
    Day
    Halsey (1904-   )
    Marathon

Monroe
    Jefferson (1922-   )

Ozaukee
    Belgium (1922-1940)
    Port Washington (-1940)

Racine
    Burlington (-1940)

Sauk
    Franklin (1912-   )

Shawano
    Washington (1905-   )

Sheboygan
    Russell

Washington
    Kewaskum

Wood
    Marshfield (1903-1940)

German Catholic Villages and Cities under 2,500 (19)

Brown
    Wrightstown (1901-   )
Calumet
    Chilton
    Hilbert
Chippewa
    Boyd
Dane
    Cross Plains (1920-   )
    Sun Prairie
    Waunakee
Dodge
    Neosho (1902-   )
Fond du Lac
    Campbellsport (1902-   )
    St. Cloud (1909-   )

Marathon
    Marathon
Ozaukee
    Belgium (1922-   )
    Saukville (1915-   )
Sauk
    Plain (1912-   )
Shawano
    Gresham (1908-   )
Sheboygan
    Random Lake (1907-   )
Trempealeau
    Arcadia
Washington
    Barton (1925-   )
Wood
    Auburndale

German Catholic Cities 2,500-10,000 (4)

Manitowoc
    Two Rivers
Outagamie
    Kaukauna

Ozaukee
    Port Washington
Winnebago
    Menasha

Norwegian Townships (35)

Adams
- Strongs Prairie

Buffalo
- Dover
- Modena

Crawford
- Freeman (1912-   )

Dane
- Christiana (1914-   )
- Perry
- Pleasant Springs

Dunn
- Colfax (1904-   )
- Grant
- Sand Creek (-1940)

Green
- York

Jackson
- Curran
- Franklin
- Garfield
- Northfield
- Springfield (1919-   )

Monroe
- Portland

Pierce
- Gilman
- Martell

Portage
- New Hope

St. Croix
- Eau Galle
- Rush River

Trempealeau
- Albion (1902-   )
- Chimney Rock
- Ettrick
- Hale
- Pigeon (-1940)
- Preston

Vernon
- Christiana
- Coon (1907-   )
- Franklin
- Jefferson

Waupaca
- Harrison
- Iola
- Scandinavia

Norwegian Villages and Cities under 2,500 (19)

Barron
    Dallas (1903-   )
Crawford
    Ferryville (1912-   )
Dane
    Blue Mounds (1912-   )
    Cambridge
    Deerfield
    DeForest (1903-   )
    Mt. Horeb (1899-   )
    McFarland (1920-   )
    Rockdale (1914-   )
Dunn
    Colfax (1904-   )
    Elk Mound (1909-   )

Jackson
    Taylor (1919-   )
Rock
    Orfordville (1900-   )
Trempealeau
    Blair
    Whitehall
Vernon
    Coon Valley (1907-   )
    Westby
Waupaca
    Iola
    Scandinavia

Norwegian Cities over 2,500 (1)

Dane
    Stoughton

Swedish Townships (14)

Burnett
- Anderson (1905-   )
- Daniels (1905-   )
  (Wood Lake)
- Grantsburg (1905-1940)
- Trade Lake
- Wood River (1905-   )

Pepin
- Pepin
- Stockholm (1903-   )

Pierce
- Isabella
- Maiden Rock

Polk
- Apple River

Price
- Hackett
- Hill
- Ogema
- Spirit (Brannan)

Swedish Villages and Cities under 2,500 (5)

Burnett
- Grantsburg

Pepin
- Stockholm (1903-   )

Pierce
- Bay City (1909-   )

Polk
- Clayton (1909-   )
- Dresser (Junction; Valley City) (1919-   )

Swedish Cities over 2,500 (1)

Price
- Park Falls (1901-   )

Danish Townships (8)

Brown
    New Denmark (1915-   )

Clark
    Hixon (1904-   )

Juneau
    Orange

Oconto
    Maple Valley

Polk
    Bone Lake
    Luck (1905-   )
    Milltown (1910-   )

Waupaca
    Waupaca

Danish Villages and Cities under 2,500 (3)

Brown
    Denmark (1915-   )

Polk
    Luck (1905-   )
    Milltown (1910-   )

Danish Cities over 2,500 (1)

Waupaca
    Waupaca

Finnish Townships (12)

Ashland
    Ashland (1910-   )
    Marengo (1908-   )

Bayfield
    Oulu (1904-   )

Douglas
    Brule (-1940)
    Cloverland (1921-   )
    Lakeside (1912-   )
    Maple (1907-   )

Lincoln
    Somo (1905-1940)

Iron
    Carey (1909-1940)
    Kimball (1914-   )
    Oma (1912-   )

Price
    Knox

Yankee Townships (22)

Adams
  Colburn
  Leola
Crawford
  Haney (1901-1940)
  Scott
Jackson
  Bear Bluff (-1940)
Monroe
  Lafayette
Oconto
  Little River
Richland
  Bloom
  Eagle
  Forest (1899-   )

Marshall
  Rockbridge
  Sylvan
  Willow
Vernon
  Forest
  Kickapoo
  Liberty
  Stark (1899-   )
  Webster
  Whitestown
Waushara
  Hancock (1902-   )
  Plainfield

Yankee Villages and Cities under 2,500 (20)

Columbia
    Fall River (1903-   )
    Pardeeville

Crawford
    Bell Center (1901-   )
    Gays Mills (1900-   )
    Lynxville
    Steuben (1900-   )

Green
    Brodhead
    Browntown

Jackson
    Merrillan

Richland
    Viola (and Vernon Co.)

Rock
    Clinton
    Evansville
    Milton (1900-   )

Vernon
    De Soto (and Crawford Co.)
    Ontario
    Readstown
    La Farge (1899-   )

Walworth
    Walworth (1901-   )

Waushara
    Hancock (1902-   )
    Plainfield

Yankee Cities over 2,500 (2)

Richland
    Richland Center

Walworth
    Delavan

English Townships (3)

Grant
   Little Grant

Iowa
   Linden (-1940)

Lafayette
   White Oak Springs

English Villages and Cities under 2,500 (2)

Grant
   Hazel Green

Iowa
   Linden

Welsh Townships (2)

Columbia
   Courtland
   Springvale

Welsh Villages and Cities under 2,500 (2)

Columbia
   Cambria

Dodge
   Randolph (and Columbia Co.)

Swiss Townships (3)

Green
  Mt. Pleasant
  New Glarus (1901-   )
  Washington

Swiss Villages and Cities under 2,500 (2)

Green
  Monticello
  New Glarus (1901-   )

Swiss Cities over 2,500 (1)

Green
  Monroe

Dutch Reformed Townships (3)

Fond du Lac   Sheboygan
  Alto   Holland (1909-   )
                                  Lima (-1940)

Dutch Reformed Villages and Cities under 2,500 (2)

Sheboygan
  Cedar Grove (1899-   )
  Oostburg (1909-   )

Polish Townships (12)

Brown
    Eaton
Clark
    Withee
Marathon
    Bevent (Pike Lake)
    Reid (Pike Lake)
Portage
    Dewey (1898-   )
    Hull (-1940)

Sharon
    Stockton
Rusk
    Strickland (1923-   )
Shawano
    Maple Grove
Taylor
    Roosevelt (1905-   )
Trempealeau
    Burnside

Polish Villages and Cities under 2,500 (2)

Brown
    Pulaski (1910-   )
    (and Oconto and Shawano Cos. to 1919)

Portage
    Junction City (1911-   )

Bohemian Townships (11)

Barron
    Bear Lake (1901-   )

Grant
    Castle Rock
    Muscoda

Kewaunee
    Carlton
    Casco (1920-   )
    Franklin
    Montpelier

Langlade
    Neva (-1940)

Manitowoc
    Franklin
    Vernon
    Union

Wood
    Milladore

Bohemian Villages and Cities under 2,500 (2)

Barron
    Haugen (1918-   )

Kewaunee
    Casco (1920-   )

Austrian Townships (1)

Pepin
    Lima

Irish Townships (9)

Brown
    Holland

Juneau
    Seven Mile Creek

Lafayette
    Kendall
    Shullsburg (1903-   )

St. Croix
    Erin Prairie
    Richmond

Sauk
    Bear Creek

Sheboygan
    Mitchell

Washington
    Erin

Belgian Townships (7)

Brown
    Green Bay (-1940)
    Humboldt

Door
    Brussels
    Gardner
    Union

Kewaunee
    Lincoln
    Red River

French Canadian Townships (2)

Iron
   Saxon (-1930)

St. Croix
   Somerset (1915-   )

Canadian Villages and Cities under 2,500 (2)

Marinette
   Coleman (1903-   )

St. Croix
   Somerset (1915-   )

Italian Townships (2)

Barron
   Crystal Lake (1902-   )

Vernon
   Genoa (1935-   )

Italian Villages and Cities under 2,500 (1)

Vernon
   Genoa (1935-   )

Dutch Catholic Townships (1)

Outagamie
   Vandenbroek (1902-   )

Dutch Catholic Villages and Cities under 2,500 (1)

Outagamie
   Little Chute (1899-   )

City Wards

Other German Wards (30)

Fond du Lac			Outagamie		
	Fond du Lac	ward 5 (-1930)		Appleton	ward 4 (-1938)
	"	ward 6 (-1930)		"	ward 5 (-1938)
Kenosha				"	ward 6 (-1938)
	Kenosha	ward 7 (-1924)	Sheboygan		
	"	ward 8 (-1924)		Sheboygan*	ward 1
La Crosse				"	ward 2
	La Crosse	ward 11		"	ward 3
Manitowoc				"	ward 4
	Manitowoc	ward 1		"	ward 5
	"	ward 3		"	ward 6
	"	ward 5		"	ward 7
Marathon				"	ward 8
	Wausau	ward 1	Winnebago		
	"	ward 2		Oshkosh**	ward 2
	"	ward 7		"	ward 3
	"	ward 8		"	ward 6
	"	ward 9		"	ward 8
				"	ward 9
				"	ward 12

* Sheboygan reapportioned c. 1933.

** Oshkosh reapportioned 1922.

Yankee Wards (5)

   Dane

      Madison   ward 10 (1904-1912)

   Rock

      Beloit   ward 2 (-1914)

      "   ward 4 (-1914)

      Janesville   ward 3 (-1920)

   Winnebago

      Oshkosh   ward 7

French Canadian Ward (1)

   Ashland

      Ashland   ward 7

Irish Ward (1)

   Rock

      Janesville   ward 5 (-1920)

Belgian Ward (1)

   Brown

      Green Bay   ward 4 (-1914)

Italian Ward (1)

   Milwaukee

      Milwaukee   ward 3

Norwegian Wards (4)

   Eau Claire

      Eau Claire   ward 7 (-1946)

      "   ward 8 (-1946)

      "   ward 10 (-1946)

   La Crosse

      La Crosse   ward 9

Swedish Ward (1)

   Ashland

      Ashland   ward 2

Danish Wards (4)

   Racine

      Racine   ward 8 (1904-)

      "   ward 11 (1904-)

      "   ward 12 (1910-)

      "   ward 13 (1910-)

Milwaukee German Wards (11)

Milwaukee	ward 7 (1912-)	Milwaukee	ward 19	
"	ward 9 (changes 1931)	"	ward 20	
"	ward 10	"	ward 21	
"	ward 13 (-1912)	"	ward 22 (1901-)	
"	ward 15	"	ward 23 (1901-)	
		"	ward 25 (1912-)	

Polish Wards (8)

Milwaukee Polish Wards

Milwaukee	ward 8 (1912-)
"	ward 11 (1912-)
"	ward 12
"	ward 14
"	ward 24 (1912-)

Other Polish Wards

Manitowoc
    Manitowoc ward 7

Portage
    Stevens Point ward 4
    " ward 7 (1936-   )

BIBLIOGRAPHY

PRIMARY SOURCES

The listing in the Bibliography of Primary and Secondary Sources is only a partial one. The footnotes provide a much more thorough description of sources used. Many of the primary sources were quantitative-- each table represents a myriad of statistical data-gathering and computation. Traditional manuscript sources and newspapers were consulted only to resolve specific questions. Thus, the New York Times was checked for the November, 1916 election, and for determining the political positions of progressives in the 1924 election.

The Wisconsin Legislative Reference Bureau maintains very comprehensive clipping files on political parties, movements, issues, and individuals. Among the files consulted for this study were those on the Republican, Democratic, and Progressive parties; Robert Marion La Follette; and Transportation for Parochial School Pupils. The latter was especially useful in analyzing the religious split in the 1946 Parochial School Bus Aid referendum. All major Wisconsin dailies, selected weeklies, and major national newspapers are among those clipped by the Reference Bureau.

I. Government Publications

Tabular Statements of the [1885, 1895, and 1905] Census Enumeration and the Agricultural, Mineral [Dairying in 1905], and Manufacturing Interests of the State of Wisconsin.

United States Bureau of the Census, Eleventh through Seventeenth Censuses, 1890-1950.

United States Bureau of the Census, Religious Bodies, 1906, 1916, 1926, 1936.

Wisconsin Blue Book, 1887-1970.

Wisconsin Bureau of Labor and Industrial Statistics, Biennial Reports. 15 vols., 1883-1910.

Wisconsin Crop and Livestock Reporting Service. A Century of Wisconsin Agriculture: 1848-1948. Research Bulletin 290. Madison: 1948.

Wisconsin Crop and Livestock Reporting Service. County Agricultural Statistics. Research Bulletin 202. Nos. 1-71. Madison: 1939-1942.

Wisconsin Crop and Livestock Reporting Service. County Agricultural Statistics, Third Series. Madison: 1952-1955.

Wisconsin Crop and Livestock Reporting Service. Wisconsin Dairying in Mid-Century. Research Bulletin 331. Madison: May, 1955.

Wisconsin Crop and Livestock Reporting Service. Wisconsin Rural Resources [Fourth County Agricultural Series]. Madison: 1956-1958.

Wisconsin Department of Transportation, Division of Highways. County Maps of Wisconsin. Madison: January, 1971.

Wisconsin Legislative Reference Bureau. A Guide to the Wisconsin Blue Book, 1853-1962. Research Bulletin 141. Madison: February, 1963. Mimeographed.

Wisconsin Legislative Reference Bureau. The Presidential Preference Primary in Wisconsin. Research Bulletin 128. Madison: April, 1960. Mimeographed.

II. Other Sources of Data

Donoghue, James R. How Wisconsin voted, 1848-1960. Madison: University of Wisconsin Extension Division, 1962.

Fuchs, Zahava, and Douglas G. Marshall. The Socioeconomic Composition of Wisconsin's Population, 1900-1960. Population Series No. 12. Madison: University of Wisconsin, Department of Rural Sociology, May, 1968.

Gaustad, Edwin Scott. Historical Atlas of Religion in America. New York: Harper and Row, 1962.

Heming, Harry Hooper. The Catholic Church in Wisconsin. Milwaukee: Catholic History Publishing Co., 1895-1898.

Marshall, Douglas G. Wisconsin's Population Changes and Prospects, 1900-1963. Research Bulletin 241. Madison: University of Wisconsin Agricultural Experiment Station, March, 1963.

National Council of Churches. Churches and Church Membership in the United States: An Enumeration and Analysis by Counties, States, and Regions. New York: 1956-1958.

National Lutheran Council. Lutheran Directory and Statistical Handbook. New York: 1953 and 1954.

Norlie, Olaf M. Norsk Lutherske Menigheter i Amerika. 2 vols. Minneapolis: Augsburg Publishing Co., 1918.

Pressly, Thomas, and William Scofield. Farm Real Estate Values in the United States by Counties, 1850-1959. Seattle: University of Washington Press, 1965.

Tien, H. Yuan, ed. Milwaukee Metropolitan Fact Book, 1940, 1950, and 1960. Madison: University of Wisconsin Press, 1962.

Wisconsin's Changing Population. Scientific Inquiries Publication IX. Bulletin of the University of Wisconsin. Madison: October, 1942. (Includes map on "The People of Wisconsin According to Ethnic Stocks, 1940.")

III. Autobiographies, Memoirs, and Other Published Sources

Anderson, Rasmus B., assisted by Albert O. Barton. Life Story of Rasmus B. Anderson. 2nd. ed. Madison: privately printed, 1917.

Campbell, William J. History of the Republican Party in Wisconsin: Under Convention Plan, 1924 to 1940. Oshkosh, Wisconsin: privately printed, 1942.

Chapple, John B. La Follette Road to Communism--Must We Go Further Along That Road? Ashland, Wisconsin: privately printed, 1936.

Evjue, William T. "A Fighting Editor." Madison: Wells Printing Co., 1968.

Frear, James A. Forty Years of Progressive Public Service. Washington, D. C.: 1937.

Haugen, Nils P. Pioneer and Political Reminiscences. Evansville, Wisconsin: privately printed, 1930. Also appeared in the Wisconsin Magazine of History.

La Follette, Philip, edited by Donald Young. Adventure in Politics: The Memoirs of Philip La Follette. New York: Holt, Rinehart, and Winston, 1970.

La Follette, Robert M. La Follette's Autobiography: A Personal Narrative of Political Experience. Madison: Robert M. La Follette Co., 1913.

The Law Makers of Wisconsin, 1899-1901: A Compilation of Biographical Sketches and Portraits of the United States Senators, Members of Congress, State Officers, and Members of the Legislature. Milwaukee: The Evening Wisconsin Co., 1899.

Platt, Chester C. What La Follette's State is Doing. Batavia, New York: Batavia Times Press, 1924.

Stephenson, Isaac. Recollections of a Long Life, 1829-1915. Chicago: 1915.

Stewart, Charles. "Prussianizing Wisconsin," Atlantic Monthly, CXXIII (January, 1919), 99-105.

"Wisconsin's Former Governors, 1848-1959," Wisconsin Blue Book, 1960, 67-206.

Work, John M. "The First World War," Wisconsin Magazine of History, XLI (Autumn, 1957), 32-44.

SECONDARY SOURCES

I. Books

Adamany, David. *Financing Politics: Recent Wisconsin Elections*. Madison: University of Wisconsin Press, 1969.

Anderson, Arlow W. *The Immigrant Takes His Stand: The Norwegian-American Press and Public Affairs, 1847-1872*. Northfield, Minnesota: Norwegian American Historical Association, 1953.

Aydelotte, William. *Quantification in History*. Reading, Massachusetts: Addison-Wesley, 1971.

Barton, Albert O. *La Follette's Winning of Wisconsin, 1894-1904*. Madison: 1922.

Benson, Lee. *The Concept of Jacksonian Democracy: New York as a Test Case*. Princeton: Princeton University Press, 1961.

Benson, Lee. *Toward the Scientific Study of History: Selected Essays*. Philadelphia: J. B. Lipincott, 1972.

Burdick, Eugene, and Arthur J. Brodbeck, eds. *American Voting Behavior*. Glencoe, Illinois: Free Press, 1959.

Burner, David. *The Politics of Provincialism: The Democratic Party in Transition, 1918-1932*. New York: Alfred Knopf, 1968.

Burnham, Walter Dean. *Critical Elections and the Mainsprings of American Politics*. New York: Norton, 1970.

Caine, Stanley P. *The Myth of a Progressive Reform: Railroad Regulation in Wisconsin 1903-1910*. Madison: State Historical Society of Wisconsin, 1970.

Campbell, Angus, Philip Converse, Warren Miller, and Donald Stokes. *The American Voter*. New York: John Wiley, 1960.

Campbell, Angus, et al. *Elections and the Political Order*. New York: John Wiley and Sons, 1965.

Capps, Finis Herbert. *From Isolation to Involvement: The Swedish Immigrant Press in America*. Chicago: Swedish Pioneer Historical Society, 1966.

Child, Clifton James. *The German Americans in Politics, 1914-1917*. Madison: University of Wisconsin Press, 1939.

Clubb, Jerome M., and Howard W. Allen, eds. *Electoral Change and Stability in American Political History*. New York: Free Press, 1971.

Curti, Merle. *The Making of an American Community: A Case Study of Democracy in a Frontier County*. Stanford, California: Stanford University Press, 1959.

David, Paul T. *Party Strength in the United States, 1872-1970*. Charlottesville, Virginia: University Press of Virginia, 1972.

Dawidowicz, Lucy, and Leon Goldstein. *Politics in a Pluralist Democracy: Studies of Voting in the 1960 Election*. New York: Institute of Human Relations Press, 1963.

Dictionary of Wisconsin Biography. Madison: State Historical Society of Wisconsin, 1960.

Doan, Edward N. *The La Follettes and the Wisconsin Idea*. New York: Rinehart and Co., 1947.

Dollar, Charles, and Richard J. Jensen. *The Historian's Guide to Statistics: Quantitative Analysis and Historical Research*. New York: Holt, Rinehart, and Winston, 1971.

Epstein, Leon D. *Politics in Wisconsin*. Madison: University of Wisconsin Press, 1958.

Epstein, Leon D. *Votes and Taxes*. Madison: University of Wisconsin Extension Division, 1964.

Fenton, John H. *Midwest Politics*. New York: Holt, Rinehart, and Winston, 1966.

Fry, C. Luther. *The New and Old Immigrant on the Land: A Study of Americanization and the Rural Church*. New York: George M. Doran, 1922.

Fuchs, Lawrence H. ed. American Ethnic Politics, New York: Harper and Row, 1968.

Gavett, Thomas W. Development of the Labor Movement in Milwaukee. Madison: University of Wisconsin Press, 1965.

Gerson, Louis L. The Hyphenate in Recent American Politics and Diplomacy. Lawrence, Kansas: University of Kansas, 1964.

Gleason, Philip. The Conservative Reformers: German-American Catholics and the Social Order. Notre Dame, Indiana: Notre Dame University Press, 1968.

Gosnell, Harold F. Grass Roots Politics: National Voting Behavior of Typical States. Washington: American Council on Public Affairs Press, 1942.

Graham, Otis L., Jr. An Encore for Reform: The Old Progressives and the New Deal. New York: Oxford University Press, 1967.

Griffith, Robert. The Politics of Fear: Joseph R. McCarthy and the Senate. Lexington, Kentucky: University of Kentucky Press, 1970.

Heberle, Rudolf. Social Movements. New York: Appleton-Century Crofts, 1951.

Hense-Jensen, Wilhelm, and Ernest Bruncken. Wisconsin's Deutsch-Amerikaner bis zum Schloss des Neunzehnten Jahrhunderts. 2 vols. Milwaukee: Milwaukee Herold Press, 1900-1902. (Portions translated and edited by Joseph Schafer, 1939.)

Hofstadter, Richard. The Age of Reform: From Bryan to F. D. R. New York: Alfred Knopf, 1955. Vintage paperback edition, 1960.

Holmes, Fred L. Old World Wisconsin: Around Europe in the Badger State. Eau Claire: E. M. Hale and Co., 1944.

Jensen, Richard J. The Winning of the Midwest: Social and Political Conflict, 1888-1896. Chicago: University of Chicago Press, 1971.

Johnson, Roger T. *Robert M. La Follette Jr. and the Decline of the Progressive Party in Wisconsin.* Madison: State Historical Society of Wisconsin, 1964.

Key, V. O., With the assistance of Milton C. Cummings. *The Responsible Electorate: Rationality in Presidential Voting, 1936-1960.* Cambridge: Harvard University Press, 1966.

Kleppner, Paul. *The Cross of Culture: A Social Analysis of Midwestern Politics, 1850-1900.* New York: Free Press, 1970.

Kolb, John H. *Emerging Rural Communities: Group Relations in Rural Society, A Review of Wisconsin Research in Action.* Madison: University of Wisconsin Press, 1959.

Kolehmainen, John, and George W. Hill. *Haven in the Woods: The Story of the Finns in Wisconsin.* Madison: State Historical Society of Wisconsin, 1951.

Korman, Gerd. *Industrialization, Immigrants, and Americanizers: The View from Milwaukee, 1866-1921.* Madison: State Historical Society of Wisconsin, 1967.

La Follette, Belle Case and Fola. *Robert M. La Follette, June 14, 1855-June 18, 1925.* 2 vols. New York: MacMillan, 1953.

Lipset, Seymour Martin. *Political Man: The Social Bases of Politics.* Garden City, New York: Doubleday, 1960. Anchor paperback edition, 1963.

Lipset, Seymour Martin, ed. *Politics and the Social Sciences.* New York: Oxford University Press, 1969.

Lipset, Seymour Martin, and Richard Hofstadter, eds. *Sociology and History: Methods.* New York: Basic Books, 1968.

Lovejoy, Allen F. *La Follette and the Establishment of the Direct Primary in Wisconsin.* New Haven, Connecticut: Yale University Press, 1941.

Lubell, Samuel. *The Future of American Politics.* New York: Harpers, 1955. Harper paperback third edition, 1965.

Lubell, Samuel. *Revolt of the Moderates.* New York: Harpers, 1956.

Luebke, Frederick C. *Bonds of Loyalty: German Americans During World War I.* DeKalb, Illinois: Northern Illinois University Press, 1974.

Luebke, Frederick C. *Immigrants and Politics: The Germans of Nebraska, 1880-1900.* Lincoln: University of Nebraska Press, 1969.

MacKay, Kenneth C. *The Progressive Movement of 1924.* New York: Columbia University Press, 1947.

Margulies, Herbert F. *The Decline of the Progressive Movement in Wisconsin, 1890-1920.* Madison: State Historical Society of Wisconsin, 1968.

Maxwell, Robert S. *Emanuel L. Philipp: Wisconsin Stalwart.* Madison: State Historical Society of Wisconsin, 1959.

Maxwell, Robert S. *La Follette and the Rise of the Progressives in Wisconsin.* Madison: State Historical Society of Wisconsin, 1956.

May, Ernest R. *The World War and American Isolation, 1914-1917.* Cambridge: Harvard University Press, 1959.

McCoy, Donald R. *Angry Voices: Left-of-Center Politics in the New Deal Era.* Lawrence: University of Kansas Press, 1958.

McDonald, Sister M. Justille. *History of the Irish in Wisconsin in the Nineteenth Century.* Washington, D. C.: Catholic University of America, 1954.

Miller, Sally M. *Victor Berger and the Promise of Constructive Socialism, 1910-1920.* Westport, Connecticut: Greenwood, 1973.

Nelson, Clifford L. *German-American Political Behavior in Nebraska and Wisconsin 1916-1920.* Lincoln: University of Nebraska-Lincoln Publication, No. 217, 1972.

O'Brien, David J. *American Catholics and Social Reform: The New Deal Years.* New York: Oxford University Press, 1968.

O'Grady, Joseph P. ed. *The Immigrant's Influence on Wilson's Peace Policies.* Lexington: University of Kentucky Press, 1967.

Plumb, Ralph G. *Badger Politics, 1836-1930.* Manitowoc, Wisconsin: 1930.

Quaife, Milo M. *Wisconsin, Its History and Its People, 1634-1924.* 4 vols. Chicago: 1924.

Raney, William F. *Wisconsin, A Story of Progress.* New York: Prentice Hall, 1940.

Rieselbach, Leroy N. *The Roots of Isolationism: Congressional Voting and Presidential Leadership in Foreign Policy.* Indianapolis: Bobbs Merrill, 1966.

Rischin, Moses. *"Our Own Kind": Voting by Race, Creed or National Origin.* Santa Barbara, California: Center for the Study of Democratic Institution, 1960.

Rogin, Michael Paul. *The Intellectuals and McCarthy: The Radical Specter.* Cambridge: MIT Press, 1967.

Rogin, Michael Paul, and John L. Shover. *Political Change in California: Critical Elections and Social Movements, 1890-1966.* Westport, Connecticut: Greenwood, 1970.

Schafer, Joseph. *Four Wisconsin Counties: Prairie and Forest.* General Studies, Vol. II. Madison: State Historical Society of Wisconsin, 1927.

Schafer, Joseph. *A History of Agriculture in Wisconsin.* General Studies, Vol. I. Madison: State Historical Society of Wisconsin, 1922.

Schafer, Joseph. *Town Studies, I. Wisconsin Domesday Book.* Madison: State Historical Society of Wisconsin, 1924.

Schafer, Joseph. *The Winnebago-Horicon Basin.* General Studies, Vol. IV. Madison: State Historical Society of Wisconsin, 1937.

Schafer, Joseph. *The Wisconsin Lead Region.* General Studies, Vol. III. Madison: State Historical Society of Wisconsin, 1932.

Schlinkert, Leroy, comp. Subject Bibliography of Wisconsin History. Madison: State Historical Society of Wisconsin, 1947.

Silbey, Joel H., and Samuel T. McSeveney, eds. Voters, Parties, and Elections: Quantitative Essays in the History of American Popular Voting Behavior. Lexington, Massachusetts: Xerox College Publications, 1972.

Silva, Ruth C. Rum, Religion, and Votes: 1928 Reexamined. University Park: Pennsylvania State University Press, 1962.

Soltow, Lee. Patterns of Wealthholding in Wisconsin Since 1850. Madison: University of Wisconsin Press, 1971.

Still, Bayrd. Milwaukee: The History of a City. Madison: State Historical Society of Wisconsin, 1965.

Stirn, E. W. Annotated Bibliography of Robert M. La Follette. Chicago: University of Chicago Press, 1937.

Swierenga, Robert P. ed. Quantification in American History: Theory and Research. New York: Atheneum, 1970.

Thelen, David P. The Early Life of Robert M. La Follette, 1855-1884. Chicago: Loyola University Press, 1966.

Thelen, David P. The New Citizenship: Origins of Progressivism in Wisconsin, 1885-1900. Columbia: University of Missouri Press, 1972.

Vidich, Arthur J., and Joseph Bensman. Small Town in Mass Society: Class, Power, and Religion in a Rural Community. Princeton: Princeton University Press, 1958.

Wefald, Jon. A Voice of Protest: Norwegians in American Politics, 1890-1917. Northfield, Minnesota: Norwegian-American Historical Association, 1971.

Wittke, Carl. German-Americans and the World War. Ohio Historical Collections, Columbus: Ohio State Archaeological and Historical Society, 1936.

II. Articles and Essays

Acrea, Kenneth. "The Wisconsin Reform Coalition, 1892-1900: La Follette's Rise to Power," *Wisconsin Magazine of History*, LII (Winter, 1968-69), 132-157.

Adamany, David. "The Size of Place Analysis Reconsidered," *Western Political Quarterly*, XVII (September, 1964), 477-487.

Allen, Howard W. "Isolationism and German Americans," *Journal of the Illinois State Historical Society*, LVI (Summer, 1964), 321-339.

Aydellotte, William. "Quantification in History," *American Historical Review*, LXXI (April, 1966), 803-825.

Baggaley, Andrew. "Patterns of Voting Change in Wisconsin Counties, 1952-57," *Western Political Quarterly*, XII (March, 1959), 141-144.

Baggaley, Andrew. "Religious Influences on Wisconsin Voting, 1928-1960," *American Political Science Review*, LVI (May, 1962), 66-70.

Bean, Louis H., Frederick Mosteller, and Frederick Williams. "Nationalities and 1944," *Public Opinion Quarterly*, VII (Fall, 1944), 368-375.

Benson, Lee. "Research Problems in American Political Historiography," in Mirra Komarovsky, ed. *Common Frontiers of the Social Sciences*. Glencoe, Illinois: Free Press, 1957, 113-181.

Bernstein, Barton J., and Franklin A. Leib. "Progressive Republican Senators and American Imperialism, 1898-1916: A Reappraisal," *Mid-America*, L (July, 1968), 163-205.

Boyer, William W. Jr. "Public Transportation of Parochial School Pupils," *Wisconsin Law Review, 1952* (January, 1952), 64-90.

Burchell, R. A. "Did the Irish and German Voters Desert the Democrats in 1920? A Tentative Statistical Answer," *Journal of American Studies*, VI (August, 1972), 153-164.

Burnham, Walter Dean. "The Changing Shape of the American Political Universe," *American Political Science Review*, LIX (March, 1965), 7-28.

Campbell, Angus. "Surge and Decline: A Study of Electoral Change," *Public Opinion Quarterly*, XXIV (Fall, 1960), 397-418.

Carter, Paul A. "The Campaign of 1928 Re-examined: A Study in Political Folklore," *Wisconsin Magazine of History*, XLVI (Summer, 1963), 263-272.

Clubb, Jerome M., and Howard W. Allen. "The Critics and the Election of 1928: Partisan Realignment?" *American Historical Review*, LXXIV (April, 1969), 1205-1220.

Cuddy, Edward. "Irish-Americans and the 1916 Election: An Episode in Immigrant Adjustment," *American Quarterly*, XXI (Summer, 1969), 228-243.

Cuddy, Edward. "Pro-Germanism and American Catholicism, 1914-1917," *Catholic Historical Review*, LIV (October, 1968), 427-454.

Degler, Carl. "American Political Parties and the Rise of the City: An Interpretation," *Journal of American History*, LI (June, 1964), 41-59.

Donoghue, James R. "The Local Government System of Wisconsin," *Wisconsin Blue Book, 1968*, 69-283.

Duff, John B. "German-Americans and the Peace, 1918-1920," *American Jewish Historical Quarterly*, LIX (June, 1970), 424-444.

Dykstra, Robert. "Town-Country Conflict: A Hidden Dimension in American Social History," *Agricultural History*, XXXVIII (October, 1964), 195-204.

Epstein, Leon D. "Size of Place and the Division of the Two-Party Vote in Wisconsin," *Western Political Quarterly*, IX (March, 1956), 138-150.

Esslinger, Dean R. "American German and Irish Attitudes Toward Neutrality, 1914-1917: A Study of Catholic Minorities," *Catholic Historical Review*, LIII (July, 1967), 194-216.

Falk, Karen. "Public Opinion in Wisconsin During World War I," *Wisconsin Magazine of History*, XXV (June, 1942), 389-407.

Flinn, Thomas A. "Continuity and Change in Ohio Politics," *Journal of Politics*, XXIV (August, 1962), 521-544.

Folsom, Burton W. "The Collective Biography as a Research Tool," *Mid-America*, LIV (April, 1972), 108-122.

Gilbert, Charles E. "National Political Alignments and the Politics of Large Cities," *Political Science Quarterly*, LXXIX (March, 1964), 25-51.

Gleason, Philip. "An Immigrant Group's Interest in Progressive Reform: The Case of the German-American Catholics," *American Historical Review*, LXXIII (December, 1967), 367-379.

Gosnell, Harold F., and Morris H. Cohen. "Progressive Politics: Wisconsin An Example," *American Political Science Review*, XXXIV (October, 1940), 920-935.

Hall, Arnold B. "The Direct Primary and Party Responsibility in Wisconsin," *Annals of the American Academy of Political and Social Science*, CVI (1923), 40-54.

Havig, Alan R. "A Disputed Legacy: Roosevelt Progressives and the La Follette Campaign of 1924," *Mid-America*, LIII (January, 1971), 44-64.

Hays, Samuel. "Political Parties and the Community-Society Continuum," in William Nisbet Chambers and Walter Dean Burnham, eds. *The American Party Systems: Stages of Political Development*. New York: Oxford University Press, 1967, 152-181.

Hays, Samuel P. "The Social Analysis of American Political History, 1880-1920," *Political Science Quarterly*, LXXX (September, 1965), 373-394.

Heberle, Rudolf. "Principles of Political Ecology," in Karl G. Specht, ed. *Soziologishe Forschung in Unserer Zeit*. Köln: 1951, 187-196.

Kennedy, Padraic. "La Follette's Foreign Policy From Imperialism to Anti-Imperialism," *Wisconsin Magazine of History*, XLVI (Summer, 1963), 287-293.

Kennedy, Padraic. "La Follette's Imperialist Flirtation," *Pacific Historical Review*, XXIX (May, 1960), 131-144.

Kennedy, Padraic. "Lenroot, La Follette and the Campaign of 1906," *Wisconsin Magazine of History*, XLII (Spring, 1959), 163-174.

Kerr, Thomas J. "German-Americans and Neutrality in the 1916 Election," *Mid-America*, XLIII (April, 1961), 95-105.

Key, V. O. "Secular Realignment and the Party System," *Journal of Politics*, XXI (May, 1959), 197-210.

Key, V. O. "A Theory of Critical Elections," *Journal of Politics*, XVII (February, 1955), 3-18.

Kinzer, Donald L. "The Political Uses of Anti-Catholicism: Michigan and Wisconsin, 1890-1894," *Michigan History*, XXXIX (September, 1955), 312-332.

Korman, Gerd. "Political Loyalties, Immigrant Traditions and Reform: The Wisconsin German-American Press and Progressivism, 1909-1912," *Wisconsin Magazine of History*, XL (Spring, 1957), 161-168.

Larson, Agnes M. "The Editorial Policy of *Skandinaven* 1900-1903," *Norwegian-American Studies and Records*, VIII (1934), 112-135.

Leary, William M. Jr. "Woodrow Wilson, Irish Americans, and the Election of 1916," *Journal of American History*, LIV (June, 1967), 57-72.

Levi, Kate Everest. "Geographical Origin of German Immigration to Wisconsin," *Collections of the State Historical Society of Wisconsin*, XIV (1898), 341-393.

Levi, Kate Everest. "How Wisconsin Came by Its Large German Element," *Collections of the State Historical Society of Wisconsin*, XII (1892), 299-334.

Lubell, Samuel. "Who Votes Isolationist and Why," *Harpers*, CCII (April, 1951), 29-36.

Luebke, Frederick C. "German Immigrants and Churches in Nebraska, 1889-1915," *Mid-America*, L (April, 1968), 116-130.

Margulies, Herbert F. "Anti-Catholicism in Wisconsin Politics, 1914-1920," *Mid-America*, XLIV (January, 1962), 51-56.

Margulies, Herbert F. "The Background of the La Follette-McGovern Schism," *Wisconsin Magazine of History*, XL (Autumn, 1956), 21-29.

Margulies, Herbert F. "The Decline of Wisconsin Progressivism, 1911-1914," *Mid-America*, XXXIX (July, 1957), 131-155.

Margulies, Herbert F. "The Election of 1920 in Wisconsin: The Return to 'Normalcy' Reappraised," *Wisconsin Magazine of History*, XLI (Autumn, 1957), 15-22.

Margulies, Herbert F. "The La Follette-Philipp Alliance of 1918," *Wisconsin Magazine of History*, XXXVIII (Summer, 1955), 248-249.

Margulies, Herbert F. "Political Weakness in Wisconsin Progressivism, 1905-1909," *Mid-America*, XLI (July, 1959), 154-172.

McCoy, Donald R. "The Formation of the Wisconsin Progressive Party in 1934," *The Historian*, XIV (Autumn, 1951), 70-90.

McCoy, Donald R. "The National Progressives of America, 1938," *Mississippi Valley Historical Review*, XLIV (June, 1957), 75-93.

Muzik, Edward J. "Victor L. Berger: Congress and The Red Scare," *Wisconsin Magazine of History*, XLVII (Summer, 1964), 309-318.

Ogburn, William F., and Lolagene C. Coombs. "The Economic Factor in the Roosevelt Elections," *American Political Science Review*, SSIV (August, 1940), 719-727.

Ogburn, William F., and Estelle Hill. "Income Classes and the Roosevelt Vote in 1932," *Political Science Quarterly*, L (June, 1935), 186-193.

Ogburn, William F., and Nell Snow Talbot. "A Measurement of the Factors in the Presidential Election of 1928," *Social Forces*, VIII (December, 1929), 175-183.

Parenti, Michael. "Ethnic Politics and the Persistence of Ethnic Identification," *American Political Science Review*, LXI (September, 1967), 717-726.

Prescott, Gerald. "Gentlemen Farmers in the Gilded Age," Wisconsin Magazine of History, LV (Spring, 1972), 197-212.

Prescott, Gerald. "Wisconsin Farm Leaders in the Gilded Age," Agricultural History, XLIV (April, 1970), 183-199.

Ranney, Austin. "The Utility and Limitations of Aggregate Data in the Study of Electoral Behavior," in Austin Ranney, ed. Essays on the Behavioral Study of Politics. Urbana: University of Illinois Press, 1962, 91-102.

Reinders, Robert C. "Daniel W. Hoan and the Milwaukee Socialist Party During the First World War," Wisconsin Magazine of History, XXXVI (Autumn 1952), 48-55.

Rieselbach, Leroy N. "The Basis of Isolationist Behavior," Public Opinion Quarterly, XXIV (Winter, 1960), 645-657.

Robinson, W. S. "Ecological Correlations and Behavior of Individuals," American Sociological Review, XV (June, 1950), 351-357.

Rothstein, Morton, et al. "Quantification and American History: An Assessment," in Herbert J. Bass, ed. The State of American History. Chicago: Quadrangle, 1970, 298-329.

Rusk, Jerrold G. "The Effect of the Australian Ballot Reform on Split Ticket Voting: 1876-1908," American Political Science Review, LXIV (December, 1970), 1220-1238.

Schafer, Joseph. "Church Records in Migration Studies," Wisconsin Magazine of History, X (March, 1927), 328-337.

Schafer, Joseph. "Documenting Local History," Wisconsin Magazine of History, V (December, 1921), 142-159.

Schafer, Joseph. "Peopling the Middle West," Wisconsin Magazine of History, XXI (September, 1937), 85-106.

Schafer, Joseph. "Who Elected Lincoln?" American Historical Review, XLVII (October, 1941), 51-63.

Schafer, Joseph. "The Wisconsin Domesday Book," *Wisconsin Magazine of History*, IV (September, 1920), 61-74.

Schafer, Joseph. "The Yankee and Teuton in Wisconsin," *Wisconsin Magazine of History*, VI and VII (December, 1922-December, 1923), 125-145, 261-279, 386-402, 3-19, and 148-171.

Sellers, Charles G. "The Equilibrium Cycle in Two-Party Politics," *Public Opinion Quarterly*, XXIX (Spring, 1965), 16-38.

Shannon, David A. "Was McCarthy a Political Heir of La Follette?" *Wisconsin Magazine of History*, XLV (Autumn, 1961), 3-9.

Shideler, J. H. "The Disintegration of the Progressive Party Movement of 1924," *The Historian*, XIII (Spring, 1951), 189-201.

Shideler, J. H. "The La Follette Progressive Party Campaign of 1924," *Wisconsin Magazine of History*, XXXIII (June, 1950), 444-457.

Smith, Guy-Harold. "Notes on the Distribution of the Foreign-Born Scandinavian in Wisconsin in 1905," *Wisconsin Magazine of History*, XIV (June, 1931), 419-436.

Smith, Guy-Harold. "Notes on the Distribution of the German-Born in Wisconsin in 1905," *Wisconsin Magazine of History*, XIII (December, 1929), 107-120.

Smith, Guy-Harold. "The Populating of Wisconsin," *Geographical Review*, XVIII (July, 1928), 401-421.

Smith, Guy-Harold. "The Settlement and the Distribution of the Population in Wisconsin," *Wisconsin Acadamy of Science, Arts, and Letters, Transactions*, XXIV (1929), 53-107.

Smuckler, R. H. "The Region of Isolationism," *American Political Science Review*, XLIII (June, 1953), 386-401.

Sorouf, Frank J. "Extra-Legal Parties in Wisconsin," *American Political Science Review*, XLVIII (September, 1954), 692-704.

Stave, Bruce Martin. "The 'La Follette Revolution' and the Pittsburgh Vote, 1932," *Mid-America*, XLIX (October, 1967), 244-251.

Steinke, John, and James Weinstein. "McCarthy and The Liberals," *Studies on the Left*, II (Summer, 1962), 43-50.

Stephenson, George M. "The Attitudes of Swedish Americans Toward the World War," *Proceedings of The Mississippi Valley Historical Association*, X (1919), 79-94.

Still, Bayrd. "Norwegian-Americans and Wisconsin Politics in the Forties," *Norwegian-American Studies and Records*, VIII (1934), 58-64.

Swierenga, Robert P. "Ethnocultural Political Analysis: A New Approach to American Ethnic Studies," *Journal of American Studies*, V (April, 1971), 59-79.

Thelen, David P. "Robert La Follette's Leadership, 1891-1906: The Old and New Politics and the Dilemma of the Progressive Politician," *Pacific Northwestern Quarterly*, LXII (July, 1971), 97-109.

Thelen, David P. "Social Tensions and the Origins of Progressivism," *Journal of American History*, LVI (September, 1969), 323-341.

Usher, Ellis B. "New England in Wisconsin," *New England Magazine*, XXII (June, 1900), 446-461.

Weibull, Jorgen. "The Wisconsin Progressives, 1900-1914," *Mid-America*, XLVII (July, 1965), 191-221.

Weinstein, James. "Anti-War Sentiment and the Socialist Party, 1917-1918," *Political Science Quarterly*, LXXIV (June, 1959), 215-239.

Wolfinger, Raymond E. "The Development and Persistence of Ethnic Voting," *American Political Science Review*, XLIX (December, 1965), 896-908.

Wyman, Roger F. "Middle-Class Voters and Progressive Reform: The Conflict of Class and Culture," *American Political Science Review*, LXVIII (June, 1974), 488-504.

Wyman, Roger E. "Wisconsin Ethnic Groups and the Election of 1890," *Wisconsin Magazine of History*, LI (Summer, 1968), 269-293.

III. Ph. D. Dissertations, Master's Theses, and Other Unpublished Works

    Acrea, Kenneth. "Wisconsin Progressivism: Legislative Response to Social Change, 1891-1909." 2 vols. University of Wisconsin Ph. D. Dissertation, 1968.

    Backstrom, Charles H. "The Progressive Party of Wisconsin, 1934-1946." University of Wisconsin Ph. D. Dissertation, 1956.

    Erlebacher, Albert. "Herman L. Ekern, The Quiet Progressive." University of Wisconsin Ph. D. Dissertation, 1965.

    Graves, Lawrence. "The Wisconsin Woman Suffrage Movement, 1846-1920." University of Wisconsin Ph. D. Dissertation, 1954.

    Hill, George W. "Man in the 'Cut-Over', A Culture Case Study of Social Relationships." University of Wisconsin Ph. D. Dissertation, 1940.

    Jackson, James E. "Wisconsin Attitudes Toward American Foreign Policy Since 1910." University of Wisconsin Ph. D. Dissertation, 1934.

    Kent, Alan Edmond. "Portrait in Isolationism: The La Follettes and Foreign Policy." University of Wisconsin Ph. D. Dissertation, 1957.

    Margulies, Herbert F. "Issues and Politics of Wisconsin Progressivism, 1906-1920." University of Wisconsin Ph. D. Dissertation, 1955.

    Meyer, Karl E. "The Politics of Loyalty from La Follette to McCarthy in Wisconsin, 1918-1952." Princeton University Ph. D. Dissertation, 1956.

    Olson, Frederick I. "The Milwaukee Socialists, 1897-1941." 2 vols. Harvard University Ph. D. Dissertation, 1952.

    Pedersen, Harald A. "Acculturation Among Danish and Polish Ethnic Groups in Wisconsin." University of Wisconsin Ph. D. Dissertation, 1949.

    Peterson, Arthur LaVerne. "McCarthyism: Its Ideology and Foundations." University of Minnesota Ph. D. Dissertation, 1962.

Schmidt, Lester F. "The Farmer-Labor Progressive Federation: The Study of a 'United Front' Among Wisconsin Liberals, 1934-1941." University of Wisconsin Ph. D. Dissertation, 1955.

Schumacker, Waldo. "The Direct Primary in Wisconsin." University of Wisconsin Ph. D. Dissertation, 1923.

Slocum, Walter L. "Ethnic Stocks as Culture Types in Rural Wisconsin: A Study of Differential Native American, German, and Norwegian Influence on Certain Aspects of Man-Land Adjustment in Rural Localities." University of Wisconsin Ph. D. Dissertation, 1940.

Sorauf, Francis. "The Voluntary Committee System in Wisconsin: An Effort to Achieve Party Responsibility." University of Wisconsin Ph. D. Dissertation, 1953.

Taggart, Glen L. "Czechs of Wisconsin as a Culture Type." University of Wisconsin Ph. D. Dissertation, 1948.

Ulrich, Robert J. "The Bennett Law of 1889: Education and Politics in Wisconsin." 2 vols. University of Wisconsin Ph. D. Dissertation, 1965.

Weaver, Norman F. "The Knights of the Ku Klux Klan in Wisconsin, Indiana, Ohio, and Michigan." University of Wisconsin Ph. D. Dissertation, 1954.

Wyman, Roger E. "Voting Behavior in the Progressive Era: Wisconsin as a Case Study." 3 vols. University of Wisconsin Ph. D. Dissertation, 1970.

Adamany, David W. "The 1960 Election in Wisconsin." University of Wisconsin Master's Thesis, 1963.

Bedford, Henry F. "A Case Study in Hysteria: Victor L. Berger, 1917-1921." University of Wisconsin Master's Thesis, 1953.

Brandes, Stuart Dean. "Nils P. Haugen and the Wisconsin Progressive Movement." University of Wisconsin Master's Thesis, 1965.

Ebling, Walter H. "Recent Farmer Movements in Wisconsin." University of Wisconsin Master's Thesis, 1925.

Harvey, Alfred. "The Background of the Progressive Movement in Wisconsin." University of Wisconsin Master's Thesis, 1933.

Johnson, Arzalia S. "The La Follette-Roosevelt Feud." University of Wisconsin Master's Thesis, 1930.

Kligora, Ira J. "The German Element in Wisconsin, 1840-1880." University of Wisconsin Master's Thesis, 1937.

Long, Robert E. "Wisconsin State Politics, 1932-1934: The Democratic Interlude." University of Wisconsin Master's Thesis, 1962.

Martin, Lawrence J. "Opposition to Conscription in Wisconsin, 1917-1918." University of Wisconsin Master's Thesis, 1952.

Moriarty, Francis J. "Philip F. La Follette: State and National Politics, 1937-1938." University of Wisconsin Master's Thesis, 1960.

Nelson, Charles A. "Progressives and Loyalty in Wisconsin Politics, 1912-1918." University of Wisconsin Master's Thesis, 1961.

Robinson, Ruth F. "The Control of the Republican Party in Wisconsin, 1904." University of Wisconsin Master's Thesis, 1930.

Schlereth, Thomas John. "The Progressive-Democrat Alliance in the Wisconsin Presidential Election of 1928." University of Wisconsin Master's Thesis, 1965.

Slatin, Alfred. "Wisconsin Progressivism in Transition, A Study of Progressive Concepts, 1918-1930." University of Wisconsin Master's Thesis, 1952.

Spellberg, William. "Wisconsin Reaction to the Versailles Peace Treaty as Revealed in Newspapers, Letters, and Resolutions of Organizations." University of Wisconsin Master's Thesis, 1953.

Steinke, John. "The Rise of McCarthyism." University of Wisconsin Master's Thesis, 1960.

Twombley, Robert C. "The Reformer as Politician: Robert M. La Follette in the Election of 1900." University of Wisconsin Master's Thesis, 1964.

Wagner, Kenneth C. "William T. Evjue and the *Capital Times*." University of Wisconsin Master's Thesis, 1949.

Whiteside, Donald. "The Use of Historical Data in a Sociological Study of Lafayette County, Wisconsin." University of Wisconsin Master's Thesis, 1960.

Zischke, Douglas A. "La Follettes and the *Progressive*: The Case Study of a Liberal Magazine." University of Wisconsin Master's Thesis, 1952.

Elser, Louise Helen. "The Change from Lumbering to Agriculture in Northern Wisconsin, 1870-1920." University of Wisconsin Bachellor's Thesis, 1923.

Kloske, Ralph. "The New Deal in the Badger State: A Look at Some County Level Data." Luther College, Decorah, Iowa Senior Thesis, 1974.

Snyder, H. M. "The Foreign Population of Wisconsin." University of Wisconsin Bachellor's Thesis, 1920.

Epstein, Leon D. *The Wisconsin Farm Vote for Governor, 1948-1954*. Madison: University of Wisconsin Extension Division, 1956. Mimeographed.

Huber, Henry. "War Hysteria." Manuscript in the State Historical Society of Wisconsin, 1928.

Ralston, Craig. "The La Follette Dynasty." Manuscript in the Wisconsin Legislative Reference Bureau, c. 1939.

Wyngaard, John W. *A Popular Front in Wisconsin: An Examination of the Farmer-Labor-Progressive Federation*. Madison: January, 1937. Mimeographed.

INDEX

-452-

Agriculture and Farming 49,
  84-85, 86, 91, 122, 125,
  128, 179, 197, 253,256,
  272, 310-311, 313, 323,
  349, 351, 355-356, 361t,
  362t
Austrians 35, 136, 182, 185,
  202t, 263, 267, 278, 297,
  301, 317, 319, 348, 420t
Belgians 35, 87, 114, 118-119,
  174, 182, 185, 192, 196t,
  236, 238, 242, 250-251, 256,
  260, 276, 278, 280, 297,
  301, 306, 319, 324, 421t
Bennett Law 171-174, 186, 190,
  196, 206
Benson, Lee v, 1, 2, 7, 12,
  36, 37
Blacks 137, 370t
Blaine, John 175, 246, 271t
  306, 321
Bohemians 35, 43, 45, 87,
  114, 117-118, 172, 174,
  182, 184, 185, 196, 201t,
  278, 297, 301, 317-319,
  348, 355, 420t
Bryan, William Jennings 163-
  165, 190, 200, 201, 204,
  207, 248
Charts 170, 176
Correlation Matrices 240,
  253, 273, 274, 298, 303,
  322, 330, 367-368, 369
Danes 35, 45, 61, 87, 126-
  127, 185, 193t-194, 232,
  243, 264, 266, 276, 278,
  301, 306, 317, 319, 324,
  329, 413t, 424t
Democrats 8, 12, 13, 48, 52,
  56, 63, 163-169, 166-167t,
  171-175, 181, 182-185,
  187, 190, 192, 194-195,
  196, 197, 198, 198-199,
  200, 201, 202, 203-205,
  205-207, 209, 226, 228t,
  231t, 237, 238, 241, 247-
  264, 250t, 251-252t, 253,
  259t, 260t, 262-263t, 265,
  267, 269, 270t, 271t, 295,
  296, 298t, 301, 306, 308,
  309, 310t, 311, 312t, 314t,
  315, 318, 320t, 323, 326,
  327, 328t, 329, 330t, 331,
  332-333t, 334t, 335, 347,
  348, 349, 350-351, 371t,
  372-373t, 373-374t, 374t,
  375-376t, 381-382t
Direct Primary Referendum
  229-230, 234, 239
English (Cornish) 35, 87, 91,
  95, 96-98, 100, 101, 165,
  182, 183, 184, 188t, 200, 235,
  243, 248, 252, 260, 280, 304,
  315, 324, 329, 348, 417t,
Epstein, Leon 15, 16, 17, 46, 50,
  327
Ethnic Group Tables 60, 88, 94-95,
  111-112, 166-167, 233-234, 239
  241, 250, 259, 260, 262-263,
  275-276, 277, 279, 307, 310,
  314, 316, 325, 332-333, 334,
  363-364, 365, 366, 367-368,
  369-370, 377-378, 379-380,
  381-382, 383-384, 385-386,
  387-391, 392-393, 394-395,
  396-397, 398-399
Finns 35, 61, 87, 127-129, 183,
  185, 192, 194t-195, 232, 243,
  265, 266, 267, 276, 304, 311,
  315, 317, 319, 324, 329, 335,
  414t
Freidel, Frank v, 261, 262
French Canadians 35, 45, 87, 95-
  96, 182-183, 184, 197t, 237,
  238, 260, 264, 276, 278, 280,
  301, 306, 317, 318, 319, 422t,
  424t
Germans v, 8, 13, 35, 37, 45, 50,
  58, 61-62t, 82, 87, 89, 99, 101,
  103-114, 106t, 111t, 121, 182;
  183, 184, 185, 188, 189, 196,
  200, 203t-206, 205t, 207t, 208t,
  209, 236, 237, 239, 242, 245,
  248, 251-252t, 255, 257, 260,
  261, 263, 264, 266, 277-278,
  286, 297, 301, 304, 305, 308,
  309, 315, 317-321, 320t, 324,
  329, 331, 335, 348-350, 352,
  400-402t, 402t, 403t, 404-405t,
  405-406t, 407t, 408t, 490t,

423t, 425t
Hays, Sam iv, v, 2, 4, 7, 163, 184
Hofstadter, Richard iv, 5, 180, 235, 273, 297, 349
Hollanders (Dutch) 35, 45, 87, 114, 116-117, 174, 182, 184, 195t-196, 202t, 238-239, 242, 243, 248, 250, 252, 260, 263, 264, 278, 280, 297, 301, 304, 310, 311, 315, 317, 318, 324, 325, 348, 418t, 422t
Hughes, Charles Evan 248, 249, 254, 257t, 258
Illustrations 173
Indians 137-138
Initiative and Referendum Amendment 229-230, 239, 273-274t
Irish 8, 35, 87, 89, 91, 99-101, 106, 119, 172, 174, 182, 184, 189, 199t, 200, 238, 250, 256-258, 260, 261, 264, 280, 301, 317, 318, 319, 320, 335, 421t, 424t
Italians 35, 45, 54, 87, 101, 133-134, 172, 182-183, 185, 198t, 237, 238, 260, 261, 263, 276, 280, 305, 317, 319, 320, 348, 422t, 424t
Jensen, Richard 18, 164-168, 174-175, 177, 184, 186, 189-190, 195-196, 206
Jews 136, 320
Key, V.O. 10, 11, 51, 163, 185, 296, 297, 350
Kleppner, Paul vi, 18, 164-168, 174-175, 184, 185, 186, 189-190, 192, 194, 195-196, 197, 200, 203-204, 206, 209
La Follette, Phillip v, 34, 321, 322t, 323-324, 326, 352
La Follette, Robert, Jr. v, 34, 321, 322t, 323-324, 325t, 36-329, 328t, 331, 352-353, 398-399t

La Follette, Robert Sr. iv, v, 15, 34, 174, 177, 179-180, 181, 182, 183-184, 191, 192, 200, 205, 207, 208, 225-281, 231t, 270t, 273-274t, 275-276t, 277t, 279t, 295, 296, 297, 298t, 301, 321, 322t, 349-352
Lubell, Sam 18, 48, 51, 261, 264, 280, 295, 296, 302, 309, 318, 320
Maps 83, 93, 102, 115, 120, 124, 130, 135
McCarthy, Joseph 14, 15, 18, 324, 328t, 330, 347
McGovern, Francis 175, 225, 230, 241, 244
Milwaukee 45, 81, 82, 100, 103, 107, 114, 117, 123, 129, 132, 133-134, 136, 139, 183, 199, 208, 239, 240t, 241, 248, 255, 267-269, 268t, 301, 306, 309, 313, 315, 323, 324, 329, 360t
Native-stock (Yankees) 35, 57, 58, 87, 89, 90t, 94, 96, 101, 165, 167, 172, 174, 178-179, 182, 183, 184, 186t-188, 200, 232, 235, 236, 240, 243, 260, 264, 266, 280, 301, 304, 306, 315, 317, 319, 324, 329, 347, 348, 349, 415t, 416t, 424t
New Deal 5, 34, 51, 273, 274, 281, 298, 299, 309, 310, 311, 313, 315, 323, 236, 350
Norwegians 35, 40, 41, 45, 59, 61, 85, 87, 119, 121t-123, 265, 172, 180, 183, 184, 189t-191, 192, 235-236, 243, 248, 261, 262, 264, 276, 301, 306, 315, 320, 324, 329, 335, 410t, 411t, 424t
Parochial School Aid Amendment 17, 101, 108-114, 111t, 119,

301, 303, 357
Philipp, Emanuel 175, 230
Poles 34, 43, 45, 87, 107,
   129, 131-133, 174, 182,
   184, 196, 198t-199, 239,
   251, 255, 260, 264, 267,
   268, 278, 280, 301, 309,
   315, 319, 320, 324, 335,
   348, 355, 419t, 425t
Populists 85, 194, 204,
   371t, 372t
Progressives iv, 4, 12, 15,
   18, 92, 175, 177, 180-
   181, 182, 225-281, 308,
   349
Progressives, 1912 233-234t,
   249-251, 299t, 371t, 372t,
   375t, 379-380t
Progressives, 1924 271-296,
   299t, 301, 371t, 373t,
   392-393t
Progressives 1934-46 176
   (chart), 281, 295, 296,
   321, 322t, 323-324,
   326-328, 331, 372-373t,
   373-374t, 375-376t
Progressives 1948 281, 329,
   371t, 373t
Prohibition Referendum 303
   303t, 304
Religion 35, 52-56, 61-62,
   91-92, 97, 98, 104, 106,
   108-114, 111-112t, 116-
   117, 118, 119, 122-123,
   125, 127, 129, 131-132,
   163-168, 171-172, 186,
   188, 190, 195-196, 198,
   203, 297-298, 301, 302,
   304-306, 308, 313, 347,
   348, 350, 356-357, 367-
   368t
Republicans 8, 12, 36, 54,
   56, 63, 163, 166-167t,
   165-169, 170 (chart),
   171-175, 176 (chart),
   177, 179-180, 181-182,
   186, 187, 188, 189, 191,
   193, 194, 195, 196, 197,
   198, 199, 200, 201, 203-
   205, 205-207, 209-210,
   226, 227, 228t, 231t, 232,
   235, 236, 238, 241, 243,
   246, 247, 254, 255, 262,
   264, 265, 270t, 271t, 272-
   273, 278, 295, 297, 298,
   306, 308-309, 311, 315,
   318, 321, 324, 327-329,
   328t, 330, 334t, 335, 348,
   349, 352, 371t, 372-373t,
   373-374t, 375-376t, 377-
   378t, 383-384t
Roosevelt, Franklin D. 13,
   51, 273, 274, 297, 300,
   301, 309, 311, 313, 316t,
   317, 318, 323, 329, 330t,
   331, 350-352, 396-397t
Roosevelt, Theodore 208,
   230, 231t, 237, 240-243,
   241-242t, 244, 248, 251,
   254, 257t, 273-274t, 299,
   300, 322t
Scandinavians 99, 182, 232,
   235, 240, 260, 278, 280,
   297, 298, 304, 317, 319,
   320t, 324, 348
Schafer, Joseph 9, 12, 16,
   41, 89, 113, 203, 205,
   358
Smith, Al 17, 295, 296, 297,
   298, 300-306, 308-309, 331,
   350-351
Socialists 193, 194, 226,
   247, 254, 255, 259, 265-
   269, 268t, 270, 271t, 278,
   317, 323, 328t, 371t, 372-
   373t, 373-374t, 375-376t,
   385-386t, 387-391t
Swedes 35, 45, 61, 87, 114,
   116, 123, 125-126, 165,
   180, 184, 191t-192, 232,
   243, 261, 264, 266, 267,
   276, 301, 306, 310, 311,
   315, 320, 324, 329, 412t,
   424t
Swiss 35, 87, 174, 183, 185,
   209t-210, 239, 242, 260,
   263, 266-267, 278, 280, 297,
   304, 305, 311, 318, 319,
   324, 329, 348, 349, 418t
Taft, William Howard 230-231t,

237, 241, 243, 254, 257t,
Union Labor Party 371t, 375t
Union Party 317, 318, 371t
Urban Areas 45, 46, 49, 50, 105, 106-107t, 116, 123, 187, 208-209, 268t, 301, 306, 309-310, 313, 315, 317, 324, 328, 329, 350, 355
Villages 39, 44, 46, 49, 98, 105, 116, 123, 187, 315, 317, 319, 350, 351
Welsh 35, 96, 182, 184, 188t, 235, 243, 250, 252, 263, 279, 301, 315, 324, 348, 417t
Wilson, Woodrow 226, 231t, 241-243, 248-258, 257t, 280, 306, 349
World War I 34, 44, 226, 227, 230, 244-246, 273, 278, 320, 321, 349
World War II 34, 318-321, 326
Wyman, Roger vi, 17, 27

Augsburg College
George Sverdrup Library
Minneapolis, Minnesota 55454